DESIGN FOR POWER

DESIGN FOR POWER

POWER

The Struggle for the World

MAPS BY

GEORGE D. BRODSKY

NARRATIVE BY

FREDERICK L. SCHUMAN

1942 · NEW YORK 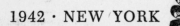 ALFRED A. KNOPF

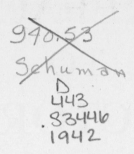

Copyright 1941 by Alfred A. Knopf, Inc.

Manufactured in the United States of America
Published simultaneously in Canada by The Ryerson Press

Published January 5, 1942
Second Printing, February 1942
Third Printing, April 1942

PREFACE TO VICTORY
1942

On the first December Sunday of 1941 America found its soul. On this day, in the twelfth month of the fourteenth year of Hirohito's blood-stained reign of "Radiant Peace," the leaders of the Fascist Triplice unleashed war against the United States. They thereby united all Americans and insured their own ultimate defeat in their battle for mastery of the planet.

The assault took place ten years and eighty days after the "Mukden incident," fabricated by the warlords of Tokyo as their pretext for the rape of Manchuria. In 1931 Mussolini was a feeble tyrant, Hitler was a madman marching toward power in a tan rain-coat, and the powerful democracies of the West were paralyzed by the Great Depression. By 1941 Mussolini was a deflated scare-crow, Hitler was a frustrated and desperate conqueror, and the surviving democracies had at long last allied themselves in arms for the liberation of the earth.

Design for Power attempts, in maps and story, to tell the tale of the ten years. The tale of the eighty days, culminating in the world-shattering climax of the most fateful decade of the 20th Century, cannot yet be told in full. Yet its outlines are plain and can here be sketched.

THE WAR OF DESPERATION

The Nazi invasion of Russia was a product of Nazi failure to conquer Britain. The Nazi attack on America is a product of Nazi failure to conquer Russia. In like fashion, the Japanese assault on the United States is a consequence of Japanese failure to conquer China and of Japanese fear of an immediate test of force with a Russia that refuses to be conquered.

In order to conquer Russia, and therewith to crush Britain and render America isolated and defenseless, the thwarted Führer of the *Furor Teutonicus* requires another year of frenzied effort on the part of his demented subjects. The effort offers hope of success only if British resources are dissipated on far-flung battle lines and American energies are immobilized by a costly

[*i*]

war in the Pacific. Hence Hitler's need of a Japanese-American war, which unmistakably bears the label "Made in Germany." By the same logic, Hitler's allies in the Orient require at least another year of butchery and terror to crush Free China and thereby pave the way for the final defeat of America, Britain and Russia and for the effective enslavement of all of Asia. But if the year is to have a harvest of victory, it must be one in which the Tokyo militarists can conquer the riches of the Indies for their depleted war machine, cut off American supplies of rubber and tin, and halt the flow of arms to China. Hence Hirohito's need of mastery of the whole vast area of land and sea between Burma and the Fiji Islands.

This adventure in arms, foredoomed to failure if Britons, Russians, Chinese and Americans act together and do their duty, became a necessity for the strategists of the Triplice not only by virtue of their military failure in China and Russia, but by virtue of their psychological failure in Britain and America. During most of the decade dealt with in this volume the astute maniacs of Berlin, Rome and Tokyo were hugely successful in befuddling and demoralizing the democratic world with the ideological weapons of anti-Communism and anti-Semitism. By the time they felt ready to unsheath the sword they had been permitted by democratic blindness and weakness to enhance their power to a point at which they felt confident of swift victory over the "decadent" democrats of the West. France and the lesser European democracies were in truth corrupted and easily struck down. But the Nazi dream was broken by the magnificent resistance of Churchill's Britain and Stalin's Russia, aided by Roosevelt's America, just as the Nipponese vision of "Greater East Asia" was shattered by the People's Front in China.

The Nazi decision to invade the Soviet Union was inspired by the expectation that the Reichswehr could speedily smash the Red Army while the agents of Göbbels spread confusion in the Atlantic democracies by preaching a new crusade against Bolshevism. Both hopes were vain. Japanese expectations of evoking a resumption of appeasement in Washington and London through new pretensions of "saving Asia from Communism" also came to nothing. The desperadoes of Berlin and Tokyo were thus confronted with two alternatives: (1) accepting slow defeat under the pressure of steadily mounting American aid to Britain, Russia and China and American embargoes against Japan and the Axis; or (2) challenging the American colossus to open battle in a suicidal endeavor to win by force the triumph which they had been unable to win by fraud. Their choice of the second alternative must lead inevitably to the same result as the first if America and its allies do what Destiny demands of them.

"NEW ORDER" IN EXTREMIS

In only one respect were the hopes of the military tyrants of Europe and Asia partially realized: their onslaught against "Bolshevism" did serve to consolidate their control of the ghost governments in the areas held by their armies.

The Quislings, the Vichymen, the Falangists of Franco's Spain and the traitors who follow Wang Ching-wei all know that their lives are forfeit if the Triplice loses its war. All serve as puppets of their masters. All strive to deceive their own people and the outer world as to their status and their purposes. All rule, or pretend to rule, by playing upon the anti-Communist and anti-Semitic sentiments of their deluded subjects.

These tawdry pro-consuls of the Caesars, with the spectre of assassination and the shadow of the gallows ever present at their council tables, necessarily welcomed the crusade of their overlords against Moscow and (with many doubts and afterthoughts) against America. The ceremonial manifestations of the new solidarity were reasonably impressive—to the participants. On the 25th of November, 1941, the "Anti-Comintern" Pact was renewed in Berlin by representatives of Germany, Italy, Japan, Hungary, Spain and Manchukuo (the original signatories) and adhered to by the shadow rulers of Nanking China, Finland, Denmark, Slovakia, Rumania, Bulgaria and Croatia. In the wake of the Triplice declarations of war against the United States, the puppets of the Triple Alliance Pact—Hungary, Rumania, Slovakia, Bulgaria and Croatia—obediently declared war on America in a sublime gesture of political buffoonery and immolation. A new recruit to the cause was won in the submission of Thailand to Japanese occupation after a few hours of "token" resistance on December 7-8.

These diplomatic vaudeville acts had little military significance save in the cases of Bangkok, Vichy and Madrid. In fear of internal revolt the top Thai-men did not dare join Japan in war on Britain and America. But by opening their frontiers to the "peacemakers" of the Orient they brought a grave military menace to Malaya and Burma. In fear of internal revolt, Pétain and Darlan did not dare sign the Anti-Comintern Pact or the Triple Alliance, but they pursued "collaboration" with a vengeance. They dismissed Weygand from his North African command on November 20. They conferred anew with Göring and Ciano. They opened the bases of French North Africa to Axis forces. They prepared to turn over the remnants of the French fleet to those who had struck France down. In fear of internal revolt, Franco and Suñer did not dare to enter the war on the side of the Powers which had destroyed the Spanish Republic, but they rejoined the "Anti-Comintern" alliance. They also prepared to aid the Axis in the Mediterranean and Africa.

These steps threatened at the turn of the year to deal grievous blows to the Allied cause. Act IV of the drama of war in Libya opened on November 20 with the British attack on the Axis forces under General Rommel, accompanied by great expectations in London of a swift victory on the pattern of Act II. The invaders, however, met with heavy reverses. Although they raised the siege of Tobruk, their progress westward was slow and costly. Even should Libya be conquered, the policies of Vichy and Madrid, unless frustrated by Nazi brutality toward the peoples of France and Spain, would merely move the African front from Libya to Tunisia, Algeria or Morocco.

The addition of Vichy's fleet to the Axis, moreover, would weaken British seapower in the Mediterranean. It might bring Nazi planes and raiders to Dakar, whence they could threaten the South Atlantic and strike toward Brazil and the Caribbean. Should the Fascist rulers of Portugal succeed in delivering the Madeiras and the Azores to the enemy, this threat might become formidable.

THE WAR OF LIBERATION

Yet these gains to the Triplice cause seemed likely to be overbalanced by losses of a less tangible quality. Russian resistance encouraged scores of thousands of the vanquished peoples during the summer and autumn to hope for Axis defeat and to risk their lives in deeds of sabotage and terrorism. Only in Serbia, where heroic bands of Chetniks resumed the war from their mountain fastnesses, did the sentiment flare into open revolt. But in Rumania, Czechoslovakia, Poland, Norway, the Low Countries and France, individuals did what their consciences demanded of them.

With America in arms the secret hopes of the conquered will rise anew and find new means of expression, highly hazardous to the "master race." Once the Allied forces win major victories, the war for the world will become a revolutionary war, with all the subjugated peoples, including the Italians, eagerly awaiting a favorable hour to rise against their exploiters. The bankruptcy of the "New Order" will then be plain. Sweeping triumphs will then lie within the grasp of those Allied commanders possessed of wit and will to supplement war by weapons with war by propaganda and war by insurrection.

If these opportunities are to be fully used during 1942, however, Moscow's defense against the Reich must be strengthened and London, Washington and Chungking must evolve new skills in the conduct of hostilities and in the instigation of revolution. Only by summoning the vanquished to rebellion against the conquerors can victory be won without the shedding of oceans of blood. Each handful of trained agitators and shrewd conspirators in Shanghai, Barcelona, Bordeaux and Brussels (and eventually in Nagasaki, Naples, Budapest and Munich) will be worth a whole division of troops in British and American Expeditionary Forces. The summons to revolt will be fully effective only when it is linked with a positive program, visible in deeds as well as in words, for a United States of Europe and a United States of the World, dedicated irrevocably to a free world order as a viable alternative to the "New Order" of tyranny. For this much more will be needed than blood, sweat and tears. The enterprise will call for revolutionary daring and imagination, for a repudiation of the musty ideas of the past, for a dynamic democracy capable of refashioning the human adventure through a new birth of freedom, and a new vision of peace and order in a realm of liberty as wide as the earth.

THE WAR OF RETRIBUTION

The ordeal of World War II is itself the consequence of the irresponsibility of the democracies in the aftermath of World War I. Charged with creating a world polity through a permanent concert of power, they sought safety and peace by shunning risks and avoiding duties. Their feckless formulas of "non-intervention" and "appeasement" were a prescription for anarchy. Step by inexorable step, they led to the aggrandizement of the Caesars, to democratic disgrace and international violence, and to the frenzied efforts of the new fanatics to build by the sword and the lash the world polity which men of good will would not build by the devices of freemen.

The people of no great democratic community, save only the victims of betrayal in France, has paid more dearly for its errors and its hallucinations than the people of the United States. Its grief at the time these words are written is still a grief of incredulity and indignation rather than a grief of suffering and sorrow. These too must come, for the people of America, like those of Britain and Russia, are doomed to pass through the "long, grim, scowling valley of war" before they find their salvation. Their trial by arms is directly attributable to their reluctance to run the dangers and pay the price of doing their duty in time of peace, albeit those dangers and that price would both have been negligible by comparison with the perils and sacrifices which must now be faced.

America has been for half a century the richest and most powerful of the Great Powers. America has therefore had the largest stake in world order and the largest opportunity to give the world leadership in the organization of peace. This has long been so because, as Henry Luce pointed out so plainly almost a year ago, nothing affects so decisively the international environment in which America must live as the influence of America upon it. But Americans preferred to ignore the call of Destiny which Woodrow Wilson addressed to them, and for twenty years sought not to remake the world environment but to flee from it and to convince themselves that they were not their brothers' keepers. The national policies dictated by this attitude have now brought their inevitable reward. In the school of anguish Americans will learn what is demanded of them by their place in the world and by their inescapable role in the history of our time. Not to learn is to perish. And the American dream is far from death.

On the very eve of the great awakening the "schism in the soul" of the American masses was still unresolved. The Administration continued on its appointed course in the face of constant attack from the appeasolationists. In mid-September Lindbergh in Des Moines alleged, à la Göbbels, that "the three most important groups which have been pressing this country towards war are the British, Jewish and the Roosevelt Administration." In mid-September the President asked Congress for six billion dollars more for the Lease-

Lend program and Secretary Knox acknowledged that the Navy was escorting merchant convoys. At the three-Power conference held in Moscow early in October, W. Averill Harriman pledged all possible American aid to the U.S.S.R. In his Navy Day address the President made it clear that America was already in a shooting war. "Hitler has offered a challenge which we as Americans cannot and will not tolerate." Yet the public remained indifferent, even after the torpedoing in the North Atlantic of the destroyer *Kearny* (October 17) and the sinking (October 30) with the loss of over a hundred lives of the destroyer *Reuben James.*

The President's proposal to Congress, originally submitted on the 9th of October, to amend the "Neutrality" Act of 1939 in order to permit the arming of American merchant ships produced dissension and delay rather than a firm resolve to act. Wendell Willkie's bold appeal for the repeal of the entire statute evoked little response from the Republicans in Congress. Not until November 9 did the Senate vote, 50 to 37, to amend the Act to allow the arming of United States vessels and to permit their sailing through combat zones and into belligerent ports. Not until November 14 did the House concur by the narrow margin of 212 to 194. The President signed the new legislation on November 18 while critics grumbled that another move had been made toward involving America in "other peoples' wars."

Meanwhile the Administration (November 7) pledged to the Soviet Union a billion-dollar loan from Lease-Lend funds and made vain appeals to Hitler's Finnish allies to halt their invasion of Russia. During five long months of war in the East, Britain and America appeased the Nazi puppets in Helsinki, Budapest and Bucharest. No British declaration of war on Finland, Hungary and Rumania was issued until December 6. Washington likewise followed London's lead in appeasing Madrid and Vichy until the dismissal of Weygand led to a revocation of all American export licenses for French North Africa and of licenses for petroleum exports to Spain and Tangiers. On November 24 Washington announced American military occupation of Dutch Guiana by agreement with Brazil and The Netherlands Government-in-exile.

On the very day before the Fascist assault, most Americans, although committed to aid to Britain and Russia, felt that the war was still not America's war. No American supposed even in his wildest imaginings that his country could be attacked by treachery and violence as a score of others had been. The Atlantic was wide. The Pacific was wider. The public which booed the notion in the spring of 1940 that the American frontier lay on the Rhine, and doubted in 1941 whether it lay in Greenland and Iceland, would never have conceded, had the question been put, that its defenses actually lay on the Don and the Oka and on the Isthmus of Kra and along the Mekong—all places of which most Americans had never heard. At the end of November the laughter of scorn would have greeted anyone who had suggested that America would be at war within a week over a question of the number of yellow men with guns who could safely be permitted at Long-xuyen or Pnom-Penh.

And yet so small and dangerous had America's world become that this question and none other was the last question under discussion by the diplomats before America was summoned to fight for its life. The great republic did not fight and would never have fought to save China from conquest by lawless aggressors. Nor Ethiopia. Nor Spain. Nor Austria nor Czechoslovakia nor yet Poland nor Rumania nor even France. Britain? Perhaps. Russia? Never. Cambodia or Thailand? Unthinkable. In fact, however, the clash of wills over Thailand and Cambodia was the ultimate event before the storm and the shocking news of the worst defeat in the history of American arms. It is all but certain that this defeat was inflicted by Japanese bombers coming from the Marshall Islands, which America had permitted in 1899 to pass from Spain to Germany and in 1914 from Germany to Japan. It is equally certain that the planes were made of American material, fueled and lubricated with American oil and supplied with bombs manufactured of American metal.

In the midst of the grim Nemesis which is always and everywhere the lot of those who seek to find safety by deflecting the forces of evil against others, Americans and Britishers alike could echo the words of their greatest poet: "All our yesterdays have lighted fools the way to dusty death." The world in truth is one and all men are brothers. For failure to recognize and act upon these facts the United States is called to fight for freedom in the most costly and most dangerous war in its history.

DEFEAT ON THE DON

"This enemy is broken and will never rise again." Thus spake the Führer to his people early in October of the year of his invasion of Russia. Had his words been true, the attack on America two months later would never have been made, for the breaking of Russian resistance would have rendered hopeless both the British cause and the Chinese cause and paved the way for the ultimate subjugation of the Americas without open war—save in the final stages. His words were false.

The gigantic offensive against Moscow launched in October by the armies of Marshal Fedor von Bock was drowned in blood by the furiously fighting defenders of the Soviet citadel. In mid-summer Timoshenko's troops had halted the Nazi Blitzkrieg beyond Smolensk. New Nazi preparations to smash the Red Army on the central front were made on a colossal scale and with meticulous care. During the first two weeks of the attack the invaders did indeed break through the Soviet lines near Kalinin and also near Orel in a great pincer movement designed to encircle the capital by way of the Volga and the Moskva to the north and the upper Don and the Oka to the south.

But the speed and daring of Soviet counter-moves, brilliantly organized by General Gregory Zhukof, halted the enemy in a great semi-circle around the outer suburbs of the metropolis.

Meanwhile impressive Nazi victories in the south were also followed by defeat. Besieged Odessa was taken (October 16) and then the great industrial center of Kharkov (October 25). By the end of November the armies of Rundstedt were overrunning the Crimea. Kleist's crack panzer divisions, never hitherto halted in any campaign, had taken Rostov-on-the-Don (November 22) and were menacing the entire Donetz Basin and the north Caucasus area. On the first day of December, however, Soviet troops recaptured Rostov and drove Kleist's men in headlong rout along the shore of the Sea of Azov. In the center the second battle of Moscow, unleashed in mid-November, ended in an even greater disaster for the invaders, leading to the displacement of Bock by List as commander of the broken Nazi armies. In the north the siege of Leningrad was lifted. Berlin announced that the front was being "stabilized" by "strategic withdrawals" and that Moscow would not be taken until spring or summer of 1942.

That the Nazi high command will strike new and terrible blows against Russia during the coming twelvemonth is scarcely open to question. But it was clear to all the Triplice leaders as winter descended upon the Russian plains that at least another year would be needed to fulfill Hitler's boast of October. For the first time the Reichswehr had tasted the bitterness of defeat. An uninterrupted flow of aid from America to Britain and Russia during 1942 might well spell total defeat for the Axis in 1943—and, in the sequel, inevitable defeat for the Japanese allies of the Axis. What to do?

DEFEAT ON THE POTOMAC

The invariable technique of the Triplice when faced with problems such as this is to confuse and divide its enemies or intended victims by offering to negotiate a settlement with some at the expense of others. Examples: the "peace" of Munich, the Nazi-Soviet pact of 1939, the Japanese-Soviet pact of 1941, the Nazi bids for peace with Britain on the eve of the invasion of Russia. Those who have yielded to such inducements have invariably been brought to ruin, for "negotiations" as conducted by Fascist diplomats are but a means of winning military victories without war or a screen to hide carefully prepared plans of aggression.

In the fall of 1941 the Triplice game was obviously to initiate elaborate Japanese-American negotiations in the hope of bringing about a resumption of appeasement in Washington—first of Tokyo and later perhaps of Rome and Berlin—and to lay plans simultaneously for a crippling blow at the United States Navy, to be launched if the "negotiations" produced no results. The gradual strangulation of Japanese economy under the pressure of the Anglo-

American embargoes necessitated swift decisions. Unless the Tokyo warlords could secure new shipments of supplies from America by the end of the year, they must seize new sources in the East Indies or face the gradual paralysis of their forces.

Following preliminary discussions initiated in April and the dispatch of an August message from Prince Konoe to President Roosevelt asking vainly for a personal conference somewhere in the Pacific, Mr. Nomura did his best to prove the truth of the old adage that an ambassador is an honest man sent abroad to lie for the good of his country. In the midst of his labors, Konoe resigned (October 18) in favor of General Hideki (Eiko) Tojo, who took unto himself the Premiership, the Home Ministry and the Ministry of War and gave the portfolio of Foreign Affairs to Shigenori Togo. The new leaders sent to Washington, for the purpose of aiding Nomura to "negotiate a settlement," none other than Saburo Kurusu, who had signed the Triplice pact in Berlin fourteen months before. Dark hints were dropped that war might come if a settlement were not reached during the special Diet session which assembled in mid-November.

Not for months and perhaps not for years will it become possible to reconstruct in detail the course of the curious negotiations which took place in Washington during the last weeks of America's uneasy "peace." All that is now clear is that Japanese hopes of renewed appeasement were dashed at the outset by the firm resolve of Hull, Welles, and Roosevelt neither to betray China nor to renounce the principles to which American diplomacy in the Orient had adhered ever since John Hay's formulation of the "Open Door" doctrine at the turn of the century. "The American Government," said the final Japanese note of December 7, "failed to display in the slightest degree a spirit of conciliation"—i.e. a willingness to desert China and recognize Japanese hegemony over Asia. The most that Tokyo was prepared to do to secure a lifting of the restrictions on trade was to pledge itself (along with the United States!) "not to dispatch armed forces into any of the regions, *excepting French Indo-China,* in southeastern Asia and the southern Pacific area" and to withdraw Japanese troops from *southern* Indo-China "upon the conclusion of the present agreement." In return the United States was asked to "supply Japan the required quantity of oil," to help reopen Japanese trade with the Dutch Indies, to restore commercial relations, to unfreeze Japanese assets, and to acquiesce in "the restoration of general peace between Japan and China" on Japanese terms, with "China" presumably meaning the puppet regime at Nanking [Japanese note of November 20, 1941].

The United States on the other hand asked Japan to join it in affirming support for the principles of non-aggression, non-intervention, equality of commercial treatment, pacific settlement of disputes and international economic collaboration for freer trade and freer access to raw materials for all countries. It further proposed the negotiation of a multilateral pact among Britain, China, Japan, The Netherlands, the U.S.S.R., Thailand and the United States in which the signatories would pledge themselves to non-aggression and to respect for the territorial integrity of Indo-China. It offered to join Japan in renouncing all extraterritorial rights in China, to negotiate a reciprocal trade agreement in which raw silk should be kept on the free list, to restore trade relations and to stabilize the dollar-yen rate. Washington asked in return that Tokyo "withdraw all military, naval, air and police forces from China and from Indo-China" and cease support of any Chinese regime other than the Chungking Government. No formal renunciation of the Triplice pact was demanded, but "both governments will agree that no agreement which either has concluded with any third Power or Powers shall be interpreted by it in such a way as to conflict with the fundamental purpose of this agreement: the establishment and preservation of peace throughout the Pacific area" [U.S. note of November 26].

These terms were rejected. "Obviously," declared the final Japanese note, "it is the intention of the American Government to conspire with Great Britain and other countries to obstruct Japan's efforts toward the establishment of peace through the creation of a New Order in East Asia, and especially to preserve Anglo-American rights and interests by keeping Japan and China at war." Commented Hull, when this note was delivered to him at 2:20 p.m. December 7 by Nomura and Kurusu: "In all my fifty years of public service I have never seen a document that was more crowded with infamous false-hoods and distortions on a scale so huge that I never imagined until today that any government on this planet was capable of uttering them."

Meanwhile President Roosevelt, on the afternoon of December 6, had ad-dressed a last appeal directly to Emperor Hirohito, recalling the century of Japanese-American friendship and pleading that "both Japan and the United States should agree to eliminate any form of military threat." He referred to the Vichy-Tokyo agreements for the "protection" of Indo-China and asserted that the movements of large numbers of Japanese troops into Cambodia raised "a reasonable doubt" as to whether the character of the concentration was defensive. "No attack has been made upon Indo-China, nor has any been contemplated. It is clear that continuance of such a situation is unthinkable. None of the people whom I have spoken of [the Filipinos, the East Indians, the Malays and the Thais] can sit either indefinitely or permanently on a keg of dynamite. There is absolutely no thought on the part of the United States of invading Indo-China if every Japanese soldier or sailor were to be with-drawn therefrom. I would even undertake to ask for the same assurance on the part of the government of China [as well as from the East Indies, Malaya and Thailand]. Thus a withdrawal of Japanese forces from Indo-China would result in the assurance of peace throughout the whole of the south Pacific area. I address myself to Your Majesty at this moment in the fervent hope that Your Majesty may, as I am doing, give thought in this definite emergency to ways of dispelling the dark clouds. I am confident that both of us, for the sake of the peoples not only of our own great countries, but for the sake of humanity in neighboring territories, have a sacred duty to restore traditional amity and prevent further death and destruction in the world."

BLITZ OUT OF ASIA

At the very moment when Secretary Hull was receiving the Japanese envoys on Sunday afternoon, news was received at the White House that the American Pacific fleet, at anchor in America's greatest naval base—Pearl Harbor on the Island of Oahu—had been attacked by Japanese bombers at 7:35 a.m. Two more attacks followed later in the day and another on Monday. American strategists and diplomats had learned in advance of Japanese preparations in Indo-China for an attack on Thailand, Malaya and the Philippines. They seemingly had no inkling of the vastly more ambitious preparations long under way in the "demilitarized" mandated islands to smash America's Pacific fleet and its billion-dollar base in the Hawaiian archipelago, two thousand miles to the east. The blow was swifter, more unsuspected and more damaging than the best of Hitler's exploits in the science of hurling speedy destruction at victims lulled into unawareness by a pretense of "negotiations." It was, said the President later, "a brilliant feat of deception, perfectly timed and executed with great skill."

The losses suffered by Admiral Kimmel's fleet and by the land and air forces near Pearl Harbor were in no sense decisive, despite their appalling magnitude. Japanese bombs demolished hundreds of planes on the ground, destroyed barracks and hangars, and slaughtered several hundred soldiers and civilians throughout the area of Honolulu. The aggressors sank three destroyers, a mine layer and the training ship *Utah*, inflicted grave damage on sundry cruisers and battleships, killed over 2600 sailors, sank the battleship *Oklahoma* and blew up the battleship *Arizona.* Two days later the two most powerful units of the British Navy in the Far East, the new battleship *Prince of Wales* and the battle cruiser *Repulse,* were sent to the bottom off the Malay coast by Japanese bombers attached to the forces invading Malaya from the north. These disasters meant that for weeks and possibly for months to come, the Allied forces in the Indies and the Western Pacific would be obliged to remain on the defensive with little hope of effective reinforcement while the aggressor attacked Hong Kong, the Philippines, Singapore and the rich and far-flung islands of the Indies.

Japan declared war on the United States and Great Britain on the morning of December 7, after the first deadly blows had been struck. For the first time in a quarter of a century, Americans were utterly united. Said the President to Congress on Monday: "We will not only defend ourselves to the uttermost, but we will make it very certain that this form of treachery will never again endanger us. We will gain the inevitable triumph—so help us God. I ask that the Congress declare that since the unprovoked and dastardly attack by Japan on Sunday, December 7, 1941, a state of war has existed between the United States and the Japanese Empire." The Senate approved, 82 to 0, the House, 388 to 1. At 4:10 p.m., December 8, the President signed the war resolution.

Said the President to the nation on Tuesday evening: "Together with other free peoples, we are now fighting to maintain our right to live among our world neighbors in freedom and common decency, without fear of assault. It will not only be a long war, it will be a hard war. The United States can accept no result save victory, final and complete. Remember always that Germany and Italy, regardless of any formal declaration of war, consider themselves at war with the United States at this moment just as much as they consider themselves at war with Britain and Russia. We are going to win the war and we are going to win the peace that follows. And in the dark hours of this day—and through dark days that may be yet to come—we will know that the vast majority of the members of the human race are on our side. Many of them are fighting with us. All of them are praying for us. For, in representing our cause, we represent theirs as well—our hope and their hope for liberty under God."

WHOM THE GODS WOULD DESTROY

Shortly before 3:00 p.m. on Thursday, December 11, 1941, a huge throng, ordered as usual to listen and cheer, listened to and cheered a four-minute address by Benito Mussolini from the balcony of the Palazzo Venezia. "The Powers of the steel pact, Fascist Italy and National Socialist Germany, ever closely linked, participate from today on the side of heroic Japan against the United States of America. One man, one man only, an authentic and democratic autocrat, wanted the war and has prepared for it day by day with diabolical obstinacy. Italians! Once more arise and be worthy of this historical hour. We shall win." At 2:30 Ciano handed to Chargé George Wadsworth a proclamation: "His Majesty, Victor Emmanuel, King-Emperor, declares that Italy from today considers herself in a state of war with the United States."

During the morning of the same day Hans Thomsen submitted to the Department of State, and Ribbentrop submitted to Chargé George Brandt in Berlin, a note charging the United States with aggression and violations of international law. "Germany, too, considers herself as being in a state of war with the United States of America." At 2:07 p.m. Hitler began an 88-minute address to the Reichstag in the Kroll Opera: "A historic revenge has been entrusted to us by the Creator, and we are now obliged to carry it out. There is a world-wide gulf between the outlook of President Roosevelt and myself. It does not impress me very much if Roosevelt sees fit to call me a gangster. I cannot feel insulted by Roosevelt because, just as with President Wilson, I consider Roosevelt to be insane. We know, of course, that the eternal Jew is behind all this. Our patience has come to the breaking point."

The same afternoon the Senate, in response to the President's request, recognized a state of war with Germany (88 to 0) and with Italy (90 to 0). The House concurred, 393 to 0 and 399 to 0. Within a few days declarations of war were voted by the governments of Cuba, Haiti, the Dominican Republic, Panama, Costa Rica, El Salvador, Guatemala, Honduras and Nicaragua. Other American Republics prepared to follow suit or proclaimed their benevolent neutrality toward the United States. China had already declared war against Germany and Italy. The British Dominions and the Allied governments-in-exile followed suit with declarations of war against Japan.

In the enemy camp a new tripartite agreement published on December 11 as a supplement to the Triplice Pact pledged Rome, Berlin and Tokyo to conduct war jointly against Britain and America, to refrain from any separate armistice or peace, and to collaborate after victory "in order to realize and establish an equitable new order in the world." Moscow refrained temporarily from open hostilities with Tokyo, though Ambassador Litvinov in Washington denounced Japan as "the common enemy." All the world was openly at war. "Neutrality" remained the refuge of only a few backward or dubious communities. The camps were united. The causes were clear. The god of battles would henceforth hold the balance between the fanaticism of slaves and the courage of freemen.

THE WAY TO LIBERTY

To speculate upon the probable future course of the titanic clash of arms in which all the earth is now engaged is a thankless and needless task. Details of armaments and tactical plans must of necessity remain military secrets. But the grand strategy of the Triplice and of the Allies is obvious for all to see.

In order to subjugate and enslave the human race the Triplice must conquer the prerequisites of victory during 1942 or else go down to doom before the slow and ponderous power of the Allied coalition. These prerequisites are writ large across the world arena. Japan must subdue Hong Kong, Malaya, Singapore, the Philippines and the East Indies, cut the Burma Road, threaten India, and immobilize the forces of the United States, China and the Soviet Union in the Far East. The Reich and its vassals in Europe must break Russian resistance, win Turkey to their cause, defend Libya, strike anew at Egypt and the Middle East, and acquire control of Vichy's navy and of French and Spanish North Africa. Given these successes, the Triplice will be able to exploit the resources under its control for the organization of an effective invasion of Britain in 1943. In the sequel it may reasonably hope to bring the United States to defeat by invading South America and exposing the North American Continent to blockade and possible invasion from both the east and the west.

In order to pave the way for the liberation of mankind from the new barbarism the Allies, by the same logic, must act together during 1942 to defend the Indies, harry Japan from Siberia, invade Manchukuo, strengthen the armies of China, maintain Russian resistance intact, clear all of Africa from Axis forces, hold the Near and Middle East secure against assault, and fuse the war production and the strategic plans of the United States and the British Commonwealth into a single mighty effort, closely coordinated with Russian and Chinese campaigns. Only on these presuppositions will it be possible to organize the subsequent invasion of the European Continent, the emancipation of the conquered peoples and the military annihilation of Hitler's Reich and of Hirohito's Japan.

Not by arms alone, nor by blindly heroic outpourings of money, goods and men can freemen save their heritage and win the world. The foe will continue to fight, cleverly and unscrupulously, with the poisons of disruption—i.e. anti-Semitism and anti-Communism—and with the heady wine of the "New Order." With many blandishments the enemy will beckon the war-weary to submission, to collaboration and to illusions of hope. Free peoples will be assaulted not only by arms and terrorism but by all the devices of disunion and demoralization through false expectations of a tolerable life in a world controlled by the Caesars. If these weapons are to be parried, if those who wield them are to be beaten, the Allied leaders must use weapons of equal power in awakening mankind to a new dawn of promise and to a new world order consecrated to a freer and richer life for all. Only through the creative dynamism and the devastating fury of a truly revolutionary democracy can the resources of the flesh and spirit be mobilized for the world-wide tasks of emancipation and reconstruction which lie ahead.

These tasks call for more than a Great Coalition in the grand manner of 1813 or 1918. They call for more than a unified command and the full integration into a single strategic design of the efforts of America, Britain, Russia, China and their lesser allies. They call for the building of a free world order during the course of the struggle to give to all who work and fight a firm conviction that the peace will not be lost, and to give the courage of a mighty revelation to all of those upon whose ultimate insurrection against the tyrants the hope of total Allied triumph must rest.

Nothing at present on the horizon offers more fruitful promise of victory in war and peace than the establishment this year of a vast Federal Union of the Atlantic civilizations, comprising the United States, Britain, the British Dominions and those Latin American Republics which are willing to join the Allies as belligerents. Such a Union, to be effective both for waging war and for guaranteeing the peace of the future might well be made as daring and ambitious in the scope of the functions entrusted to the new federal authorities as was the grant of powers to the government of the United States by the Constitution of 1787. Such a Union, if it is to offer hope for tomorrow, should be open to membership to the European democracies, as and when they are liberated. Their government-in-exile should be committed to membership now. The promise of eventual participation as equals should be held out as well to the people of Germany, Italy and Japan, once they are purged of their soul-sickness by the pitiless surgery of war and by social and moral revolution within.

Meanwhile such a Federation of the Free could and should make the Covenant of the League of Nations the basis of its relationship with the Soviet Union and China, with an emancipated India, with the peoples of Africa and Oceania, and with such States as might prefer to hold aloof from the Federation or be found inadmissible by virtue of insufficient guarantees of individual freedom within their frontiers. Such a new League would be inspired and led and made effective by the Atlantic Federation, which would constitute its largest and most powerful member. It would avoid the danger of post-war rivalry with Russia and China by uniting all in a looser concert of power for the service of those purposes common to all. It would avoid the danger of developing a new persecution complex among the vanquished by opening its ranks at once to a new Germany, a new Italy and a new Japan. It would contain within itself, as the old League did not, one preponderant Great Power whose leaders and people would be dedicated in deeds and not in words to immediate action against law-breakers. That Great Power would itself be a Federation of democracies capable of indefinite extension as other States, including both present allies and present enemies, gradually came to accept its principles and to make themselves ready for the advantages of full membership.

Here is no demand for the millennium and no program for Utopia, but merely a practicable means, and in all likelihood the only means and the minimum means, of winning the war and the peace at smallest cost and guaranteeing the future against a repetition of the tragic irresponsibilities of 1919–1939. Such a design for power as this, supplemented by creative thought and constructive action toward a more fruitful and enduring design for social and economic security throughout the World Society, will rally all the world to the cause of freedom. Such a vision as this, translated in the heat of battle into life-giving deeds of foresight and valor, will give new content to Woodrow Wilson's dream and transmute into vital reality in the daily lives of all the world's peoples his inspired words of 1917:

"In every discussion of the peace that must end this war, it is taken for granted that that peace must be followed by some definite concert of power which will make it virtually impossible that any such catastrophe should ever overwhelm us again. Every lover of mankind, every sane and thoughtful man, must take that for granted. It is inconceivable that the people of the United States should play no part in that great enterprise. To take part in such a service will be the opportunity for which they have sought to prepare themselves by the very principles and purposes of their polity and the approved practices of their Government, ever since the days when they set up as a new

[*xv*]

nation in the high and honorable hope that it might in all that it was and did show mankind the way to liberty. They cannot in honor withhold the service to which they are now about to be challenged. They do not wish to withhold it. But they owe it to themselves and to the other nations of the world to state the conditions under which they will feel free to render it.

"That service is nothing less than this—to add their authority and their power to the authority and force of other nations to guarantee peace and justice throughout the world. Such a settlement cannot now be long postponed. No covenant of cooperative peace that does not include the peoples of the New World can suffice to keep the future safe against war. Peace cannot be had without concessions and sacrifices. There is no entangling alliance in a concert of power. When all unite to act in the same sense and with the same purpose, all act in the common interest and are free to live their own lives under a common protection. These are American principles, American policies. We can stand for no others. And they are also the principles and policies of forward looking men and women everywhere, of every modern nation, of every enlightened community. They are the principles of mankind and must prevail."

FREDERICK L. SCHUMAN

CONTENTS

DESIGN FOR POWER

"There's glory for you!" "I don't know what you mean by 'glory,'" Alice said. Humpty Dumpty smiled contemptuously. "Of course you don't—till I tell you. I meant, 'there's a nice knock-down argument for you!'" "But 'glory' doesn't mean 'a nice knock-down argument,'" Alice objected. "When I use a word," Humpty Dumpty said in a rather scornful tone, "it means just what I choose it to mean—neither more nor less." "The question is," said Alice, "whether you can make words mean so many different things." "The question is," said Humpty Dumpty, "which is to be Master— that's all."

X MARKS THE SPOT

Hon. Army gentlemen tried hard to make all clear. It happened one night, they said. At ten o'clock sharp. It was the end of summer in the fourth year of Showa, reign of "Radiant Peace." On the throne sat Hirohito—"Magnanimous Exaltation"—a god, a king and a priest in one, and lineal descendant through twenty-six centuries of Amaterasu, Goddess of the Sun. A lieutenant and six privates were marching southward along the tracks of the South Manchurian Railway toward Mukden, ancestral capital of the Manchus. Behind them they heard a loud explosion. Hurrying back, they found a yard of rail blown away. Bullets whizzed from nearby fields. They fired back. Chinese began to run northward toward the Peitaying barracks of China's Northeastern Army. Four or five were killed. The lieutenant telephoned for help. The southbound express from Changchun roared down the tracks toward the broken rail. . . .

By a happy miracle, the train jumped over the gap and arrived on time (10.30) in Mukden. Meanwhile some 600 Japanese warriors had assembled

[*3*]

under Lieut. Gen. Shimamoto. "Offense," he said, "is the best defense." He boldly ordered his men to storm the barracks. All night, his story ran, the battle raged: 600 little men against 10,000 fiercely fighting troops. It was another Charge of the Light Brigade. The outcome, however, was different. By dawn the barracks were wrecked and burned and the survivors put to flight. Chinese dead: 320. Japanese dead: 2.

Said Shimamoto, it was "wonderful" and due to "the Grace of God, the Glory of the Imperial Throne and Divine Protection." "What army with a grain grit left," asked *The Manchuria Daily News,* "could remain still passive? The Japanese soldiers blood boiling in rage might have delivered their attack with redoubled ferocity but, as the saying runs, 'All is fair in War and Love.' The above is the truth in a nutshell."

Lieut. Gen. Honjo, Commander-in-Chief of the Imperial Japanese Kwantung Army, explained that China's Northeastern Army had challenged the Empire and must be taught a lesson. He therefore ordered the occupation of all barracks, and of Mukden, and of roads and rails and towns all over the vastness of Manchuria. Five days later foreigners were allowed to see the site of the explosion. They saw some new rails and ties, and several dead Chinese. The Lytton Commission held later that "the damage, if any, was not sufficient to justify military action." Others recalled that earlier in the year the wandering Captain Nakamura, "agricultural expert," had been murdered by Chinese soldiers. Tokyo had demanded "satisfaction." An investigation was ordered by young Manchurian Marshal Chang Hsueh-liang. An agreement was about to be reached when the rail flew and the leaping locomotive passed into legend. Some hon. Army gentleman perhaps wished no agreement. Therefore . . . ?

Such was the "Mukden incident" of September 18, 1931. Solutions of many mysteries would be possible if Honjo's aides were willing to speak. The Kwantung Colonels knew their goal and the means of reaching it. Among them was Seishiro Itagaki, destined for a Generalship and the Ministry of War. There was Kenji Ishihara. There was Jiro Minami, the "Little Hitler." Before all others, there was the fabulous Kenji Doihara, Chinese expert, "Lawrence of Manchuria," and a past master of the art of intrigue. Soon after the night of the broken rail Doihara became Mayor of Mukden. Years before he had rescued a young Chinese friend from Peking. He was to rescue him again two months later from "rioters" in Tientsin, and to keep him safe for future use. His friend was ex-"Emperor" Henry Pu-yi, who was destined to become again an "Emperor." The officers of the Kwantung Army were a power in Manchuria. They were on the march to power in Japan. They knew, no doubt, the

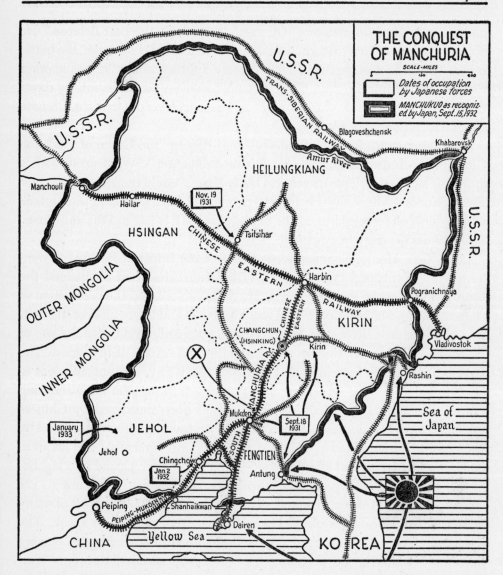

THE CONQUEST OF MANCHURIA

whys and hows of the bomb and the barracks, and the story of the six and the six hundred. But what they knew and what they said were not the same.

The flaming brands at Peitaying spread sparks far afield. Shanghai was to burn, and Addis Ababa, and Almeria, and city after city in many lands, for the world is one and all men are brothers. In the end this fire would consume the books of poets and the benches of lawmakers in Berlin, homes of workers in Vienna, huts of natives in Harar, university classrooms in Madrid, hovels in Warsaw, offices in Rotterdam, palaces in London, churches in Belgrade, docks in Hamburg, children everywhere, women anywhere, wrecks of ships on seven seas. When people choose to live without government, whether in a little neighborhood or in a world society, each clash of wills means violence. The great violence of our time began along the railway tracks north of Mukden.

SCHOOL FOR CRIME

Within the memory of people still alive, Japan emerged from the mists of a feudal kingdom of monks and armored knights to become a great State of industrial tycoons and bankers, holding the reins of power in the Western Pacific. Before the middle of the 19th century the realm of the Rising Sun was a mysterious medieval empire, remote from the West and determined to safeguard itself from Western contamination. But the impact of barbarians with guns and steam-engines was not to be resisted. In 1853 Commodore Matthew Perry, bearing letters and gifts, led a squadron of five steamers and six sailing ships into Yedo (Tokyo) Bay. In accordance with instructions from Washington, he cajoled and coerced the alarmed Japanese into signing a treaty with the United States opening their ports to American merchants. Other Powers at once insisted on similar privileges.

The nobles of the Satsuma and Choshu clans, long rivals of the decadent Tokugawas, saw the wisdom of adopting Western ways if Japan was to escape the fate already overtaking China. In 1867 they overthrew the Shogun, whose office for several centuries had overshadowed the Throne. They restored full power to the young Emperor Mutsuhito, later known as Meiji. They set about to transform their country into a State capable of coping with the Western nations. All the mechanical gadgets of the Christian world were copied. The new way of life made Japan a Great Power.

Once supplied with Western tools of war, Tokyo's statesmen cast covetous eyes on the mainland of Asia. Perceiving that Britishers and Russians vied with Frenchmen and Germans in plundering China, they strove to follow the example of their teachers. They also strove to emulate the ancient deeds of Empress Jingo, who invaded Korea while Septimius Severus reigned at Rome, and of Hideyoshi who did the same when Elizabeth ruled England. In 1894 Tokyo sent troops into the Korean "hermit kingdom," long a dependency of the Chinese Empire. War with China followed. In less than a year Korea and South Manchuria were overrun.

With Peking menaced, China sued for peace. By the Treaty of Shimonoseki, China was obliged to recognize the "independence" of Korea, to pay an indemnity of 150 million dollars, and to cede to Japan Formosa, the Pescadores Islands and the Liaotung Peninsula, key to Manchuria. At this point Russia, Germany and France intervened and forced Japan to give up the Liaotung Peninsula in return for an increased indemnity. Japanese expansion was thus thwarted by rival Western imperialisms. Tokyo perceived that it must be prepared to defy the Western Powers if Japan was to have her rightful share in the dismemberment of a helpless China.

The vast Tsardom of Muscovy was the first obstacle. Japan strengthened her position in 1902 by concluding an alliance with Britain, hereditary enemy in Asia of "the bear that walks like a man." Two years later Japan challenged the bear to battle. The soldiers of Nippon captured Port Arthur and routed the Slav armies at Mukden. At sea the Russian squadrons were destroyed by Admiral Togo's new fleet. Under the Treaty of Portsmouth, signed in New Hampshire under the beneficent eye of Roosevelt I, Japan acquired Port Arthur and the Liaotung Peninsula (Kwantung territory). Russian railway and mining rights in South Manchuria also passed into Japanese hands, along with the southern half of the long island of Sakhalin.

Japan was now on the march. The British alliance was renewed in 1905. By pacts with Paris and St. Petersburg, Tokyo became a partner of the Triple Entente, with a free hand in South Manchuria and in Korea which was annexed in 1910. Should the Entente clash with the Reich, Japan could displace Germany in Shantung as she had already displaced Russia farther north.

LARGE-MINDED LARCENY

On August 15, 1914, Tokyo urged Berlin to withdraw German warships from the Far East and to deliver the Kiaochow leased territory to Japan "with a view to the eventual restoration of the same to China." No reply came. Japan declared war and swiftly seized Kiaochow and its Shantung hinterland, along with the German islands north of New Guinea. In the following January the Japanese Minister politely presented twenty-one demands to the President of China. By their terms Tokyo asked Chinese approval of any disposition Japan might make of Kiaochow and Shantung; the granting to Japan of a 99 year lease on Port Arthur and Dairen; Japanese participation in the Hanyehping Company, producing iron and steel in the Yangtze valley; and the transfer to

Tokyo's control of mining, railway and banking concessions in South Manchuria and Inner Mongolia. Peking was also asked to agree "not to cede or lease to a third Power any harbor, bay or island along the coast of China." Group V of the twenty-one demands provided for Japanese supervision of China's political, financial and military affairs; a joint Sino-Japanese police force in important Chinese cities; the purchase of at least half China's munitions from Japan; and the granting to Tokyo of a sphere of influence in Fukien, opposite Formosa.

Under threats of violence, the Chinese Government yielded. The first sixteen demands were embodied in treaties and notes of May 25, 1915. Other Powers were too preoccupied to interfere. The Allies secretly agreed to support the Japanese claims at the Peace Conference. Even the United States, in the Lansing-Ishii agreement of November 2, 1917, recognized that "territorial propinquity" gave Japan "special interests" in China. Tokyo was not deterred by China's entry into the war on the Allied side. New concessions were wrested from Peking during the last year of the conflict.

By the time of the Armistice, Japanese power in Asia had been blown up to the bursting point. Tokyo controlled Shantung, Fukien, all of Manchuria, Inner Mongolia and the German islands north of the equator. Revolution in Russia had enabled Japan to expand her conquests to the north. In agreement with the Allies and America, Japan had embarked upon military intervention in Siberia in the summer of 1918. Washington, London and Paris sought to aid the "White" Armies in overthrowing the Soviets. Tokyo sought to acquire real estate. Northern Sakhalin was occupied. Japan poured 70,000 troops into eastern Siberia with a view toward retaining permanent control of the Maritime Provinces and perhaps of the whole region east of Lake Baikal. Friction developed between the American and Japanese armies of intervention, and between Tokyo and Washington. But Japan was supreme in eastern Asia—for a brief but glorious moment—and the protests of other States were in vain.

RETREAT WITHOUT REPENTANCE

Had the Kaiser's Germany defeated the Allies in 1918, Japan's leaders, despite their "alliance" with the Allies, would have done then what they were to try to do in 1940 in the wake of the defeat of the Allies by Hitler's Germany. Had Russia's Red regime been destroyed in 1918-1919 (as Tokyo was to hope it would be in 1941), the little men of Nippon would have entrenched them-

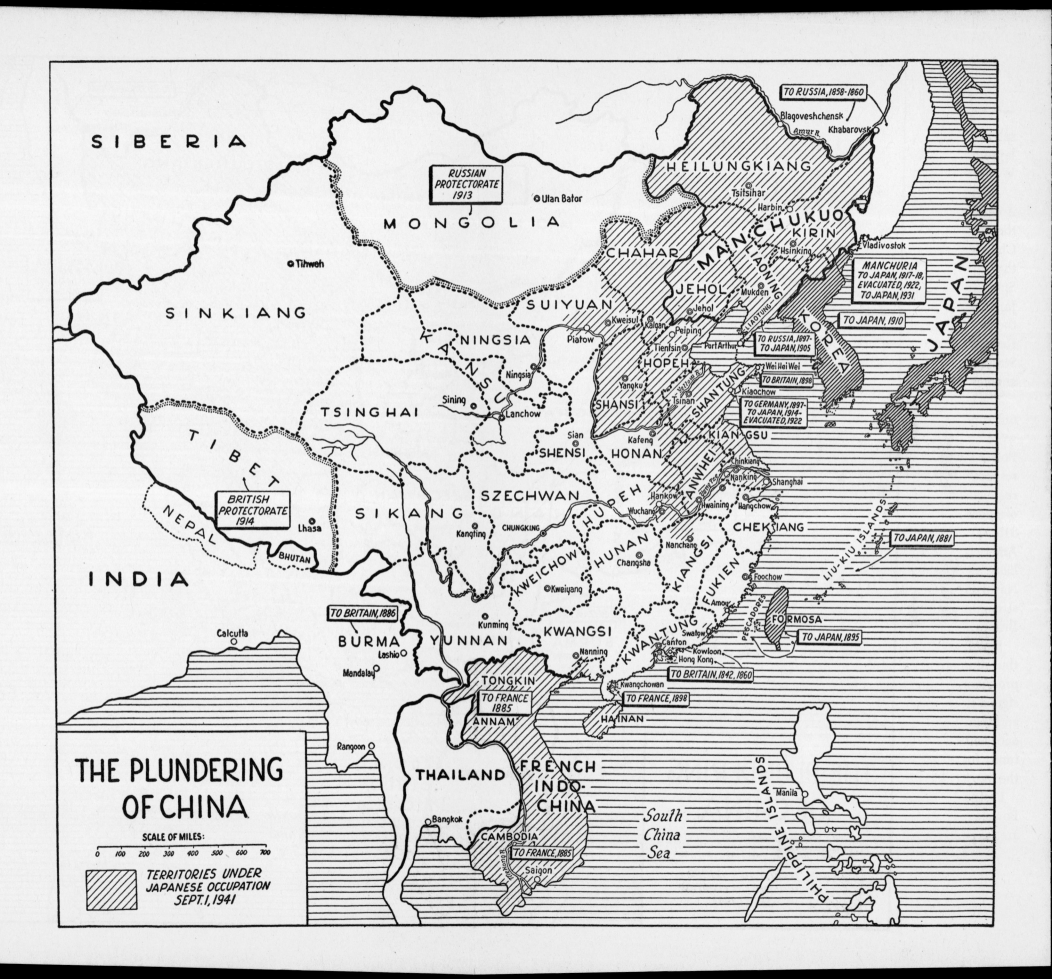

SIBERIA

RUSSIAN
PROTECTORATE
1913

MONGOLIA
○Ulan Bator

○Tihwah

SINKIANG

SUIYUAN

CHAHAR

HEILUNGKIANG

TO RUSSIA, 1858-1860
Blagoveshchensk
Amur R.
Khabarovsk
Tsitsihar
Harbin○
MANCHUKUO
KIRIN
Hsinking
Vladivostok
LIAONING
MANCHURIA
TO JAPAN, 1917-18,
EVACUATED, 1922,
TO JAPAN, 1931
JEHOL
○Kweisui Kalgan Peiping
Jehol
Mukden LIAOTUNG
Piatow
Tientsin Port Arthur
KOREA
TO RUSSIA, 1897-
TO JAPAN, 1905
TO JAPAN, 1910

NINGSIA
Ningsia
Yangku
HOPEH
Wei Hei Wei
TO BRITAIN, 1898
KANSU
Sining○
Lanchow
SHANSI
○Tsinan
Kiaochow
TO GERMANY, 1897-
TO JAPAN, 1914-
EVACUATED, 1922
SHANTUNG

TSINGHAI

TIBET

NEPAL

BRITISH
PROTECTORATE
1914

○Lhasa

BHUTAN

INDIA

Sian
SHENSI
Kaieng
HONAN
KIANGSU
Chinkiang
Nanking ○Shanghai
SZECHWAN
HUPEH
Hankow
Wuchang
ANWHEI
Hwaining Hangchow

SIKANG

Kangting○
CHUNGKING
HUNAN
Changsha
KWEICHOW
○Kweiyang
KIANGSI
Nanchang
CHEKIANG
TO JAPAN, 1881
LIU-KIU ISLANDS

TO BRITAIN, 1886

BURMA
Lashio○
Mandalay○

Calcutta○

Kunming○
YUNNAN
KWANGSI
Nanning○
FUKIEN
Amoy
Foochow
PESCADORES
FORMOSA
TO JAPAN, 1895

KWANGTUNG
Swatow
Canton
Kowloon
Hong Kong
TO BRITAIN, 1842, 1860
Kwangchowan
TO FRANCE, 1898

TONGKIN
TO FRANCE
1885
ANNAM
HAINAN

Rangoon○

THAILAND

FRENCH
INDO-
CHINA

PHILIPPINE ISLANDS
○Manila

South
China
Sea

Bangkok○

CAMBODIA
TO FRANCE, 1885
Saigon○

JAPAN

THE PLUNDERING
OF CHINA

SCALE OF MILES:
0 100 200 300 400 500 600 700

TERRITORIES UNDER
JAPANESE OCCUPATION
SEPT. 1, 1941

selves in eastern Siberia. But the defeat of the Central Powers and the collapse of the White Armies left Japan standing alone against the victorious Western democracies.

At the Paris Peace Conference Tokyo's delegates were induced, under American pressure, to agree to retain only economic privileges in Shantung, though Germany's rights in the province were transferred to Japan despite China's plea for justice. Tokyo also kept possession, as League "mandates," of the Caroline, Marshall and Mariana Islands which Germany had bought from Spain in 1899 and lost to Japan in 1914. But the more ambitious hopes of Japan's empire-builders were thwarted. They could not hope to compete with the new American naval building program. They shrank from challenging the Red Army to battle. At the Washington Conference of 1921-1922 the United States and Britain cooperated to bring Japan to terms. The Anglo-Japanese alliance was ended. The Tokyo Cabinet judged it wise to compromise.

The ensuing bargain was incorporated in a series of treaties—most of which unhappily were to become "scraps of paper" as soon as Americans and Britons were to show that they would run no risks to enforce them. By the "Four Power Pacific Pact" of 1922 Washington, London, Paris and Tokyo agreed "to respect their rights in relation to their insular possessions and dominions in the region of the Pacific Ocean" and to "consult" one another in case of any threat of aggression. In the naval treaty of February 6, 1922, Japan was granted 315,000 tons of battleships as against 525,000 tons each for Britain and America. All the Powers agreed to maintain the *status quo* as regards naval bases and fortifications in the Western Pacific. A decade later, at the London Naval Conference of 1930, Tokyo achieved the right to maintain a naval strength in cruisers and auxiliary vessels in the ratio of 7:10:10 in relation to Britain and the United States.

Japan was recognized as the third greatest naval Power. The United States thus renounced ambitions of naval supremacy in the Orient. As for the *quid pro quo,* Tokyo agreed to restore Shantung to China. Most important, Japan signed the Nine Power Pact of 1922 for the preservation of the "Open Door" and thereby repeated her pledge of 1899 and 1908 to respect the independence and integrity of China and to support the principle of equality of opportunity for the traders of all nations in Chinese markets. Northern Sakhalin and the Maritime Provinces were restored to the Soviet Union in 1925.

Postponement of hopes was not a renunciation of hopes. Like other Great Powers on the march, Japan sought to extend her dominion over as wide an area as possible. The objectives of her quest reflected the interests of her ruling classes: the new bourgeoisie, the old nobility, and the military, naval and diplomatic bureaucracy. The goals at first were the usual goals of imperialists everywhere in the age of merchandising and money-making. They later became more glamorous. A ready excuse for aggrandizement was "surplus population." America and the British Dominions closed their doors to Japanese immigrants. Crowded China could furnish no outlet for Japan's teeming millions. Australia and New Zealand, however, were empty, as was much of Siberia. Control of China might pave the way for control of greener pastures abroad.

The Great Depression created insecurities in Japan much like those experienced in other States with small margins of wealth. They led, as elsewhere, to political fanaticism, to frantic efforts to recapture vanishing markets, and to a resurgence of militant imperialism. Bankers and business men, dominating a capitalism which was already monopolistic rather than competitive, spoke through the politicians of the Minseito party. Feudal aristocrats were better represented by those of the Seiyukai. Neither group was ever firmly devoted to the ideals of Western liberalism. The lower middle class was politically inarticulate, save in the Army. The impoverished peasantry, heavily in debt to the landlords, demanded relief but did not embrace radicalism nor lose its reverence for the Emperor-god and the divinely established social order. A few city workers listened longingly to Marxist agitators, but never became a significant factor in Japanese politics. The real rulers of the land were the professional specialists in violence.

THE DUTY OF ASSASSINATION

Power in feudal Japan rested with the Daimyo or lords of the land, and with the Samurai who commanded their peasant troops. In the new Japan born out of the "Meiji Restoration," power went ultimately not to the new class of business men but to the officers of the new Army, inspired by Samurai traditions and equipped with modern machines of war. From the outset this conscript force was a school for the best of the youth. Its officers rose from the ranks of the best among the best. Most were poor and of humble origin. Most were imbued with deathless love of the Emperor, deep devotion to "Shinto" or the way of the gods, and half-hidden contempt for business men and bankers.

The new lords of war had power to make or break cabinets by naming, or refusing to name, the ministers of war and navy. These ministers were not civilians but always active officers. Alone among their colleagues they had direct access to the Emperor. The fiercely tribal patriotism of the militarists was (sometimes) sane and respectable. The fiery underlings who followed them were less patient with politicians who sought peace by wrong formulas. Armies and navies exist for war. Wars are fought to establish peace. Whoever opposes war is therefore the enemy of peace, the foe of all good warriors and, quite obviously, a traitor to the Throne. A patriotic officer confronted by disgrace commits *hara-kiri* to save his face and the honor of his ancestors. By the same token, a patriotic officer who sees others disgracing the nation must not suffer them to live.

By these quaint customs many Japanese politicians have been enabled to avoid the boredom of dying of old age. Premier Hara prepared the way for the Washington naval treaty. A patriot therefore stabbed him to death. A decade later Premier Hamaguchi prepared the way for ratification of the London naval treaty. A patriot therefore shot him to death. So perished also Premier Inukai, who believed in peace with China, and Baron Takuma Dan, head of the House of Mitsui, and Finance Minister Inouye—all within the year which followed the "Mukden incident." Most of the murderers were lightly dealt with. To punish patriots would be absurd.

Army-inspired patrioteers had hotly assailed the Minseito Cabinet in 1930, demanding an end of the "corrupt" alliance between politicians and capitalists, and insisting on military leadership, a "strong" foreign policy, the suppression of all radicalism, and a kind of national socialism to relieve agriculture and control industry. Liberal Baron Shidehara, Foreign Minister during the 1920's, was pledged to compromise with the Western Powers and cooperation with China. Bankers and merchants supported him. But the militarists, following more heroic gods, denounced his "weakness" and resolved to achieve their ends by fair means or foul. The excursion into Manchuria had helped them toward their goal. But the help was not enough. Following a Seiyukai victory in the election of February, 1932, the moderate Admiral Makato Saito, six times the target of would-be assassins, formed a coalition cabinet. Two years later, in July, 1934, the moderate Admiral Keisuke Okada succeeded to the premiership, with Saito later replacing the moderate Count Makino as Keeper of the Privy Seal and adviser to the Emperor.

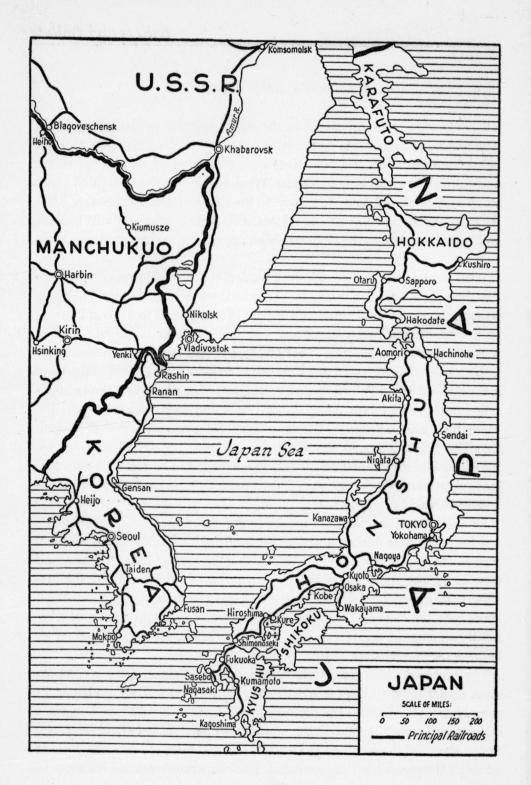

BALLOTS AND BULLETS

All moderation was distasteful to the Army apostles of dangerous living. The seizure of Manchuria had failed to produce its expected results on the home front. Admirals and politicians were still spurning the martial virtues and cultivating sweet reasonableness. What was worse, the benighted voters stubbornly preferred sanity to lunacy. In the Diet elections of February, 1936, they repudiated the Seiyukai candidates, with their Fascist-militarist backers, and gave a majority to the moderate Minseito men who supported the Okada Cabinet.

Such insults from the masses were intolerable to the Hotspurs who knew that their patriotism alone was pure. They forthwith decided to act. Their plan was simple: they would murder all the ministers opposed to Army rule, along with sundry "uncooperative" officers, and then set up an undiluted regime of warlords. At dawn of February 26, 1936, a number of regiments, including the Imperial Guards, began seizing public buildings in Tokyo. One group went to the home of Saito. They shot him dead and wounded his wife. Other soldiers called on General Jotaro Watanabe and slew him with a machine-gun. The venerable Finance Minister, Korekayo Takahashi, was murdered in his bedchamber. Admiral Suzuki was shot but recovered. The aged Prince Saionji, last of the Genro, was also on the list, but managed to be missed. Count Makino, vacationing in the country, fled to the hills while mutineers killed his bodyguard and burned his house.

Premier Okada, awakened at sunrise by the shooting of four policemen before his home, was pushed into a secret vault by his brother-in-law, Colonel Matsuo. The patriots killed the Colonel, mistaking him for the Premier, and then withdrew. The Imperial Palace announced Okada's death. But the "deceased" disguised himself and on the following morning slipped out of his house with the mourners, in the wake of his own funeral procession. His belatedly announced survival embarrassed the Throne. He was obliged to relinquish the premiership.

The mutineers had meanwhile surrounded the Palace. They waited for some leader of the higher warlords to take command. They explained in pamphlets that politicians and plutocrats were traitors, and that the Emperor's evil retainers must be removed. But none of the upper officers would act. Loyal troops encircled the rebels and ultimately induced them to surrender. Fifteen minor plotters were tried and executed. Their superiors remained immune. In any other land the Army leadership would have been disgraced and discredited by such deeds as these. But in the land of *Kokoku*—Empire of *Tenno*, "Heavenly King," whose descendants rule forever in eternal devotion to the way of the sword—the glory of the warlords could never be dimmed.

Their most effective weapon, they now perceived, was not holy murder at home but holy war abroad. To fight with the neighbors keeps peace in the family. The effects of the Manchurian adventure were wearing off. Another war was needed. The new Premier, Koki Hirota, offered hope, for he was a member of the Black Dragon Society of super-patriots and a militant champion of Japan-over-Asia. In the end, however, he was to prove disappointing. Other devices would be needed. The ingenuity of the warlords would prove equal to their problem.

WORDS AT GENEVA

Weak minds and wills in Paris, London, and Washington had long since convinced the adventurers in Tokyo that new crusades would involve few risks. No other conclusion could be drawn from the aftermath of the rape of Manchuria. Three days after the Mukden "bombing" of 1931 Dr. Alfred Sze, China's spokesman at Geneva, had asked the League of Nations to fulfill the pledges of its members. He summoned them to action to preserve the peace, to restore the *status quo*, to fix the reparations due his country. Ambassador Yoshizawa, spokesman for Japan, pleaded "self-defense" and asked "direct negotiations." The Council of the League sent pleas to halt the fighting. Tokyo made excuses. The Council asked America to join in an investigation. President Herbert Hoover, grappling dismally with business woes, was doubtful. His Secretary of State, Colonel Henry Stimson, feared that a joint inquiry would embarrass the civilian men-of-good-will in Tokyo and provoke the Army hotheads into rasher deeds. He accordingly declined Geneva's invitation.

It soon was plain that the Japanese Army was a law unto itself and that the chief function of the Foreign Office was to make excuses for what the Army did. Geneva and Washington felt called upon to act. They "invoked" the Kellogg Pact. To insure that Tokyo would be impressed, Prentiss Gilbert, American Consul in Geneva, sat at the Council table in October. Tokyo was not impressed. The Council met in Paris in November. Washington ordered Ambassador Dawes from London to watch the proceedings—but not to attend the meeting, lest American isolationists be outraged. Tokyo still declined to be impressed. The invaders moved into North Manchuria. In December, 1931, the Council at last appointed an investigating commission, headed by Lord Lytton and including an American, General Frank McCoy. It went. It saw. But it did not conquer. A year and a fortnight after the Mukden incident it issued a report of 100,000 words. The words were admirably reasonable, but much too late. Tokyo rejected them. So sorry.

Secretary Stimson had meanwhile learned that force cannot be overcome by words. Yet his colleagues and his countrymen would use no counter-force and authorize no threats. He cast about for stronger words and finally announced his "doctrine": let no one recognize the fruits of conquest. He knew, however, that gestures of ostracism would be without result unless America and Britain stood together. He appealed to Britain's Foreign Minister, Sir John Simon, to join him in invoking the Nine Power Pact. Sir John gave lawyers' answers. During February, 1932, Stimson phoned Sir John four times to plead for common action. Sir John was vague. "I finally became convinced," wrote Stimson later, "that the British Government felt reluctant to join in such a demarche. . . . My plan was therefore blocked. . . . I seemed doomed to inaction, while a great tragedy was following its predestined course."

The tragedy was more bitter than he knew. Japanese forces began a bombardment and invasion of Shanghai at the end of January, 1932. Thousands died. China invoked more articles of the Covenant. At Geneva 232 delegates from 57 countries pathetically opened the General Disarmament Conference of the League of Nations. The League Assembly met in March while Shanghai's defenders sought safety in flight. The Assembly asked Japanese withdrawal and endorsed the "Stimson Doctrine." In May a Shanghai truce was signed. Japan withdrew. The League had won a victory. Yet the victory was a defeat, for Tokyo had no thought of quitting Manchuria.

In March of 1932 the incantations of the Army leaders resurrected a forgotten man: Henry Pu-yi, friend of Doihara and last of China's Manchu rulers. At the age of four Henry had succeeded his grand-aunt, the Dowager Empress Tzu Hsi, on the celestial throne. Immediately thereafter his dynasty was ended by the revolution of 1911. The royal boy grew up in obscurity, save for a few days of 1917 when a monarchist *coup* restored his imperial title. At twenty-five he was harmless, amiable and fond of his Japanese friends. He was now made "Regent" and later "Emperor Kang Teh" of "Manchukuo." In September of 1932 Tokyo formally recognized Henry's new realm and signed a treaty making it a protectorate of Japan.

China thus lost a great province, larger than France and Germany combined, with more than 30,000,000 people living on its fertile plains. The West lost more. The Western Powers were paralyzed. Britain had abandoned the gold standard on the very day on which Dr. Sze had made his first appeal. The shadow of bankruptcy hung over the white man's world. Britain's "National Government," under renegade Laborite Ramsay MacDonald, was quite content to let simple Simon defend Japan at Geneva. No one would risk blood or treasure to rescue Manchuria from its conquerors. Inaction was simpler and safer than action. Apart from verbiage, nothing was done. In February, 1933, the League Assembly condemned Japan and endorsed the report of the Lytton Commission. Tokyo announced withdrawal from the League.

Here the West's design for chaos was woven for the years to come. The warp was the faith of Patriotism forbidding men to pay the price of checking crime so long as their Fatherlands seemed safe. The woof was the cult of Property inspiring secret love among the well-to-do for all adventurers, however foul their deeds, who proclaimed themselves crusaders against the fiends of Moscow. Western Christians said they believed that all men everywhere were brothers. But no Christian State would be its brother's keeper if such a role required sacrifice. Western men of money said they believed in law and order. But none would act for justice in Manchuria if action meant discomfort or danger. Safety now and danger later were preferred to danger now and safety later—the more so as Sir John and all his kind were sure that later would be safer. But those who misunderstand the present have no future.

UNFINISHED BUSINESS

Nippon's little men-at-arms had never lost a war. In the decade of the '30's they looked with hungry eyes on China's helplessness. With quick contempt they watched the West, immensely strong in gold and goods, neglect its weapons and lose its will to act. When the strong grow weak, the weak must strive for strength.

"The battlefield," says the Field Service Code of Japan's Ministry of War, "is where the Imperial Army, acting under the Imperial Command, displays its true character, conquering wherever it attacks, winning wherever it engages in combat, in order to spread *Kodo* far and wide so that the enemy may look up in awe to the august virtues of His Majesty. . . . The destiny of the Empire rests upon victory or defeat in battle. Never give up. Never tarnish the glorious history of the Imperial Army with its tradition of invincibility. . . . Faith is strength. He who has faith in combat is always the victor."

The warriors of Japan had faith. Their faith bred works. For years their works were clever in sowing seeds of discord across the China Sea. For years their wits were equal to befuddling Western leaders. Their foe, they said, was Bolshevism. All good men agreed and wished them well.

Jehol was annexed to Manchukuo in 1933. Step by step the intruders pushed on southward and westward during the years which followed. Chahar was seized. Chinese forces were compelled to quit Tientsin and Peiping. Much of northern China was taken over by a group of puppets shrewdly labelled the "Autonomous Federation for Joint Defense Against Communism." Another "autonomous" regime assumed control of Peiping, Tientsin and Chahar, along with Hopei and Shantung. With Tokyo's aid, Manchukuan forces occupied Suiyuan and strove to establish still another "autonomous" administration, partly encircling Outer Mongolia. Japan's officials meanwhile flouted China's tariff laws and fostered (for a price) a vast smuggling of opium and other goods into northern China, thus doping their victims, conquering new markets and reducing the revenues of Nanking. During the course of tedious talks in the autumn of 1936 Japan solicited Chiang Kai-shek's "cooperation." Tokyo offered "advisers." Tokyo pledged support in fighting the Chinese Soviets. Tokyo asked suppression of all anti-Japanese agitation and the grant of privileges to Japanese concessionaires. Chiang was tempted but dared not quite accept.

To realize more sweeping plans for expelling the West from Asia more artful formulas were needed. In April, 1934, Tokyo announced a "Japanese Monroe Doctrine": henceforth Japan alone would be "guardian of the peace of the Pacific." The militarists were cheered by the Philippine Independence Act of 1934 and by the first of the new American "neutrality" statutes, enacted in 1935. With the most powerful of the Powers in full flight toward fancied safety, the soldiers of the Son of Heaven felt new courage. Tokyo demanded naval parity with Britain and America. London and Washington refused. Tokyo then declined to renew the naval treaties of 1922 and 1930, and called its delegates home from the futile London naval conference of 1935-36. As the new naval race began, Rome and Berlin borrowed leaves from Tokyo's book and embarked anew on conquests in Africa and Europe. Most leaders of the West welcomed every victory of those who said their only goal was defense against the Marxists. The conquerors were more than willing to foster this delusion.

[*17*]

TRIAL AND ERROR

On November 25, 1936, Ambassador Mushakoji and Joachim von Ribbentrop signed their names in Berlin to a document cleverly called a "German-Japanese Agreement against the Communist International." They pledged their States to act together against the menace from Moscow. Stalin scoffed. But Western Tories cheered. Italy joined the "Anti-Comintern" a year thereafter—and then Hungary, Manchukuo and Franco's Spain. This façade of righteousness achieved its purpose. Most pious men of property and many politicians in the Western States gave silent thanks and blessed their would-be saviors. The warriors of the Rising Sun thus chloroformed the democratic Powers and won potential allies for despoiling them of their empires.

The stage was now prepared for further moves on other fronts. The home front was most crucial. Following legislative criticism of its course the Army, led by Gen. Terauchi, overthrew the Hirota Cabinet in January, 1937, by refusing to supply a minister of war. The militarists once more demanded an end of rule by "politicians." When the Emperor named the moderate Gen. Kazushigi Ugaki to replace Hirota, they still withheld approval. Ugaki said: "Japan is now standing at the crossroads of Fascism or parliamentary government." Early in February a Cabinet acceptable to the warlords was formed by Gen. Senjuro Hayashi. The political parties were ignored. The new Premier dissolved the Diet.

But the militarists rejoiced too soon. In the election of April, 1937, all the major parties opposed Hayashi. Of the 466 seats in the House of Representatives the voters filled 421 with anti-Hayashi candidates. For a time the General-Premier tried to keep office with Army support. In June, however, he yielded his post to Prince Fumimaro Konoe who appeased the Army, named Koki Hirota as Foreign Minister and cryptically announced that "our external policy will seek peace based upon justice, which is not the same thing as the mere maintenance of the *status quo.*"

What to do? A new slaughter of moderate leaders might further alienate the masses. Better to win them by new wars abroad. Whom to fight? To attack the Western Powers would be unsafe until they should be immobilized by Japan's allies in Europe. To attack the U.S.S.R. was tempting. The West would cheer. Men of means in both Japan and China would rally to the cause.

On June 20, 1937, Japanese forces clashed with Soviet detachments along the Amur south of Blagoveshchensk. An ultimatum to Moscow demanded Soviet evacuation of several disputed islands. But the invaders were quickly beaten by the Far Eastern Red Army. A year later they tried once more. In July, 1938, Japanese troops stormed the heights of Changkufeng (on the Manchurian border near Possiet Bay), claimed by Tokyo but held by Soviet forces. Within two weeks Red divisions retook the stronghold and put their foes to flight. In Moscow Ambassador Shigemitsu hastened to sign an armistice with Litvinov. In February, 1939, desultory fighting broke out on the Argun River, northwest of Manchuli. In September, 1939, Japanese troops attacked Soviet guards on the Manchu-Mongol frontier near the Khalka River. Once more they were defeated with numerous casualties.

Since all experiments led to the same result, the Tokyo militarists refrained from challenging the Soviets to war. To fight those who are willing to fight and who fight too well is always inexpedient if other and easier victims are at hand. The would-be conquerors in Japan, like those in Italy and the Reich, decided to defer a reckoning with the U.S.S.R. War on China in the name of "anti-Communism" seemed a safer course.

A HOUSE DIVIDED

No one can tell, save those who will not speak, just what was planned in secret by the guiding spirits of the Imperial Army in the spring and summer of 1937. They willed a war. They chose China as their victim. Konoe and Hirota acquiesced in their desires. At first perhaps they sought no more than a few cheap local victories. Perhaps they believed that all of China could be subdued at little cost or risk. They scarcely sought a struggle to the death. Yet they felt alarmed at late events in China. The sick and sleepy dragon was stirring with new life. A sacred war for "peace" would rally all Japan behind the warlords. If successful it would likewise shatter the dream of Chinese unity and pave the way for full scale conquest. The Army's double goal was to keep China divided and Japan united. The warlords' choice of time was shaped by the April election returns at home. It was also shaped by the curious course which Chiang Kai-shek was forced reluctantly to follow after January.

Well worth retracing are the steps by which this cold and callous Christian was changed from rebel to tyrant, from conqueror to weakling, from China's hope to China's grief, and then from a grief to a hope once more despite himself. In his youth this talented man of means perceived what many other young Chinese saw: that China's survival in a hard new world required revolution and a copying of Western ways. In his youth he turned, as others did, to Sun Yat Sen, father and founder of the Kuomintang or National People's Party. With Sun he saw that victory for the cause of China's freedom required alien aid against the Western Powers. From only one source could such aid be had. In 1923 Chiang Kai-shek journeyed to Moscow in quest of help.

The men of the Kremlin were then still moved to succor all the oppressed. They pledged support. To Canton came Michael Borodin, Adolf Joffe, Vasily Bleucher (alias General Galen) and other advisers and organizers. Such men as these helped to forge the Kuomintang into a sword for China's emancipation. Sun Yat Sen approved. Chiang, his faithful aide, rejoiced. Sun, however, was not to taste the fruits of victory. He died of cancer in Peiping in March of 1925. His mantle fell to Chiang Kai-shek.

Love and money played their roles in things to come. Sun and Chiang married sisters, whose father was wise old "Charley" Soong, Americanized Methodist with three daughters and three sons. He made his fortune selling Chinese Bibles. His oldest daughter, Ai-ling Soong, was wed to H. H. Kung, a Christian descendant of Confucius who went to Yale and later amassed great riches with the help of his practical spouse. The middle daughter, gentle Ching-ling Soong, became the wife of Sun Yat Sen. Young Chiang, divorced in 1921 from a wife he never loved, became enamoured of the youngest daughter, Mei-ling Soong—Wellesley-bred and blessed with beauty and strength of will. Chiang wooed her while he took command of the Soviet-trained armies of his cause. He pressed his courtship even as he carried the Nationalist banners northward to the Yangtze and beyond. In his year of triumph, 1927, he and Mei-ling were wed. The marriage was childless but happy. The victory was barren and tragic.

China's grief was the fruit of Chiang's perfidy in the wake of his own success. Had he remained loyal to the vision of Sun Yat Sen, he might have kept the Kuomintang intact as a united brotherhood of leaders. For China's common future he might have kept the faith with his Soviet assistants and his followers, millions strong, among the lowly. By such a course he might have built a strong new China and forever balked the hopes of Japanese adventurers.

That these things were not to be was due to war within the ranks of China's saviors. This war would later have its counterparts in many forms in many lands and bring them all alike to ruin. This war was the old and ugly war of rich and poor. No sooner had Generalissimo Chiang Kai-shek mastered the Yangtze and won the Shanghai bankers to his cause in the spring of 1927 than the strife of classes among his followers broke out in open violence. Like Martin Luther in the Peasants' War, he was forced to choose. He was rich. He had married riches. He cast his lot at once with the men of money and the land-lords. To keep control against the masses he made himself a tyrant.

DIVISION AND REUNION

Terror followed—White and Red. The Generalissimo suppressed the Left regime at Hankow. He dealt out torture and death to hundreds of Communists, Russian and Chinese, and to thousands of farmers and coolies who had looked to the Kuomintang for support against their exploiters. At Nanking he set up a government of Right-wing Nationalists. Borodin and Bleucher fled to Russia. Chiang's own son by his first wife became a Communist. Chiang's sister-in-law, Madame Sun Yat Sen, denounced him as a traitor to the revolution. Unmoved by mercy or remorse, he slaughtered those who were once his friends. Peiping fell into his hands in 1928. All China was his. But in winning his land he lost it. Ten years of civil strife ensued, with Chiang now quitting all his posts, now resuming his bloody leadership, now battling local chieftains, now bribing them and begging their support. Through all this futile struggle his course toward Tokyo was appeasement. His eyes saw only one enemy: the Communists who had escaped his wrath.

Many of these stubborn fighters had fled the terror along the Yangtze and established themselves in Kiangsi Province near Shanghai. Wherever they went they organized local Soviets and waged war on the well-to-do. Peasants and workers rallied to their cause. Each year Chiang's armies moved against them in a crusade of extermination. But all of Chiang's horses and all of Chiang's men were unable to bring them to defeat. When the pressure in Kiangsi became too heavy in 1934 the two Red leaders, Mao Tse-tung and Chu Teh, led their followers on the "Long March" of a year and a day across twelve provinces to safety. Harassed at every step, one hundred thousand men marched 6,000 miles until half their number reached Shensi in the far northland. Here they reestablished their soviet regime, declared war on Japan and defied Chiang Kai-shek to conquer them.

The tragedy closed as a farce. When the Reds reached Shensi, Chiang ordered Chang Hsueh-liang, ex-ruler of Manchuria, to attack them. But the Young Marshal refused and pleaded for unity against the Japanese, who had killed his father and robbed him of his patrimony. His men made friends with

Chiang's Red foes. The Generalissimo went to Sian to investigate in December, 1936. He bitterly denounced the Young Marshal for insubordination. He spurned all pleas for a common front against Tokyo. At this the Marshal boldly kidnapped the Generalissimo and spent the next twelve days apologizing to his captive, pleading for peace, threatening punishment and begging forgiveness. All about were Communist troops who could easily have killed the man who had brought death to tens of thousands of their comrades. They preferred unity to vengeance. At length the deadlock between captor and captive was complete. Chiang and his wife, who had flown to his side, were then prevailed upon to receive the Communist leader, Chou En-lai. He it was who arranged for Chiang Kai-shek's release.

Chiang's sojourn at Sian brought about the end of China's civil war. The Generalissimo made a virtue of necessity. Left and Right were reconciled. Communists and Nationalists closed ranks. Chiang agreed that a test of force with Japan must come. The later it came the stronger would China be to meet it. The Army men of Tokyo took thought together. They resolved to strike while China was still weak.

THE COMING OF THE PEACE-MAKERS

On the night of July 7, 1937, a battalion of the Japanese North China garrison went out for "night manoeuvers" southwest of Peiping near Lukouchiao. They were searching, they said, for a soldier whom Chinese troops had seized or slain. (He later turned up safe and sound.) At the Marco Polo Bridge over the Yungting River they clashed with part of the Chinese 29th Army. For several weeks skirmishes, truces, sieges and negotiations followed one another in bewildering disorder.

Japanese troops poured into North China from Manchukuo. Tokyo refused to talk with the Chinese Government at Nanking and demanded that the local authorities in the north withdraw all troops, suppress all anti-Japanese agitation and "cooperate against Communism." On July 27, Hirota told the Diet that a new buffer State would be established south of the Great Wall. "The Japanese policy in East Asia," he explained, "is directed solely toward the realization of stability through conciliation and cooperation between Japan, Manchukuo and China and the halting of the Communist invasion of the Orient." By the end of the month general hostilities were in progress in the north. Japanese flyers slaughtered thousands of helpless civilians in Tientsin and harried the nearby provinces with savage fury.

Chiang Kai-shek had no choice but to resist. He declared in late July: "It is obvious that the Peiping-Tientsin warfare marks the beginning of a war of invasion. I am sure that our people, finding the Fatherland at this crucial point, will fight to the finish like one man. I am confident that final victory will be ours." A month later he concluded a non-aggression pact with the U.S.S.R. In September the Chinese Communist party announced the dissolution of the "Soviet Republic of China" and the establishment of a People's Front with the Kuomintang in resistance to Japanese aggression.

Whatever the original intentions of Nippon's warmakers may have been, they now were forced to strike at all of China with all the strength at their command. They called their war "the China incident." They summoned their simple countrymen, blinded by ignorance and bewitched by tribal pride, to give their money and their sons in order that the simple countrymen of China might be taught the virtues of obedience. They showed quite clearly how the wicked must be brought by torture to the ways of love and how their ancient dream of peace on earth could only be served with fire and sword.

CHINA'S SORROW

In the appalling holocaust which ensued, the invaders took city after city and province after province. They found, however, that they had at last aroused the slumbering Chinese masses to fierce patriotism. Victories in the field over the ragged troops of Chiang Kai-shek and bestial massacres of Chinese civilians were alike futile in inducing surrender. Each outrage steeled the Chinese will to resist. Effective resistance was made possible by the willingness of the defenders to take frightful punishment without flinching, and by the small but steady stream of military supplies which flowed into central China from the Western world and the Soviet Union. A new Japanese attack on Shanghai was launched in mid-August of 1937. Battleships, bombers and land artillery reduced much of the native city to a flaming shambles. By mid-November Chinese troops were forced to quit the vicinity of China's greatest port. The capital was moved from Nanking to Hankow and later to Chungking in remote Szechwan province.

The invaders came up the Yangtze and entered Nanking on December 10, 1937, pillaging and burning wherever they went. Thousands of women were violated. The aged, the infirm and even the children were slaughtered. Disarmed soldiers and non-combatants were butchered with machine-guns and artillery or made living targets for bayonet practice. Forty thousand victims died. In the gutted capital the victors set up a provisional puppet regime. "Imperial benevolence," declares the Field Service Code, "is extended to all without favor, while the Imperial virtues enlighten the world. The Army, under command of the Emperor, assists in furthering the Imperial fortunes by enhancing the glories of the Empire through the embodiment of the lofty spirit of valor. This spirit is the basic factor in realizing universal peace. Modest in its strength, unostentatious in its kindness, the Imperial Army becomes the object of admiration when it quietly displays its valor and benevolence."

When these deeds of loving-kindness produced no will to yield, Tokyo enlisted Nazi mediation to negotiate peace with Chiang Kai-shek. Hirota asked Chinese repudiation of "Communism" and of the Soviet non-aggression pact, recognition of Manchukuo, payment of the costs of the war, and appointment of Japanese "advisers." Chungking refused to surrender. Prince Konoe then announced in January, 1938, that Japan would have no further dealings with the Kuomintang but would promote the establishment of a new Chinese regime.

During Europe's year of Anschluss and Munich, the Imperial Army won further Pyrrhic victories but failed to crush its foe. An attempt to take Suchow in Kiangsu, at the junction of the Peiping-Nanking and Sian-Haichow railway, met at first with disaster. Chinese forces, aided by thousands of guerrillas throughout North China, inflicted costly defeats on the invaders near Taierchwang in early April and again in May, 1938, but were forced at length to quit Suchow. In the south Amoy was lost. Thousands died in air-raids on Canton. When Japanese columns sought to take Chingchow, west of Suchow, and to cut the Peiping-Hankow railway, they were halted with heavy losses by the opening of the dikes of the Yellow River. Foiled in the north, they renewed their attack in the south where they seized Canton and Hankow in October. Early in 1939 Hainan was occupied and then Spratley Island. These conquests threatened Indo-China and Singapore but inflicted no injury on the Chinese armies. Brutal air raids on defenseless Chungking failed to break the deadlock. When Europe's war of nerves became a war of blood, the would-be conquerors of China were deeply tangled in a seemingly hopeless enterprise.

Following the rejection of new pleas to Chungking to capitulate, Tokyo announced the creation on March 30, 1940, of a new puppet regime at Nanking. Its leader was the poet Wang Ching-wei, who had been expelled for treason from the Kuomintang a year before. On November 30, 1940, Tokyo recognized

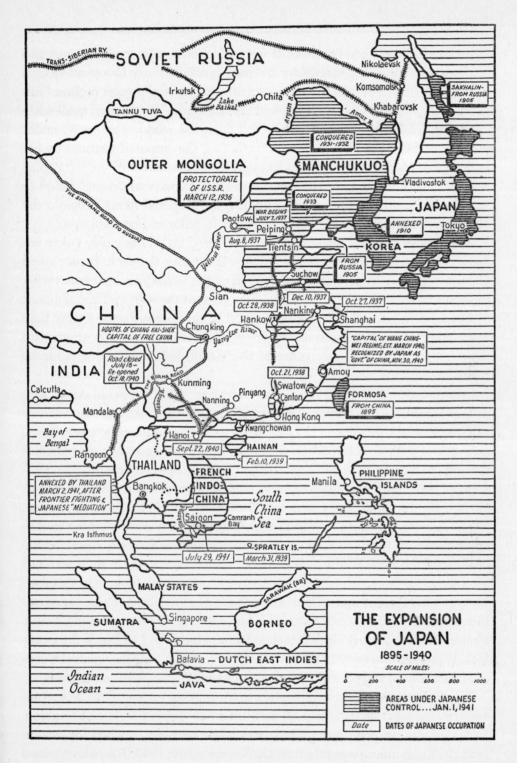

THE EXPANSION
OF JAPAN
1895-1940

SCALE OF MILES:

0   200   400   600   800   1000

AREAS UNDER JAPANESE
CONTROL ... JAN. 1, 1941

Date   DATES OF JAPANESE OCCUPATION

this regime as the "Government" of China and concluded with it a series of treaties, still disguised in the verbiage of "anti-Communism," making China a Japanese protectorate. But Wang Ching-wei had no authority. His aides were highly allergic to assassins. The Japanese puppet mayor of Shanghai was murdered in his bed, despite a score of guards.

In late October Chinese forces had retaken Nanning. They later drove the invaders from Kwangsi and from much of Kwangtung. Japanese troops held most of the larger cities, all of the principal railways and much of the coast of China. With trucks, tanks, planes, guns, oil and munitions largely purchased in Britain and America, they continued their crusade for "peace." By the close of 1940 the Imperial Army estimated that 100,000 Japanese had lost their lives and that 3,500,000 Chinese had been slain. Fifty millions or more were homeless. But no victory was in sight. Free China refused to yield and looked to Moscow and the West for aid.

HOME FRONT VICTORY

The costs of the "China incident" to the Japanese masses were staggering. Workers, peasants and business men dumbly followed the warlords along a stony road. The warlords won no triumph over China. But they won something which most of them valued more: triumph over Japan.

Their rivals for power at home were vanquished step by step. Following police raids on headquarters of both major parties in February, 1938, the Konoe Cabinet was bitterly attacked in a riotous session of the Diet. But the Army leaders paid little heed to politicians. In the name of "Great Japanism" fiery Baron Kichiro Hiranuma and frenzied General Sadao Araki demanded a totalitarian State. A "National Mobilization Bill," pushed through parliament in March, foreshadowed the full subordination of the industrialists to the militarists. In May Hirota was replaced by Ugaki as Foreign Minister. Araki became Minister of Education. A week later the bellicose Sugiyama was succeeded by the more bellicose Itagaki as Minister of War.

In the aftermath of a bitter dispute over State control of corporation funds, Konoe's "Quick Victory" Cabinet resigned on January 4, 1939. Hiranuma, the bachelor fanatic, took the premiership with Arita as his Foreign Minister. A month later the once liberal "Social Mass" party merged with the ultra-Imperialist Tohokai.

The warlords' progress toward their goal was briefly interrupted by events abroad. The Nazi-Soviet pact evoked consternation in Tokyo. The Cabinet resigned five days after its signature. General Nobukuyi Abe, with Admiral Kichisaburo Nomura as his Foreign Minister, held the premiership during the second half of 1939. Admiral Mitsumasa Yonai held it during the first half of 1940, with Arita again at the Foreign Office. But this confusion at the top was soon resolved. On July 16, 1940, Prince Konoe returned to the premiership at the head of a solidly militarist regime. His Foreign Minister was Yosuke Matsuoka.

It fell to these two men to complete the transition toward totalitarianism and to link Japan irrevocably with Europe's Fascist Axis. The tall and languid Premier was a pure aristocrat who traced his descent from ancient days to Amenokoyane, a legendary ancestor-god. At the age of 13 he had been left an orphan. He became, he said, "a gloomy youth in my student days, with an inclination to read extremist literature from the West." His early mentors were Marx and Tolstoi. But when old Prince Saionji, his father's friend, gave him counsel and took him as secretary to the Paris Peace Conference, he began to see new light.

After assuming his ancestral seat in the House of Peers, he became, like his father before him, the president of that noble body. He played no role in party politics. He had no commitments save admiration for Hitler and concurrence with the views of the warlords. He was thus the militarist's ideal premier. Undiluted totalitarianism was his program. He induced the old political parties and the trade unions to decree their dissolution. He founded the "Imperial Rule Assistance Association" and strove for a one-party State. And yet he was no Duce or Führer. Parliament was not at once abolished. The conservative forces of money and democracy were allowed to fight a stubborn rear-guard action against the military apostles of the "new structure." Yet few could doubt the final outcome.

Yosuke Matsuoka, like his chief, was a child of the aristocracy. At the age of 12 he came to America. He later worked his way through the University of Oregon, serving at times as a bell-boy in a Seattle hotel. Following his entry into the Japanese diplomatic service, he distinguished himself at Geneva in 1932 by his evasive but effective defense of Japanese policy in Manchuria. His greatest victories there were won by his good friend of Downing Street, Sir John Simon. Sir John, he declared warmly, "had said in half an hour, in a few well chosen phrases, what he—the Japanese delegate—had been trying to say in his bad English for the last ten days." He later became a deputy of the Seiyukai but resigned in 1933 to urge the abolition of all parties and of parliament. His "Neo-Nippon" movement was premature. But his appointment as president of the South Manchurian railway paved the way for his return to power. Like Prince Konoe and the army fanatics, he had no doubt but that Japan's destiny was conquest and world hegemony achieved through the downfall of the "pluto-democracies."

THE WEST'S LOST FACE

"We shall build our capital all over the world, and make the whole world our dominion." So reads the alleged Imperial Rescript of the Emperor Jimmu Tenno, legendary founder of the oldest reigning dynasty on earth. "It is my conviction," said Yosuke Matsuoka some twenty-six centuries later, "that the mission of the *Yamato* people is to prevent the human race from becoming devilish, to rescue it from destruction and lead it to the world of light."

The West's strange course made possible the partial fulfillment of this vision. At any time between 1931 and 1939 Britain or America with the greatest of ease could have paralyzed the Japanese war machine. All that was needed was an interruption of its source of supplies from abroad, or effective aid in goods and arms to China. But London and Washington preferred to arm their enemies. The Imperial Army regularly bought 80% of its imports of arms, oil, iron, fuel and motors from American and British companies. Between 1937 and 1940 the United States shipped to Japan $700,000,000 worth of metal scrap, finished steel, machine tools, gasoline, copper and zinc.

The West's neglect of the diplomacy of business was matched only by its folly in the business of diplomacy. Insults were answered by feeble words, outrages by notes of protest, injuries by futile conferences. In the fighting at Shanghai in August, 1937, several Americans were killed, several American ships were damaged and the British Ambassador, Sir Hughe Montgomery Knatchbull-Hughesson, was machine-gunned and gravely wounded by Japanese flyers. London and Washington sent wordy dispatches to Tokyo. They produced polite apologies but nothing more. Despite Chinese objections, President Roosevelt in mid-September, 1937, forbade vessels owned by the United States Government to ship arms or munitions to China or Japan and warned that private vessels so engaged would be given no protection. Three weeks later he pleaded eloquently for a "quarantine" of all aggressors in his Chicago address. Tokyo knew that speeches were empty so long as neither

America nor Britain would run any risk to aid China or protect their own interests.

Following a new epidemic of political paralysis at Geneva, London made the proposal on October 4 which Stimson had made (and London had rejected) six years previously: that the Nine Power Pact be invoked against Japan. Washington agreed and followed Britain's lead in denouncing Japanese aggression. In November, 1937, all the signatories of the pact, save Japan, sent delegates to a conference at Brussels. But no one would take any action or run any risk. The conference breathed pious hopes and adjourned. On December 13, 1937, Japanese aviators bombed and sank the gunboat U.S.S. *Panay* along with three American oil tankers on the Yangtze. Roosevelt protested to Hirohito and ultimately accepted an apology and indemnity. During 1938 Chamberlain furiously appeased Tokyo as well as Rome and Berlin. Washington sent periodical notes of protest to Japan in the name of humanity, international law and the Open Door.

Fools and their empires are soon parted. Three weeks after Munich Japanese troops occupied Canton, cut Hong Kong off from its hinterland and closed the Yangtze to foreign shipping. Japanese planes bombed British gunboats. Tokyo induced Paris to halt arms shipments to China by making threats against Indo-China. Chamberlain complacently told Commons on November 2, 1938, that no one need fear a Japanese monopoly of the China trade. British capital, he said, would eventually be needed to reconstruct China, and the longer the war went on the more capital would be required!

The logical culmination of these developments coincided with the approach of conflict in Europe. On June 14, 1939, Japanese forces began a "blockade" of the British concession in Tientsin to compel British "cooperation." Chamberlain asserted that the beating of British gentlemen and the stripping of British ladies by Japanese soldiers made his "blood boil." He hinted darkly that "in certain circumstances" the fleet might be sent to the Far East. But on July 24, he told Commons that the text of a "formula" had been accepted as a basis for continuing the discussions over Tientsin. He recognized that "the Japanese forces in China have special requirements for the purpose of safeguarding their own security and maintaining public order in the regions under their control and that they have to suppress or remove such causes or acts as will obstruct them or benefit their enemy." His Majesty's Government would cooperate to this end.

But Tory hopes of enlisting American support in arranging an Oriental Munich were disappointed. Two days after Chamberlain's announcement the

State Department gave notice of termination of the Japanese-American commercial treaty of 1911. On January 26, 1940, following the required six months' interval, Washington secured full freedom of action to embargo exports of war supplies to Japan. No embargoes were imposed, however, until July, and then only in a half-hearted fashion. Under further pressure from Tokyo, Prime Minister Churchill had meanwhile agreed in June to prohibit transport of war materials to China through Hong Kong and over the Burma Road for a period of three months. This move was as displeasing to Washington as Chamberlain's earlier moves had been. After the Anglo-American destroyer deal of September, the Burma Road was reopened.

TRIPLE ALLIANCE

The warriors of Righteous Justice were not in doubt as to how to meet these feeble counter-measures from the West. An alliance with Italy and Germany would threaten Britain and America with war in two oceans. After much urging from Berlin, Tokyo accepted the formula in the autumn of 1940. Premier Hiranuma had said in January, 1939: "We will shake hands with those who agree to the establishment of a new order in East Asia by Japan, but we cannot shake hands with those who oppose such a policy." Three months later War Minister Itagaki had said: "I wish to express heartfelt homage to Germany and to Italy for their spirited endeavors in the cause of a projected new order in Europe." Hiranuma had expressed approval of the German-Italian alliance but declined to make Japan a signatory.

The chagrin evoked in Tokyo by the Hitler-Stalin accord on the eve of Armageddon slowly faded as the warlords realized the opportunities which Nazi victory over the West would present to them. Hesitation waned during 1940 with the fall of France, the warnings from Washington to respect the *status quo* in the East Indies, the development of Anglo-American cooperation and the arrival in Tokyo of Ribbentrop's special envoy, Heinrich von Stahmer, bearing the gift of French Indo-China. On September 27, 1940, Ribbentrop, Ciano and Ambassador Saburo Kurusu attached their signatures in Berlin to a treaty of alliance.

This pact of blackmail, couched in terms of "prosperity and welfare" and "world peace," was to run for ten years. It bound the Axis Powers to "recognize and respect the leadership of Japan in the establishment of a new order in Greater East Asia." It bound Japan to "recognize and respect the leadership of Germany and Italy in the establishment of a new order in Europe." More important, it bound all three "to assist one another with all political, economic and military means" should any one of them be "attacked by a Power at present not involved in the European war or in the Chinese-Japanese conflict." But "the aforesaid terms do not in any way affect the political status which exists at present as between each of the three contracting parties and Soviet Russia." America was thus warned clearly to stand aside while the conquerors completed their tasks.

Emperor Hirohito voiced "deep satisfaction" and declared that Nippon's mission was "to enhance justice on earth and to make the world one household." Ambassador Kurusu asserted that the pact would "become a sword in the hand of the righteous warrior and thus contribute to the reestablishment of universal peace." Ciano said that the three empires would "shatter every attempt to spread the conflict beyond its present confines." Ribbentrop warned that any State which might "harbor the intention of mixing in the final phase of the solution of these problems in Europe or Eastern Asia or attacking one State signatory to this three Power pact will have to take on the entire concentrated might of three nations with more than 250 million inhabitants." The new allies, commented Konoe, were "ready to display the power of their military alliance in case of necessity" in order to create "a new era in the entire world." "If the United States," he warned, "refuses to understand the real intentions of Japan, Germany and Italy, there will be no other course open than to go to war." Matsuoka threatened hostilities "if the United States entered the European struggle." If America, he added, "is going to stick blindly and stubbornly to the *status quo* in the Pacific, then we will fight America."

THE AMERICAN WAY

Washington declined to be impressed by loud barking from dogs unable to bite. So long as China and Britain still fought a good fight, the Triplice allies could scarcely take action against America. Hull asserted that the pact changed nothing. Sumner Welles avowed that an "equitable settlement" with Japan was still possible. An American loan of $25,000,000 to China was announced, followed by another of $100,000,000 after Tokyo's recognition of Wang Ching-wei. American sales of scrap iron and steel and of high test gasoline to Japanese buyers were further restricted.

But Tokyo was still quite free to buy finished iron and steel, old ships and all forms of low grade oil products. During 1940 two million barrels of oil per month flowed across the Pacific from American refineries to supply the Japanese tanks and planes that brought death to a million Chinese. By the summer of 1941 a million barrels a month continued to flow, much of it in American-owned tankers, transferred to Panamanian or other foreign registry. Englishmen lost battles for lack of tankers. New Englanders paid more and more for gasoline. The American oil companies were guided by the State Department which insisted that shipments to Japan must continue lest Tokyo be tempted to seize the oil fields of the Dutch Indies. The diplomatic bureaucrats in Washington hinted that serious restrictions on trade with nations friendly to the Axis would be unwise lest such nations become friendly to the Axis. Americans thus continued to give generous aid to China and to denounce Japanese aggression while selling to Japan the means of continuing the aggression. Bomb-blasted Chungking found Occidental ways hard to understand.

Despite their quiet satisfaction over this happy state of affairs, Tokyo's warlords were disturbed by other American moves. The signing of the Berlin pact produced no visible slackening of American efforts to aid Britain. Said Roosevelt: "No combination of dictator countries will stop the help we are giving. Our decision is made." Ten days after the pact was signed the State Department urged all Americans in the Far East to return home. Tokyo jumped at what looked like an anticipation of war. "There is no reason," said Mr. Suma of the Foreign Office, "to be so nervous. We wish Americans would understand that there is nothing to be alarmed about." Matsuoka bit his moustache, chewed on his pipe and explained that the pact was not "against" the United States but "for" the United States—as a means of keeping America out of war. The American fleet remained at Hawaii. American bombing planes moved to Manila. The American program for a conscript army, a huge air force and a "Two Ocean Navy" moved into faster tempo. Britain reinforced Singapore. Anglo-American consultations began on the defense of the East Indies. Matsuoka wondered what to do.

SOUTHWARD BOUND

Prince Konoe and his wily Foreign Minister did not consent to the Triple Alliance out of love for the Axis leaders. Neither were they sure that the threat would immobilize America. Their *quid pro quo* was more tangible and was delivered in advance. It was control of northern Indo-China. Tokyo, to be sure, might have seized control of this rich French colony without consulting Pétain or Hitler. London could not, and Washington would not, risk defending it. Neither the vanquished at Vichy nor the victors at Berlin could have said Tokyo nay. But such a step would have antagonized useful friends. And it might have led to local hostilities with unpleasant complications in their wake. To secure by force favors which can be had by fraud is foolish.

Five days before the ceremony of signature in Berlin, Vichy and Tokyo signed another pact as the sequel to sundry "incidents" and skirmishes along the northern border of Indo-China. This pact was Tokyo's price for joining the Axis. On Ribbentrop's advice Laval agreed herewith to the dispatch of Japanese troops to Haiphong and to the nearby inland city of Hanoi. He also agreed to the establishment of three Japanese air bases in northern Indo-China. These convenient arrangements, declared Gen. Maurice Martin, the local French commander, were "the first manifestation of a durable friendship between France and Japan." Access to Indo-China enabled the Army of Righteous Justice to bomb the Burma Road more easily. It also enabled Tokyo to secure new supplies of rice by browbeating the French authorities, and new supplies of oil by threatening the Dutch in the East Indies. In mid-November, by a "compromise" agreement signed in Batavia, the Dutch colonial officials and the agents of Shell and Socony Vacuum consented to quadruple sales of oil from the Netherlands Indies to Japan.

Meanwhile Tokyo saw a chance to fish in the troubled waters of the Mekong. This tropic river wanders for almost a thousand miles through western Indo-China. Some of the steaming jungles and rice fields which it drains were once part of the ancient kingdom of Siam. This curious country, of late renamed Thailand, was long a buffer between the rival imperialisms of Britain and France. With France conquered, Britain busy and Japan a friendly counsellor, the top Thai men at Bangkok now asked of Governor-General Jean Decoux that he restore to them the lands of Laos and Cambodia which once were theirs. When he refused, they launched a small-scale border war in late September, 1940. Hanoi and Bangkok each accused the other of aggression. Matsuoka, ever the friend of "peace," deplored this violence. Japan, he said, must show the way to rectitude by rectifying the vexed frontier.

In January, 1941, he announced that Bangkok, Hanoi and Vichy had accepted Japanese "mediation." An armistice signed on the last day of the month was followed by negotiations aboard a Japanese cruiser in Saigon harbor. The negotiators soon moved to Tokyo. Matsuoka, whom French Ambassador Charles Arsené Henry called "the peace-maker," made it quite clear that both Thailand and Indo-China were now part of Japan's "co-prosperity sphere" in East Asia. In early March, after the armistice was thrice extended, a boundary protocol was signed, and on May 9, 1941, a formal peace treaty. By its terms Thailand bought at a nominal price some 25,000 square miles of Indo-Chinese territory along the Mekong. All future disputes would be submitted to Japanese mediation. Thailand and Indo-China both gave pledges to abstain from any cooperation with third Powers against Japan.

All these diplomatic victories, reflected Matsuoka, were made possible (or at least made easier) by the Triplice Pact. And yet many in Tokyo still were worried. The Chinese war went on in hopeless and costly deadlock. The November "peace" with Wang Ching-wei brought no peace. New friction in China between Chiang Kai-shek and his Communist allies stirred hopes. But such hopes also brought no peace. By mid-May of 1941 the *Japan Times-Advertiser* was saying of China that "ideas of overcoming this mastodon of nations must have little more appeal even to the most sanguine of soldierly minds." When asked his opinion of this view, Lieut.-Col. Kunio Akiyama, Army spokesman in China, complained: "We can't catch the Chinese. This continental area is too large. It is difficult for us to run about it."

To move farther south with dangers still threatening from the west and north seemed unwise to the men of Tokyo, the more so as Britishers, Americans, and Dutchmen were standing together behind the great guns and bombing squadrons at Singapore. The Dutch government in London stoutly declared that the Netherlands Indies would never be incorporated in "any new order under the leadership of any Power whatsoever." By mid-June the long negotiations in Batavia between Kenkichi Yoshizawa and Minister H. J. Van Mook broke down. Van Mook and his colleague, Governor-General A. W. L. Hjarda Van Starkenborgh Stachouwer, stubbornly refused to make new economic concessions to Tokyo without assurances that the goods thus sold would not be sent to Germany. Tokyo hinted at force. But no attack on Java could be safely launched without reducing Singapore. No reduction of Singapore was possible without the connivance of Thailand to facilitate an overland attack through the narrow jungle-covered isthmus of Kra, north of heavily fortified British Malaya. Any attack on Singapore, moreover, would mean war with Britain and probably with America. This in turn would create a danger of a Soviet stab-in-the-back from the north. Tokyo's warlords shrank from the risks of war so long as Hitler's war was still unwon. Mr. Matsuoka reflected further.

THE MEANDERINGS OF MR. MATSUOKA

One of his friends was a bluff and hearty admiral, Kishisaburo Nomura, who had once been a popular naval attaché in Washington. In 1939 he had served as Foreign Minister. In 1940, on the eve of the signing of the treaties with the puppets at Nanking, Matsuoka persuaded Nomura to accept the post of Ambassador to the United States. Americans must be induced to understand Japan's high motives. Said Matsuoka in December to the Japan-American Society of Tokyo: "Japan is not waging an imperialist war of aggression. We are engaged in a moral crusade. We have a great mission as a civilizing and stabilizing force. Japan's foreign policy will revolve in the future around the Three Power Pact." Ambassador Joseph Grew drily replied: "The only thing that counts is the concrete evidence of facts and actions regardless of the persuasive garb in which such facts and actions may be dressed."

Nomura reached Washington in February. The winter was mild but his reception was chilly. Hull and Welles conferred with the envoys of Britain, Australia and The Netherlands. Halifax announced that British forces in the Far East were being substantially increased. Dr. Louden declared that "the Dutch East Indies will fight any aggressors." Matsuoka registered disappointment. He complained that there was no reason for any "campaign of fear." But a few days later he suggested that "the white race must cede Oceania to the Asiatics."

To relieve the gloom of the melancholy Prince Konoe and to assuage his own regret at American lack of "comprehension," Matsuoka tried other tricks. He now declared that his government was unable "to see any good purpose to be served by prolonging the war" and was "fully prepared to act as mediator, not only in East Asia but anywhere else in the world." Major General Ott, Nazi Ambassador in Tokyo, at once conveyed Hitler's displeasure to Matsuoka. Sumner Welles observed that "the United States is far more interested in deeds than in statements." Churchill welcomed assurances that Japan had no anti-British moves in mind but rejected any thought of mediation between London and Berlin. By threatening war as the Reich's ally, Matsuoka had angered America and Britain. By proposing peace he had angered Germany. By shrieking from making good his bluff, he had lost face at home. To retrieve his fortunes he decided to make a long journey.

On March 12, 1941, Matsuoka left Tokyo for Manchukuo whence he rode across Eurasia on the tedious Trans-Siberian and finally reached Berlin and

Rome. Behind an outward show of solidarity, much was probably said by his Axis friends which was not too pleasant to his ears. But at least an open break was avoided and doubtless plans were laid for future action. In Italy, Matsuoka later explained, he composed a poem: "A flowery country is brightened with pretty faces and a spring sky." He spent an hour with the Pope ("the prettiest moment of my life," he said) and assured His Holiness that Japan's sole purpose was the salvation of Asia from Communism.

Early in April the visitor left the Axis lands to return to the East. He had apparently given no new pledges to the Caesars. But neither had he secured any promises or prizes to bring back home with him in triumph. But he had one more stop to make and one more chance for the success he needed badly. His last stop was Moscow.

PAX VOBISCUM

From Moscow he brought back a victory which won him an ovation. Strangely enough that which Stalin granted him was something which Stalin had many times asked of Tokyo earlier and been as many times refused: a peace pact. But Japan was now the beggar and Russia the giver. In January the Kremlin had driven a hard bargain in the annual renewal of the fisheries treaty. The new agreement was signed in the Kremlin on Easter Sunday, April 13, 1941, by Molotov, Matsuoka and Ambassador Yoshitsugu Tatekawa. For a five year period it pledged Japan and the U.S.S.R. to "maintain peaceful and friendly relations between them and mutually respect the territorial integrity and inviolability of the other contracting party." "Should one of the contracting parties become the object of hostilities on the part of one or several third Powers, the other contracting party will observe neutrality throughout the duration of the conflict." An appended declaration bound Moscow to respect the territorial integrity and inviolability of Manchukuo, and bound Japan to do the same for Outer Mongolia.

On coming home Matsuoka declared that he had talked to Stalin for thirty minutes. Stalin had said "Yes." They drank toasts. The guest beamed and chortled: "The treaty has been made. I do not lie. If I lie, my head will be yours. If you lie, be sure I will come for your head." The host replied: "My head is important to my country. So is yours to your country. Let us use care to keep our heads on our shoulders. You are an Asiatic. So am I." Matsuoka rejoined: "We are all Asiatics. Let us drink to the health of the Asiatics!"

Like other Asiatic bargains, the pact had many meanings. Matsuoka had

[*36*]

done what Ribbentrop had done two years before: made peace with Muscovy in order to be free to act against others. The Nazi and Fascist press rejoiced at this new sign of solidarity. The Japanese press rejoiced for a different reason. Prior to the Easter agreement, Japan was pledged to aid the Reich should it be attacked by the U.S.S.R., but the Reich, under the terms of the Triple Alliance, had no corresponding duty toward Japan. Now Japan's relations to Moscow were the same as Germany's. Moscow had pledged its neutrality to Tokyo as well as to Berlin in the event of a joint Triplice crusade against the "pluto-democracies."

So far so good. Yet there were doubts. There is honor among thieves, but no real trust among treaty-breakers. Hitler had double-crossed Hiranuma by his pact with Stalin of August, 1939. Who had double-crossed whom by Matsuoka's pact with Molotov of April, 1941? Perhaps Stalin was the winner. If he had any inkling of Berlin's plans, he stood to gain by pledging Tokyo to neutrality. And if Matsuoka had any inkling of Berlin's plans, he stood to gain by keeping his hands free. Yet he tied his hands and regarded the new bond as a triumph.

Despite loud lip-service to the Triplice, Tokyo was seeking to recover "independence" of action. Rumor held that Nomura sought in Washington, with no success, to conclude a similar pact with the United States. Like all good players of the game of power, Matsuoka and Konoe were seeking something for nothing, or at least much for little. With China unconquered, they could not fight the Soviet Union. They could not even induce the Kremlin to cease its aid to Chungking. They had no appetite for fighting Britain and America. Such a war, they said, would "ruin civilization." Such a war, they meant, would ruin Japan. But to blackmail London and Washington by pacts with Berlin and Rome was cheap. And to blackmail Berlin and Rome by pacts with Moscow was equally cheap. And to blackmail Moscow . . . ? Should Hitler win his war, Tokyo could move from words to deeds and pick up pieces of the wreckage. But what if the Reich should fail and fall?

At the end of April, on the 40th birthday of the divine Hirohito, the *Japan Times-Advertiser*, organ of the Foreign Office, proposed "exploratory" peace terms to America. The Triplice should have parity of sea power with the Anglo-American fleets. The Mediterranean and North Africa should be abandoned by Britain. Gibraltar, Malta, Aden, Singapore, Hong Kong and all American bases west of Hawaii should be demilitarized. All the world should be divided into spheres. But in the American sphere (South America) the United States should grant full equality to the Axis and its allies. Said Konoe two months later: "Japan is very anxious to maintain friendly relations with the United States and we see no reason why our two countries cannot remain friendly. We consider that the German-Japanese alliance is designed to keep the United States from involvement in the European war."

THE TREPIDATION OF PRINCE KONOE

The unleashing of Hitler's war against Stalin in June created as much consternation in Tokyo as the signature of the Hitler-Stalin accord twenty-two months before. A double double-cross was almost too much. The Führer made partial amends: on July 1, 1941, his puppets in Italy, Spain, Slovakia, Croatia and Bulgaria joined him in granting diplomatic recognition to Tokyo's puppets in Nanking. But this "government" of China remained a joke. The Nazi-Soviet clash ended Communist-Kuomintang friction in Chungking. It made China a *de facto* member of a great anti-Triplice bloc. It confronted Japan with the threat of "encirclement" which Matsuoka's Moscow pact had been designed to prevent.

Konoe's Foreign Minister was clearly not in Hitler's confidence, despite his long journey to Berlin. His face was lost. Early in July the Cabinet reached a "decision" regarding the Nazi-Soviet war. But it was a deep secret. Konoe hinted at a Japanese "neutrality zone" to shut out American ships from Vladivostok. Konoe made himself President of a "Great Japan-East Asia Construction League" to unify all organizations pledged to Nipponese mastery of Asia. "Shining as the sun and stars," he said, "is the goal of the Japanese Empire. It is the greatest honor and life mission of every Japanese to do his part in the construction of the co-prosperity sphere in East Asia."

But whether "prosperity" was to be had by attacking Siberia or by moving farther south was anybody's guess. Hitler, like some of the American isolationists, preferred that Japan should be embroiled with the Western Powers in the South Seas, since this would presumably keep the American fleet in the Pacific and hamstring American aid to Britain. Yet this calculus presupposed a speedy Nazi victory over Russia. By mid-July the Blitz was stalled and Hitler was hoping for a Japanese move against Siberia. The Tokyo warlords reflected, however, that they had never been able to beat the Red Army. If Schicklgruber the Great could do no better, then prudence dictated observance of the Moscow pact and a move toward the greener pastures of the Indies.

Konoe was received by the Emperor on July 15. "Filled with trepidation," said the official communiqué, "the Premier retired from the presence of His Majesty and reported to the Cabinet Ministers concerning the Imperial message." Matsuoka did not attend. He was suffering from chills and fever. On the following day the Cabinet resigned. The new Cabinet of July 18 was headed once more by Konoe. It contained three admirals and four generals, with Hiranuma as Vice Premier, Gen. Eiko Tojo in the War Office, Admiral Koshiro Oikawa at the Naval Ministry, and Vice-Admiral Teijiro Toyada at the Foreign Office. Otherwise there were few changes, save that "political party influences" were further diminished. Matsuoka was out. "Now that I am a free man," he explained, "I shall devote myself to reading. There will be no necessity for me to take office again."

TOWARD SINGAPORE

Even before the Cabinet shift at Tokyo, Admiral Jean Decoux, Governor-General of Indo-China, had received new demands from his Japanese friends. Konoe's decision was to move once more along the paths of least resistance. To gobble up the rest of Vichy's rich colony would involve no risks. A face-saving formula for the Vichymen was easy, for they had already all but effaced themselves in their grovelling before the Führer.

A Vichy spokesman declared on July 23 that Japanese demands had been accepted "in principle." Japan would be granted new bases "as a temporary military measure to defend Indo-China against a combination of followers of Gen. Charles de Gaulle and British and Chinese. Japan has made no territorial demands. We merely want to protect Indo-China." Nippon's warlords were specialists in "protection." Berlin cooperated. Darlan and Ambassador Sotamatsu Kato signed a protocol at Vichy on the 29th day of the 7th month of the 16th year of Showa, reign of "Radiant Peace": "The two Governments agree to cooperate militarily for the common defense of Indo-China." The military clauses were secret. But Japanese officers flew to Saigon. Japanese warships moved to Cam Ranh Bay. Japanese army trucks brought troops by thousands down through the rice fields toward the mouth of the Mekong and westward toward the Thai frontier.

The British "threat" to the colony was fantasy. Despite their success in Syria, the British leaders lacked wit and will to occupy southern Indo-China before Japan should move. Such action might precipitate a clash. To act after

[*39*]

Japan had moved would surely precipitate a clash. The way to avoid clashes (and also avoid survival) is not to act. Tokyo counted on the Anglo-American appeasers doing nothing to defend Indo-China, and probably nothing to defend Thailand, even though the Philippines, the Indies, Malaya and Burma were all alike menaced by Tokyo's new drive.

Tokyo's assumptions were right in regard to action by arms. But they were otherwise wrong. The democracies had long acted as suffer States and duffer States and almost as buffer States. They now on a sudden became huffer States. On July 25 President Roosevelt ordered the "freezing" of all Japanese assets in the United States—and, at the request of Chungking, of Chinese assets as well, lest the Nanking puppets use them to serve Tokyo's purposes. Gen. Douglas MacArthur was recalled to active service to take over the Army of the Philippine Commonwealth which was placed on a war footing under American command. Silk imports were halted and oil exports were licensed anew, with a threat of full suspension. London followed suit and denounced the commercial treaties of Britain, Burma and India with Japan, at the same time reinforcing Singapore, Malaya and the road to Mandalay. The Netherlands Indies suspended the agreement by which Japan had been promised 1,800,000 tons of oil per year.

These moves were most unkind. Japanese stock prices fell to a ten-year low. The Silk Exchange closed its doors. When Washington protested sharply at the end of the month over the bombing of the U.S. gunboat *Tutuila,* anchored in the Yangtze off much-bombed Chungking, Tokyo apologized. So sorry. Incident closed. Japan retaliated, measure for measure, for the economic blows struck by Anglo-Saxony. Thanks to Anglo-American folly for four years past, the Army and Navy of Righteous Justice had ample stocks of oil for another year. But Japan could not survive a full economic boycott. If the democracies meant business (i.e. no business), Japan would be ruined—unless Japan could conquer the Indies and defeat the Western Powers in war. But Konoe shrewdly doubted whether business was really meant, despite the sound and fury from the West.

Threats of war had sufficed before to bring the West to terms. Why not again? Britain found one war more than enough. America found no war better than one. If Indo-China was not deemed worth a fight, then Thailand too might well be yielded. Beyond this Tokyo could afford once more to pause, meanwhile moving troops into Manchukuo—just in case Herr Hitler should reach Moscow after all.

WARLORDS' DILEMMA

In truth, however, the masters of Nippon found themselves beset by agonizing perplexities at the beginning of the third year of World War II. Their own war in China was in its fifth year. Nothing remotely resembling victory was in sight in spite of (or because of) the shameful spoliation of the conquered provinces and the savage bombing of undefended civilians in Free China. From its ruins Chungking hurled defiance.

To confess defeat and seek a rapprochement with Chiang Kai-shek and with the western foes of Hitler would precipitate violence at home. The younger Army hotheads and the professional patrioteers, long encouraged in their fanaticism by the leading militarists, would turn upon those who had never hitherto admitted that their course could ever be wrong. In mid-August, 1941, the new Vice Premier, Baron Hiranuma, who was himself a bellicose extremist, was gravely wounded by a youthful member of the Black Dragon Society who found his victim's "moderation" intolerable. Further vacillation in high places might well lead to a new wave of assassinations, with the mighty militarists themselves serving as targets.

What to do? Konoe and Toyada alarmed public opinion by their silence. It was obvious that they had no answer. London and Washington warned Tokyo that any Japanese move into Thailand would have grave consequences. Did this mean that Britain and America would fight? Nobody knew. But Tokyo's spokesmen hastened to declare that Japan had no designs on Thailand, and no desire even for a "joint defense" agreement. Further moves southward now involved acute danger of a clash with the English-speaking Powers.

President and Prime Minister in their Atlantic meeting of mid-August made secret plans not only for defeating the Axis but for coping with Japanese aggression. "It is certain," declared Churchill on August 24, "that this has got to stop. Every effort will be made to secure a peaceful settlement," but if the effort fails "we shall, of course, range ourselves unhesitatingly on the side of the United States." The newspaper *Asahi* commented: "Jews are conspiring to overthrow the world-ruling Powers. Jews want bases in the Atlantic and Pacific, at Burma and bases in China from which to bomb Japan. These remarks may be laughed off as the dream of a fiction writer but they are most important." But important or not, such remarks furnished no solution for Japan's problem.

To move northward against the Soviet Union seemed equally dangerous, for America, Britain and Russia were now acting together. As American war supplies flowed toward Vladivostok, Moscow warned that any interference with trade would be an "unfriendly act" and Washington reiterated its championship of "freedom of the seas." Tokyo suspended all shipping services to Australia and the United States, and sought to detain American and British nationals as hostages. Japanese commanders moved more troops and ships northward and southward. But each new move was now met by a counter-move. So long as Hitler was unable to inflict a decisive defeat on Britain or Russia, and so long as Americans were seemingly committed, in deeds as well as in words, to opposing further Japanese aggression, so long would the frustrated madmen of Tokyo be immobilized. For they knew, even in their madness, that Japan would be beaten if they challenged other Great Powers to open combat.

"The essence of total war," explained Lieut.-Gen. Teiishi Suzuki, President of the Planning Board, "is to live and die for the State. I don't like to deal with fools and those mentally affected. Let us live with a conviction of race and elevate ourselves to a more glorious history with light heart." Perhaps the only solution would be national *hara-kiri*. Or an attempted retreat on the model of 1918-1922, despite the domestic danger from patriotic murderers. Or watchful waiting—in the expectation that American morale would disintegrate and that Hitler would yet win his *Kampf*.

War with America might not only prove disastrous to Japan but might wreck the Reich as well by inspiring an all-out American war effort on a world scale. The United States could better be immobilized and demoralized by pleas for "peace." For a decade Tokyo had played upon the fears and hopes of American isolationists with sufficient skill to keep Washington quiescent. The formula which had worked so well and so long might work once more. Three weeks before the tenth anniversary of the "Mukden incident" Nomura submitted to Roosevelt a message from Prince Konoe. The warlords' decision, for the moment at least, was to attempt "negotiations" for the purpose of gaining time, disrupting the democratic front and strengthening the hand of America's appeasers.

If this technique achieved results, the flag of Japan might yet fly over all of Eastern Asia and the Pacific. If it failed, if America held firm, if Tokyo was forced to make a choice between war and retreat, then all might be lost. The masters of the land of the Rising Sun looked dubiously toward sunset over China and toward the shadows creeping out of the east. Was America willing to fight? If so, dusk would fall upon them—either gently amid the shades of quiet repentance, or thunderously in a flaming fury of destruction such as they themselves had hitherto inflicted upon others. The mode of their demise would be for them to choose. Their bloody banners, besmirched with infamy, were dragging in the dust. Yet they had been saved before and might be saved again by the irresponsibility and defeatism of the great democracies. From this malady the greatest of the democracies had not yet recovered. Therefore, even in their desperation, the warlords of Nippon were still hopeful.

I passed by his garden, and marked, with one eye, how the Owl and the Panther were sharing a pie: the Panther took pie-crust, and gravy, and meat, while the Owl had the dish as its share of the treat. When the pie was all finished, the Owl, as a boon, was kindly permitted to pocket the spoon: while the Panther received knife and fork with a growl, and concluded the banquet by . . .

LITTLE MAN'S MISERY

To be poor is hard. Yet poverty is bearable if only one has a place he can be sure of. What is galling beyond endurance is to be treated as an outcast, to have one's self-respect destroyed, to be alone and afraid and friendless in a world which is brutal or condescending. For men, and for nations of men, such a lot fills the spirit with bitterness. Some who suffer thus become helpless, resigned, without will. Others are consumed by a fierce thirst for vengeance, for violent self-assertion, for power over those who are callous or contemptuous. Power to command obedience, power to inspire fear, power to deprive others of all dignity and all semblance of selfhood—this brings peace of soul. Men escape fear by acting like beasts in order that they may feel like gods.

So ran the lessons of life for many of Europe's poor in an epoch of fear and poverty. So ran the lesson of living for one among them destined for fame and for disgrace. Benito Mussolini, born July 29, 1883, in the village of Dovia di Predappio near Forlí, was a son of *les miserables*, living poorly in a poor province of a poor land. His father, Alessandro, was a farmer and a blacksmith. His mother, Rosa, was a country school teacher. Like many others who struggled hard for bread, Alessandro was a revolutionary Socialist. He braved prison for his beliefs and became a leader of his fellows. His eldest son he named after Benito Juarez, the Mexican rebel. The boy absorbed his father's radicalism and spurned his mother's piety.

When at the age of nine he was sent to a school of the Salesian Fathers at Faenza, he hotly resented the third-class status which his own poverty and the snobbery of others imposed upon him. After two stormy years he got himself expelled. Later he went to normal school. In the first year of the new century he secured a license as an elementary school teacher. "Discipline obtained by coercive methods," he wrote after his first few months as a substitute teacher, "is not discipline. That sort of discipline represses the child's individuality and generates bad feeling. The teacher must forestall and remove the causes of evil in order not to have to resort to painful repression."

This hopeful young man, like millions of others, became the victim of those with wealth and power who would not or could not apply this doctrine. Long afterward he found it necessary to reassert his importance by coercing and repressing his pupils in a larger school. Between the generous teacher and the power-driven tyrant lay years of anguish and turmoil. In the summer of 1902 he went to Switzerland—to evade military service, some said later. He worked for a few days as a hod-carrier. The toil was killing, the pay a pittance. "I chafed with the terrible rage of the powerless."

He left his job. He begged and starved in Lausanne where he was arrested for vagrancy. He found contentment only when he became a labor organizer and a Socialist orator and journalist. He was arrested and expelled from Bern. The police began to watch him as a dangerous radical and a "violent character." In Geneva he became *duce* or leader of the local Italian Socialist Club. Here too the authorities expelled him. He preached Marxism; wrote inflamatory articles; harangued the crowd; mingled with international firebrands; enrolled for (but apparently never took) a course from Vilfredo Pareto at the University of Lausanne; and at length returned to Italy late in 1904 to do the military service which he had hitherto avoided.

His two years in Switzerland fixed the pattern of his life. In a society which he feared and hated, he found reassurance only by winning the public plaudits of others as discontented as himself. In his private life he made no friends and found no peace. He pursued women, made love, begot illegitimate children, but all without joy or tenderness. By 1910, when his father died, he was living at Forlí with Rachele Guidi, a quiet woman whom he met when she was working in a small tavern which the elder Mussolini had acquired.

[45]

Their first child was a girl whom they named Edda. Not until the coming of the Great War did he marry Rachele. Other women came and went. But his only grand passion was for rebellion.

His one true love was a love for the applause of rebels and for the power which command over mobs can give. His vocation as a pedagogue he pursued intermittently. His avocation as an agitator he pursued incessantly, getting himself arrested at Forlí in 1908, expelled from Trent in Austria-Hungary a year thereafter, and arrested and imprisoned once more in 1911 for agitating against Italy's war upon Turkey. This was the way to become *someone*. "I am possessed by this mania," he told his official biographer years later. "It inflames, gnaws and consumes me, like a physical malady. I want to make a mark on history with my will, like a lion with his claws."

TRANSFIGURATION

His doctrine of revolt was borrowed from his father and from the companions of his youth. In 1910 he founded a paper in Forlí: *The Class Struggle*. He played Socialist politics as an uncompromising extremist. He opposed all cooperation with bourgeois groups. He attacked the Republicans of Forlí so viciously that their paper replied in kind, calling him "Vulgar; indecent; nauseating; insensate; a vagabond in the pay of Jewish societies; pretentious; conscienceless; paranoiac; a ferocious madman; a rancorous inciter; an unscrupulous liar; a most vile and delinquent sower of hatred; a trickster; a hack-writer; a maniac; an imbecile; and, to boot, a disgusting reptile."

By 1912 he was a national leader of the Socialists and editor of *Avanti!* He held that God was a fraud, the Pope a charlatan, the King a fake, the ruling classes a set of thieves, the national flag "a rag to be planted on a dunghill." He was all fury and violence. Yet he differed from other fanatics. As early as 1912 one of his mentors, Georges Sorel, the founder of revolutionary syndicalism, predicted: "You will one day perhaps see him as the head of a sacred battalion, saluting the flag of Italy with his sword. He is an Italian of the fifteenth century, a *condottiere*. No one knows it yet."

In the end his insatiable thirst for power proved more potent than his attachment to the cause through which his thirst had first been slaked. When war broke out in 1914, with Italy neutral, he first supported the Socialist position of uncompromising opposition to intervention. But by October he was asking the Executive of the Party to declare against unconditional neutrality. All were against him. He resigned the editorship of *Avanti!* In November he founded a new paper, *Il Popolo d'Italia,* to urge intervention. He was expelled from the Party as a renegade and traitor. He breathed defiance to his erstwhile comrades: "Today you hate me, because in your hearts you love me still." In fact he had done more than change his mind. He had changed his paymasters. *Il Popolo d'Italia* was established with money supplied by French agents whose task was to bring Italy into the war.

But Mussolini's acceptance of bribes was "pure." He wanted power, not money. He wished to serve not France, not democracy, not even socialism any longer, but only his own ambition, disguised in the poetry of violence. "Is not to cry, 'we want war!' more revolutionary than to cry 'down with war!'?" "We must act, move, fight and if it be necessary die. Neutrals have never dominated events. They have always been overwhelmed by them. It is blood which gives movement to the wheels of history."

He rode on the wave of the future. Italy became a belligerent. Mussolini joined the army in November, 1915. He saw little service at the front, but in January, 1917, a shrapnel shell exploded behind him during trench mortar practice. Not until August was he sufficiently recovered from his forty flesh wounds to leave the hospital at Milan and to resume the war—not as a soldier but as editor of *Il Popolo d'Italia.* He was to find his golden moment later in the agony and disenchantment of a nation defeated in victory, thwarted in triumph, economically prostrate, socially divided, politically impotent.

SACRED SELFISHNESS

Mussolini's Marxism and Mussolini's Fascism were alike products of the poverty and weakness of himself and his people, and of the fierce anger and sly scheming which weakness and poverty begot. Italian foreign policy was no less a product of the poverty and weakness of Italy as a Power. In the arts of gracious living Italy stood long in the forefront of Western civilization, from the Renaissance to the *Risorgimento* and beyond. In the scales of power, however, the Kingdom of Italy was the weakest of the Great Powers at the time of its establishment in 1861. It remained so thereafter. The ambitions of the patriots and politicians of the new Rome were often beyond attainment. Italy's only military asset was a teeming population. But Italians were the least warlike of peoples. Numbers count for little without iron, coal, capital, control of seaways and possession of bases—and in these things Italy was poor.

Under such circumstances the quest of Italian diplomats and strategists for martial glory and the gaudy baubles of empire was from the outset incongruous and pathetic. From beginning to end Italy's role in *Realpolitik* was that of a jackal, attacking only the small and weak or snatching bones from the feasts of others. "Insatiable Italy, with furtive glances, roves restlessly hither and thither," said Bismarck, "instinctively drawn on by the odor of corruption and calamity—always ready to attack anybody from the rear and make off with a bit of plunder. It is outrageous that these Italians, still unsatisfied, should continue to make preparations and to conspire in every direction."

The foreign policy of Italy after 1870 was pulled alternately in opposite directions by two irreconcilable ambitions: the desire to secure the "unredeemed" Italian-speaking provinces still held by the Hapsburgs (*Italia Irredenta*), and the desire to create an African empire. The first could be realized only at the expense of Austria, the second only at the expense of France. The French seizure of Tunis precipitated Italy into the waiting arms of Germany and Austria-Hungary in the Triple Alliance of 1882. But Italy remained an unreliable ally. Nationalistic aspirations in the north and in the Adriatic were more powerful driving forces than hopes of aggrandizement in Africa. France, for a price, was prepared to approve the fulfillment of at least a portion of these hopes. In 1896 Italy at last recognized the French protectorate in Tunis, in return for commercial concessions. In 1899 a commercial convention put an end to the long Franco-Italian tariff war. In 1900 France extended assurances that she harbored no designs on Tripoli, and Italy acquiesced in French designs on Morocco.

By an agreement of 1902, Italy, acting contrary to the spirit if not the letter of her compacts with her allies, agreed to remain neutral in the event of an attack upon France, even if France should be obliged to take the initiative in a declaration of war. In 1909 Italy agreed to view with benevolence Russia's designs upon the Straits in return for Russian approval of her project of seizing Tripoli (Libya) from Turkey, Russia's hereditary enemy and satellite of Italy's allies, Germany and Austria-Hungary. Libya was accordingly seized in the Italo-Turkish war of 1911. But in form Rome retained its commitments to Berlin and Vienna. Italy thus had a foot in both camps and was prepared to bargain for terms in the event of a crisis in which each of the great coalitions should seek her support.

When World War I broke out, Italy remained neutral on the specious plea that the war was aggressive and not defensive on the part of her allies

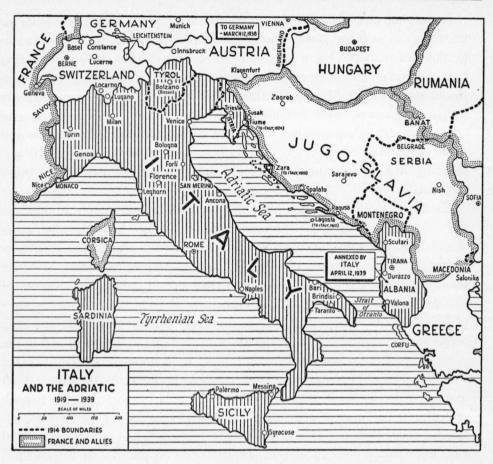

ITALY
AND THE ADRIATIC
1919 — 1939
SCALE OF MILES
0   50   100   150   200
- - - - 1914 BOUNDARIES
FRANCE AND ALLIES

and thus did not involve the *casus foederis*. With her long, open coast line exposed to attack by the British and French fleets, Italy had more to lose than to gain by joining the Central Powers, even if eventual victory might enable her to seize a large portion of the French African colonies. During the winter of 1914–15 the Italian Government, acting frankly on a policy of *sacro egoismo* (holy selfishness), bargained with both coalitions for promises of territorial compensation and agreed to enter the war on the side which promised most. Though Germany and Austria-Hungary were lavish with promises of French territory in Africa, they were unwilling to surrender Trieste, the Tyrol, and Trentino as the price of Italian aid. The Allies, on the other hand, promised Rome all these territories and part of the Dalmatian coast besides, plus compensations in the Near East and "rectifications" of the African frontiers. These terms were embodied in the secret Treaty of London of April 26, 1915.

[*49*]

On May 24, Italy declared war on Austria-Hungary. Italy's military contribution to the Allied cause was not impressive. When the Italian front collapsed in the disaster of Caporetto in the fall of 1917 and most of Venetia fell into the hands of the enemy, British and French divisions had to be sent to the Piave to stem the German invasion. In the summer of 1918, however, the Italian armies checked an Austrian offensive and counter-attacked with sufficiently telling effect (Vittorio Veneto) to claim a share in the glory of final victory.

At the Peace Conference, Italy found her claims thwarted by Wilsonian idealism, by Serbian aspirations in the Adriatic, and by French and British reluctance to permit Italy to dominate the Mediterranean. Small "rectifications" of the Libyan frontiers were secured. In the north, *Italia Irredenta* was indeed acquired, plus the Austrian Tyrol south of Brenner Pass, which was demanded for strategic reasons. Fiume was likewise seized, as well as Zara and the island of Lagosta. But the Italian acquisitions included territory claimed by Serbia on grounds of language and self-determination. Italy was faced across the Adriatic by an embittered and resentful Jugoslavia in alliance with France. In the Near East Italy gained nothing save the Dodecanese and the confirmation of her occupation of Rhodes. While Kemal Pasha's Turkish Nationalists frustrated Italian aspirations in Anatolia, France retained Syria and Great Britain acquired Iraq and Palestine. All Italian patriots felt that Italy had won the war but had lost the peace. Italy, despite her gains, emerged from the Conference an unsatiated State.

THE VIOLENCE OF THE WEAK

Italy also emerged from war and peace impoverished and divided against itself by a bitter class struggle. For decades Italian democracy had been a half-anarchic rule of political gamblers, typified by the gray and wily Giolitti, over miserable and ignorant masses—all for the benefit of politicians, plutocrats, priests and nobles. The Socialist leaders who now won a huge following vied with the Communist secessionists from their ranks in preaching revolution to the poor. Land-owners and business men were terrified into a frantic quest for a savior. Democrats were paralyzed. Even Don Sturzo's energetic Populist Party of Catholic liberals seemed to offer no hope to the insecure. Strikes and riots swept the land. The disgruntled war veterans, jobless, desperate and restless after plunging from the excitement of battle and victory into the miseries of a shameful peace, furnished a fertile field for political scoundrels and idealists, for reformers, rebels and demagogues. They formed sundry leagues, societies and *fasci* (groups) of the discontented under rival leaders who preached a dozen fanatic gospels of salvation.

One such group, calling itself the *Fasci di Combattimento*, was established in Milan on March 23, 1919, under the leadership of Benito Mussolini. Its program was democratic, patriotic, republican, socialistic, anti-imperialist, pro-League of Nations. Its *duce* demanded land for the peasants and bullets for profiteers. The Socialist Party denounced him as a turncoat and a buffoon. Mussolini denounced the Socialists as lukewarm opportunists and betrayers of the workers. Only *he* could lead the revolution! When the patriot-poet D'Annunzio, at the head of a motley horde of young adventurers, seized Fiume in September in defiance of the government, Mussolini applauded. He adopted as his own the black shirts, the Roman salute, the rites and titles and slogans which D'Annunzio had devised to glorify his lawlessness. In the election campaign of November, 1919, the *Fascisti* championed universal suffrage, votes for women, minimum wages, an eight-hour day, workers' participation in industry, social insurance, nationalization of the arms industry, anti-clericalism, a pacific foreign policy and a capital levy. But no Fascist candidates were successful. In Milan Mussolini got 5,000 votes out of 346,000.

In 1920 came more strikes and riots, the lockout of the metal workers and finally widespread seizure of factories by revolutionary proletarians. The old Giolitti, once more Premier, did nothing, on the correct assumption that the workers would fail in their efforts and come to their senses. They did. The "Red Peril" was ended by this episode. But the propertied classes were panic-stricken at the government's inaction. Mussolini seized his chance and promised "to destroy the Bolshevik plans of the Socialist Party." Money flowed from the well-to-do to the Fascist coffers. By the spring of 1921 the Fascisti were 100,000 strong. They elected 35 members to parliament, including their leader. They formed military gangs or squads to beat up or murder Socialists, to wreck and burn the headquarters of trade unions, cooperatives and Left newspapers. Army officers joined in the fun. The police were "neutral." Giolitti used the Fascist ruffians against both the Socialists and the Populists —and succeeded only too well.

CROSSING THE RUBICON

Mussolini, now a member of a hopelessly divided parliament, urged an end of murder and arson, lest civil war break out before he was ready for victory. But his fiery followers had tasted blood and wanted more. Italo Balbo, Dino Grandi, Robert Farinacci and other specialists in brutality assailed his pleas for a political truce. Violence continued. In November, 1921, Mussolini transformed his loose following into a formal Party and insured his own control in the name of sharing it with others. Violence redoubled. The belated and feeble efforts of the government to suppress it were futile. The Socialists were helpless. "They were too long suffering," wrote Herman Finer later, "and too divided—the nemesis of free men." They had once expelled and denounced Mussolini. He was taking his revenge. But he wanted more.

To Henry IV, Paris was worth a mass. To Mussolini, Rome was worth the renunciation of his Republicanism. "Our program," he said, "is simple: we wish to govern Italy. It is not programs that are wanting for the salvation of Italy, but men and will power." He ordered a "March on Rome"—that is, a national mobilization of the Fascist legions to terrorize the weak-willed and wobbling Premier Facta, and to persuade the King to give him the Premiership. On October 27, 1922, the Cabinet resigned and then decided, before its resignation was accepted, to order a state of siege to thwart the Fascist coup. The King refused. The Army was passive. The legions marched. Mussolini tarried safely in Milan. On October 29 the King called him to the capital. He crossed the Rubicon in a sleeping car. On the next day he formed his Cabinet and begun what was to become "the Fascist era."

This was a revolution of frightened little men, driven to fury by the disorders and dangers which flowed from the weakness of decrepit politicians. The revolutionists were brought to power not by strength of numbers (they were but a handful), nor by the attractiveness of their program (they had none), but by their ruthlessness, by the support of the well-to-do, and by the paralysis of their foes and victims. Once in power, they were enabled by the blindness and self-defeating folly of their rivals to devise a program, to bewitch the masses, to brutalize parliament, to abolish all other parties (1925) and to establish a despotism.

Patriots were persuaded that the Duce would save the State. Priests were convinced that he would save the Church. Plutocrats and aristocrats were certain that he would save Property. All were deceived by their own illusions.

Those no longer capable of governing themselves must be governed by others. Those unable to act together to preserve their freedom must separately and contemptibly lose their birthright. The result of the weakness of freemen is tyranny—a form of governance which men seldom prefer to liberty (if liberty gives them safety and self-respect), but always prefer to anarchy.

THE SEARCH FOR WAR

"A tyrant," wrote Plato, "must always be stirring up some war or other, in order that the people may require a leader." This necessity flows from the very nature of tyranny. People who are not allowed to quarrel peaceably among themselves will quarrel with their ruler unless he sets them to quarrelling with their neighbors. In 1925-26 no less than four attempts were made on Mussolini's life. To repress by naked force the aggressions which tyranny engenders is always more difficult and invariably less successful than to deflect them on to scapegoats at home and enemies abroad. Intolerance and conquest are unavoidable devices of despotism.

But tyrants whose subjects love peace and whose State is weak must make haste slowly. The Duce's first task was to militarize his countrymen by preaching the gospel of "Believe, Obey, Fight" and by inculcating faith in the glory of the fatherland. Rome's ancient grandeur was to be restored. Mussolini was to be imperator and conqueror. Italy was to be made formidable and therefore respected. Every phase of life was to be mobilized to the supreme end of the power of the nation. In the name of national solidarity, the old trade unions were dissolved and the right to strike suppressed. In the name of unity and power, youth was imbued with tribal mysticism. The tyranny was rationalized and sanctified. The State concluded its long struggle with the Papacy. By the Treaty and Concordat of 1929 it restored the temporal authority of the Pope and recognized Vatican City as a "sovereign" territory. The Republican who made peace with the King was the atheist who made peace with the Pope. Principles were nothing. Power was all.

The foreign policy of Fascismo was frankly directed toward aggrandizement. Italy, however, could afford to use violence only against small and feeble States. When an Italian General was assassinated by Greek patriots near the Albanian frontier, Mussolini ordered the bombardment and seizure of the island of Corfu (August 31, 1923) and defied the League of Nations to say him nay. The victory was glorious: fifteen orphan children were killed

[*53*]

by the shells. An indemnity and apology were exacted from Greece. But under British pressure Corfu was evacuated and Rome gained no conquests.

By the Treaty of Tirana (November, 1926) Albania became an Italian protectorate, to the alarm of the Cabinets in Belgrade and Athens. Mussolini looked greedily toward Croatia and the Dalmatian coast. But Jugoslavia was the ally of France and a member of the Little Entente. The Fascist Caesar was obliged to modify Theodore Roosevelt's advice to "speak softly and carry a big stick." He spoke loudly and recognized that the Italian stick was ineffective against the bigger stick of French hegemony over the Continent.

Mussolini was nonetheless impelled by the slow impoverishment of the masses under Fascism to counteract popular unrest by fulfilling long-deferred promises of war and glory. The Nazi revolution in Germany gave him his chance. He sponsored the futile (and unratified) Four Power Pact of 1933, whereby Rome, Paris, London and Berlin agreed to "consult" one another to promote peace and disarmament. He blocked Hitler's designs on Austria by subsidizing the Austrian Heimwehr and supporting the diminutive clerical dictator, Engelbert Dollfuss. He secured British and French diplomatic support against the Reich in common championship of Austrian "independence." In May, 1934, following Dollfuss's bloody suppression of the Vienna Socialists, Mussolini formed an "Italian bloc" by concluding a series of diplomatic and commercial accords with Hungary and Austria. A month later he met Hitler for the first time near Venice. But the two tyrants could come to no agreement. When the Austrian Nazis murdered Dollfuss in July and unleashed a putsch to deliver the country to Germany, Mussolini moved troops to the frontier and threatened intervention unless Hitler desisted. The putsch failed. Mussolini was not yet ready to sell out Austria for larger stakes. Hitler saw no need of quarrelling with the Duce over a prize he felt sure of getting later without a quarrel.

THE CALL OF THE WILD

In truth Mussolini's road to Vienna was actually his road to Africa. Bad geography made good politics for reasons which became clear only later. The Duce took new aim at an old target: Ethiopia. Following the dismal failure of the first Italian attempt (blessed by Britain and opposed by France) to conquer Ethiopia in 1896, a stable balance of power had emerged in East Africa with the ancient Coptic kingdom enjoying the position of a buffer State. Britain,

France and Italy had agreed in 1906 to maintain the *status quo* and to make "every effort to preserve the integrity of Ethiopia." By the Treaty of London of 1915 Italy was promised "compensations" in the event of British and French annexations of German territory in Africa. The failure of the Allies to fulfill this pledge embittered all Italian imperialists. The small British cessions to Eritrea in 1924 and the larger Anglo-Egyptian cessions to Libya a decade later were deemed wholly inadequate. Fascist dynamism required that an African empire must somehow be conquered.

Mussolini was long in doubt as to how to solve his problem. As early as March of 1932 he dispatched to Africa his comrade of *squadrista* days, General Emilio de Bono, to investigate and report. In the fall of the following year he decided tentatively on an invasion of Ethiopia. He perceived from the fate of Manchuria that Britain and France, despite their pledges to enforce peace, would do nothing against aggression where their own interests were not directly endangered. Yet he feared that their leaders might regard an attack on Ethiopia as a threat to their own African colonies. And Italy was too weak to risk a clash with the democratic Powers.

His solution was to sell them Italian support against Germany—and Italian sponsorship of the "independence" of Austria—in return for their support of his African ambitions. The solution hung fire as long as Louis Barthou was French Foreign Minister. He was too shrewd to be tricked. But on the 9th of October, 1934, Barthou and King Alexander of Jugoslavia were murdered in Marseille. The assassin was an agent of the Ustaschi, a Croat terrorist organization headed by a certain Ante Pavelich, with headquarters in Hungary and Italy. Pavelich enjoyed Mussolini's protection. Pierre Laval, butcher's son from the Auvergne and Foreign Minister of France after Barthou's death, fell into Caesar's trap. He feared Communism. He admired Fascism. He could see only one means to make France secure against Germany: an alliance with Italy. He could see only one means of making Fascist Italy a strong and willing ally: cooperation in Mussolini's African designs. To buy Italian friendship at the expense of a remote kingdom of barbarians seemed cheap and easy. On January 5-7, 1935, Laval conferred with Mussolini in Rome.

The result was the signature of elaborate accords, pledging peace, friendship and consultation. Laval got no alliance but only a vague promise to "consult" in case of any threat to Austrian independence or any danger of Nazi repudiation of disarmament obligations. He consented to "collaboration" in developing African colonies and to Italian participation, to the extent of 7% of the shares, in the French-owned railway from Jibuti to Addis Ababa.

He agreed to redefine the status of Italians in Tunisia and to cede to Italy 44,000 square miles of desert in the Tibesti region south of Libya and 309 miles of desert south of Eritrea. These concessions were accepted by the Duce as a "definitive" settlement of Italian claims against France under the Treaty of London. The ceded regions had no resources and almost no inhabitants. Those who were astonished at the modesty of Italian demands did not know that Laval had also agreed to acquiesce in Mussolini's plan for conquering an empire. "Of course," said Laval privately to Jules Romains, "I gave him Ethiopia." Despite his repeated public denials, Laval had given to the Duce precisely such a promise.

One month before this pledge was given, Italian and Ethiopian forces had clashed at Wal Wal. When Mussolini refused to arbitrate the resulting dispute, the Ethiopian Government appealed to the League of Nations—with no immediate results. In fear of invasion Haile Selassie, Emperor of Ethiopia, Negus Negusti (King of Kings), Chosen of God and Conquering Lion of the Tribe of Judah, instructed the ministers of his medieval realm to invoke Article 11 of the Covenant early in January. But Laval made his bargain with Mussolini immediately thereafter. Rome informed London of its terms. Downing Street appointed a Foreign Office Commission headed by Sir John Maffey to make recommendations. In June it recommended that Britain should not oppose Italian designs on Ethiopia but should on the contrary "seize the occasion to obtain, if possible, rectifications of the frontiers of British Somaliland, Kenya and the Sudan."

Under these circumstances, which were unknown at the time to all save the "insiders," Ethiopian efforts to secure effective support against impending aggression were foredoomed to failure. Sir Samuel Hoare, British Foreign Minister, cooperated with Laval in obstructing all Ethiopian efforts at Geneva to initiate League action. Italian troops, planes, tanks and poison gas poured through the Suez Canal in preparation for the blow to come. A resolution of the League Council (May 25) dealt only with the arbitration of the Wal Wal incident. An arbitral commission finally settled this dispute in September by holding that neither Ethiopia nor Italy was responsible for the original clash. Mussolini was thus deprived of his pretext. But he was determined to invade Ethiopia without any pretext. The leaders of Britain and France were resolved to connive in his plans.

THE WEAKNESS OF THE STRONG

The most they were disposed to do to fulfill their pledges under the League Covenant was to threaten feeble economic penalties (chiefly for the edification of the British electorate and neutral opinion) in the event that Mussolini should resort to war. Meanwhile they sought to dissuade him from taking the sword by offering him control of Ethiopia without war. The Western Powers offered the prospective victim of aggression not protection but a choice between assassination and suicide. Anthony Eden went to Rome in June to offer an exchange of territories whereby Ethiopia would cede land to Italy, and Britain would make small cessions to Ethiopia. Mussolini rejected it. While the invaders gathered in Eritrea and Italian Somaliland, the exports of arms to Ethiopia was forbidden by France, Britain and other States. The United States offered Haile Selassie "moral support" and promptly passed the "Neutrality" Act of 1935, barring arms to Ethiopia (and to Italy which had no need of them) if Caesar should strike. At a three Power conference in London in mid-August, the British and French Ministers offered Baron Aloisi a plan for "territorial adjustments" and "collective assistance" to Ethiopia, "particular account being taken of the special interests of Italy." Mussolini rejected it. A month later a League Commission of Five proposed "international assistance to Ethiopia"—i.e. Italian domination. Mussolini was not interested. "If you offered me all of Ethiopia on a silver platter," he is reported to have said to the French Ambassador, "I would refuse it, for I have resolved to take it by force."

Laval and Hoare reluctantly concluded that Mussolini would attack and that they must make a pretence at Geneva of imposing sanctions. Otherwise the voters of Britain and France, convinced that their own safety lay in support of the League and enforcement of the Covenant against aggressors, might turn them out of office and elect honest men in their places. On September 10, 1935, Hoare and Laval secretly agreed at Geneva to rule out military sanctions, naval blockade, closure of the Suez Canal—"in a word," said Hoare later, "everything that might lead to war." On the next day Hoare declared publicly at Geneva that his government stood "for the collective maintenance of the Covenant in its entirety, and particularly for steady and collective resistance [meaning "assistance"?] to all acts of unprovoked aggression." Said Laval: "France is faithful to the Covenant." Both men privately assured Mussolini that he had nothing to fear.

The Duce loudly threatened war against all who might oppose his designs, knowing that the bluff was safe. In the name of "peace," the Anglo-French leaders told their countrymen that sanctions must be kept innocuous lest all Europe be plunged into bloodshed. Laval consented to weak sanctions as a means of aiding the British Tories to win the parliamentary election scheduled for November. But Hoare quibbled when his French friends, recalling that Hitler had repudiated the military clauses of Versailles in March, asked a promise of sanctions against Germany in the event of further treaty-breaking. "There may be degrees of aggression," explained Hoare. "Elasticity is part of security." London and Paris assured Rome that sanctions would be purely "economic" and would not impede the Fascist program. Rome assured Laval and Hoare that Italy would not retaliate with force but would remain "on the defensive." Hoare assured Hitler that Britain would not join France in any future sanctions against the Reich. Hitler assured Hoare that Germany would not join Italy or move against France during the crisis.

On October 1, 1935, Mussolini ordered the invasion of Ethiopia. Rome informed the League that Ethiopian mobilization was a threat, aggravated by the withdrawal of Ethiopian troops from the frontier, and that "the warlike and aggressive spirit of Ethiopia has succeeded in imposing war against Italy." Four days later the League Council reassembled to consider the report of its Committee of Thirteen which refuted the Italian charges and noted that Rome was solemnly bound by numerous treaties to refrain from resorting to force. With Italy in the negative, the Council and Assembly both held "that the Italian Government has resorted to war in disregard of its covenants." Aloisi argued that Italy was a victim of aggression. He waxed eloquent: "Caught as she is in the tide of her full spiritual and material development but confined within territorial limits that are stifling her, Italy must make her voice heard in this Assembly as the voice of the proletariat calling for justice." By mid-October the Assembly's "Committee for Coordination of Measures Under Article 16" had appointed a smaller Committee of Eighteen to propose sanctions.

The farce of sanctions helped Mussolini to make an unpopular war popular by pretending that he was successfully defying the British Empire and the world. Five proposals for sanctions were put forward at Geneva. The first contemplated lifting the arms embargo against Ethiopia and keeping it in force against Italy. The second proposed a ban on all loans to Italy. The remaining three forbade purchases of Italian exports, banned the sale to Italy of certain raw materials, and provided for cooperation among League members to reduce commercial losses resulting from sanctions.

The "economic siege" of Italy was begun on November 18, 1935, with the adoption of the sanctions proposals by almost all the League members. Shocked by Italian lawlessness and fearful for their own security, they were willing to accept trade sacrifices for the purpose of discouraging aggression. The Baldwin Cabinet was victorious in the general election of November 14 largely because of its pretended championship of sanctions. Yet it was clear to even the dullest observer that the sanctions already imposed would not halt the war. Fighting could easily have been stopped by closing the Suez Canal, by blockading Italy or by barring oil exports to the aggressor. Italian tanks, trucks and planes in Ethiopia were dependent upon foreign oil. The great democracies in the League were not prepared to apply military sanctions. Were they prepared to extend economic sanctions to a point at which they might become effective?

THE SHAME OF GENEVA

This question was soon answered in the negative. At the end of November London and Paris agreed to postpone all discussion at Geneva of oil sanctions. Early in December London asked Turkey, Greece, Jugoslavia, Rumania and Czechoslovakia how far they were prepared to go in assisting any sanctionist State attacked by Italy. These governments agreed to grant full support to Britain against any Italian assault in the event of an application of oil sanctions. But Downing Street intimated early in January that American refusal to halt oil shipments to Italy would make oil sanctions useless. More delay ensued while Italy laid in huge oil supplies. No oil sanctions were ever imposed.

Meanwhile the Western statesmen, again in the name of "peace," had done all in their power to give Ethiopia to the aggressor. On December 8, 1935, it became known that Hoare and Laval had agreed to a "peace plan" whereby Italy was to be rewarded with two-thirds of Ethiopia. The two Foreign Ministers did not communicate their plan to the League Council until the 13th, exactly a year after Ethiopia had first appealed for protection. Laval requested the Council to express no opinion until Rome and Addis Ababa had been heard from. The plan failed because of Italian indifference. A storm of British indignation forced Hoare out of office. His successor, Anthony Eden, pursued a policy of masterly inactivity while the Italian armies plunged ever deeper into Ethiopia.

Haile Selassie was forced to flee from his capital early in May of 1936. Before his flight he asked a question and made a prophecy: "Do the peoples of the world not yet realize that by fighting on until the bitter end I am not only performing my sacred duty to my people but standing guard in the last citadel of collective security? I must still hold on until my tardly allies appear. If they never come, then I say prophetically and without bitterness, 'The West will perish. . . .'" From Jerusalem he wired the Secretary-General of the League that he had left his country to "avoid the extermination of the Ethiopian people" and to devote himself to "the preservation of the age-old independence of Ethiopia and the principles of collective security and the sanctity of international obligation, all of which are threatened by Italy." He asked the League not to recognize the conquest and to continue its efforts to secure respect for the Covenant.

When the Council met in May Aloisi withdrew in protest at the presence of an Ethiopian delegation. Ethiopia asked a full application of Article 16. Ecuador asked that sanctions be lifted since the war was over. Chile agreed. The Council postponed a decision, but resolved to keep sanctions in force meanwhile. Argentina called for an Assembly meeting, convoked for June 30. Rome announced that it would take no part until sanctions were abandoned. Joseph Beck announced that Poland had already abandoned them.

GOLGOTHA

Britain now assumed leadership in destroying the League. Early in June, while Eden welcomed Haile Selassie to his lonely exile in England, Sir Samuel Hoare reentered the British Cabinet. Neville Chamberlain declared: "If we have retained any vestige of common sense, surely we must admit that we have tried to impose on the League a task which it was beyond its powers to fulfill." Italy had lost half of its gold reserve. Italian imports had been sharply reduced. Continued sanctions might well have undermined the Fascist regime despite its victory in Ethiopia. But precisely this was what the Anglo-French appeasers desired to avoid. They now scrambled with indecent haste to betray the victim of banditry and to embrace the bandit.

The Assembly of June 30-July 4, 1936, abandoned Ethiopia to her fate.

Assembly President Van Zeeland, Premier of Belgium, read a note from Rome: "The Ethiopian populations welcome the Italian troops as champions of freedom, justice, civilization and order. Italy views the work she has undertaken as a sacred mission of civilization and proposes to carry it out according to the principles of the Covenant of the League and of other international agreements which set forth the duties of civilizing Powers." Eden had already announced British abandonment of sanctions on June 18. Anglo-French efforts to dissuade Haile Selassie from speaking in Geneva failed. As he mounted the rostrum, Italian journalists in the press gallery shrieked curses and insults until they were expelled by the police. To an Assembly shamed into silence the King of Kings spoke simply: "I am here today to claim that justice that is due to my people, and the assistance promised to it eight months ago by fifty-two nations who asserted that an act of aggression had been committed in violation of international treaties. I decided to come myself to give Europe warning of the doom that awaits it if it bows before the *fait accompli*. God and history will remember your decision. What answer am I to take back to my people?"

The answer was desertion. Léon Blum spoke of the beauties of peace. Anthony Eden suggested that the Covenant should be amended. Maxim Litvinov snorted his contempt. M. Ter Waters of South Africa said that the impending decision would "shatter for generations all international confidence and all hope of realizing world peace. Order is losing to chaos. The spectacle of power has hypnotized the world." Ethiopia asked the Assembly to declare that it would recognize no annexation obtained by force and to recommend a loan of ten million pounds to Ethiopia under conditions to be fixed by the Council. The latter proposal was rejected, 23 to 1, with 25 not voting. As for the former, the Assembly ignored it and closed its session with the adoption of an ignominious resolution expressing "firm attachment to the principles of the Covenant," soliciting proposals for the reform of the League, and recommending an end of measures taken under Article 16. Sanctions were abandoned. Ethiopia was abandoned. Collective security was abandoned.

The last curtain fell in May of 1938. London proposed that the League Council, then holding its 101st meeting in Geneva, scrap the Stimson Doctrine and approve recognition of Italian title to Ethiopia on the part of League members, as promised in the Ciano-Perth Accord of April 16, 1938—another tragic milestone along the appeasers' road toward disaster. Washington was silent. Haile Selassie sought to prevent this final betrayal by making a token payment on Ethiopia's defaulted dues. Halifax declared: "Nothing is gained and much may be lost by refusal to face facts. Great as is the League of Nations, the ends it exists to serve are greater than itself and the greatest of those ends is peace. . . ."

Haile Selassie, small and dark, a ruler of barbarians but every inch a king, replied in words of Judgment Day: "The Ethiopian people, to whom all assistance was refused, are climbing alone their path to Calvary. No humiliation has been spared the victim of aggression. Many threatened Powers have uttered the cry of panic and rout: 'Everyone for himself.' It is a certainty that they would be abandoned, as Ethiopia has been, and between two evils they have chosen one which the fear of aggression led them to consider the lesser. May God forgive them. There are different ways to maintain peace. There is maintenance of peace through right and there is peace at any price. The League would be committing suicide if after having been created to maintain peace through right it were to abandon that principle and adopt instead the principle of peace at any price, even the price of immolation of a member State at the feet of its aggressors."

The Council chose suicide. Council President Wilhelm Munters of Latvia declared that each member should decide for itself whether to recognize Italian title to Ethiopia. Only four delegations objected: New Zealand, Bolivia, China and the U.S.S.R. Britain and France recognized Italian title to Ethiopia in November. Seventeen months later Mussolini reciprocated with a declaration of war against those who had sought to buy peace by giving him an empire.

IMPERATOR AFRICANUS

With the aid of his Anglo-French friends the Duce thus destroyed the League of Nations, humiliated Britain and rendered France ripe for defeat at the hands of the Reich. He also conquered a kingdom. In the winning of it much easy glory went to Mussolini and to the members of his family. Daughter Edda had married young Count Galeazzo Ciano who had served in the diplomatic corps and as Minister of Propaganda. Italo Balbo, made too popular by his flight to Chicago in 1933, had been "exiled" as Governor of Libya and was given no part in the Ethiopian campaign. But son-in-law Ciano heroically bombed defenseless black men and became Foreign Minister in the aftermath. De Bono was soon replaced in the north by Marshal Pietro Badoglio. Rodolfo Graziani led the invaders from the south. Mussolini's two sons, like Ciano, played their parts in planes—by far the safest branch of the service since the

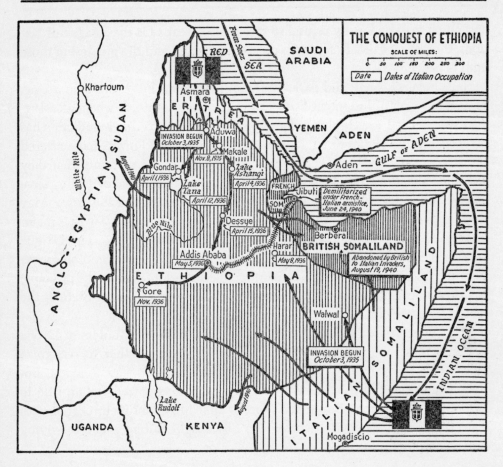

Ethiopians had no air force and no anti-aircraft guns. Vittorio Mussolini bombed Red Cross detachments and machine-gunned the doctors and nurses and the wounded. He also sprayed poison gas, dropped incendiary bombs for the pleasure of seeing good fires, and experimented with aesthetics: "I still remember the effect I produced on a small group of Galla tribesmen massed round a man in black clothes. I dropped an aerial torpedo right in the center and the group opened up just like a flowering rose. It was most entertaining."

Mussolini's son Bruno was also entertained: "We had to set fire to the wooded hills, to the fields, and to the little villages. It was all most diverting. I thought of the animals. God, how they ran! After the bombracks were emptied I began throwing bombs by hand. It was most amusing. A big 'Zariba' surrounded by tall trees was not easy to hit. I had to aim carefully at the straw roof and only succeeded at the third shot. The wretches who were inside, seeing their roof burning, jumped out and ran off like mad. Surrounded by a circle of fire about five thousand Abyssinians came to a sticky end."

On the fifth day of May, 1936, Mussolini addressed a cheering throng from the balcony of the Palazzo Venezia: "Blackshirts of the Revolution, men and women of all Italy, Italians and friends of Italy beyond the mountains and seas: Marshal Badoglio telegraphs: 'Today, May 5, at 4 p.m., at the head of the victorious troops, I entered Addis Ababa.' Ethiopia is Italian. It is Italian in fact because it is occupied by our victorious armies. It is Italian in law because of the law of Rome and civilization which triumphs over barbarism, justice which triumphs over cruel whims, redemption of miseries which triumph over slavery."

Four days later he addressed the populace once more: "The territory and peoples which appertain to the empire of Ethiopia are hereby placed under full and complete sovereignty of the Kingdom of Italy. The title of Emperor of Ethiopia is assumed for himself and for his successors by the King of Italy." Badoglio was named Viceroy. Graziani was promoted to the rank of Marshal and soon succeeded Badoglio in the new post. Caesar beamed: "Italy at last has her empire. It is a Fascist empire. The Italian people have created it with their blood. They will defend it against anyone with their weapons. In this supreme certainty, lift your flags, your swords, your hearts to salute the reappearance after fifteen centuries of an empire on the fateful hills of Rome. Will you be worthy of it?" The mob howled: "Yes! Yes!" "Is this cry a sacred oath?" demanded the Duce. "Yes!" "Is it an oath that binds you before God and man?" "Yes!" "Is it an oath which binds you for life or death?" "Yes! Yes!"

This successful aggression placed Italy in a far stronger position than she had hitherto enjoyed. Having effectively played off Berlin against Paris and London, Mussolini could (so he thought) bargain with each camp for favors under threat of joining the other. An Austro-German agreement of July 11, 1936, represented (on paper) an abandonment of Nazi designs against Vienna in return for Italian support against France. An Italian-German accord of October 25, 1936, appropriately negotiated by the heroic Ciano, foreshadowed a possible alliance between the Fascist Powers. Austria became a bridge instead of a barrier between Rome and Berlin.

Italy's enhanced prestige in the Mediterranean offered opportunities in other directions. The Sudan and the headwaters of the Nile lay adjacent to Italian Ethiopia. The British route to India through the Red Sea was apparently at the mercy of Italy. French communications with North Africa might be severed by Italian air power, particularly in the event of cooperation from a Fascist Spain. Intrigues against Britain and France throughout the

Arab world offered hope of further weakening the influence of London and Paris in the Near East. Perhaps *Mare Nostrum* could, after all, be made once more a Roman lake. Perhaps Libya and Italian East Africa could be united over the ruins of British imperial power. Perhaps. . . .

Mussolini was driven forward to new adventures by the economic dilemma of Fascism and by the psychological compulsion of a despotism obliged to give the masses circuses instead of bread. At the end of August in the year of his African victory the Duce declared: "We can mobilize eight million men. We reject the absurdity of eternal peace, which is foreign to our creed and to our temperament. We must be strong. We must be always stronger." Two months later he declaimed at Milan: "Collective security never existed, does not exist and will never exist. The League of Nations can perish. Today we raise the banner of anti-Bolshevism. For us Italians the Mediterranean is life."

THE SALVATION OF SPAIN

Meanwhile, the next adventure in aggression had been launched. In Rome, as in Berlin, it was obvious to the tyrant in power that his ambitions could be furthered by converting Spain into a Fascist ally or vassal. To threaten Gibraltar from Algeciras and Ceuta, to menace French communications from the Balearic Islands, to control the coasts of Spain would enable the Axis to levy further blackmail against France and Britain and perhaps ultimately to destroy them. The means for the enterprise were at hand in the determination of the army officers, industrialists, feudal grandees, and priests of reactionary Spain to destroy the liberal Spain of the "People's Front" which won the election of February 16, 1936. Although there were neither Socialists nor Communists in the People's Front Cabinet, the Axis crusade could be readily disguised in terms of "saving Spain from Bolshevism." Mussolini and Hitler assumed correctly that most men of Property and Piety in France, Britain, and America would be deceived by this slogan and would therefore acquiesce or even cooperate in the destruction of the Spanish Republic.

As early as March, 1934, Spanish monarchist leaders were received by Mussolini and Balbo in Rome and encouraged to hope for Fascist support against the Republic. In the spring of 1936, Spanish generals and plutocrats made repeated visits to Rome and Berlin and laid their plans for a military uprising with Axis support. General Francisco Franco, dispatched to the Canaries because his loyalty to the Republic was suspect, conferred before his departure with Generals Mola and Varelo, millionaire Juan March, Colonel Yagüe, and José Primo de Rivera, son of the former Spanish dictator and leader of the Fascist *Falange Española*.

A private British plane arrived at Las Palmas in the Canaries on July 15, 1936. On the same day a squadron of bombers of the Royal Italian Air Force was ordered to be ready for duty in Spain. On July 17, Franco received a wire from Yagüe in Tetuán, Spanish Morocco. "The troops in Africa revolted on the 16th at 11 a.m." Franco boarded the plane, reached Tetuán on July 19, took command of the revolting Moors and Foreign Legion, and proclaimed that Spain was "saved." But this Nazi-Fascist *putsch* failed in its immediate purpose. General Sanjurjo, flying from Lisbon, was killed in an air crash. General Goded, flying from the Balearic Islands, was captured and shot. Mola was subsequently killed and Rivera executed. Army uprisings were successful in the south and in the north but were crushed in Madrid, Barcelona, and other centers by a hastily organized People's Militia which rallied to the defense of the Republic. What was to have been a military coup became a "civil war."

In reality this "civil war" at once assumed the form of an Axis invasion of Spain. Italian bombers were immediately placed at Franco's disposal. Nazi agents, technicians, and aviators poured into Rebel territory from German ships and from Portugal. Italian troops landed in Seville and at other points. The first joint diplomatic action of Rome and Berlin, following their secret agreement of October 25, was simultaneous recognition of Franco as ruler of Spain on November 18, 1936. The better to lend plausibility to the enterprise, Germany and Japan concluded the "Anti-Comintern" Pact of November 25. Italy adhered on November 6, 1937, and Franco's Spain on March 27, 1939. Britain and France in the name of "nonintervention," followed by the United States in the name of "neutrality," forbade their citizens to sell arms to Spain and thereby cooperated with the Axis Powers in the murder of Spanish democracy. An international "Nonintervention" Committee was set up in London with Lord Plymouth as chairman to supervise the enforcement of the obligations assumed.

These obligations were well observed by France and Britain and systematically violated by Italy, Germany, and Portugal—and also, in retaliation for Fascist intervention, by the U.S.S.R. After the event, when all need for subterfuge was gone, Mussolini's *Popolo d'Italia* boasted, "We have intervened from the first moment to the last." In June, 1939, Italian and German troops returned to their homelands and enjoyed triumphal receptions in Rome and Berlin. Ciano and Göring revealed that Axis soldiers, sometimes disguised as "tourists," had gone to Spain at the outset of the rebellion and had been prepared for action long in advance.

The courageous struggle of the Spanish people to defend their liberties in the face of the united opposition of the Vatican, the Caesars of the Axis, and the appeasers and isolationists of Paris, London, and Washington was fore-doomed to failure. No government, save only that of the U.S.S.R., would give or even sell them arms to resist their enemies. By mid-August, 1936, Franco's mercenaries had taken Badajoz, where they massacred several thousand help-less prisoners, and effected a junction with Mola's forces in the north. By the end of October they raised the Loyalist siege of the Alcázar in Toledo. In early November, four Rebel columns, supported by Italian and German planes, tanks, and artillery, advanced on Madrid, expecting a "Fifth Column" of sympathizers within the city to give them speedy mastery of the capital. But the Loyalist "International Brigade," assisted belatedly by Soviet arms, smashed the assault and compelled the invaders to lay siege to Madrid. On January 2, 1937, as German and Italian cruisers fired on Loyalist shipping, Ciano and Perth exchanged letters pledging respect for the *status quo* in the Mediterranean and the territorial integrity of Spain. Under the new "Non-intervention" plan of February 16, 1937, designed to "prohibit" volunteering and arms exports to both sides, Axis warships "patrolled" the Loyalist coasts while British and French vessels did likewise off Rebel ports. The United States imposed its own unilateral arms embargo upon Spain on January 8, 1937. "President Roosevelt," declared Franco, "behaved in the manner of a true gentleman."

On March 13, 1937, an Italian armored column seeking to outflank Madrid from the north via Guadalajara was crushingly defeated by the defenders. Rome refused to withdraw its "volunteers." The London Committee and its local observers were at no time able to detect any violation of the "Non-intervention" agreements. In May, Loyalist planes bombed the Italian cruiser *Barletta* at Palma and the German pocket battleship *Deutschland* at Iviza. Hitler retaliated by ordering a naval bombardment of Almeria on May 31. Rome and Berlin announced their withdrawal from the sea "patrol." They resumed "cooperation" in mid-June. Nazi dive-bombers meanwhile destroyed Guernica, holy city of the Catholic Basques, on April 26. Italian forces occu-pied Bilbao. On June 23, Mussolini and Hitler alleged further Loyalist out-rages against their ships and withdrew permanently from the naval patrol, simultaneously demanding belligerent rights for Franco. The hypocritical tergiversations of the London Committee now became incredibly complex.

Italian efforts to blockade Republican Spain by torpedoing merchant ships all over the Mediterranean were abruptly halted by a conference at Nyon in September, 1937, where it was agreed by nine Powers (not including Italy and Germany which refused to attend) that "unknown" submarines should be attacked and destroyed on sight as pirates.

THE VICTORY OF NONINTERVENTION

Despite these setbacks, the Duce and Führer were enabled by Paris, London, and Washington to achieve their goal of victory for Caudillo ("Chief") Franco. Almost 100,000 Italian troops were operating in Spain. Rome acknowledged 40,000. A League Assembly resolution of October 2, 1937, declared "there are veritable foreign army corps on Spanish soil." It urged "immediate and complete withdrawal." Rome and Berlin refused to withdraw "volunteers" unless the Western Powers should grant Franco belligerent rights and thus enable the Axis navies to impose an effective blockade upon Loyalist ports. Downing Street and the Quai d'Orsay were willing to negotiate forever over this question while the Fascist conquest of Spain continued. Santander fell to the invaders on August 22 and Gijón in the Asturias on October 21, 1937. The summer offensive of the Loyalists in Aragon failed. The Republican capital was moved from Valencia to Barcelona on October 20. On St. Patrick's Day, 1938, Axis bombers raided Barcelona twelve times in twenty-four hours. The slain victims included 245 women and 118 children. In New York, Patrick Cardinal Hayes publicly prayed for a Franco victory. The Earl of Perth negotiated amiably with Ciano in Rome.

Franco's forces reached the Mediterranean at Vinaroz on April 15, 1938. On the following day Ciano and Perth signed the pacts whereby Britain agreed to recognize Italian title to Ethiopia and accepted an Italian pledge to withdraw volunteers from Spain only after the end of the "civil war." Chamberlain and Mussolini exchanged congratulatory telegrams. Roosevelt expressed "sympathetic interest." Daladier and Bonnet approved. Early in May Hitler visited Rome to return Mussolini's visit to Berlin of the preceding September. Austria was dead. Spain was dying. The Axis was "steel." In mid-May Alvarez del Vayo, Loyalist Foreign Minister, infuriated Halifax and Bonnet at Geneva by indelicately recalling the Assembly resolution on the withdrawal of volunteers. During June British ships and French towns were "accidentally" bombed by Franco's allies. Chamberlain went fishing. On July 5,

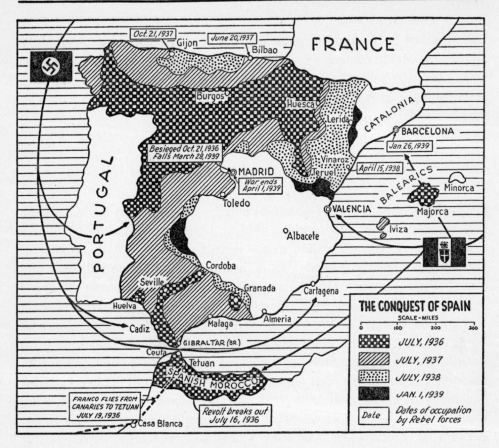

THE CONQUEST OF SPAIN

SCALE - MILES

0   100   200   300

JULY, 1936

JULY, 1937

JULY, 1938

JAN. 1, 1939

Date — Dates of occupation by Rebel forces

1938, the London Committee adopted an eighty-page "formula" for the withdrawal of volunteers. Franco rejected it. The Duce and Führer laughed. In the aftermath of Munich, Britain put into effect (November 16, 1938) the Ciano-Perth accord which had specified that "a settlement of the Spanish question" was "a prerequisite of entry into force" of the agreement.

The nature of this "settlement" was no longer in doubt. Chamberlain and Daladier were as eager for Fascist victory in Spain as were Hitler and Mussolini. The final Rebel offensive against Catalonia was launched two days before Christmas, 1938. Chamberlain and Halifax conferred with Mussolini, Ciano, and Pius XI in Rome, January 11–14, 1939. On January 18 Chamberlain and Daladier declared that "nonintervention" must continue to the end. Barcelona fell to the Rebels. Mussolini shouted to cheering crowds outside the Palazzo Venezia, "Our enemies are biting the dust!" Early in March a group of defeatists and appeasers in Madrid, headed by General Sigismundo Casado, repudiated the authority of Loyalist Premier Juan Negrin, raised the banner of "anti-Communism," and asked Franco for peace terms. He demanded unconditional surrender. Casado fled. The Fifth Column in Madrid took over the ruined capital. Rebel forces entered on March 28, 1939. Bloody vengeance was visited on thousands of Loyalists. Half a million refugees were grudgingly admitted to France, there to be herded wretchedly into concentration camps and condemned to misery. Since Franco and his executioners, trained by the Gestapo and blessed by the bishops, would grant no amnesty, the fugitives could not be repatriated.

On February 27, 1939, Chamberlain and Daladier granted *de jure* recognition to the Franco regime. London sent as Ambassador to Burgos Sir Maurice Peterson, one of the authors of the Hoare-Laval plan to give Mussolini Ethiopia. Paris sent eighty-three-year-old Marshal Henri Philippe Pétain, clerical reactionary and favorite hero of the French Fascist leagues. The United States recognized Franco on April 1 and lifted the arms embargo. The democratic Powers hoped to appease Franco with loans. The Caudillo's brother-in-law and Minister of the Interior, Ramon Serrano Suñer, leader of the Falange (who was to become Foreign Minister in October, 1940), hinted broadly that the new Spain would aid the Axis to destroy France and Britain and to combat the United States in Latin America. "Our enemies," declared the Duce, "are too stupid to be dangerous."

PACT OF PUTTY

But victory in Spain was not an undiluted blessing for the Caesar of Rome. Italian losses had been heavier than in the Ethiopian campaign. No territories had been won. Fascist Spain was dominated more by Germany than by Italy. Franco was in no position to make an alliance for war in aid of the Axis. A million Spaniards had been slain. The vanquished were starving, sullen, bitter. The country was in ruins. Yet Mussolini had again demonstrated that the class prejudices of the Anglo-French ruling groups incapacitated them for defending the interests of their States. He had likewise improved his opportunities for blackmailing the French Republic and further weakening British power.

When French Ambassador André François-Ponçet came to Rome in November, 1938, bearing the gift of French recognition of Italian title to Ethiopia, he was greeted in the Italian chamber with loud outcries for "Tunisia! Jibuti! Corsica! Nice! Savoy!" On December 17, Rome informed Paris that the

Laval-Mussolini accord of 1935 was no longer regarded as binding. France must give more. Daladier breathed feeble defiance. Bonnet intrigued obscurely through his secret agents—Fernand de Brinon in Berlin, Paul Baudouin in Rome—to give away additional French territory. But he failed. The psychological and diplomatic aftermath of Hitler's seizure of Prague in mid-March rendered further appeasement inexpedient. The Duce's potent ally had won another major victory. The Roman Caesar was left empty-handed.

Mussolini sought solace by seizing Albania and concluding a formal military alliance with the Reich. On April 7–8, 1939, Italian troops drove King Zog and Queen Geraldine out of their backward Balkan kingdom. On April 15, King Victor Emmanuel assumed the Albanian crown. Although this action was a flagrant violation of the Ciano-Perth accord, France and Britain took no counteraction beyond extending guarantees to Greece and Rumania on April 13 and concluding an alliance with Turkey on May 12. On April 15, Roosevelt addressed an appeal to Hitler and Mussolini to refrain from attacking their neighbors. The Führer replied at length on April 28 with bitter and effective sarcasm. The Duce contemptuously refused to be moved by "Messiahlike messages." Ribbentrop conferred with Ciano at Milan on May 6. On May 22, 1939, the two Foreign Ministers affixed their signatures at Berlin to an apparently unlimited military alliance threatening the Western Powers with war should they continue to oppose Axis demands.

By this pact, which was to run for ten years, Germany and Italy agreed to "stand side by side and with their united strength to render secure their *Lebensraum* and for the maintenance of peace. Proceeding along this path pointed out to them by history, Germany and Italy desire in the midst of a world of unrest and disintegration to serve the task of rendering safe the foundations of European culture." "Constant contact," "consultation" and "mutual support" were pledged. "If contrary to the wishes and hopes of the contracting parties it should happen that either of them should become involved in military entanglements with one other Power or with other Powers, the other contracting party will immediately rally to his side as ally and support him with all his military resources on land, at sea and in the air. The contracting parties obligate themselves now, in the event of war conducted jointly, to conclude an armistice and peace only in full agreement with each other."

But this "pact of steel" was in part compounded of *Ersatz*. Ciano admitted in December that Rome had told Berlin at the time of its conclusion that Italy would not be ready for war for three years. Hitler had agreed not to raise issues likely to lead to armed conflict during this period. In the summer crisis of 1939, Rome sought to avert an open test of force. Mussolini was not favored with any advance information regarding the German-Soviet Pact. When a general conflagration appeared imminent, Mussolini and Ciano cooperated with Bonnet in efforts to localize the German-Polish conflict and to arrange an armistice and a conference. Their plans foundered on German refusal to halt the *Blitzkrieg* and British refusal to negotiate unless it were halted. If Mussolini contemplated joining Germany in hostilities, he was dissuaded by his Chief of Staff, Marshal Pietro Badoglio, by the King and perhaps even by Hitler who realized full well that Italy as a belligerent would soon crack under the full brunt of Anglo-French attack. Much greater advantages were to be had by retaining the benefits of neutrality while cooperating secretly with the Reich. This policy presupposed that the Western Munichmen would be too timid and blind to force an immediate showdown with Rome. The assumption was correct.

THE HOUR OF DECISION

On September 1, 1939, the Italian Government accordingly announced that it "would take no initiative whatever toward military operations." The Fascist formula was "nonbelligerency" which meant in practice all aid to Germany short of war and blackmail against the Allies. Early in March, 1940, Britain yielded on the issue of Italian imports of German coal. Ribbentrop conferred in Rome with Mussolini, Ciano, and Pius XII on March 10–11. Hitler and Ribbentrop conferred with Mussolini and Ciano at Brennero on March 17. Sumner Welles, departing from Rome on March 19 after a tour of the belligerent capitals, declared that he had neither received nor conveyed any peace plans and was not carrying any home to the President. The *Popolo d'Italia* asserted early in May: "Italy has been in the war from the beginning. When she changes her policy of waiting is a matter which concerns only him who has the responsibility of guiding and safeguarding the interests of the Italian people." The answer to the question of when depended upon calculations of safety. To attack while the Allies could still counterattack would be too soon. To attack after the Reich had won complete victory would be too late. To attack after the Allies had been decisively defeated but before they had capitulated would be to attack at the right moment.

As the moment seemed to be approaching in the wake of Allied disasters in

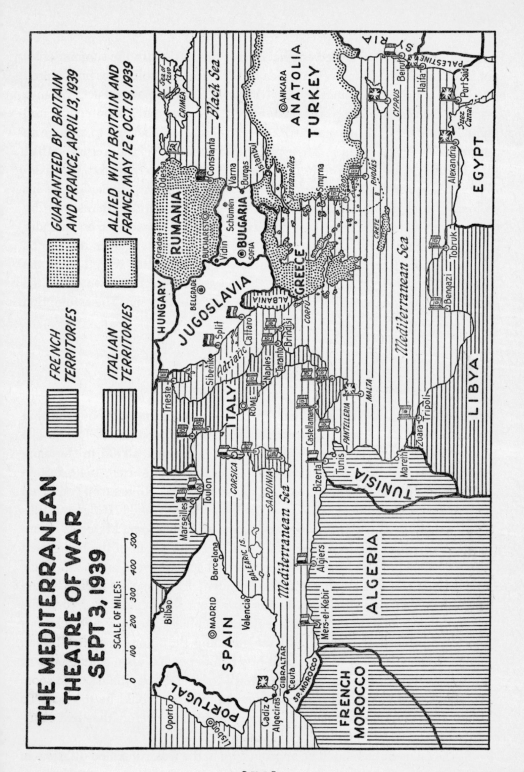

THE MEDITERRANEAN THEATRE OF WAR SEPT 3, 1939

SCALE OF MILES:

0 100 200 300 400 500

FRENCH TERRITORIES

GUARANTEED BY BRITAIN AND FRANCE, APRIL 13, 1939

ITALIAN TERRITORIES

ALLIED WITH BRITAIN AND FRANCE, MAY 12 & OCT. 19, 1939

PORTUGAL
Oporto
Lisbon
Cadiz
Algeciras

SPAIN
Bilbao
⊙MADRID
Barcelona
Valencia
GIBRALTAR
Ceuta
S.P.MOROCCO

FRENCH MOROCCO
Mers-el-Kebir
Algiers

ALGERIA

TUNISIA
Bizerta
Tunis
Mareth
Zuara

LIBYA
Tripoli
Benazi
Tobruk

BALEARIC IS.

CORSICA

SARDINIA

Mediterranean Sea

Marseilles
Toulon

ITALY
ROME⊙
Naples
Castellamare
Taranto
Brindisi

PANTELLERIA
MALTA

Trieste
Sibenik
Split
Cattaro

Adriatic

JUGOSLAVIA
BELGRADE⊙

HUNGARY

RUMANIA
Oradea
BUCHAREST⊙
Vidin

ALBANIA
CORFU

GREECE
SOFIA⊙
BULGARIA
Schumen
Varna
Burgas

CRETE

Mediterranean Sea

BLACK SEA
Odessa
CRIMEA
Sea of Azov
Constanta

Istanbul
Dardanelles
Smyrna

ANATOLIA
TURKEY
⊙ANKARA

RHODES

CYPRUS

SYRIA
Beirut
PALESTINE
Haifa
Port Said
Suez Canal
Alexandria

EGYPT

[73]

the north and west, efforts were made from Paris, London, and Washington to bribe or cajole the Duce into continued neutrality. Reynaud made proposals. They were rejected. Laval went to Rome and returned empty-handed. On May 16, 1940, Churchill sent a secret message of good will, coupled with a plea and a warning. "Whatever may happen on the Continent, England will go on to the end, even quite alone as we have done before; and I believe, with some assurance, that we shall be aided in increasing measure by the United States and, indeed, by all the Americas. I beg you to believe that it is in no spirit of weakness or of fear that I make this solemn appeal, which will remain on the record. Hearken to it, I beseech you in all honor and respect, before the dread signal is given. It will never be given by us." Mussolini replied weakly on May 18 with references to "grave reasons of a historical and contingent character which ranged our two countries in opposite camps [*e.g.*, sanctions and Mediterranean 'servitude']. The same sense of honor and of respect for engagements assumed in the Italian-German treaty guides Italian policy today and tomorrow in the face of any event whatsoever." President Roosevelt through Ambassador William Phillips offered to Mussolini his good offices to adjust Anglo-Italian differences. "I proposed that if Italy would refrain from entering the war I would be willing to ask assurances from the other Powers concerned that they would faithfully execute any decision so reached and that Italy's voice in any future peace conference would have the same authority as if Italy had actually taken part in the war as a belligerent." Rome rejected all overtures.

By early June Mussolini and his advisers had decided that France was doomed and that Britain would be crushed by the end of the summer. On June 10, 1940, the Duce informed a cheering throng in the Piazza Venezia that Italy had declared war on France and Britain and that hostilities would begin at 12.01 a.m., June 11. "The hour destined by fate is sounding for us. The hour of irrevocable decision has come. We want to break the territorial and military chains that confine us in our sea. It is a conflict between two ages, two ideas. Now the die is cast and our will has burned our ships behind us. I solemnly declare that Italy does not intend to drag other peoples bordering on her by sea or land into the conflict. Switzerland, Jugoslavia, Greece, Turkey and Egypt, take note of these words of mine. We will conquer in order, finally, to give a new world of peace with justice to Italy, to Europe, and to the universe." On the same day, at the University of Virginia, Roosevelt asserted, "The hand that held the dagger has struck it into the back of its neighbor."

The calculation behind this decision was right as to France and wrong as to

Britain. For his rightness, the Duce got small reward. For his wrongness, his subjects were to suffer grievously. On June 16, 1940, Pétain telephoned Madrid to seek an armistice from Hitler. The Duce and the Führer met in Munich two days later. On June 22 the French-German armistice was signed. A French-Italian armistice was made a condition of its execution. On June 23, Ciano, Badoglio, and Cavagnari met French emissaries near Rome. At 7.15 p.m., June 24, an agreement was signed. Hostilities in France ceased at 12.35 a.m., June 25, 1940. The twenty-six articles of the Italian armistice required French demilitarization of a fifty-kilometer zone on the European frontier and of comparable zones in Tunisia, Algeria, and French Somaliland, as well as disarmament of the French naval bases at Toulon, Bizerte, Ajaccio, and Oran. Italy secured control of Jibuti and the French railway to Addis Ababa. But Rome got nothing more. In the interest of "collaboration" with Vichy, Berlin denied to Mussolini the pleasure of immediate annexation of French territory. Despite Laval's intrigues, the French fleet did not pass to the Axis. The British navy remained master of "Mare Nostrum." Nazi assaults on England in the summer and autumn failed of their purpose.

THE WEAKNESS OF THE VIOLENT

Mussolini sought to solve his problem by joining Germany and Japan in the Triple Alliance of September 27, 1940, and by invading British Somaliland, Kenya, the Sudan, Egypt, and Greece. Only the first of these invasions attained its objective. With the evacuation of Berbera on August 19, British Somaliland passed into Italian hands. Attempts to invade Kenya and the Sudan from Ethiopia achieved only local successes. Marshal Rodolfo Graziani's Libyan army of 250,000 invaded "nonbelligerent" Egypt in mid-September in a drive aimed at Alexandria and Suez. It quickly reached Sidi Barrani, some seventy-five miles from the border, only to be stalled on the narrow coastal plain pending the arrival of stores and equipment which never came in sufficient amounts because of control of the sea by Sir Andrew Cunningham's battle fleet. On October 28, Hitler and Mussolini conferred in Florence. On the same day the Italian army in Albania launched an invasion of Greece. This adventure proved disastrous. The Duce had been deceived by the wily Greek dictator, John Metaxas, who had studied war and politics in Germany, into supposing that "Little John" and King George II would flee at the first blow and deliver Athens into the hands of a pro-Italian Fifth Column. Metaxas and his able Chief of Staff, General Alexander Papagos, had secretly made all preparations for a warm reception of the unwelcome guests.

The Italian ultimatum to Greece of October 28, 1940, asking "free passage" and "control of strategic points," was at once rejected. The invaders were thrown back. Albania was invaded in turn. British air and sea forces now had access to Greek bases and used them to raid Naples, smash Italian battleships at Taranto (November 11), bomb Valona and Durazzo, and harry communications across the Straits of Otranto. The Greeks took Koritza on November 22, Porto Edda on December 6, and Argyrokastron on December 8. On the next day, General Sir Archibald Wavell's "Army of the Nile" launched a motorized *Blitzkrieg* against Graziani's troops, retaking Sidi Barrani, invading Libya, capturing Bardia, pushing on to Tobruk and Bengazi and seizing 150,000 prisoners and huge stores at a cost of 438 killed, 1,249 wounded and 87 missing.

These events brought Italy to the brink of disaster. Early in December, Marshal Badoglio, who had opposed the Greek adventure, resigned. He was replaced by General Ugo Cavallero as Chief of Staff. Admiral Domenico Cavagnari, whose fleet had suffered successive defeats at British hands, was displaced by Admiral Arturo Riccardi. Other shifts of military and political personalities reflected confusion in Rome. On December 23, 1940, Churchill broadcast an appeal to the Italian people: "Our armies are tearing your African empire to shreds. It is all because of one man—one man and one man alone has ranged the Italian people in deadly struggle against the British Empire. After 18 years of unbridled power he has led your country to the horrid verge of ruin. One man has arrayed the trustees and inheritors of ancient Rome upon the side of the ferocious pagan barbarians. There lies the tragedy of Italian history and there stands the criminal who has wrought the deed of folly and shame. The people of Italy were never consulted. The army of Italy was never consulted. No one was consulted. What hard choice is open now? It is to stand up to the battery of the whole British Empire on sea, in the air and in Africa, and to the vigorous counterattack of the Greek nation. Or, on the other hand, to call in Attila over the Brenner Pass with his hordes of ravenous soldiery and his gangs of Gestapo policemen to occupy, to hold down and to protect the Italian people, for whom he and his Nazi followers cherish the most bitter and outspoken contempt that is on record between races."

FROM FRYING PAN TO FIRE

Whoever might win the war, it was clear by the first anniversary of Mussolini's stab-in-the-back that Fascismo had lost it. The pseudo-Machiavellian mountebank who sold Italy's birthright for a delusion of glory had forgotten Machiavelli's best advice: "A Prince ought to take care never to make an alliance with one more powerful than himself for the purpose of attacking others, because if he conquers you are at his discretion." By June of 1941 the Duce's East African empire was lost and his own land was in the hands of the Reichswehr and the Gestapo. Balbo was dead, mysteriously slain at the very outset of the Libyan campaign. Badoglio was out. Graziani resigned his North African command at the end of March, following the overwhelming defeat of his armies. The remnants were rescued by divisions from the Reich. Veteran Fascist Achille Starace, Chief of Staff of the Blackshirt Militia, was replaced in May by a nonentity. All important decisions affecting Italians were now made at Berlin or Berchtesgaden. The Duce's military forces were impotent, his navy was wrecked, and his people were more and more aware that he himself was not a creator of any "new order" but only a creature of Hitler.

The Nazi Caesar was quite willing to throw bones to the deflated Benito, not from gratitude but because puppets, to be useful, must seem to be sovereign. After the German conquest of Jugoslavia and Greece, Italy's disheartened soldiery was permitted to police the vanquished while the Reichswehr prepared its greater *Drang nach Osten*. Mussolini was allowed to annex to Italy the port of Susak and the Dalmatian shore down to Split, and to annex to Albania the rocky coast between Cattaro and the old Jugoslav-Albanian frontier. Montenegro was groomed for puppetry under the Roman puppet's rule. An "independent" Croatia became an Italian protectorate by treaty.

A ceremony of gilt and tinsel took place in Rome on May 18, 1941. The central figure was the puppet of Zagreb, Ante Pavelich, who had plotted the murders of Barthou and Alexander and was now dubbed "Poglavnik" (Duce) of Croatia. In the uniform of a Ustaschi terrorist he appeared before the tiny Victor Emmanuel to ask the King of the Italians to name a King for the Croats. The Italian monarch graciously named his nephew, Aimone, Duke of Spoleto.

Among the subjects of the House of Savoy only the blind and the stupid rejoiced. Others knew that on the very same day Aimone's brother, the Duke of Aosta, Viceroy of Ethiopia, had abandoned the defense of besieged Alagi, last important Italian stronghold in East Africa, and asked the British for terms of surrender. They also knew that Haile Selassie had re-entered his capital on the fifth anniversary of Badoglio's triumphant occupation of Addis Ababa. And they knew that "Mare Nostrum" was half-German and half-British, that Italy was hopelessly in chains, and that the South Slav Quislings who were now to be "ruled" from Rome were not in the power of Rome but in the power of the Reich.

The aging tyrant of the Palazzo Venezia was bald and dyspeptic. He was sick in both body and soul. His theatricality was no longer glamorous but pathetic. His efforts to preserve appearances deceived no one. On the 2nd of June, 1941, Hitler condescended to meet him at Brennero for a mysterious "conference." Seven years before a strutting Duce had met a fumbling Führer for the first time and had laid down the law. Now he came to be told. His own slogan had always been, "Believe, Obey, Fight!" He obeyed, since he had no choice. He no longer believed. He declared war on Russia twenty days later, since this was Hitler's will.

But neither he nor his enslaved people any longer had a will to fight. He mouthed stale phrases and feebly defied America to declare war. "I firmly believe," he said without faith, "that in this immense struggle between gold and blood the just God, which lives in the souls of young people, has made his choice. We shall conquer!" But those who sell themselves to the conqueror can never conquer. Italy was a lost land. Its civilians at home were cynical and weary. Its soldiers abroad, policing Greece and Croatia, fighting Serb guerrillas, or dragging themselves toward death on the Russian steppes, performed their tasks without enthusiasm. Their embittered Caesar, who had long ago defined war as "justice, nobility and brotherly pity," lost his son Bruno in an air crash near Pisa early in August. The grieving father perhaps envied the young man's fate. For he knew that his realm was in alien hands and that the deluded masses whom he had led to misery through his blunders no longer had a cause or a Fatherland.

The Walrus and the Carpenter were walking close at hand: They wept like anything to see such quantities of sand. "If this were only cleared away," they said, "it would be grand!" "O Oysters, come and walk with us!" the Walrus did beseech. "A pleasant walk, a pleasant talk, along the briny beach: we cannot do with more than four, to give a hand to each." And four young oysters hurried up, all eager for the treat. Their coats were brushed, their faces washed, their shoes were clean and neat— And this was odd, because, you know, they hadn't any feet. Four other oysters followed them, and yet another four; and thick and fast they came at last, and more, and more, and more— All hopping through the frothy waves, and scrambling to the shore. "A loaf of bread," the Walrus said, "is what we chiefly need. Pepper and vinegar besides are very good indeed— Now, if you're ready, Oysters dear, we can begin to feed." "But not on us!" the Oysters cried, turning a little blue. "After such kindness, that would be a dismal thing to do!" "The night is fine," the Walrus said, "Do you admire the view?" "I weep for you," the Walrus said. "I deeply sympathize." With sobs and tears he sorted out those of the largest size, holding his pocket-handkerchief before his streaming eyes. "O Oysters," said the Carpenter, "you've had a pleasant run! Shall we be trotting home again?" But answer came there none. And this was scarcely odd, because they'd eaten every one.

FROM ARMINIUS TO SCHICKLGRUBER

The inner life of nations is often revealed by their symbols of leadership. The history of Germany begins with a man-symbol, continues with three successive dynasty-symbols, and ends with a man-symbol: Hermann, the Hohenstauffens, the Hapsburgs, the Hohenzollerns, Hitler. The first of these leaders, called by the Romans Arminius, was the chieftain of the Cherusci who led his pagan followers out of the long darkness of barbarism to butcher the legions of Varus in Teutoberger Wald (A.D. 9), thereby compelling Imperial Rome to abandon the dream of a frontier on the Elbe. The early dynasties typified the "First," or Holy Roman, Reich, established in its initial form eight centuries after Hermann by Karl der Grosse (Charlemagne) when the Germanic tribes had long since learned to revere and imitate the great world of ancient Rome which their ancestors had destroyed. Under Hohenstauffen and Hapsburg Emperors, this curious realm endured as a living polity for eight centuries more, symbolizing the catholic universality of medieval Christendom and the common culture of Frenchmen, Germans, Czechs, Poles, Italians, and others—bound together by Church and Empire until the "seamless robe" of unity was torn beyond all mending by Protestantism and Nationalism. The life span of the Hohenzollern dynasty was the life span of the modern cult of the nation-state in Germany—from the Mark of Brandenburg through the Kingdom of Prussia to the German Empire (the "Second Reich") of 1871–1918. Hitler, the little man of Austria who became tyrant over Europe, symbolized the twilight time of nationalism and Christianity when Germans returned to a debased cult of imperial power, reverted to barbarism and paganism, and dreamed of a world State conquered by the sword of a "Third Reich."

To most Germans of the 20th century this leader was a Holy Man and a Redeemer, sent by the Teutonic gods to "save" Germany and the world from the Jews and the Communists. To all other Western peoples, and to many Germans as well, he was a diabolical synthesis of Julian the Apostate, Caligula the Degenerate, Attila the Hun and Tamerlane the Scourge of God. On the day on which he launched the greatest of his aggressions, he was described by Winston Churchill, in words reflecting the hatred of half of mankind, as "a monster of wickedness, insatiable in his lust for blood and plunder." In these qualities he resembled, many times magnified, the tawdry Caesar of Fascismo and the Japanese warriors of righteous justice who had turned another continent into a charnel-house. He resembled them also in his power-mad frenzy and in the fury of his fanatic followers. Yet this sickness of the soul, which in the Age of Hitler swept over much of the earth like a plague, was less the product of the innate viciousness of evil men than of the fierce resentment of millions of desperately frightened little people, terrified of their own loneliness in a harsh and ill-ordered world that denied them security and love.

Hitler, like Mussolini and Stalin, became a leader of such people because he

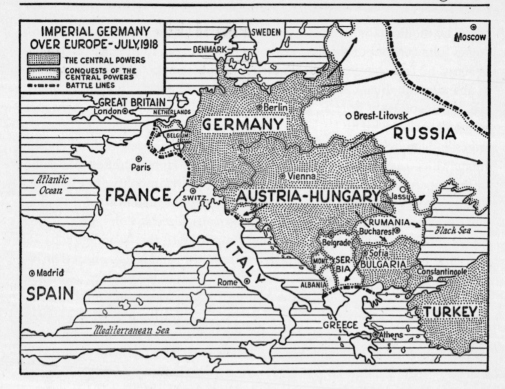

was one of them. Like all geniuses, he was more talented than the rest. Like all politicians, he was in need of public acclaim to bring peace to his twisted soul. But essentially he was a little man, transformed by his own magic and by the paranoid delusions of his followers into a Savior with a Sword. His father (like Stalin's) was a shoe-maker. This shoe-maker long called himself Alois Schicklgruber. He was the illegitimate son of Maria Anna Schicklgruber. She married her boy's father when Alois was five. Not till the boy was a man of forty did he change his name to Hitler, after the Austrian peasant family from which his father came.

Alois Hitler was helped by his first wife to secure a post in the Austrian customs service. His second wife died within a year after their marriage. His third wife was a distant cousin, Klara Poelzl, who had been a maid in his first wife's home. With Klara he lived and worked in Braunau-am-Inn, a little town northeast of Salzburg on the Austrian-Bavarian frontier. Here, on April 20, 1889, Klara gave birth to the son whom they named Adolf.

When the son was seven, his father retired on a pension to Leonding. When the son was almost fourteen, his father died. Three years later his mother died. Adolf had hated his father and quarrelled with his mother. They wanted him to become a respectable official. He wanted to be an artist. Now he was free. But he was alone and poor. He went to Vienna to study art. He failed. Having no money, he worked as a building trades laborer and learned, out of his poverty and bitterness, to hate Social Democrats and Jews and Slavs. Since no one loved him, he loved no one. In his early twenties he painted post-cards and lived in misery, first in Vienna and then in Munich. His hero fantasies came true in 1914. War brought meaning to an otherwise empty life. He joined the German forces, tasted mud and blood, won a corporalship and an Iron Cross, and at the end was gassed at Ypres in October, 1918. He was convalescing when defeat and revolution drove him once more to morbid despair.

MEMBER NO. 7

All misfits are not agitators. But all agitators are misfits. Adolf Hitler could not go back to civilian life. He stayed with the Army and returned to Munich where he watched with loathing the rise and bloody fall of the Bavarian Soviet Republic of 1919. Marxists and Jews seemed to him more than ever the enemies of the mystical Fatherland which he worshipped with all the ardor of a repressed romanticist incapable of normal passion. He shunned women and lectured the members of his regiment on the duties of patriotism. Munich was full of riff-raff—revolutionists, reactionaries, political revivalists and salvationists of a dozen brands. Hitler attended meetings, seeking some outlet for his hatreds and his cloudy ambitions.

On a June evening of 1919 he chanced to attend a little anti-Semitic gathering arranged by a group calling itself the "German Labor Party." Here in a beer-hall a certain Gottfried Feder expounded the difference between "international Jewish" capitalism and "national German" capitalism, and between "Jewish-Marxist" socialism and "patriotic" socialism. Hitler was impressed. A few days later he went again and was invited to join. On a hunch he did. His membership card made him member No. 7.

He took his duties seriously and soon discovered that he was an orator. Crowds gathered in beer-halls to hear his bitter denunciations of the Jews, the Marxists, the Allies. He persuaded his fellow-soldiers to join. The "party," like its Italian counter-part, was primarily a movement of disgruntled war veterans, seeking through political gangsterism to recapture the thrills of the martial spirit. By the following spring Hitler was leader of the group, now renamed the "National Socialist German Workers' Party." He adopted Gottfried Feder's weird economics. From besotted Dietrich Eckart, an elderly would-be poet, he took the slogan "Germany, Awake!" From the detested Marxists he took red banners, proletarian catch-words and the title of "comrade" for party members. A platform of twenty-six points was adopted at a great mass-meeting at the Hofbräuhaus on February 24, 1920. It was a jumble of Pan-Germanism, anti-Semitism and pseudo-socialism. Every week Hitler harangued the crowds, damning Jews and Masons, capitalists and Communists, democrats and monarchists with impartial fury and preaching the liberation of Germany from "interest slavery" and the chains of Versailles. Every week more members and more money flowed to the Party.

Art, discovered Hitler, should have social significance. He designed placards. He equipped the husky "bouncers" at his meetings with brown shirts and organized them into a *Sturm-Abteilung* or Storm Division of the Party. He copied the Roman salute of the Italian Fascists and devised the black-white-red Hakenkreuz flag, representing anti-Semitism, nationalism and socialism. Symbols, songs and pageantry won converts. The fevered oratory of hatred imbued them with fanaticism. Other able malcontents and adventurers joined the cause: Hermann Göring, wealthy war ace and dope-addict; Rudolf Hess, soldier and anti-Semite, called "the Egyptian" because of his birth in Alexandria; Ernest Röhm, war veteran, terrorist and homosexual; Edmund Heines, patriotic murderer; Gregor Strasser, soldier and druggist; Alfred Rosenberg, Baltic German and rabid anti-Bolshevik; General Erich von Ludendorff, ex-warlord and political lunatic; and thousands of smaller misfits.

By the autumn of 1923, disastrous year of invasion and inflation, the Party had 70,000 members. Like Mussolini's movement, it had support from the wealthy and influential who hoped to use it for their own ends. The Nazis were encouraged by Generalstaatskommissar Gustav von Kahr; by Gen. von Lossow, Reichswehr commander in Bavaria; and by Lieut. von Seisser, Munich police chief. All three were engaged in obscure intrigues aiming at a restoration of the monarchy and the secession of Bavaria from the Reich. With their supposed support, Hitler planned his "revolution" for the fifth anniversary of the "Jewish-Marxist" revolt which ousted the Kaiser.

THE PUTSCH THAT FLOPPED

On the evening of November 8, 1923, the Führer and his stormtroopers surrounded the Bürgerbrau where Kahr, Lossow and Seisser were addressing a

[*83*]

patriotic rally. Firing a revolver at the ceiling as he dashed down the aisle, he mounted the rostrum and proclaimed the overthrow of the Bavarian and Reich Governments. By threatening murder and suicide, he induced his three powerful friends to promise cooperation while Göring bellowed at the crowd. But the three pleaded sleepiness and asked that the new regime be organized on the morrow. Hitler agreed.

The three departed, but not for their beds. They at once called out police and troops to suppress the rebels. Dawn found the armed forces of the State guarding all public buildings against the stormtroopers. What to do? Hitler ordered a noon parade. Kahr ordered the dissolution of the Party. As the marchers, with Ludendorff and Hitler at their head, approached the Feldherrnhalle on Odeonplatz, the police opened fire. Eighteen of the paraders died. Göring fled, slightly wounded. Hitler threw himself on his belly. He was spirited away by his followers, but was later arrested. The "revolution" was a bloody farce. The Party was outlawed and smashed.

Hitler's trial for treason was held before a court which, like most German courts under the Republic, was savagely severe in dealing with Leftists but invariably lenient in dealing with patriotic murderers and plotters. The principal defendant was permitted to orate: "The future of Germany means the annihilation of Marxism. Who is born to be a dictator will not be halted, but must himself press forward. I wish to be the drummer of the Third Reich. Of the young men who fell, it will some day be said: 'These, too, died for the liberation of the Fatherland.'" Ludendorff was found "not guilty." Hitler was sentenced to five years' imprisonment, with praise of his war record and his patriotism and a recommendation of clemency for good behavior. He was released in December, 1924. His "imprisonment" in the fortress of Landsberg-am-Lech was pleasant but tedious. He was frustrated and gloomy. Hess persuaded him to begin the writing of his political autobiography. He decided to call it *Mein Kampf*.

THE REPUBLIC WITHOUT REPUBLICANS

In the life of the German Republic the "beer-hall putsch" in Munich was but a small episode in a year of troubles. No one (save Hitler) believed that it ever would or could have an aftermath. Germany's face was turned toward freedom. Between the fall of the Hohenzollern regime and the establishment of the Nazi despotism, fifteen years elapsed. These were the years when German

Liberalism and Social Democracy belatedly came into their own. They were years of hope.

But the hope was always deferred and forever frustrated, since the democrats and socialists of the defeated Reich were never able to please patriots or convert to their cause the old ruling classes whose prerogatives they dared not disturb. They fought Communism on the left (and defeated it in 1919–1920) but compromised endlessly with reaction on the right. French insecurity, enhanced by British indifference and American isolationism, drove Paris to policies of oppression which the German Republic had no means of resisting. Its weakness promoted disloyalty; its hopelessness provoked desperation.

Despite limited and belated diplomatic successes, the Weimar Republic never lived down its early associations with the military débâcle, the "Diktat" of Versailles, indemnities, disarmament, weakness, disgrace, inflation, disaster. In the struggle over reparations between victors and vanquished the Republic lost the first great battle in "the war after the war." On April 27, 1921, the Reparation Commission fixed the total bill at 132 billion marks, or about 31 billion dollars. Germany was compelled to accept this total, under threat of the occupation of the Ruhr. But the financial condition of the German Government led to huge budgetary deficits, which were met by inflation, with a resulting depreciation of the mark. A temporary moratorium had to be granted to Germany. But at the end of 1922 the determination of the Poincaré Government in France to use force and seize "productive guarantees" was reflected in the action of the Reparation Commission in declaring Germany in voluntary default on timber, coal, and cattle deliveries. In January, 1923, French and Belgian troops seized Düsseldorf, Essen and other mining and smelting centers in the Ruhr valley. Germany countered by stopping all reparation payments and organizing passive resistance against the invaders. The forces of occupation resorted to reprisals, arrests, courts-martial, and other repressive measures. But coal could not be mined with bayonets, and the occupation was fruitless. The German Government, however, was reduced to bankruptcy. In August of 1923 Chancellor Gustav Stresemann abandoned passive resistance and surrendered.

Germany's efforts to bring about the end of foreign military control and to secure equality in armaments were more successful. The Allied occupation of the Rhineland was terminated in June of 1930, five years before the expiration of the period specified in the treaty, and the Allied military and financial control commissions were withdrawn. This was a substantial gain and the fruit of the Briand-Stresemann era of *rapprochement*. By abandoning passive resistance and flirtations with the Soviet Union, by accepting as permanent the Reich's western frontier, guaranteed in the Locarno treaties of 1925, and finally by accepting the Young Plan, Stresemann gained membership in the League of Nations for Germany in 1926 and achieved the end of foreign supervision of German armament. But this was a negative victory and only a small step toward that equality of military status which was the prerequisite of effective political equality with other Powers. Germany insisted upon the fulfillment of the pledge of the Treaty of Versailles that the unilateral disarmament of Germany would be followed by general disarmament. In the sessions of the Preparatory Commission for the Disarmament Conference between 1925 and 1929, and in the General Disarmament Conference of the League of Nations which met at Geneva in February, 1932, the German representatives pleaded eloquently for general disarmament to the German level or, as an alternative, the granting to Germany of the right to rearm to the level of her neighbors. France and her eastern allies, with qualified support from Great Britain, stood steadfast against both demands, for the acceptance of either would destroy the strategic bases of French hegemony and enable Germany to challenge the 1919 *status quo* in other respects. Not until December of 1932—much too late—was the German demand for equality of armaments granted—and then only "in principle."

In the matter of territorial readjustment, the German Republic achieved nothing. In the Locarno treaties, it accepted the loss of Alsace-Lorraine and of Eupen and Malmédy as permanent. But the loss of Danzig, the Polish corridor, and Upper Silesia remained a festering wound in the hearts of all patriots, and none could abandon hope of recovering these territories in the future. Their recovery, however, demanded a new dismemberment of resurrected Poland—and behind Poland stood France and the Little Entente, firmly resolved to maintain frontiers as they were. Here was a stake of German diplomacy which could be attained only at the risk of war. And so long as Germany was impotent, war could not be risked. At Locarno, Germany refused to guarantee the eastern frontiers but agreed not to resort to forcible measures of revision. Stresemann and his successors were consequently obliged, like Gambetta, to cherish in silence the memory of the new "lost provinces" and to await a more favorable conjuncture of events before assaying their recovery. As for the lost colonies, the most that Germany was able to attain was a seat on the Permanent Mandates Commission of the League of Nations. German colonial aspirations remained unfulfilled. Efforts at *Anschluss* with Austria led to further humiliation, compelling Foreign Minister

Curtius to resign under French pressure in 1931 and further weakening Chancellor Brüning, last hope of German democracy.

In summary, Republican Germany's foreign policy encountered a succession of defeats at the hands of France and attained none of its major objectives. This circumstance helped to discredit democracy. The psychic insecurities bred of national defeat and impotence were aggravated by social insecurities engendered by currency inflation and general impoverishment. Even in its early days, the Weimar Republic was bitterly assailed by monarchists, ultra-patriots, and adventurous leaders of disgruntled ex-soldiers. Liberals and Social Democrats, in the name of freedom, tolerated reactionary enemies of the Republic on the right and Communist enemies of the Republic on the Left and won the contempt of both. *Junkers* and industrialists, left undisturbed in possession of their privileges, saw visions of greed and glory and plotted with reactionary politicians against the new regime. Only the false prosperity of the 1920's, nourished by American and British loans, enabled the Republic to survive as long as it did.

[87]

LITTLE MAN, WHAT NOW?

When the Great Depression descended upon the Reich, paralyzing the money markets, halting the wheels of heavy industry, bankrupting anew the insecure middle class, and depriving millions of workers of their jobs, the foes of the Republic for the first time found a mass following. Conservatives and liberals were spurned by the desperate masses. Armies of converts flocked to the banners of reactionaries and radicals. Hungry laborers joined the Communist cause. Frightened peasants and burghers looked to the extreme Right for protection. Aristocrats and plutocrats conspired to feather their nests. The Nationalist Party of Alfred Hugenberg—power-mad, money-mad magnate of press and cinema—gained new recruits. Intrigue in high places was matched by fear-bred fanaticism among the poor.

In every corner of the land the agitators whose shrieking was shrillest, whose cursing was most colorful and whose promises were most extravagant were the preachers of "National Socialism." They cried from the house-tops and in the market places that Germany was undefeated in 1918 but was stabbed in the back by the Jews and the Marxists; that the "November criminals" of the "Weimar Jew Republic" must be destroyed; that the Reich could recover "freedom and bread" through a new Messiah who would save all souls and fill all stomachs in a glorious "Third Reich." The Messiah, garbed in a tan raincoat and a battered fedora, flew like a madman from town to town. At a thousand meetings he climaxed a grand drama of pageantry and music with the hoarse eloquence of hysteria, arms waving, hair flying, sweat streaming, voice screaming, choking and thundering in fury. Under his spell millions found their souls by losing their minds. Their Savior was Adolf Hitler.

Upon his release from prison in 1924, he had bestirred himself mightily to revive the "Movement" with the aid of Feder and Rosenberg and the Strasser brothers, Gregor and Otto. A lame dwarf, possessed of the morals and wisdom of Satan, brought his talents to the cause: Dr. Paul Joseph Göbbels. His task, he said, was "to unchain volcanic passions, to arouse outbreaks of fury, to set masses of men on the march, to organize hate and suspicion with ice-cold calculation." In 1927 the first of the impressive "Party-Days" was celebrated in Nürnberg. Hitler was now absolute Führer of his followers. His stream-lined machine of propaganda and terrorism won few converts as long as Germans had jobs and hopes. But when the temple of Mammon crumbled, when want and worry turned masses of little men and women into neurotics, then huge throngs joined the parade of the swastikas and thrilled to the cry of *"Deutsch-land, Erwache!"*

With banners, drums, and trumpets the brown-shirted Nazi stormtroopers, subsidized by businessmen and aristocrats, carried the *Hakenkreuz* flag throughout the land and shouted their battlecries: "Freedom and bread!" "Out with the Jews!" and "Break the bonds of interest slavery!" In the Reichstag election of September 14, 1930, they won 6,400,000 votes. In the presidential election of April 10, 1932, in which the "wooden Titan," Hindenburg, was re-elected by a slim margin, 13,400,000 votes were cast for Hitler. In the Reichstag election of July 31, 1932, 13,745,000 Nazi votes were cast—37 per cent of the total. Hitler seemed about to be swept into power by a great mass movement which would give him a majority of the electorate. But business conditions improved slightly in the autumn of 1932. In the Reichstag balloting of November 6, 1932 (the last free election in Germany), the Nazis polled only 11,737,000 votes—less than one-third of the total. By the end of the year their movement was bankrupt and disintegrating. Göbbels was desperate. Hitler threatened suicide.

THE TRICKSTERS

The Reich was delivered to Fascism not by an electoral victory but by a conspiracy, entered into against the last republican Chancellor, Kurt von Schleicher, whose old friend, Franz von Papen, resolved to use Hitler to put himself back in power. Papen, arch muddler of the German reaction, had been head of the "Baron's Cabinet" which Hindenburg had appointed after ousting Chancellor Heinrich Brüning in May, 1932. In December Papen was forced out of office and replaced by Schleicher. In January, 1933, Papen spun his plot. His tools, so he thought, were Hitler, the mob hypnotist; Hugenberg, the ultra-nationalist publisher; Fritz Thyssen, the steel magnate; the *Reichsverband der Industrie;* and the *Junker Landbund.* Hindenburg, who had been re-elected to the Presidency nine months previously by the support of Brüning and of all the liberals and Socialists in order that he might save the Reich from Hitler, was persuaded to "save agriculture" (*i.e.,* the *Junkers*) from "agrarian Bolshevism" (*i.e.,* an exposure of the use to which they had put State subsidies) by dismissing Schleicher on January 30, 1933, and appointing Hitler Chancellor, Papen Vice Chancellor, Hugenberg Minister of Economics, and other reactionaries to the remaining posts. Hitler dissolved the Reichstag and ordered an election for March 5, 1933.

Six days before the balloting the Reichstag building was burned. Hitler at once accused the Communists of arson and bloody revolution. He posed as the savior of the nation from the Red menace. He ordered the arrest of thousands of Communists and Social Democrats, suppressed the campaign activities of the anti-Nazi parties, induced Hindenburg to abolish civil liberties in the name of defense against the Communist peril, and threw the electorate into a panic. His followers polled 44 per cent of the vote. They promptly secured a majority in the new Reichstag by excluding and arresting all the Communist deputies. An "Enabling Act" transferred dictatorial powers to the Cabinet.

The story of how Hitler astutely tricked his non-Nazi colleagues, wiped out all other parties, suppressed the social radicals in his own ranks, and established the Nazi despotism cannot be reviewed here. Suffice it to note that the multitudes were exalted by the mass pageantry of great festivals, by the masterly propaganda of Göbbels and by the demagoguery of the Führer. They were prevailed upon to give the regime almost unanimous support in a series of referenda. Dissidence was suppressed by the ruthlessness of Göring and the espionage of Himmler. Heavy industry and the *Junkers* had paid the piper and were, for a time, able to call the tune. On "Bloody Saturday," June 30, 1934, critics within the ranks were silenced and old scores were settled. Among those shot for "treason" were Gregor Strasser, Ernst Röhm, Edmund Heines, Karl Ernst, and other Nazi radicals who resented Hitler's dependence on the propertied classes or who aspired to replace the *Junker*-controlled Reichswehr with the stormtroopers as Germany's new army; the aides of the incautious Papen, who barely escaped death and was bundled off to Vienna as German Ambassador; Kurt von Schleicher and his wife; Erich Klausener; General von Bredow; and scores of others.

With Hindenburg's death on August 2, 1934, and Hitler's assumption of the powers of the Presidency, the Führer's control of the German State became absolute. Hjalmar Schacht remained his liaison with Big Business. Defense Minister Blomberg and the General Staff remained his liaison with the *Junkers*. With the trade unions abolished and strikes forbidden, with the press, radio, motion pictures, theatre, and school system shackled, and with all social organizations "coordinated" under Nazi control, the dictatorship was as unlimited as human ingenuity and lust for power could make it. Popular unrest was deflected into Jew-baiting and into hatred of foreign enemies. Germany thus became a new citadel of Fascist totalitarianism, dedicated to militarism, revenge, and imperial expansion.

"TO FORGE A MIGHTY SWORD . . ."

The Third Reich pursued the same general diplomatic objectives as the Weimar Republic but utilized in place of conciliation and compromise the methods of treaty-breaking, threats, and defiance. But to these old objectives were added new ones far more alarming to Germany's neighbors. Mystical racial Pan-Germanism contemplated the ultimate "liberation" of all Germans abroad and the union with the Reich of Austria, German Switzerland, the Sudeten-Deutsch of Czechoslovakia, the Germans of Danzig, the Corridor, the Baltic States, and other irredentist areas. Beyond these lived other "Nordics" who ought also, willy-nilly, to join the Reich—the Flemings, the Dutch, the Scandinavians. The building of this greater Reich in the name of *Deutschtum* and *Grossraumwirtschaft* would require the partition or extinction of most of Germany's neighbors. In militant National Socialism, moreover, was a new *Drang nach Osten*—a dream of controlling the Danube valley and the Balkans. And here also, bred of middle-class hysteria and the fanatical thirst for revenge of Alfred Rosenberg and other Russian émigrés in the Nazi ranks, was a vision of a great crusade against Bolshevism, involving a restoration of the terms of Brest-Litovsk, with White Russia, the Baltic States, and the Ukraine in German hands. "To forge a mighty sword," Hitler had written in *Mein Kampf*, "is the task of the internal political leadership of a people; to protect the forging and to seek allies in arms is the task of foreign policy." "Today we have conquered Germany," sang the Nazi youth, "Tomorrow the world is ours."

That these objectives meant war was fully realized by the Nazi leaders. War is seldom embarked upon, however, even by desperate autocrats, unless it offers at least a gambler's chance of victory. Hitler's problem was one of building up an overwhelming military force, dividing and weakening his prospective enemies, and finding allies. Rearmament was dangerous because it involved treaty violations and might precipitate a preventive war by the French bloc before the Reich was prepared to resist. Hitler moved cautiously and calculated correctly that French pacifism and British muddlement would prevent any concerted effort to coerce Germany. Amid loud protestations of peace and further pleas for "honor" and "equality," he announced Germany's withdrawal from the League and the Disarmament Conference on October 14, 1933. This gesture of protest against the refusal of other Powers to grant arms parity to the Reich won wide approval at home and provoked no retaliation from Paris or London.

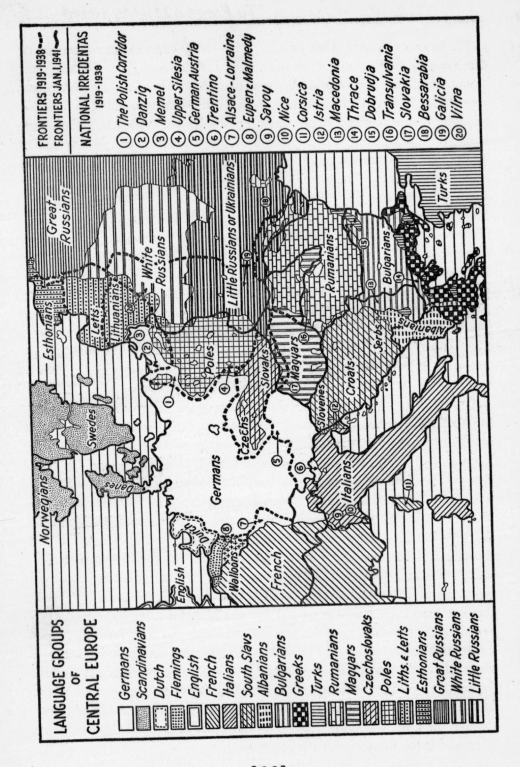

LANGUAGE GROUPS OF CENTRAL EUROPE

FRONTIERS 1919-1938
FRONTIERS JAN. 1, 1941

NATIONAL IRREDENTAS
1919-1938

① The Polish Corridor
② Danzig
③ Memel
④ Upper Silesia
⑤ German Austria
⑥ Trentino
⑦ Alsace-Lorraine
⑧ Eupen & Malmedy
⑨ Savoy
⑩ Nice
⑪ Corsica
⑫ Istria
⑬ Macedonia
⑭ Thrace
⑮ Dobrudja
⑯ Transylvania
⑰ Slovakia
⑱ Bessarabia
⑲ Galicia
⑳ Vilna

Germans
Scandinavians
Dutch
Flemings
English
French
Italians
South Slavs
Albanians
Bulgarians
Greeks
Turks
Rumanians
Magyars
Czechoslovaks
Poles
Liths. & Letts
Esthoniars
Great Russians
White Russians
Little Russians

[99]

The second step was taken on March 16, 1935, with the announcement of the "Law for the Reconstruction of the National Defense Forces" which reintroduced military conscription and greatly enlarged the Reichswehr in open repudiation of Part V of the Treaty of Versailles. This led, after considerable fumbling and wrangling, to the Anglo-French-Italian "Stresa Front" of April and to Germany's condemnation by the League Council. There were warnings and threats but again no action, save the signature of the Franco-Soviet Pact on May 2 and of the Czech-Soviet Pact on May 16. The united front was soon shattered. On June 18, 1935, Downing Street connived in Hitler's treaty-breaking by accepting his offer of a naval pact limiting the German fleet to 35 per cent of the British. Since Berlin was anxious to conciliate London, the agreement was most satisfactory. A German fleet one-third the size of the British could easily dominate the Baltic and thus aid in the projected crusade against Russia. Within three months, Britain and Italy were at swords' points in the Mediterranean and Hitler could proceed with his plans unhindered. The German General Staff was reestablished in October with General Ludwig Beck as its Chief. Unemployment waned and munition profits mounted, as government loans financed an enormous production of guns, tanks, artillery, bombing planes, submarines, and battleships.

The third step toward military domination of the Continent was taken on March 7, 1936, while the Western Powers were hopelessly split over Italy's impending conquest of Ethiopia. Hitler announced the abrogation of the Locarno treaties of 1925 and the remilitarization of the Rhineland (in violation of Locarno and of Articles 42 and 43 of Versailles), alleging that the Franco-Soviet Pact violated the Locarno engagements. He proposed a twenty-five year nonaggression pact with France and Belgium, guaranteed by Italy and Britain; the reciprocal demilitarization of the frontier (involving the scrapping of the Maginot Line); bilaterial nonaggression pacts with Germany's eastern neighbors (excluding the U.S.S.R.); and other ingenious devices designed to safeguard the western frontier and leave Germany free in the east. Had French armies moved into the Rhineland, the Reichswehr was prepared to withdraw, since it was not yet ready for war. But the French armies did not march. Again protests, warnings, and League condemnation were followed by inaction. Britain pledged France support against German invasion but pledged nothing as to eastern Europe where conflict would come first. The British memorandum of May 8, designed to discover Hitler's intentions in the East, was judged in Berlin unworthy of a reply. German troops remained in the Rhineland. Paris acquiesced.

Although German strategists perfected a new Schlieffen Plan to crush France through Holland and Belgium, Hitler's professed objective was to keep the peace in the West while he moved forward in the East. A Fascist or conservative France could be expected to abandon Moscow and strike a bargain with Berlin, however suicidal, at Russia's expense. A liberal or socialist France would be sufficiently pacifist to acquiesce in whatever Hitler might do, short of open war. In the event of French military aid to Czechoslovakia or the U.S.S.R., the Reichswehr would remain on the defensive in the west as a means of keeping Britain neutral. Such a defensive strategy, made possible by the building of the "West Wall" in the Rhineland, would render French aid to Prague or Moscow impossible. Britain would scarcely fight unless France or the Low Countries were invaded. With France checkmated and British neutrality assumed, the *Drang nach Osten* could be carried forward until the Western Powers should be outarmed, outmanoeuvered and made ripe for conquest.

In August, 1936, German military service was extended from one to two years. The Nürnberg Party Congress of September was devoted to denunciations of Bolshevism. The Führer declared wage increases impossible. He demanded new sacrifices and promised to make the Reich economically self-sufficient within four years. Rosenberg declared: "The Soviet Union's Government is controlled by Jewish interests and it is money stolen from the Russian people by the Jews which is being used in an attempt to awaken the underworld in all nations to march against European culture and against the holy traditions of all peoples." Said Göbbels: "Bolshevism must be annihilated. The idea of Bolshevism could have emanated only from the Jewish brain." Hitler, denouncing Russia and the "Bolshevist Jews" before massed thousands of marching troops, shouted, "We are ready any hour. I cannot permit ruined States on my doorstep."

ANTI-COMINTERN AXIS

By such mouthings of anti-Bolshevism the leaders of the Western Powers were effectively anesthetized to their doom, precisely as the leaders of German liberalism had been a few years before. So long as the Anglo-French ruling classes could be induced to believe that the Third Reich was "saving civilization from the Reds" and arming only to attack the Soviet Union, so long could Hitler and Mussolini move from victory to victory. Their violations of treaties and their aggressions against the weak were not only tolerated by Downing Street and the Quai d'Orsay but were even encouraged. The Führer's threats against the U.S.S.R. were doubtless "sincere" up to the point at which his experimentation convinced him that the Soviet Union, far from being a weak State in process of reduction to helplessness by the "Jewish ferment of decomposition," was a strong State whose leaders and people were able and willing to fight not only in defense of their frontiers but in defense of their allies. The weak Powers were obviously France and Britain since their governments, despite the enormous resources at their disposal, had no will to fight and preferred to desert their allies so long as they believed that they could find safety by deflecting the Reich against Moscow. Hitler accordingly prepared for war against the West.

For this a mighty sword was needed—and control of Austria, Czechoslovakia, and Poland to protect the German rear. For this allies were also needed. Hitler originally dreamed of a coalition with Britain and Italy to crush France before undertaking the conquest of Russia. Experience demonstrated that a formal alliance with Britain was not to be had. Berlin could merely rely on British opportunism to afford a strong likelihood of nonintervention in any war in eastern or central Europe. As for Italy, the fly in the ointment was Austria. Mussolini could not tolerate at the Brenner Pass a Germany of 75 million people pushing southward toward Bolzano and Trieste. Therefore he must oppose German designs on Austria. Propaganda from Berlin and Munich converted perhaps 40 per cent of the Austrian electorate to the Nazi faith—and to union with the Reich—during 1933. But the conservative clerical Chancellor, Engelbert Dollfuss, established an Austrian Fascist State to block the Hitlerite menace. Spurning support against the Nazis from the Social Democrats who controlled the municipality of Vienna and another 40 per cent of the Austrian electorate, he placed himself in the hands of Mussolini and of the reactionary Heimwehr militia which was subsidized from Italy. At the behest of Rome and of the Heimwehr leaders, Emil Fey and Prince von Stahremberg, Dollfuss crushed the Social Democrats in February, 1934, by accusing them of rebellion, bombarding the apartments of the Vienna workers, and executing or imprisoning their leaders. In May, he signed a series of political and economic protocols at Rome with Hungary and Italy.

Hitler journeyed to Italy to confer with Mussolini at Venice on June 15, 1934. But the two tyrants could come to no agreement. Seemingly in despair over the prospects of securing power by peaceful penetration, the Austrian Nazis resorted to force in the *Putsch* of July 25, 1934. Armed Nazis seized the

Chancellery building, shot Dollfuss, and permitted him to bleed to death. But the uprising failed in the provinces. The Duce threatened to send troops over the border if Germany intervened or the Nazis seized Austria from within. Chancellor Kurt Schuschnigg succeeded Dollfuss and continued to enjoy Italian support.

At last, however, Hitler pretended to come to terms on July 11, 1936, and agreed to respect Austrian independence and to reopen German trade and travel with Vienna. In October, Schuschnigg dissolved the Heimwehr and subsequently dropped its representatives from the Cabinet. With the Nazi menace at least temporarily removed, he could afford to dispense with the support of Mussolini's mercenaries. The Duce acquiesced, for he had fallen into Hitler's arms. On October 25, Ciano struck a bargain with the Führer at Berlin and Berchtesgaden. Germany recognized the conquest of Ethiopia and was promised economic concessions. Italy agreed with the Reich that any new Locarno must be limited to western Europe, that Article 16 should be removed from the Covenant, and that the two Fascist Powers must cooperate against "Bolshevism." Both Powers expressed their approval of General Franco's cause in Spain. Both agreed to cooperate in the Danube valley within the framework of the Protocols of Rome and the Austro-German accord of July 11. This entente apparently signified Italian acquiescence in the German domination of an "independent" Austria and joint German-Italian support of Hungarian revisionism, tempered by continued efforts to isolate Czechoslovakia. After the discussions at Berchtesgaden in the Bavarian Alps, Italy was, for all practical purposes, Germany's ally, even though Berlin would not forget that desertion of allies was an old Italian custom. An ally which might definitely place Britain in the enemy camp, moreover, was dangerous. But this could be risked in order to isolate France.

In other quarters, varying degrees of success were encountered in Nazi efforts to build a coalition. On January 26, 1934, a ten-year nonaggression pact with Poland was signed. Claims on the Corridor were deferred in return for Poland's detachment from the French bloc. But Nazi aggressiveness in Danzig, coupled with the alarming scale of German rearmament and the obvious fact that Germany could attack Russia effectively only through Poland, caused Warsaw to veer back toward Paris in the summer of 1936. Poland remained an incalculable factor. Hungary would be certain to cooperate in any attack on Czechoslovakia if protected against Rumania and Jugoslavia. Premier Duca of Rumania was murdered by pro-Nazi Iron Guardists in December, 1933. The toleration at Bucharest of anti-Semitic and pro-German conspirators, and the dismissal of Titulescu in August, 1936, all encouraged hopes at Berlin that Rumania might be won to the Fascist cause. Bulgaria's conservative regime, with irredentist ambitions scarcely less passionate than those of Hungary, was sympathetic.

If Italy, Hungary, and Bulgaria became Germany's allies, Jugoslavia would be immobilized. The successful Fascist coup of General John Metaxas in Greece on August 5, 1936, placed in power at Athens a regime sympathetic toward Germany. Nazi support of the Fascist Rebels in the Spanish civil war was based on the hope that a Fascist Spain could be used to complete the isolation and encirclement of France. In Asia, Turkey remained committed to a policy of friendship with Moscow. But Japan, with designs on Siberia, was prepared to enter into commercial, political, and military understandings with Germany and Italy promising an eventual assault upon the U.S.S.R. from the east and west simultaneously. The German-Japanese agreement of November 25, 1936, ostensibly against the Comintern, was a significant step in this direction, although Ribbentrop secretly envisaged it as so much dust thrown into the eyes of Britain and France to blind them to the blows being prepared against them.

REUNION IN VIENNA

The stage was thus set for territorial expansion. Prior to 1938, no "lost provinces" had been recovered save the Saar district which was restored to the Reich March 1, 1935, following an overwhelmingly pro-German plebiscite in January. Recovery of Danzig and the Corridor required that Poland be first rendered defenseless. This in turn required the liquidation of Czechoslovakia, since German armies in Bohemia and Slovakia could outflank Poland's Reich frontiers. The reduction of Czechoslovakia to helplessness (and its consequent destruction without war) required German control of Austria in order to outflank the Czech border fortifications. Italian acquiescence in the liquidation of Austria was already assured. Berlin felt confident of British acquiescence following the visit of Lord Halifax to the Reich in November, 1937. The war in Spain had demonstrated that the Western Powers were paralyzed and self-defeated. It had furnished a useful testing ground for the new Nazi arms. It had confirmed Axis hypotheses regarding the best slogans for befuddling London and Paris. Hitler thus began to outline the plot of the third and most terrifying volume of his *Kampf*, destined to be written in deeds rather than words.

In early February, 1938, Hitler made important changes in his entourage. Minister of Defense, General Werner von Blomberg, then on his honeymoon with his secretary, was retired in disgrace. The Führer took his post and named General Wilhelm Keitel as his adjutant. General Werner von Fritsch, Commander-in-Chief of the Reichswehr (who was to die mysteriously in Poland twenty months later), was replaced by General Walter von Brauchitsch. Baron Constantine von Neurath, Foreign Minister since May, 1932, was replaced by Joachim von Ribbentrop. Hjalmar Schacht was succeeded as Minister of Economics by Walter Funk. Henceforth the army command, the diplomatic bureaucracy, and the industrialists would be pliant tools in the hands of the Nazi radicals.

On February 12 the last Chancellor of Austria, Kurt Schuschnigg, was invited to Berchtesgaden at Papen's suggestion. He was there browbeaten by Hitler's threats of invasion into granting amnesty and full freedom of action to the Austrian Nazis and admitting into his Cabinet several leaders of the Nazi Fifth Column in Vienna, including Edmund Glaise-Horstenau, Guido Schmidt, and Arthur Seyss-Inquart. On February 20 Hitler denounced Russia before the Reichstag, promised "protection" to all Germans outside the borders of the Reich, demanded a free hand in central Europe, and condemned British critics of National Socialism, in particular Foreign Minister Anthony Eden. The same night Eden resigned and was replaced by Lord Halifax. The Führer now felt that he could take Austria with few risks.

On March 9 Schuschnigg announced in desperation that a plebiscite would be held on March 13 on the question of Austrian independence. He was confident of overwhelming support from the older voters. On the same day the French Cabinet fell. Ribbentrop visited British leaders in London as he took his leave as Ambassador. On March 10 the German press and radio shrieked that a "Communist" uprising in Vienna was imminent and that Germany must act to protect its nationals. On March 11 Glaise-Horstenau returned from a visit to Berlin and delivered a Nazi ultimatum to Schuschnigg: Abandon the plebiscite, or face invasion. The same afternoon a second ultimatum arrived: Resign by 7.30, or face invasion. Nazi rowdies were already attacking Jews and rioting in the doomed capital. Schuschnigg was alone. He announced his resignation that evening. Seyss-Inquart assumed the Chancellorship and invited the Reichswehr to "protect" Austria. On March 12, 1938, after the German Minister in Prague assured himself and the Wilhelmstrasse that Czechoslovakia would not interfere, the German Army poured into Austria.

Hitler crossed the bridge at Braunau where, as a small boy, he had often gazed across the Inn from the Austria of the Hapsburgs to the Germany of the Hohenzollerns. After visiting the graves of his parents, he entered Vienna in triumph on March 14. Here he named Seyss-Inquart *Statthalter* of the *Ostmark*, and ordered a "plebiscite" for *Anschluss* on April 10. In both Germany and Austria, 99 per cent of the electors voted "*Ja*." Meanwhile, Schuschnigg was imprisoned and never heard from thereafter. Fey was found shot to death, along with his wife and dog. Stahremberg survived by virtue of being in Switzerland. The assassins of Dollfuss became heroes. Scores of liberals, Socialists, and Jews committed suicide. Thousands fled the country. More thousands stayed behind to face persecution, imprisonment, or death. Austria was conquered.

"SELF-DETERMINATION"

The next victim was Czechoslovakia. Here the leader of the Nazi Fifth Column was Konrad Henlein, leader of the Nazified *Sudeten Deutsche Partei*, subsidized from Berlin and pretending to represent the 3½ million German-speaking citizens of the Czech Republic. The Sudetens had lived within the Bohemian borderlands for centuries and had never been nationals of any North German State. They were better treated than any other national minority in central Europe. But Hitler found it useful to provoke disorders, to raise a great cry of "persecution," and ultimately to demand the "liberation" (and then the annexation) of Sudetenland in the name of a specious "self-determination." Chamberlain announced on March 24 that Britain would assume no commitments to defend Czechoslovakia. He intimated that Hitler could have his way if only he would refrain from force. In April Henlein (*i.e.*, Hitler) demanded "autonomy." In May Henlein visited London, and Hitler alarmed Britain and France and precipitated partial Czech mobilization by threatening force. On June 3, the *London Times* opined that "self-determination" for the Sudetens would afford "a welcome example of peaceful change. It would be a drastic remedy for the present unrest, but something drastic may be needed."

There followed the fantastic "war crisis" of the summer of 1938 and an even more fantastic "peace." The determining elements were simple. Hitler was resolved to destroy Czechoslovakia. If Prague could be induced to yield Sudetenland, which included all the Czech border fortifications, the rest of the country would be indefensible. President Eduard Beneš, Premier Milan Hodza, Foreign Minister Kamil Krofta, and General Jan Syrovy were determined to fight rather than surrender. Czechoslovakia was guaranteed by France and the Soviet Union, allied with Rumania and Jugoslavia, and linked through France with Britain and Poland. Hitler was at no time prepared to risk war with any such combination. But he quickly perceived that no Power save the U.S.S.R. was prepared to come to Prague's defense. Daladier and Bonnet were groping for ways of evading French obligations. Chamberlain and Halifax were resolved to sacrifice Czechoslovakia on the altar of the Nazi *Drang nach Osten.* The Nazi bluff could be called and Czechoslovakia protected by accepting Soviet offers of joint defense. This, however, was the last thing desired by the Anglo-French appeasers. Their calculus was based on the assumption of an eventual Nazi-Soviet conflict, and for this Czechoslovakia must be sacrificed. To "sell" the sacrifice to the Western parliaments and publics, a war panic must be manufactured. Hitler was quite willing to coöperate. The result was the "Peace" of Munich.

Both Hitler and Chamberlain played their roles with consummate skill. On July 18, Hitler sent a confidential message to Halifax through Fritz Wiedemann, his aide-de-camp. It presumably suggested a non-violent "solution" of the Sudeten problem through a Four Power Pact. On July 25 it was announced that Chamberlain was sending Viscount Runciman to Prague as an "investigator" and "mediator" between Henlein and the Czech Cabinet. Runciman arrived on August 4, conferred with sundry persons, and pressed Beneš to yield. He departed on September 16. In a final letter dated September 21 he recommended the immediate cession of the Sudeten areas to the Reich without a plebiscite. He also urged that Prague forbid all anti-German agitation, terminate its alliances, accept a guarantee from the Powers against unprovoked aggression, and conclude a commercial treaty with the Reich on preferential terms.

The war panic was meanwhile fully developed. On August 23 the Little Entente committed suicide by granting to Nazi-supported Hungary equality of rights in arms in return for projected nonaggression pacts which were to become effective only after Prague's "minority problem" was solved to Budapest's satisfaction. Each day the Nazi press and radio screamed more loudly about "Czech outrages," "barbarous persecutions," and the "Red menace." The Reichswehr gradually mobilized. Armored divisions and bombing squadrons gathered near the Czech borders. On September 6 the *London Times* unofficially urged the partition of Czechoslovakia. On September 12, last day of the tenth Nürnberg *Parteitag,* Hitler shrieked terrifying threats and dedicated the Reich to the "liberation" of the Sudetens.

Immediately thereafter, Henlein's followers attempted a military *Putsch* in Sudetenland but were speedily dispersed. The leaders fled into Germany where they were received as "refugees" from the "Czech terror." On September 15 Chamberlain flew to Munich and conferred with Hitler in Berchtesgaden. There he made the "discovery" that Hitler was contemplating an immediate invasion of Czechoslovakia unless Chamberlain could promise "self-determination." The Prime Minister returned to London to confer with Simon, Hoare, and Halifax and then with the full Cabinet. On Sunday, September 18, Daladier and Bonnet flew to the British capital. The King, the Queen, and the Archbishop of Canterbury led England in prayers for peace. On September 19 an Anglo-French ultimatum was presented to Prague, demanding the surrender of Sudetenland and offering in return an international guarantee against unprovoked aggression to what would be left of the Czech Republic. A reply was asked "at the earliest possible moment." When Prague inquired of Paris whether France would honor its obligations in the event that a rejection of the ultimatum was followed by German aggression, Daladier and Bonnet made no answer. A new ultimatum demanding an immediate decision was presented to Beneš at 2.15 a.m., September 21, by the British and French Ministers, Basil Newton and M. De la Croix. They warned that Britain and France would not only abandon Czechoslovakia in case of a German invasion but would even aid the Reich.

Despite all pretense to the contrary, then and later, Anglo-French policy was not dictated by military weakness. With the Soviet Union as ally, the Western Powers could crush the Reich, as Hitler well knew. Chamberlain and Daladier desired to save the Reich and turn its might against Moscow over the body of Czechoslovakia. The Soviet Union was not bound to defend Prague after the French desertion, but it nevertheless offered to do so and to compel Poland and Rumania to grant passage to the Red Army. Beneš debated the offer with the party leaders. Rudolf Beran, leader of the reactionary Agrarians, threatened to call in the Nazis and precipitate civil war if Beneš relied on Communist support against Hitler. Brokenhearted, Beneš yielded and accepted the Anglo-French ultimatum. "Nothing else remained, because we were alone." Said Minister Hugo Vavrecka: "It is a case without parallel. We shall not blame those who left us in the lurch, but history will pronounce a judgment about these days."

"PEACE WITH HONOR"

The end was not yet, for more panic was needed to secure public acceptance in the West of so base a betrayal. Shame and indignation began to sweep British and French opinion. On September 22, Chamberlain flew to Godesberg on the Rhine where he conferred again with Hitler and Ribbentrop. He returned with dark hints that Hitler had enlarged his demands and was threatening immediate war unless they were met. The Czech army was mobilized. Daladier ordered partial mobilization in France. Gas masks were distributed in London. Air-raid shelters were hastily dug in public parks. Hitler's "Godesberg Memorandum" asked military occupation of certain Czech areas by October 1, with plebiscites to follow in others. Daladier, Bonnet, and Gamelin flew to London. Downing Street and the Quai d'Orsay belatedly pledged defense of Czechoslovakia if Germany attacked. Chamberlain pleaded with Hitler for a conference.

The Führer breathed blood and fire. "If this problem is solved, there will be no further territorial problems in Europe for Germany. We do not want any Czechs. We are resolved! Let Herr Beneš choose!" Roosevelt pleaded for negotiations. Hitler intimated to Mussolini that he would invade Czechoslovakia on September 28. Chamberlain told the world on September 27 that it was "horrible, fantastic, incredible that we should be digging trenches and fitting gas masks because of a quarrel in a faraway country among people of whom we know nothing. I was taken completely by surprise [by Hitler's demand for immediate military occupation]. I must say that I find that attitude unreasonable. [But] if we have to fight it must be on larger issues than that. But if I were convinced that any nation had made up its mind to dominate the world by fear of its force, I should feel that it must be resisted."

By September 28 all the democracies were in a frenzy of fear, precisely as Hitler (and Chamberlain) intended. The Commons met at 2.45. The Prime Minister spoke in funereal tones to a House fully expecting immediate war. He reviewed the negotiations lugubriously and revealed that he had appealed to Hitler and Mussolini for a conference to arrange the transfer of Czech territory. At 3.40 a messenger dashed madly to Lord Halifax in the balcony. The message was hurriedly relayed to Chamberlain. He paused, read it, and beamed: Hitler had invited him to Munich the next morning. The whole House burst forth in cheers. Chamberlain and Simon smiled and wept. Continental banking circles had known early the same day that a four Power con-

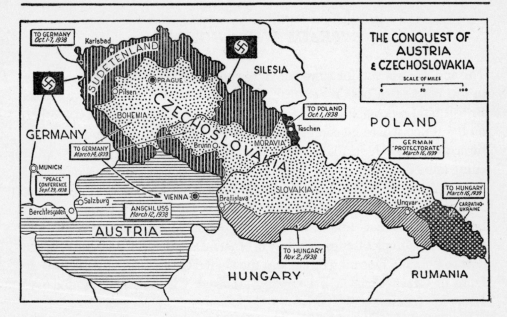

ference would be held in Munich on the morrow. But Parliament, public, and all the Western world were led to believe that war had been averted at the very last moment.

During the afternoon and evening of September 29, 1938, Chamberlain, Hitler, Daladier, and Mussolini conferred in the Munich *Führerhaus*. Czech representatives were kept in waiting in an anteroom. Shortly after midnight all four leaders attached their signatures to a document whereby German forces were to begin occupation of Czech territory on October 1 and continue their advance by stages until October 10. An "international commission" would fix the conditions governing the evacuation, prepare and supervise plebiscites in additional territories, and finally determine the frontiers. An annex declared that Britain and France "stand by the offer" of September 19 "relating to an international guarantee of the new boundaries of the Czechoslovak State against unprovoked aggression. When the question of the Polish and Hungarian minorities in Czechoslovakia has been settled, Germany and Italy for their part will give a guarantee to Czechoslovakia."

In bitterness and tears, Prague yielded to what Beneš knew was a death sentence. He resigned and was presently succeeded by weak and elderly Emil Hacha, with Beran as Premier. Chamberlain concluded his work by signing with Hitler a pledge "never to go to war again." He came home to announce that he had "saved" Czechoslovakia and brought "peace with honor. I believe it is peace for our time."

The Peace of Munich was the greatest triumph to date of Hitler's strategy of terror. It was the culmination of appeasement and the warrant of death for the Western Powers. The fate of the last surviving Continental democracy east of the Rhine was the smallest part of the price to be paid for the agreement signed in Hitler's house. Poland seized 400 square miles of Czech territory with a population of 240,000, including 160,000 non-Poles. Hungary seized 5,000 square miles with a million inhabitants, including 250,000 non-Magyars. The "international guarantee" of the rump "Czecho-Slovakia" never materialized. The "international commission" became a farce. Ambassadors Henderson, François Ponçet, and Attolico yielded at once to Nazi demands (going far beyond even the "Godesberg Memorandum") as presented by Count Ernst von Weizsäcker, leaving Dr. Mastny, the Czech representative, helpless. Berlin groomed Carpatho-Ukraine as the nucleus of the Great Ukraine which was to be carved out of Poland and the U.S.S.R. Bonnet signed a nonaggression pact with Ribbentrop in Paris on December 6—interpreted in Berlin to mean that France had renounced all interest in eastern Europe. The Munichmen of Paris and London comforted themselves with the happy thought that the Third Reich would now strike toward Kiev and the Black Sea and clash with Moscow. In this assumption, which was the whole meaning of Munich, they were completely and tragically mistaken.

Hitler's genius lay in his ability to persuade the hollow men of the West that they should grant him the means wherewith he could bring the Western Powers to ruin. Munich left Poland more helpless than *Anschluss* had left Czechoslovakia. Munich reduced the French-Soviet mutual assistance Pact of 1935 to waste paper and compelled Stalin to seek new roads toward safety. Munich left Hitler free to complete the economic and military domination of the Danube and the Balkans, to blackmail Warsaw, and to make a bargain with Moscow to protect his rear for the war against the West. He assumed that the Western Munichmen would be too blind to conclude a new Russian alliance even when they should awaken to their danger. He assumed that the enfeebled democratic Powers could be driven from surrender to surrender or, if they resisted belatedly, could be defeated in arms at small cost. That most of these things were to come to pass was the measure of Hitler's astuteness and of the incredible folly of the Western appeasers.

THE IDES OF MARCH

Whatever Ukrainian dreams were entertained by the Führer were indefinitely postponed during the winter of 1938–1939. He likewise decided to liquidate the pitiable remnant of "Czecho-Slovakia." The technique was already perfected. Nazi agents fanned separatist sentiment in Slovakia and Carpatho-Ukraine. When Prague sought to hold the State together by curbing such agitation, the separatists appealed to Berlin against "Czech persecution." When Hacha on March 9–10 dismissed the Slovak Cabinet, ordered the Fascist "Hlinka Guards" disarmed, and discharged from his post Father Josef Tiso, pro-Nazi Premier at Bratislava, Tiso flew to Berlin to confer with Ribbentrop and Hitler. On March 14 he returned and proclaimed the "independence" of Slovakia.

On the same day Hitler summoned President Hacha and Foreign Minister Frantisek Chvalkovsky to Berlin while German armored divisions gathered in Sudetenland. In the Chancellery building shortly after midnight, Hacha was given a document to sign placing Czecho-Slovakia under German "protection." When he refused, Göring declared that Prague would be destroyed by Nazi bombers at 6 a.m. Hacha fainted and was revived by injections. The Nazi officials hounded him around the table with threats and imprecations. At 4.30 a.m. he signed.

German troops were already across the frontiers. They entered Prague at 9.15 a.m., March 15, followed by the Schutzstaffel (Black Guard) and the Gestapo. Hitler came in the afternoon and proclaimed from Hradcany Castle that Czecho-Slovakia was part of Germany's *Lebensraum*. Bohemia and Moravia were annexed, with Neurath as "Protector." Budapest was covetous of the Carpatho-Ukraine and a common frontier with Poland. Pro-Nazi and anti-Semitic Premier Bela Imredy had resigned in February on discovering that he had "Jewish blood." On March 16, with Berlin's consent, his pro-Nazi and anti-Semitic successor, Paul Teleki, announced the annexation of Carpatho-Ukraine to Hungary. "Independent" Slovakia was obliged to sign a treaty on March 23 making it a German protectorate. On the preceding day the Reich occupied Memel and signed a "nonaggression" pact with Lithuania.

IN AND OUT OF THE RED

These events led to the belated abandonment of appeasement by London and Paris and to Anglo-French guarantees to Poland, Rumania, Greece, and Turkey. Hitler retaliated on April 28, 1939, by denouncing the Anglo-German Naval Accord of 1935 and the Polish nonaggression Pact of 1934. On May 22 he concluded his treaty of alliance with Italy. When the Western Powers, in the course of prolonged negotiations with Moscow, declined to pay Stalin's price for an alliance against Germany (*i.e.*, Soviet military control of the Baltic States and access to eastern Poland), Hitler secretly offered Stalin a nonaggression pact on the same terms. On August 23, 1939, the world was shocked by the signature in Moscow by Molotov and Ribbentrop of a ten-year pact of nonaggression and neutrality between the Third Reich and the U.S.S.R. The self-appointed savior of European civilization from Bolshevism proclaimed his friendship with Stalin. He thus rejected, temporarily, Alfred Rosenberg's dream of conquering Russia, and returned to the Bismarck tradition of "reinsurance" in the East as a means of avoiding the danger of the two-front war which had brought the Second Reich to disaster.

Stalin did not foresee that Hitler would honor this pact for only twenty-two months and would attack the Soviet Union as soon as Soviet neutrality had enabled him to conquer the rest of the Continent. The Western appeasers were equally blind. For the moment all that was clear was that Stalin had outchamberlained Chamberlain and turned the Reich against the West. Germany and the U.S.S.R. had agreed "to refrain from any act of force, any aggressive act and any attacks against each other." Should either become "the object of warlike action on the part of a third Power, the other contracting party will in no way support the third Power." Neither would join any group of Powers directed against the other. Each would consult the other on questions of common interest. All disputes would be solved "exclusively by friendly exchanges of views or if necessary by arbitration commissions."

Said Hitler to Ambassador Henderson: "Make no mistake. It will be a treaty lasting for many years. Germany is unalterably resolved never again to enter into a conflict with Russia." Since Poland was now isolated and beyond all possibility of protection by Britain and France, Hitler invited Chamberlain and Daladier to be "reasonable" and make another Munich at Warsaw's expense. If they would not, then . . . ?

PREFACE TO MURDER

The assassination of Poland was prepared with all the Führer's customary care. Three weeks after Munich Ribbentrop had asked Ambassador Josef Lipski to submit to Foreign Minister Josef Beck and Marshal Edward Smigly-Rydz a German proposal for the return of Danzig to the Reich and the creation of a German extraterritorial highway and railway across the Corridor. A reciprocal guarantee of the new frontiers was offered as a *quid pro quo*. The Polish leaders, who fancied that their State was a Great Power, refused. In January, 1939, Beck visited Berchtesgaden and Ribbentrop visited Warsaw without result. After the fall of Prague, Berlin became more insistent. Ribbentrop repeated the German proposals to Lipski on March 26. The first British guarantee to Poland of March 31 was inspired by fear of a swift Nazi blow at Danzig and the Corridor. Beck breathed defiance in his address to the Diet of May 5. Poland would not yield. Neither would Poland consider any defensive arrangement with the only Power which could possibly protect Poland: the U.S.S.R. The Polish Colonels and feudal gentry feared and hated Bolshevism no less ardently than Beran, Bonnet, Daladier, Halifax, and Chamberlain. Suicide was preferable to salvation at the hands of Moscow.

Hitler, no less than Stalin, drew the necessary conclusions. The Führer's well-known "patience" was now "exhausted." Beyond Danzig and the Corridor, he had again "no further territorial demands" to make. He discovered that the German minority in Poland was being outrageously persecuted. In Danzig the Nazi Senate President, Arthur Greiser, and the Nazi *Gauleiter*, Albert Förster, kept up a running fire of controversy with Warsaw while the Nazi press and radio fabricated a campaign of hatred and fear even more impressive than that unleashed against Prague a year before. The Anglo-French Munichmen were already crying that "Danzig is not worth a war." Chamberlain and Daladier toyed with new appeasement schemes. Given half a chance to compel Poland to yield, they might have cooperated with Berlin once more. But in the end Hitler decided that the time had come to strike Poland down and to seek a reckoning by arms with the Western Powers.

The war crisis of August, 1939, began with a Danzig-Polish controversy over customs duties on herring and margarine and ended with an Anglo-German dispute over diplomatic etiquette and the meaning of "negotiations." Amid the scurryings of the diplomats the central issue for Berlin was whether the Allies would compel Warsaw to yield to German demands. For London and Paris the issue was whether Berlin would abstain from force and refrain from jeopardizing Polish independence. Berlin half-hoped that the announcement on August 21 of the impending Soviet pact would lead to capitulation, since Poland was now obviously beyond the power of the Allies to defend. Chamberlain addressed a letter to Hitler on August 22, however, declaring that "no greater mistake could be made" and that Britain would fight if Poland were attacked. But Britain was prepared to do all it could to promote a negotiated settlement. Hitler told Henderson that "he was 50 years old: he preferred war now to when he would be 55 or 60." He was really an artist, he said, and wanted to retire in peace to his studio.

In his reply to Chamberlain, he insisted that Germany must have Danzig and the Corridor. He had always wanted Anglo-German friendship. If the Reich's just demands led to war with Britain, it would be Britain's fault. On August 25, he asked Henderson to fly to London with an offer of an alliance. On the same day the tentative Anglo-Polish Pact was converted into a binding commitment of mutual defense. On August 28, Henderson returned with a reply: The prerequisite condition of any Anglo-German understanding was a settlement of German-Polish differences which would not endanger Poland's independence. An effort should therefore be made for a negotiated solution to be guaranteed by the Powers. Warsaw was "prepared to enter into discussions on this basis." Hitler and Ribbentrop told Henderson on August 29 that they were quite ready for negotiations, provided that a Polish plenipotentiary should arrive on Wednesday, August 30. The Ambassador commented that this "sounded like an ultimatum." Hitler denied it. He stressed the urgency of the moment and accused Henderson of not caring "how many Germans were being slaughtered."

Halifax replied that it was "unreasonable" to expect Britain to produce a Polish plenipotentiary on Wednesday. Beck recalled the fate of Schuschnigg and Hacha and refused to go to Berlin. Warsaw ordered mobilization on August 30. London urged negotiations but did not envisage them in terms of acceptance of a Nazi ultimatum. At midnight of August 30, Henderson saw Ribbentrop again in a stormy interview. The Foreign Minister declared that everything was now too late, since the time limit had expired. But to show German good faith he hurriedly read a sixteen-point proposal which was amazingly moderate. Danzig should be forthwith returned to the Reich. The Corridor should be placed under international supervision and a plebiscite held a year later. If the residents (as of 1918) voted to remain Polish, Germany should be granted an extraterritorial traffic zone to East Prussia.

If Germany won, Poland should be granted a similar zone to Gdynia. All this was quite reasonable and implied neither a new Munich nor the destruction of the Polish State. But Ribbentrop declared contemptuously that the proposal was "outdated" since no Polish plenipotentiary had arrived by midnight. He refused to transmit a copy of it to either Henderson or Lipski. "I returned to the Embassy that night," wrote Henderson, "convinced that the last hope for peace had vanished."

The sixteen points were never officially delivered to Warsaw or to London. Lipski saw Ribbentrop at 6.30 p.m., August 31, not as "plenipotentiary" but as Ambassador come to say, on Beck's instructions, that Warsaw was examining favorably British suggestions for direct German-Polish negotiations and would give its reply in a few hours. He did not ask for the sixteen points. Ribbentrop did not offer them. When Lipski tried to telephone Warsaw in the evening, he found the wires cut. At 9 p.m. the sixteen points were printed in the evening extras in Berlin and broadcast over the German radio as evidence of Nazi moderation. Henderson was told at Wilhelmstrasse that the Führer had "now waited for two days in vain for the arrival of an authorized Polish delegate" and could not but regard his proposals "as having been once more virtually rejected." In the small hours of September 1, Halifax wired Warsaw to urge that the Polish Government receive German proposals, provided that they were not accompanied by any ultimatum. The British Ambassador replied later in the day that this would be useless since Poland had been invaded at dawn.

NINETEEN THIRTY-NINE

Hitler had in fact launched his *Blitzkrieg*. At 4 a.m. of Friday, September 1, 1939, Förster issued a decree proclaiming the incorporation of Danzig into the Reich. German troops had already entered the Free City. By 5 a.m. the German cruiser *Schleswig-Holstein* was pouring shells into the near-by Polish fortifications on the Westerplatte. By 5.30, German bombs were falling on Polish air bases. Into the Corridor raced 29 German divisions, into southern Poland 40 divisions, all preceded by *Panzerdivisionen* of tanks and armored cars which tore through the Polish defenses and the half-mobilized Polish armies like deadly scythes. Göring's air force carried raids deep into Polish territory, destroying airdromes, railways, and mobilization centers and terrorizing noncombatants with fire, bullets, and bombs. There was no

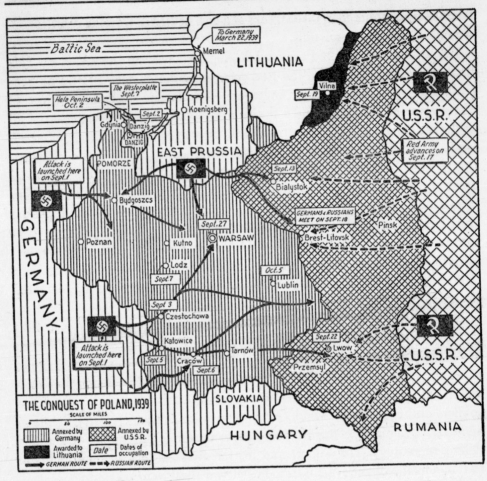

THE CONQUEST OF POLAND, 1939

"front." The German High Command had devised the means of breaking the stalemate of 1914-1918. Mobile warfare was restored. The superiority of the attack over the defense was reestablished. Western strategists, hypnotized by the outdated doctrines of Liddell Hart and André Maginot, drew no conclusions from the Polish *Blitzkrieg* until their own vastly superior armies fell victims to identical tactics in the following spring.

Poland crumpled like a deflated balloon. Within two weeks, all the western provinces were lost, Warsaw was surrounded, and the Cabinet was fleeing toward Rumania. The Polish capital was besieged and all but demolished by artillery and dive-bombers. Its defenders surrendered on September 27. How many scores of thousands of Poles perished in the holocaust may never be known. In a war of machines against men the casualties of the aggressor were negligible. A nation of 34,000,000 people with an army of 1,500,000 was completely conquered in three weeks at a cost of 10,572 German dead, 30,322 wounded, and 3,404 missing.

Britain and France had meanwhile declared war on the Reich on September 3. Moscow ordered the Red Army to enter eastern Poland on September 17—possibly by prearrangement with Berlin, probably because of alarm over the *Blitzkrieg* and a desire to prevent German occupation of all of the old Polish State. Ribbentrop again flew to Moscow on September 27. On September 28 the Reich and the U.S.S.R. reached an agreement to partition Poland between them, Germany taking the Polish-speaking industrial areas of the west, the Soviet Union taking the White Russian and Ukrainian farm lands to the east. So perished the State whose leaders had appeased the Reich, spurned all cooperation with the U.S.S.R., and eagerly joined in the partitioning of Czechoslovakia. At Christmas Hitler sent "best wishes" to Stalin and "to the peoples of the friendly Soviet Union." Stalin replied: "The friendship of the peoples of Germany and the Soviet Union, cemented by blood, has every reason to be lasting and firm."

That the war in the West remained stalemated for the next eight months was a result of Allied inability to penetrate or even attack the German West Wall. The Nazi warlords had means at their disposal for smashing the Maginot Line, as events were to show, but they wisely preferred to demoralize their victim with peace overtures and military inactivity which would cause Allied soldiers and civilians to wonder why they were fighting (or not fighting) and cause commanders to sink ever deeper into the fatal morass of a purely defensive strategy. The Führer and his fanatic followers had no doubts as to the outcome of the fearful miracles of war they were preparing.

TREACHERY IN OSLO

On April 9, 1940, Hitler struck his first great blow at the West. It was an operation of outflanking and diversion. Before dawn, strange events took place all along the far-flung coast of Scandinavia from the Arctic Circle to the Danish frontier. German troops poured into Denmark, with which Hitler had solemnly concluded a ten-year nonaggression pact only ten months previously, and at once occupied the whole kingdom without resistance. German bombers roared over Oslo. The *Blücher* brought troops up Oslo fjord to capture the Norwegian King and his Ministers and occupy the capital before anyone should know what was afoot. By a mere accident in plans

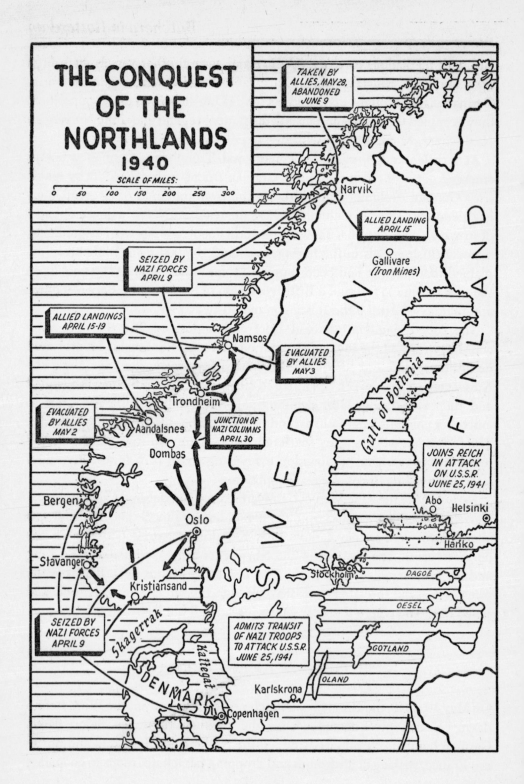

THE CONQUEST
OF THE
NORTHLANDS
1940

SCALE OF MILES:
0 50 100 150 200 250 300

TAKEN BY
ALLIES, MAY 28,
ABANDONED
JUNE 9

Narvik

ALLIED LANDING
APRIL 15

SEIZED BY
NAZI FORCES
APRIL 9

Gallivare
(Iron Mines)

ALLIED LANDINGS
APRIL 15-19

Namsos

EVACUATED
BY ALLIES
MAY 3

S
W
E
D
E
N

F
I
N
L
A
N
D

Gulf of Bothnia

Trondheim

EVACUATED
BY ALLIES
MAY 2

Aandalsnes

JUNCTION OF
NAZI COLUMNS
APRIL 30

Dombas

JOINS REICH
IN ATTACK
ON U.S.S.R.
JUNE 25, 1941

Bergen

Oslo

Abo

Helsinki

Stavanger

Hanko

Stockholm

DAGOE

Kristiansand

OESEL

SEIZED BY
NAZI FORCES
APRIL 9

Skagerrak

Kattegat

ADMITS TRANSIT
OF NAZI TROOPS
TO ATTACK U.S.S.R.
JUNE 25, 1941

GOTLAND

OLAND

DENMARK

Karlskrona

Copenhagen

laid with meticulous care, the *Blücher* and several other vessels were fired upon and sunk. King Haakon and his Cabinet had time to flee to the north. German planes brought 1,500 soldiers to the Oslo airport. Without opposition, they occupied the capital and installed a puppet regime under the Norwegian Nazi leader, Major Vidkun Quisling.

At Kristiansand, Bergen, Stavanger, and Trondheim, German warships emerged out of the morning mists. German troops materialized as by magic from German "freighters" at the docks and from the ranks of German "tourists." Traitors and Fifth Columnists gave them aid. At Narvik a dozen German destroyers came out of a snowstorm, torpedoed two Norwegian gunboats, seized British vessels in the harbor, and landed 2,000 men. Ribbentrop explained that Norway had been "unneutral" and that Germany was acting in the nick of time to forestall a British invasion of Scandinavia. Between dawn and midday of April 9 the Reich conquered two kingdoms.

The Allied counterattack was brief and inglorious. The Swedish army could have ousted the invaders from their foothold. But Stockholm preferred neutrality. Small and ill-equipped British forces made landings along the Norwegian coast between April 15 and 19. A blow at Trondheim was planned and then abandoned. Nazi columns penetrated inland from the coast to join other columns from Oslo ascending the Gudbrandsdal and the Osterdal. The feeble Norwegian army scattered before them. On April 25 the British rescuers were obliged to abandon everything south of Namsos. Five days later the invading forces effected a junction.

Early in May the Allied forces quit Namsos and Aandalsnes. On May 28–29, Narvik was indeed wrested from the Nazis, but on June 9 the enterprise was abandoned. German naval units sank the aircraft carrier *Glorious* off the northern coast. The vestiges of the Norwegian army capitulated. The King and his Ministers fled to London. The last Allied troops departed from the ruins of Narvik, threaded their way through the wreck-strewn harbor, and sailed for home where their cause was already all but lost.

BUTCHERY IN ROTTERDAM

On May 10, 1940, the German war machine struck directly at the West. Before dawn, German forces occupied Luxemburg without resistance. Before dawn, German bombers by hundreds raided the Netherlands, Belgium, and northern France, striking at airdromes and dropping parachute troops to cooperate with spies, traitors, Fifth Columnists, and German "tourists." Ribbentrop explained that Belgium and the Netherlands were about to cooperate with the Allies in invading the Ruhr. The fearful wonderwork of destruction and conquest which followed was truly unique in the annals of warfare, thanks to the genius of the German High Command and the prevalence of blindness, treason, and unmitigated ineptitude among those who led the Allied forces.

The Netherlands was subjugated in five days. The Hague was attacked by German agents inside the city. German motorized divisions, guided by traitors behind the Dutch lines, poured across the lowlands and decimated the small Dutch army before it could resist, open the dikes, or even destroy roads and bridges. At Rotterdam, German troops concealed in "freighters" joined the followers of the Dutch Nazi leader, Anton Mussert, in disorganizing the defenses of the city. When surrender was delayed, Göring's dive-bombers went into action to terrorize all Holland into surrender. On May 14 a quarter of Rotterdam was laid in ruins within a few hours. Scores of thousands of helpless inhabitants were burned, crushed, or blown to death in the flaming wreckage of homes, apartments, offices, and factories. German cameramen filmed the spectacle, as they had filmed the agony of Poland, for the terrorization of other peoples who might contemplate resistance to the Nazi Juggernaut. Later the same afternoon, General Henrik Winkelman ordered his troops to cease fighting, save in Zeeland and at sea. The Hague fell on May 15. Zeeland surrendered. The Government fled to London. Seyss-Inquart became Nazi Commissar over the vanquished.

From her English exile, Queen Wilhelmina lamented the fate of her people: "At this immensely grave moment in the history of mankind, black silent night has settled on yet another corner of this earth. Over free Holland the lights have gone out, the wheels of industry and the plows of the fields that worked only for the happiness of a peace-loving people have come to a dead stop. The voices of freedom, charity, tolerance and religion have been stilled. Where only two weeks ago there was a free nation there is now the desolation and stillness of death, broken only by the bitter weeping of those who have survived the extinction of their relatives and the brutal suppression of their rights and liberties."

Belgium suffered a like fate. Allied efforts to rescue the State whose King and Cabinet had insisted upon neutrality proved disastrous not only to Belgium but (as Brauchitsch intended) to the Allied cause in France as well. The invaders smashed through the Dutch province of Limburg to attack Maastricht and swarm across the heavily fortified Albert Canal,

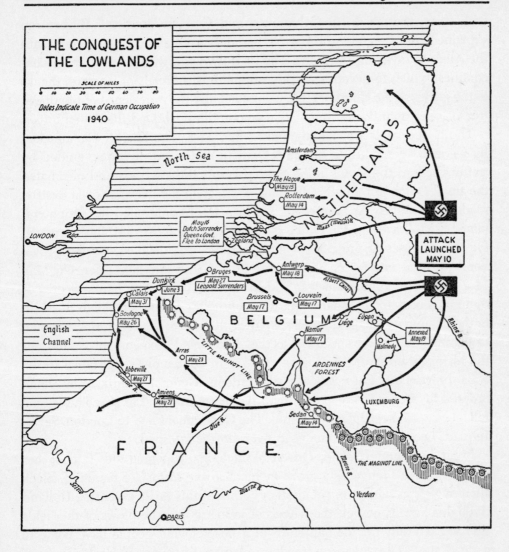

THE CONQUEST OF
THE LOWLANDS

SCALE OF MILES

Dates Indicate Time of German Occupation
1940

where bridges fell mysteriously into German hands. The *Rexist* followers of Léon DeGrelle, apostle of Belgian National Socialism and self-appointed defender of "Christ the King," played the roles which their Nazi patrons had designated for them. The tide overwhelmed Namur, Malines, and Louvain, where the library burned in 1914 was burned once more. Brussels fell on May 17 and Antwerp on May 18. On May 19, Hitler proclaimed the reannexation of Eupen, Malmédy, and Moresnet to the Reich.

Generals Maurice Gamelin and Edmund Ironside fell into the trap which Hitler's commanders had set for them. Allied divisions were rushed from behind the "Little Maginot Line" to the defense of Belgium. The Sedan-Montmédy sector along the Meuse was stripped of defenders on the assumption that the forest of the Ardennes, just across the Belgian frontier, was impenetrable. General André Corap's Ninth Army had not yet occupied the evacuated positions when the invader appeared on the hither side of the Ardennes in the hideous guise of shrieking dive-bombers, flame-throwing tanks, and eighty-ton armored monsters made at the Skoda works in Pilsen which Chamberlain and Daladier had delivered into Hitler's hands in the name of "peace for our time." Sedan was taken on May 14. The Ninth Army was destroyed. Corap's successor, General Henri Giraud, blundered into German forces and was captured with his staff. Panic reigned in Paris, for nothing stood between the enemy and the capital. Documents were burned at the Quai d'Orsay. The Cabinet prepared to flee. But the invader had other plans.

Instead of descending on the French capital, the German armored divisions crossed the Meuse and descended the valleys of the Aisne and the Somme until they reached Abbéville on the Channel on May 21. The entire Belgian army, most of the British Expeditionary Force, and numerous French divisions were thus trapped in the north. The Flanders pocket was hemmed in on three sides by Reichswehr divisions possessed of immense superiority of fire power, motorized units, heavy tanks, and air squadrons. King Leopold III, whose closest advisers were of ambiguous allegiance, ordered the surrender of the Belgian army on May 28, despite the opposition of his Cabinet which had taken refuge in London. The Belgian capitulation left the B.E.F. in a hopeless position. The armored divisions which had reached Abbéville tore up the Channel coast to cut off its only avenue of retirement. By a miracle of courage and organization, 384,000 British troops were safely evacuated from Dunkirk before its fall on June 3. All their arms and equipment were lost, along with 40,000 prisoners and 13,000 dead. Belgium was lost, Flanders was lost. France was also lost.

VICTORY IN PARIS

Before dawn of June 5, 1940, the Reichswehr attacked the hastily improvised "Weygand Line" along a 100-mile front south of the Somme. The new French Generalissimo, Maxime Weygand, was bewildered by what he called "means of war of a hitherto unknown formula." Reynaud hoped for a "miracle." But the battle was lost before it was begun. The armored divisions with their escorts of dive-bombers, acting as mobile artillery, cut the French armies to ribbons. By June 12, Weygand had given up hope. "All is lost." Vice-Premier Pétain agreed: "There are no more military possibilities." The invaders took Paris on June 14. A week later, Adolf Hitler toured the lost capital and visited Napoleon's tomb. Italy entered the war in order to be in on the "kill." At Bordeaux a new French government sued for peace on June 16. The entire Western campaign had cost the Third Reich no more than 27,000 dead and 130,000 wounded and missing. France was prostrate under the conqueror's heel.

In Compiègne forest near Rethonde, forty-five miles northeast of Paris, stands a monument bearing the inscription, "Here on November 11, 1918, perished the criminal arrogance of the Imperial German Reich, defeated by the free peoples whom it sought to enslave." Nearby was a railway coach in which Foch and Weygand had accepted the German capitulation. Here on June 21, 1940, Hitler, Keitel, Göring, Raeder, Hess, and Ribbentrop received the French armistice delegation. At 6.50 p.m., June 22, the document was signed. Hostilities ceased at 12.35 a.m., June 25, six hours after notification of the signing of an armistice with Italy. The terms defined the occupied territory and provided for French demobilization and disarmament. Vichy was required to pay the costs of the German forces of occupation and to surrender on demand all military and civil prisoners as well as German anti-Nazi exiles still within its jurisdiction. Almost 2 million French prisoners remained in German camps. A definitive peace was to wait upon the expected defeat of Britain. Berlin decreed the reannexation of Lorraine in November.

DEFEAT OVER LONDON

"You have just one more battle to win," said Göbbels in July to parading troops in Berlin. "Then bells of peace will ring. Then we will build a better Europe." But the winning of last battles is a British rather than a German habit. In war, as in love, the saddest words are those that tell what might have been. Had the Reichswehr and the Luftwaffe laid their plans for an immediate invasion of Britain after the fall of Dunkirk, a Nazi world victory in 1940 might well have been won. Britain was all but defenseless. The remnants of the French Army, even before their capitulation, were scarcely a factor worth reckoning with. The Nazi Fifth Columnists, the French defeatists and the Panzer divisions had done their work in the decadent French Republic better than Hitler knew.

Yet the very swiftness of the French collapse left the German High Command unprepared to strike across the Channel. Victory by diplomacy might prove easier than victory by arms. Obscure discussions took place in Stockholm and also in Madrid, where appeaser Hoare was British Ambassador and where the Duke of Windsor and his bride lingered before their departure for the Bahamas. With the Continent lost and all of England's allies vanquished, the Führer doubtless hoped that Britain's leaders would consider peace. When they showed themselves too stupid and stubborn to accept salvation (i.e., enslavement) at Hitler's hands, he hesitated as to what his next step should be.

He mouthed threats and promises. On July 19 he told his puppet Reichstag that his conscience compelled him "to appeal to reason and common sense in Great Britain." Let Britons entertain no false hopes. "A veritable wandering Jew among these hopes is the belief in the possibility of a fresh estrangement between Germany and Russia. German and Russian relations have been finally established." Germany had no designs on the Ukraine or Rumania or Turkey. "All hope of fresh tension between Germany and Russia is futile." There was no reply from London save contempt. Early in September in the Sportpalast Hitler breathed defiance: "Whatever comes England will break down. The people of England are very curious and ask: 'Why in the world don't you come?' We are coming . . ."

Man-mountain Göring had the formula for victory. Early in September his Luftwaffe opened an all-out assault on London. Thousands died. To save the capital and protect the helpless who daily faced death the Royal Air Force, reasoned Göring, would risk all to beat back the aerial attack. Since the Luftwaffe outnumbered the R.A.F. by at least 4 to 1, the end would be the destruction of most of Britain's planes. Once mastery of the air was won, the invasion barges could be safely turned toward the white cliffs across the narrow stretch of choppy waves which separated Nazidom from its last foe.

But the formula failed. The people of London cried defiantly from their ruins: "We can take it!" The R.A.F. did not risk destruction, though its men shot down hundreds of Nazi bombers. By October it was clear that Hitler's commanders had lost the first phase of the Battle of Britain. No invasion could be attempted so long as British air power, British sea power and British morale were unbroken. What to do?

VICTORY ERSATZ

Hitler in 1940, like Bonaparte in 1804, was stopped at the Channel. Like Bonaparte, he was forced to seek Britain's defeat not by a frontal attack but by completing his conquest of the Continent, by organizing it against Britain, by making new pacts and bargains which would, he believed, render Britain's cause hopeless. The slowly growing danger of American aid to Britain obliged him to resort to grandiose schemes of a "New World Order" and to elaborate devices of intimidation. America could be outflanked and immobilized only by Japan. To win Tokyo's aid no price was too high to pay. Ribbentrop sent Heinrich von Stahmer to work on Konoe and Matsuoka, while Hitler pushed the Vichymen into abandoning northern Indo-China to the Army of righteous justice.

The fruit of these moves was the Triple Alliance pact of September 27, 1940. Rome, Berlin and Tokyo agreed to threaten America with war and to cooperate, in the words of the Preamble, in order to realize "their ultimate aspirations for world peace." But the effect was scarcely what was hoped for. The United States declined to be impressed and increased its aid to China and Britain. London reopened the Burma Road. Despite the saving clause in the treaty regarding relations with the U.S.S.R. Stalin began to wonder about the wisdom of appeasing the Reich. The Triplice accord had some value in impressing Germans and Japanese and some of the conquered peoples of the Continent. But it produced no victory on the broader stage of *Weltpolitik*. The "war of nerves" fails when its victims refuse to be nervous.

Only one convenient arena was available for continuing the war of weapons: the Mediterranean. Here much could be done by intrigue and perhaps a mortal blow could be struck at the "life-line" of the British Empire. Hitler therefore "appeased" Vichy and sought French "collaboration," much to the Duce's disgust. He likewise wooed Franco and his pro-Nazi Foreign Minister, Ramon Serrano Suñer. But Vichy was too weak and Madrid too poor to risk open war with Britain. More could be achieved at less cost in the Balkans. Beyond the Danube lay the Aegean, and beyond the Aegean lay Egypt. Napoleon, too, had once struck at Egypt—and in the sequel had conquered neither Egypt nor Britain but Italy. Hitler believed he could do as much, and perhaps much more. . . .

Mussolini was no help. With adroit handling, Greece's little Hitler, John Metaxas, might have been won to the Axis. But the Duce threatened and

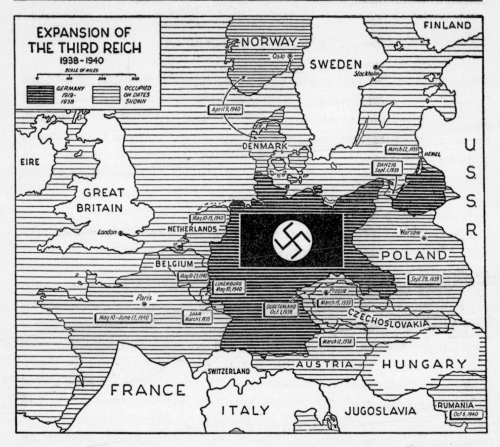

EXPANSION OF
THE THIRD REICH
1938-1940
SCALE OF MILES
GERMANY 1919-1938   OCCUPIED ON DATES SHOWN

bluffed and blundered in his eagerness to snatch part of the Balkans for himself before his German partner should act. King Carol's ramshackle kingdom of Greater Rumania, already robbed by Moscow of Bessarabia and Northern Bukovina, was meanwhile at sixes and sevens with Hungary and Bulgaria, both of which sought to recover their own "lost provinces" from Bucharest. At the end of August the Axis "mediated." Northern Transylvania was ceded to Hungary and southern Dobruja to Bulgaria. The Axis "guaranteed" what was left of Carol's shrunken realm.

The ensuing Rumanian disorders gave Hitler his opportunity to strike. The anti-Semitic terrorists of the Iron Guard, long subsidized from Berlin, unsuccessfully attempted a coup early in September. General Ion Antonescu assumed the Premiership. Weak-chinned Carol and his red-haired Magda Lupescu fled the country. Carol's son, 18 year old Michael, took the throne. Reichswehr divisions moved through Hungary into Rumania early in October to "train" the Rumanian Army and to "protect" the oil fields.

NAZIFYING BALKANIA

Whether Mussolini was consulted on this move is doubtful, despite his "conference" with Hitler at Brennero four days before the Reichswehr crossed the Rumanian frontiers. On October 28 they conferred again in Florence. But at dawn of the same day, Italian troops invaded Greece from Albania, Italian planes bombed Greek towns and the Italian Minister presented an ultimatum to Athens—all in imitation of Hitler's "Through-the-Looking-Glass" technique whereby the execution comes first, the trial next and the indictment last of all.

It is probable that the Duce struck at Greece not by agreement with the Führer but as a means of compensating himself, by what he hoped would be a cheap victory, for Hitler's easy triumph in Rumania. But his diplomats were as big dunderheads as his generals. Metaxas made promises—and then refused to resign or surrender. Within three weeks the Greeks were victoriously invading Albania, and Britain's Mediterranean fleet, now enjoying the use of Greek bases, was pounding into junk all the units of Italy's navy that came within its reach.

However embarrassing this state of affairs might be to Rome, it served Berlin's purposes admirably. The swastika marched southward. At the end of November Hungary, Rumania and Slovakia, all already occupied by the Reichswehr, became junior signatories of the Triple Alliance. Molotov on his visit to Berlin in mid-November refused to "cooperate" in forcing Bulgaria and Jugoslavia into line, despite Hitler's tempting suggestion of an Axis-Soviet partition of Turkey. (Turkish leaders were simultaneously assured by Ambassador von Papen of Hitler's eternal friendship.) Moscow in fact frowned sternly on the Nazi *Drang nach* the Bosphorus. But Soviet frowns were futile. Bulgaria's King Boris was pro-Axis, as was the Cabinet of Premier Cvetkovitch in Belgrade. The Turks, no longer terrible but timid, clung to suicidal "neutrality" despite their alliance with Britain, and made it clear that they would not fight to prevent Axis control of their neighbors.

Following a winter of preparation, during which his Roman ally suffered grievous blows at the hands of Greeks and Britons, Hitler moved to complete his march to the Mediterranean. At the close of the old year he declared: "God up to now has placed the stamp of approval on our battle. It is the will of the democratic war-inciters, and their Jewish-capitalist wire-pullers, that the war must be continued. The year 1941 will bring completion of the greatest victory in our history." With the approach of spring, he acted.

The program was to bring Bulgaria and Jugoslavia under Nazi control by threats and blandishments, to force "peace" on Greece, and then with Vichy's aid and Moscow's acquiescence to strike through Turkey or around Turkey at Palestine, Iraq and Egypt. Slavic stubbornness and British tenacity were to halt this campaign short of its goal. Yet its partial execution brought new glory to Hitler's arms and new shame and horror to his victims.

BLITZ IN BELGRADE

On the first day of March, 1941, Bulgarian Premier Bogdan Philov called (by request) at the Belvidere Palace in Vienna. There he signed a document, with Hitler, Ribbentrop, Ciano and Japan's Berlin Ambassador as "witnesses." By its terms Bulgaria became the fourth junior member of the Triple Alliance. Two hours later German divisions poured over the Danube and hastened to the Greek and Turkish borders. By the 3rd of March, when Bulgarians wryly celebrated the anniversary of their liberation from the Turks, the Reichswehr had the country firmly in its grip.

Thanks to fatal hopes of noninvolvement and neutrality, Jugoslavia was now encircled, as Czechoslovakia had been by Anschluss, and Poland by the Peace of Munich. Papen submitted reassuring messages from Hitler to President Ismet Inonu in Ankara, thus insuring Turkish neutrality until Turkey, in turn, should be encircled. In Belgrade Regent Prince Paul and Premier Cvetkovitch were induced to consider Nazi proposals of a "nonaggression" pact. Berlin secretly offered Salonika to Jugoslavia as bait. But the Prince and Premier encountered strong domestic opposition to their program of delivering their country to the Axis. Not until the 25th of March did Cvetkovitch and his Foreign Minister, Cincar-Markovitch, go to Vienna to make their Kingdom a signatory of the Triplice. Hitler cheerfully promised to respect Jugoslav sovereignty and integrity and to abstain from demands for the transit of troops. They signed.

But even as the Axis press celebrated another bloodless victory, Jugoslavia found her soul. Before dawn of March 27 an Army coup in Belgrade overthrew the Regency. Young Peter II took the throne while General Dusan Simovitch assumed the Premiership. The venerable Croat leader, Vladimir Matchek, became Vice-Premier. The new government did not publicly repudiate the pact of March 25, but declared that it would be strictly "neutral" and abide only by "open" treaties. The South Slavs, concluded Hitler, could not be corrupted but would have to be conquered.

The preliminaries were brief. Mussolini sought in vain to "mediate" between Belgrade and Berlin. The Nazi press screamed that Germans were being "persecuted" in Serbia. Reichswehr divisions massed in Hungary and Bulgaria. King Boris was cooperative. Hungary's Premier, Paul Teleki, the "tight-rope walker," put a bullet through his head rather than connive in the murder of a neighboring State with which he had concluded a non-aggression pact only a few months before. His successor, Ladislaus de Bardossy, had no such scruples. At 6.30 a.m. April 6, Ribbentrop informed the world that "England is about to commit another crime against Europe. The German Army is marching," he said, against "the clique of brigands" in Belgrade who "continuously threatened" Germany and Italy with war.

The Luftwaffe and the Panzer divisions, directed by General Sigmund List, had already struck at Jugoslavia and Greece. On the first day much of Belgrade was laid in ruins and the Aegean was reached through Thrace. On the third day Skoplje and Nish were seized by swift invaders from the east who found Serbia's mountains as easy to pierce as Holland's level plains. On the fourth day they descended the Vardar valley and occupied Salonika. On the fifth day Zagreb and Ljubljana fell and Berlin announced the formation of an "independent" Croat government headed by the terrorists Ante Pavelich and Sladko Kvaternik. Italian troops took Susak and harried the Dalmatian coast, while Hungarians invaded the Banat to seize Subotica and Novi Sad.

Belgrade, with its thousands of dead and its blocks of rubble, was in German hands a week after the Blitz began. This war was, if possible, even more one-sided than its predecessors. The half-mobilized Jugoslav Army, poor in all the weapons of modern war and permeated by traitors, crumbled at every point. Its remnants surrendered on the eleventh day of the campaign. King Peter and General Simovitch fled to Greece and then to England to join the melancholy host of governments-in-exile while their unhappy land was crushed and partitioned.

BARBARIANS IN THE ACROPOLIS

Against Mussolini's Fascist soldiery, with no skill in arms and no heart for war, the Greeks had covered themselves with glory. Against Hitler's machines, descending on the land like locusts from the Balkan hills, the Greeks were helpless, even with such aid as the British rushed from Egypt. Down the valleys of the Struma and the Vardar poured a formidable host to take Salonika, to trap the Greeks in Thrace, to wheel westward and southward and thread their way through the northern highlands. Metaxas had died in January. His successor, Premier Alexander Korizas, committed suicide two days before the Führer celebrated his 52nd birthday at his Balkan Headquarters.

The Hakenkreuz flew over Mount Olympus on the 19th of April. From Trikkala the invaders fanned out over the plains of Thessaly. Four days thereafter the Greek armies in Epirus, cut off from their bases by the Nazis, surrendered to the Italians. King George and Manuel Tsouderos, Foreign Minister and later Premier, fled from Athens to Crete. The pass at Thermopylae was stormed. The islands of the Aegean, strung like gems across the sapphire sea, were pounced upon one by one by the new Persians out of the north.

While parachute troops took the Corinth Canal and the cities of the Peloponnesus, the main body of the conquerors swept into Athens three weeks to a day after Hitler had unleashed his troops and issued his promise that "the last Briton will find his Dunkirk in Greece." Jugoslavia was carved up and subjected to savage reprisals for the continued resistance of stubborn Serb guerrillas in the hills. Greece, like other conquered lands, was robbed of its goods by the simple device of Reichswehr currency, backed by bayonets. General George Tsolakoglou became head of a puppet regime which collaborated as best it could with its German and Italian "protectors."

On the 4th of May, as his bombers began blasting Crete and raiding Suez, Hitler assured his Reichstag that Germany and its allies could defeat "any possible coalition in the world." At the end of the month there followed the ten days' war which wrested Crete from British hands. Stukas strafed the British forces under General Bernard Freyburg and the British ships of war which sought in vain to guard the island stronghold. Transport planes and gliders, filled with the Nazi infantry of the sky, landed hundreds and then thousands of armed men near Suda Bay, Rethymna and Candia. With the seizure of the airport at Maleme, near Canea, the R.A.F. was forced to quit its Cretan fields. The Greek King and Cabinet fled to Egypt. By the 1st of June all of Crete was in Nazi hands.

The subjugation of Jugoslavia and Greece, according to the German High Command, cost the invaders only 2,559 killed, 5,820 wounded and 3,169 missing. The Reichswehr took 344,000 Serb prisoners, 218,000 Greeks and

GERMANY

SEPT. 27, 1940

INVASION BEGINS
APRIL 6, 1941

NOV. 20, 1940

APRIL 10, 1941

Triesto

Fiume

Zagreb

ZARA
(IT)

MARCH 25, 1941

SEPT. 27, 1940

Ragusa

Scutari

ITALY

Naples

Brindisi

Taranto

Valona

Durazzo

Tirana

ALBANIA

Koritza

CORFU

Janina   Trikkala

GREECE

Ionian Sea

SICILY   Catania

Budapest

HUNGARY

Szeged

Subotica

Sarajevo

JUGOSLAVIA

Belgrade

JUGOSLAV ARMY
SURRENDERS
APRIL 17, 1941

Nish

APRIL 8, 1941

Skoplje

Bitolj

Monastir
Pass

GREEK ARMY IN THE
EPIRUS SURRENDERS
TO ITALIANS APRIL 23

Mt. Olympus

Volo

Lamia

Thermopylae
Pass

Patras

Corinth

TO HUNGARY
AUG. 30, 1940

NO. TRANSYLVANIA

OCT. 8, 1940

RUMANIA

NOV. 23, 1940

Bucharest

NO. BUKOVINA

U.S.S.R.

TO U.S.S.R.
JUNE 28, 1940

BESSARABIA

Black Sea

TO BULGARIA
AUG. 21, 1940

Danube R.

MARCH 1, 1941

Sofia

BULGARIA

INVASION BEGINS
APRIL 6, 1941

Rupel Pass

Xanthe

Kavalla

APRIL 9

Salonika

SAMOTHRACE

APRIL 22

LEMNOS

Larissa

APRIL 19

APRIL 22

Aegean Sea

GUARANTEED
BY BRITAIN
APRIL 13, 1939

Istanbul

Gallipoli

TURKEY

Dardanelles

Smyrna

CONCLUDES ALLIANCE
WITH BRITAIN AND
FRANCE, OCT. 19, 1939,
AND NEUTRALITY
PACT WITH GER-
MANY, JUNE 18, 1941

Athens

LEROS

THE CONQUEST
OF THE BALKANS
1940-1941

SCALE OF MILES:
0   50   100   150   200

DATE OF ADHERENCE TO
TRIPLE ALLIANCE

DATE OF OCCUPATION
BY NAZI TROOPS

CRETE

Canea

Maleme
Airport

MAY 28

MAY 22

SUDA BAY

MAY 29

Candia

CRETE

BRITISH EVACUATE
CRETE, JUNE 1

11,000 Britishers—most of them from Australia and New Zealand. London claimed that of the 58,000 troops sent to Greece, 45,000 had been evacuated, with 14,000 (out of 27,000) later withdrawn successfully from Crete to Egypt. More serious to the British cause was the admitted destruction from the air of four transports and two destroyers off the Greek mainland, and of three cruisers, four destroyers and an uncertain number of lesser vessels in Cretan waters. After so great a victory all the world expected the Führer to strike at once at Cyprus, Palestine and Egypt.

[125]

HERR HITLER, WOHIN?

The Caesar of the Teutons had taught the world to expect of him only the unexpected. Yet the world, to its grief, was slow to learn. Victory, he had often found, came with the swift *volte face*, the sudden stab-in-the-back, the startling blow against those disarmed by their own illusions.

Yet the strange decision of June, 1941—the most important and the most dangerous in his career—was not arrived at without much brooding at Berchtesgaden and much secret bickering among his aides. Three plans of attack against Britain were open after the close of the Balkan campaign: (1) He could strike at the Delta of the Nile, at the Red Sea and at the Persian Gulf—by air from Crete, by land from Libya (where Nazi divisions had rescued the Italians from defeat), and by intrigue and revolt among the Arabs of Iraq. (2) He could aim at Gibraltar and the west coast of Africa, with such support as could be gotten from Vichy and Madrid, and thus distract America from the Battle of the North Atlantic. (3) He could strike at England with all his air force and then launch an invasion of the British Isles before American supplies could arrive in large amounts.

In the chronicles of wasted time it may yet be written that the Nazi war-lord made a fatal error in not attempting one or another of these campaigns in the summer of 1941. Yet the difficulties in the way of each were great. Rightly or wrongly, they were finally judged insuperable in Berlin.

To invade Britain was far more difficult than it would have been a year before. Britain's defenders were now rearmed. The R.A.F. was far more formidable. The British fleet was still in command of the northern seas, despite the triumphs of U-boats, bombers and surface raiders in sinking half a million tons of merchant shipping a month. On May 24 the new and mighty Nazi battleship *Bismarck* sank the *Hood*, largest vessel in the British Navy, in the Straits of Denmark between Greenland and Iceland. But four days later the *Bismarck* was tracked down, crippled by aerial torpedoes and destroyed by the guns of British dreadnaughts. Without command of the air or of the sea, an invasion of Britain could scarcely succeed. The attempt, moreover, might bring America openly into the war, a consummation devoutly to be postponed.

The second plan involved a similar risk. Vichy indeed was "collaborating" nicely, despite American warnings and threats, but Vichy's collaboration was limited and feeble. Franco, too, was Hitler's stooge. But Franco's subjects were starving. Even if Gibraltar fell, the Axis lacked means to destroy the British Mediterranean fleet. Beyond Gibraltar and Morocco lay the vast deserts and jungles of Africa—no treasure house of wealth, no land for Nordics and no arena where any fatal blow at the foe could possibly be struck.

Nazi hopes were highest at first regarding the Near East, rich in petroleum and intrigue. Western Egypt was already invaded. Turkey, drugged by new assurances brought by the oily Papen, was already immobilized. Axis agents had stirred revolt in Iraq and pressed the Vichymen in Syria to serve Berlin. The result was war in Iraq in May, and war in Syria in June. The Luftwaffe crossed the French mandate to reach the oil fields near Mosul. But it did not act in force or in time. The British won in Iraq before Crete was safely in German hands. And by the time the Anglo-Free French forces invaded Syria, Hitler had changed his plans.

THE THRESHOLD OF DESTINY

How, why, when and where the master-minds of the Third Reich came to Bonaparte's conclusion of 1812—that world victory over England was to be found on the road to Moscow—cannot yet be told. Yet the calculus in both cases was somewhat the same. The Little Corporal from Corsica attempted the conquest of the realm of Tsar Alexander (with whom he had concluded a pact of eternal friendship five years before) in order to perfect his "Continental System" by which Britain was to be excluded forever from Europe and starved into submission. With Russia vanquished, he might safely attempt an invasion of England. The Little Corporal from Braunau-am-Inn had similar need for consolidating his "New Order" and protecting his flank from perfidious Russia for an ultimate assault on Perfidious Albion. In one respect, moreover, the conqueror of the Continent in 1941 felt safer in invading the realm of Stalin (with whom he had concluded a pact of eternal friendship twenty-two months before) than the conqueror of the Continent in 1812 felt in invading Alexander's empire: the England of 1812 had already invaded Spain and re-established a Western Front. The England of 1941 was still appeasing Franco and had no means of invading the Continent at any other point. As for allies, Hitler hoped to manoeuver Japan into war with either or both of his major foes, as Napoleon had succeeded in manoeuvering the United States into war with Britain in 1812.

The crucial difference between the two adventures in Hitler's scheming mind was the difference between Tsarism and Bolshevism. Fascism had won most of its greatest victories by terrifying the propertied élites of the democracies with the bugaboo of Communism. To resume the "defense" of "civilization" against the "Red menace," reasoned the Nazi conspirators, might well recapture the pattern of *Weltpolitik* of 1933–39. The conquered Continent could be rallied in a great crusade against Moscow. Britain's Tory appeasers might lift their heads anew to urge peace with the Reich at the expense of Russia. America's appeasolationists would gain new strength to denounce and impede their government's course. With Russia beaten, or even unbeaten or half-beaten, Berlin could offer "peace" to London and Washington with more than half a hope of acceptance. Göbbels and Ribbentrop saw new vistas looming . . .

On the 12th day of May, 1941, Rudolf Hess, Nazi No. 3 and successor-designate to the Führership after Hitler and Göring, flew a Messerschmitt 110 from Augsburg to the estate of the Duke of Hamilton near Glasgow. What would have followed had he reached his destination no one will ever know. He may have flown on the Führer's secret orders, with his own person as a pledge of "sincerity," to propose peace in the name of an anti-Bolshevik front. He may have flown to meet the "leaders" of a "Scotch rebellion" which the British secret service fabricated out of moonshine and sold to him as bait. He may have acted on his own initiative in the conviction that peace with Britain should be arranged *before* the assault on Russia should be launched. But he lost his way in the dark and ran out of gas. Bailing out short of his goal, he suffered a broken ankle, was captured by a Scotch farmer and was publicly identified. After a brief sojourn in a Glasgow hospital, he was sent for safekeeping to a secret haven. Official London would admit no more than that he had come to arrange a peace. Official Berlin concurred, but said he was "deluded" and "deranged."

Shortly after the Hessian visitation, John G. Winant, United States Ambassador to Britain, returned to Washington to "report." Whether he came to reveal to the President the real nature of Hess' mission, or to warn of the danger of Tory interest in Nazi overtures, or for some less sensational purpose is still untold by those who know. Roosevelt contented himself with intimating on the 6th of June that all rumors of Anglo-German peace feelers were of Nazi origin. He said that Winant had not brought "even the tenth cousin of a peace offer or anything like that or any discussion of peace. Absolutely nothing like it."

Dashed were the hopes that Hess or Hitler may have entertained of defeating Britain and immobilizing America by a specious peace at the expense of the Kremlin prior to a Nazi invasion of Russia. The hope remained that such a manoeuver might yet succeed during the course of a war in the East. Should the invasion fail, then all the dupes and dunces of the Continent and of the English-speaking world could the better be confused by a new cry of saving Europe from a Bolshevik counter-invasion. Should it succeed, the legend of Nazi invincibility, coupled with the vast resources which would then be at the Reich's disposal, might well discourage and demoralize the "pluto-democracies."

In either case, the risks seemed slight. Hitler saw little reason to believe that America would seize upon the occasion to force a show-down with Japan or to join Britain in organizing an invasion of the Continent. America lacked will. Britain lacked means. There could be no such danger before 1942. By then Britain might "see reason" or might be starved into submission. By then Russia might be prostrate and the Nazi legions might be striking into India and across Iran and Iraq toward Egypt. By some such calculus as this the frustrated and furious Führer concluded, with shrewd method in his madness, that his *Kampf* for the world was to be won on the steppes of Eurasia.

VORSPIEL

Napoleon's "victory" in Moscow led to disaster at Leipzig and Waterloo and to lonely exile on St. Helena. Wilhelm Hohenzollern's defeat of Russia led to Chateau-Thierry and Compiègne and to lonely exile at Doorn. There in the conquered Netherlands the last Kaiser, aged 82, breathed his last on the 4th of June, 1941, unwept even in the Reich.

These somber precedents were probably not discussed at Brennero. Here, two days before the Kaiser's death, Hitler and Ribbentrop met Mussolini and Ciano. For five long hours they conferred in the armored train which the Führer had given to the Duce the year before. No doubt the Tyrant of the North told the Tyrant of the South of his hopes and plans. And no doubt Mussolini agreed, since he was no longer free to disagree. Two weeks later, in a ceremony in Venice, terrorist Pavelich made the puppetry of Croatia a signatory of the Triple Alliance.

One other empty pact preceded the drive to the East. On June 18 Shukru Saracoglu, Foreign Minister of Turkey, signed with Franz von Papen another scrap of paper "on a basis of mutual confidence and sincere friendship" and "without prejudice to present obligations of both countries." It bound the parties for ten years (the same period for which the Nazi-Soviet nonaggression pact was to run!) to "respect the integrity and inviolability of their territories" and to abstain from any measure "aimed directly or indirectly against the other." They would confer "in friendly manner" on all questions of mutual interest. Supplementary notes pledged economic collaboration and control of press and radio to insure respect for "the spirit of friendship and mutual confidence that characterizes Turkish-German relations." On the following day, as Berlin hinted that all rumors of German-Soviet tension were of "foreign origin," Hitler and Inonu exchanged messages of "mutual trust."

This farce at the expense of Britain's only surviving ally was intended, like all Nazi treaties, to impress opinion abroad, to commit the other signatory to obligations which Berlin would observe only so long as expedient, and to anesthetize another victim of aggression into helplessness until the Reich should be ready to strike. The leaders of Turkey, like those of a dozen vanished States, had already rendered their country helpless by their policies of nonintervention and neutrality. The new pact was but the open acknowledgment of their impotence and the visible sign of another British defeat. It was also an added assurance (as if one were needed!) that Ankara would do nothing while the Reich invaded Muscovy, as it had done nothing while the Reich had chloroformed Bucharest and Sofia and violated Belgrade and Athens.

The Führer's secret was well kept. Apart from chronic rumors of troop movements and German "demands" on the U.S.S.R., there was no hint of things to come save in Finland. On the day of the signature of the Turkish pact London extended its blockade to Petsamo on the ground that German troops in Finland made the country no longer a neutral. Two days later the Finnish Cabinet ordered general mobilization. Otherwise silence. No complaints to Moscow. No demands on Moscow. No press campaign in preparation for aggression.

THE GREAT CRUSADE

Before break of day on the first Sunday of summer, 1941, the bombers of the Luftwaffe roared out of their hidden hangars along the eastern reaches of the Reich to rain death on Kaunas, Kiev, Zhitomir and Sevastopol and to strike at far-flung Soviet airfields. At the same moment the Stukas, tanks and armored cars of three great mechanized armies crossed the Soviet frontiers.

One from East Prussia was to pierce the Baltic provinces and aim at Leningrad in cooperation with Finnish forces from the north. Another, from central Poland, was to head for Minsk, Smolensk and Moscow. The third, in southern Poland, was to invade Bessarabia and the Ukraine in cooperation with Rumanian forces from the south. By dawn all the monstrous machines of murder in the arsenal of the Reich, never hitherto halted by any foe, were clanking or rumbling or shrieking their message of doom to the defenders of the western borders of Stalin's Red empire.

Once the assault was well under way, the Axis potentates announced that Germany and Italy were at war with the U.S.S.R. as of 5.30 a.m. June 22, 1941. Ribbentrop made the customary before-breakfast accusations. Hitler issued a long proclamation: "Weighted down with heavy cares, condemned to months' long silence, the hour has now come when at last I can speak freely." He charged a plot of "Jews and democrats, Bolshevists and reactionaries with the sole aim of inhibiting the establishment of the new German people's State and plunging the Reich anew into impotence and misery. For over ten years Jewish Bolshevist rulers have been endeavoring from Moscow to set not only Germany but all Europe aflame. This has brought us to the hour when it is necessary for us to take steps against this plot devised by the Jewish Anglo-Saxon war-mongers and equally the Jewish rulers of the Bolshevist center."

If Hitler was disappointed by the almost immediate declaration of British and American solidarity with the U.S.S.R., he was cheered by the swift response of the puppet politicians of Nazi Europe. The Rumanians were summoned by Antonescu to a Holy War to "free your oppressed brothers from the Red yoke of Bolshevism." Bardossy in Budapest severed relations with Moscow on the 23rd and declared four days later that Hungary was at war with Russia—in "self-defense." In Finland, bloody Baron Mannerheim, put in power by German arms in 1918, launched his war of revenge against Russia. Premier J. W. Rangell told the Finn parliament on the 25th that the U.S.S.R. was committing "acts of war." A day later President Risto Ryti avowed that "we shall fight for the freedom of our country and for the creed of our fathers." The Swedish Government consented to Nazi-Finn demands for the movement of troops from Norway to Finland, with the curious explanation that it was "compelled to allow transit of one German division if it was to be possible to keep its neutrality." In Ankara Papen's approach to the British Ambassador with a plea for a common anti-Soviet front was in vain. But the Turkish parliament unanimously ratified the German pact, amid professions of devotion to peace and—*mirabile dictu*—to the British alliance. This happy decision was taken the day after the loss of almost a hundred officers of the Turkish Navy in the torpedoing of the Turkish ship *Refah*, which had been guaranteed safe passage to Egypt by Berlin and Rome.

In Madrid a mob of Falangists attacked the British Embassy and cried "On to Moscow!" Franco, like Mussolini, prepared to send troops to join the Reichswehr, conveniently disguised (like the Italian troops that put Franco in power) as "volunteers." Sweden likewise approved of "volunteering." So did the Vichymen. They severed relations with Moscow on June 30, alleging threats by Soviet diplomats to the social order. (Commented Lozovsky, Soviet Vice-Commissar of Foreign Affairs: "It is unknown what social order exists there.") Only the Pope failed to give full cooperation, since he declined to espouse publicly the Axis crusade to save Christianity from the Red atheists. But the Italian Catholic hierarchy and a few of the German prelates gave their blessing.

Even the German High Command, with its communiqués now "edited" in person by Hitler, sang Fascism's old sweet song. The fantastic quantities of prisoners, tanks and planes which it claimed to have captured showed, it said, "the quantity of the menace that had grown on the eastern frontier of the Reich. It is likely that, at the last minute, Middle Europe was spared an invasion the consequences of which cannot be conceived." Red resistance from ambush along the River Bug was "a typical Bolshevist trick." "Unbelievable chaos," declared the communiqué of July 2, "has closed over the Soviet Army which was mobilized as an offensive wedge in order to fall upon Germany from the rear and carry the firebrand of Bolshevism into Europe." The American occupation of Iceland, screamed the German press, was a dastardly stab-in-the-back while Hitler was trying to save Europe from the Red peril.

THE BLITZ THAT STALLED

The opening phases of the invasion of Russia closely resembled the campaigns that had gone before. "The German eruption," said Churchill of the Battle of Flanders, which was the intended prototype of the eastern operations, "swept like a sharp scythe to the rear of the armies of the north. It severed our communications. Behind this armored and mechanized onslaught came a number of German divisions in lorries, and behind them again plodded comparatively slowly the dull brute mass of the ordinary German Army and

German people, always ready to be led to the trampling down in other lands of liberties and comforts they never have known in their own."

In the Soviet borderlands, as on a dozen other fields, the Luftwaffe and the Panzer divisions pierced through the lines of the defenders and dashed forward to outflank, encircle and destroy. The territories in Poland and the Balticum which Moscow had gained in 1939-1940 were largely overrun in a fortnight. By the first week of July Lvov, Luck, Dvinsk and Riga were in Nazi hands and the Berezina was crossed. Minsk was taken and passed. An immense Soviet army (of over 300,000 men, said the German High Command) was enveloped between Bialystok and Minsk and obliged to surrender. By mid-July Kishinev, Vitebsk and Smolensk were claimed. The fortified zone of the "Stalin Line," said Berlin, was broken "at all decisive points." The fall of Kiev and Leningrad was "imminent" and the road to Moscow was "clear," with the broken Red armies fleeing everywhere in disorder. Hitler named Alfred Rosenberg as high administrator of the conquered country and parcelled out its subdivisions among the lesser Nazi gentry. Within a month all would be over. Most British and American military authorities concurred in this judgment.

Then, unbelievably, all across the hot and dusty Russian plains, marched a mid-summer miracle. The two weeks' respite gained by earlier annexations made possible full Soviet mobilization. The vast armies which moved out to meet the invaders were not inspired by Maginots or Liddell Harts, nor were they led by Gamelins or Weygands or Ironsides. Their philosophy was the creed of attack. Their weapons were thousands of tanks and planes and heavy guns, wielded with skill and daring. Their men had faith and a will to fight. When trapped, they resisted like tigers. When free, they slashed and harried the German divisions with an adroitness and a fury of fanaticism equal to their foe's. When they retreated they destroyed all in their wake and left thousands of guerrilla fighters in the forests and swamps to assail the enemy's rear.

By early August the German communiqués reporting "successful operations," fresh "battles of annihilation" and new advances "according to plan" had become dull reading. In order to maintain the fading illusion of speedy victory the German High Command, in the seventh week of the conflict, claimed the seizure or destruction of 13,000 Soviet tanks, 10,000 guns and 9,000 planes and asserted, contrary to all reason, that three million Russians had been slain and almost a million captured. By the end of the month Berlin's optimists had captured a million and a quarter Russians and inflicted five million casualties on the foe.

The fact remained that the Blitz had failed. The Nazi-Finn forces under Mannerheim and General Nikolaus von Falkenhorst, conqueror of Norway, laid siege to Hanko and made slow and costly progress toward the White Sea and Leningrad. The northern armies under Field Marshal Ritter von Leeb overran Lithuania, Latvia and Estonia, but after ten weeks of fighting had not reached the city on the Neva which was the cradle of the Russian Revolution. The southern forces of invasion, under Field Marshals von Rundstedt and von Reichenau, took almost two months to come within striking distance of Kiev. The central armies, under General von Bock, passed Minsk and Smolensk but made no progress toward Moscow. The Red Army was still intact. The strategists who had smashed all the other armies of the Continent in campaigns of a few weeks' duration had at last met their match.

The encirclers were often encircled in a gigantic war of movement among millions of fighters. Air raids on Moscow, which began July 21, had little result save the loss of scores of raiders. As for the Soviet troops, Berlin explained that they were too stupid to surrender when defeated; they refused to fight fairly; they declined to be demoralized "because all the prerequisites of such a collapse are lacking." Communism had "bestialized" all Russians and killed their souls. How could soulless beasts be beaten?

Keitel had not found the answer as summer waned. His first big push had succeeded. His second was stopped. His son was slain, and Frick's son and thousands of other officers and celebrities. As for the "dull, brute mass," it tasted wholesale death for the first time. Russian losses were doubtless heavier. But there were endless millions of Russians. Hundreds of thousands of German youths soaked the steppes with their blood while the High Command called for new recruits.

The third major offensive, to be sure, carried the invaders to the Dnieper by the third week of August and gave them mastery of the Western Ukraine. Early in September Leningrad was encircled by land and besieged, as was Odessa in the south. After a slow start, the invaders of the Ukraine inflicted a crushing defeat on the defenders in mid-September through a vast encirclement movement which netted them Kiev and Poltava and paved the way for an assault on Kharkov, the Crimea and the Donetz basin. At the end of the third month of fighting the High Command claimed over 2,000,000 prisoners, including some 600,000 trapped east of Kiev, at an alleged cost (up to August 31) of only 725 planes, 85,000 German dead, 300,000 wounded and 19,000 missing.

These figures, though double the total of admitted German casualties in the conquest of all the rest of Europe, were received with justified skepticism abroad and even in Germany. The Reichswehr had inflicted heavy losses on the Red Army and had occupied valuable agrarian areas and industrial centers. But its own divisions had suffered grievously, and they had by no means broken Russian resistance. In the summer of 1812 Napoleon's Grand Army, moving by foot and horse, had taken Moscow in less than three months. Hitler's motorized divisions, after three months of terrific struggle, had reached only one of their three major objectives: Kiev. The defenders of Leningrad continued to fight like madmen. The defenders of Moscow had not only halted the Nazi onrush but had pushed the invaders back to the gates of Smolensk. A costly and bitter winter campaign was inevitable. The Reichswehr would not share the fate of the Grand Army. It might even reach the lower Volga and the Caucasus. Its war, however, was no longer a Blitz but a contest of exhaustion. Red tanks and guns, though destroyed or captured by thousands, continued to mow down the invaders. The Red air force, though officially "annihilated" at the outset of the struggle, rained death on their ranks and even bombed Berlin and other German cities. If Americans and Britons should do during the winter what destiny demanded of them, Russian resistance would continue through 1942.

TOMORROW THE WORLD IS . . . ?

The Reich had conquered Russia once before in a long and bloody battle of attrition. In doing so the Reich had lost its war. Germany might again win victory over Muscovy. But the cost was appalling. And there would be no psychic collapse and defeatist revolution in the U.S.S.R. in the aftermath of Nazi victories. With great war industries in Siberia, the Russians would continue to fight—in front of Moscow or behind Moscow, throughout the Ukraine or in the Caucasus, west of the Urals or east of the Urals. The Reichswehr might be bogged down as the Army of Righteous Justice was bogged down in China. Each month lost was six months gained for Britain and America. At the end the Führer might find his armies deep in a beaten Russia while the Allies crushed him in the west.

"I go my way," said Hitler long ago, "with the assurance of a sleep-walker, the way which Providence has sent me." But sleep is dangerous in the face of foes at last awake. And the ways of Providence are strange. The world might

HITLER OVER EUROPE
SEPT. 1, 1941
SCALE OF MILES
0 100 200 300 400 500
- - - - *Pre-1939 frontiers in Central Europe*
Nazi-held territories
Allies and Puppet States
Date of adherence to Triple Alliance

yet be won. Russians could not forever fight unaided. Americans and Britishers were slow of mind and slower of deed. Britain was a citadel of heroic muddling. America was a madhouse whose inmates feared to fight and perhaps would only fight too late. The poisons of anti-Communism and anti-Semitism, of isolationism and pacifism, slyly spread by Nazi agents and by thousands of dunces and dupes, might yet benumb the Anglo-Saxon Powers and prepare them for a "peace." Let them give Russia to the Führer, let the Reich restore its trade with South America, Africa and Asia, and Anglo-Saxony would be brought to ruin. But the days of the Blitz were past. The circle of the Führer's opportunities was narrowing. All over conquered Europe, from Paris to Pinsk and from Oslo to Athens, men and women were finding new courage to risk their lives by shooting German officers, blowing up bridges, wrecking trains and summoning their fellows to revolt against Hitler's minions.

The answer was terror. By early fall Heinrich Himmler's Gestapo was shooting and hanging hundreds of hostages and suspects in France, Norway, Jugoslavia and elsewhere. The new "Protector" of Bohemia-Moravia, Reinhard Heydrich (Gestapo terrorist No. 2), arrested Puppet-Premier Alois Elias for "treason" and butchered the Mayor and Councillors of Prague, along with scores of patriot-rebels. The reply of the vanquished was counter-terrorism. Ghosts haunted the Führer.

If victory eluded him, if Russia held out, if the Western Powers could not be drugged anew into appeasement, he and his horde of terrorists might yet win terms by threatening to starve or massacre those already conquered. Such a step, however, would be an admission of defeat. His own deluded subjects followed him only in victory. It is better for a tyrant to be feared than loved, said Machiavelli—but only when the tyrant is triumphant. Tyrants who fail seldom die in bed. In the Garden of Berchta the Evil Fairy, the strange man from Austria who was the son of Alois Schicklgruber wondered mournfully how his last days might be spent.

He had been driven to conquer half a world because the world denied him love. Now all the world detested him as a "bloodthirsty guttersnipe" (Churchill) with a hatred fiercer than any evoked before by the vilest human monsters of the past. Churchill's words echoed among the mists of Berchtesgaden: "He has lighted a fire which will burn with a steady and consuming flame until the last vestiges of Nazi tyranny have been burned out . . ."

Loge, god of the Magic Fire, danced in the glare of a hundred burning cities. How bright the light! But in the end dark Hagen, slayer of Siegfried, had suffered retribution, and Valhalla had perished with all its pagan gods. Could the Reich for which Hitler had promised a life of a thousand years suffer a similar fate so soon? It could and would—unless the freemen of the West once more shirked their duty. Here was Hitler's last hope. Democratic irresponsibility and blindness had raised the Nazi realm to the dazzling heights from which its leaders saw all the world below them ripe for looting. Democratic irresponsibility and blindness might yet deliver all of that world into the hands of the hosts of darkness.

Yet the pasty-faced Führer, flabby of body, bulging of hips and nervous of stride, felt fear gnawing at his vitals. He had promised his people final victory in 1941. He would repeat the promise for 1942. But behind all his posturing was doubt.

[*137*]

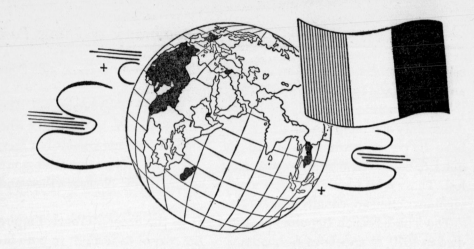

She found a little bottle, and tied round the neck of the bottle was a paper label, with the words "DRINK ME" beautifully printed on it in large letters. It was all very well to say "Drink me," but the wise little Alice was not going to do that in a hurry. "No, I'll look first," she said, "and see whether it's marked 'poison' or not"; for she had read several nice little stories about children who had got burnt, and eaten up by wild beasts, and other unpleasant things, all because they would not remember the simple rules their friends had taught them: such as, that a red-hot poker will burn you if you hold it too long; and that, if you cut your finger very deeply with a knife, it usually bleeds; and she had never forgotten that, if you drink much from a bottle marked "poison," it is almost certain to disagree with you, sooner or later. However, this little bottle was not marked "poison," so Alice ventured to taste it, and, finding it very nice (it had, in fact, a sort of mixed flavor of cherry-tart, custard, pineapple, roast turkey, toffy, and hot buttered toast), she very soon finished it off . . . "What a curious feeling!" said Alice. "I must be shutting up like a telescope!" And so it was indeed: she was now only ten inches high. She felt a little nervous about this; "for it might end, you know," said Alice to herself, "in my going out altogether, like a candle. I wonder what I should be like then?" And she tried to fancy what the flame of a candle looks like after the candle is blown out, for she could not remember ever having seen such a thing.

RES JUDICATA

Blind men wandering in strange streets often stumble unless helped by their friends or neighbors. Dishonest men who corrupt others and themselves sooner or later run afoul of the law. The sick of soul frequently injure themselves and others unless taken in hand by the community. These afflictions are seldom fatal to the individuals who suffer from them.

When a nation is thus diseased, however, survival is problematical. The community of nations is a jungle. Its law is the law of force: let those take who have the power, let those keep who can. Neighbors are not friends but foes, quick to take advantage of every weakness. Those who forget these things are lost. Those who remember them and yet are incapable of clear vision and vigorous action are equally lost.

The Third French Republic died in 1940, as the Second French Empire died in 1870, of unbelievable blindness on the part of its leaders. In both instances corruption ran rampant in a society hopelessly split by an incurable schism. In the earlier case the consequence was the débâcle of Sedan, followed by defeat and chaos and the bloody class war of the Paris Commune. In the later case the consequence was a long period of inner strife between Munichmen and *"bellicistes,"* reactionaries and liberals, pro-Fascists and anti-Fascists—followed by the second débâcle of Sedan, the capitulation of Bordeaux and the establishment of a government of traitors and defeatists. France was betrayed from within, partly by isolationist stupidity, partly by malice prepense on the part of the well-to-do, long before France was crushed from without by the hereditary foe. The latter result was the product of the former cause. In this there is perhaps no "moral." In Hegel's phrase, the only lesson which history teaches is that history teaches no lessons. Decadent peoples and degenerate ruling classes learn nothing and forget nothing. Yet the anatomy of disaster is worthy of dissection.

REMEMBRANCE OF THINGS PAST

The French nation-state is, with the possible exception of England, the oldest of the Great Powers in the Western State System. It was the first State of Continental Europe to attain political unity under its medieval kings. It was in France that Royal absolutism and centralized power first triumphed over feudal anarchy and medieval localism. It was in France, some three centuries later, that bourgeois democracy first triumphed over absolutism and the landed aristocracy. Corresponding changes had taken place earlier in England, but England was across the Channel and was no longer able to act effectively on the Continent after her knights and barons were driven out of Normandy, Aquitaine, and other "French" provinces in the Hundred Years'

War (1337–1453). The same conflict which ousted England from the mainland launched France on her career as the largest, richest, and most populous State of Europe. From 1500 to 1815 French kings, statesmen, and patriots took pride in the fact that *la belle France* was ranked first among the nations in military might, in diplomatic prestige, and in the arts of civilization.

For Paris, City of Light and eternal shrine of the best in European culture, it was the tragedy of the nineteenth century that *la grande nation* ceased to be the most powerful State of Western Europe. French policy under the Second Empire of Napoleon III (1852–1870) was directed toward imperial expansion and toward preventing the political unification of Germany. The effort to forestall this misfortune failed. The Franco-Prussian War spelled the end of French supremacy on the Continent. In the dust of Sedan and the agony of besieged and captured Paris, there perished the possibility of retaining in the hands of the Quai d'Orsay the reins of power which those hands were no longer strong enough to hold. The Rhine frontier was lost. Alsace-Lorraine was lost. Germany was a united nation. And Italy to the south was also a united nation.

French foreign policy after 1871 sought to recover for France what had been lost and to re-establish traditional French hegemony over Europe. How this purpose—seemingly impossible of realization—was attained and how French soldiers and diplomats finally achieved, and for a time preserved, a new position of uneasy preponderance over the Continent in the post-Versailles period need not here be told. It will suffice to suggest how and why that preponderance was thrown away and France was brought to ruin.

In 1918, after four years and three months of bloodshed, France achieved the goal which her diplomats and soldiers had so long pursued. But only a world in arms against the Central Powers enabled France to achieve victory. The Republic's Russian ally had been ground to pieces by the enemy and was in the throes of social revolution. Great Britain, Italy, the United States, and a host of lesser allies stood in the way of a purely French peace. They opposed French annexation of the Rhineland. They opposed outright annexation of the German colonies. They refused to conclude an alliance against Germany for the future. But much had been gained despite these obstacles. Austria-Hungary was destroyed. German military and naval strength was reduced to impotence by the Treaty of Versailles. The French Army became the most powerful force on the Continent. French power and prestige were restored almost, if not quite, to their old status. French hegemony was successfully reasserted. A new distribution of territory and power, embodying the realities of this hegemony, was written into the public law of Europe. If Poincaré and other extreme nationalists were bitter over the "leniency" of the peace settlement, at least the new Europe offered ample opportunities for the permanent humiliation of Germany and the perpetuation of French ascendancy.

Post-Versailles French foreign policy was directed almost exclusively toward the attainment of this end, although differences of opinion developed as to the best means thereto. "Security" became at once the guiding slogan of the Quai d'Orsay. "Security" meant assurance against invasion from the East. Assurance against invasion was not to be had, in the opinion of most patriotic Frenchmen, unless the prospective invader were kept in a position of political inferiority and military helplessness. No chances were to be taken with German good will, for France had been twice invaded in fifty years. Germany, moreover—defeated, truncated, disarmed—was still the most populous Power of Europe west of Russia, and still had a magnificent industrial establishment for the making of modern war. There could be no security unless the Republic possessed overwhelming power to paralyze at once any threatened resort to force on the part of the foe. Since the political, territorial, military, and reparations clauses of the Peace Treaty afforded a large measure of such security, it was natural that the French Government should not only insist upon their preservation intact but should interpret them as liberally as possible from the point of view of French interests.

IN QUEST OF SAFETY

The attainment of French security, *i.e.*, the maintenance of French hegemony over the Continent, required that Germany be kept weak and that France be kept strong. To achieve this goal, the dismemberment of the German federal State was at first contemplated. "Separatist" intrigues in the Rhineland were indulged in extensively between 1918 and 1925 and were then abandoned when it appeared that the Rhineland was not detachable. But the territorial clauses of the Treaty of Versailles were kept intact, and any union, political or economic, between the Reich and German Austria was prevented. Germany was kept disarmed, for a rearmed Germany, bent upon a counter-*revanche*, would be a formidable foe. Germany was kept diplomatically isolated, for if she gained allies she might conceivably at some future date undo the verdict of 1919, as France, with the aid of allies, was able earlier to undo the verdict of 1871. And Germany was kept economically and financially pros-

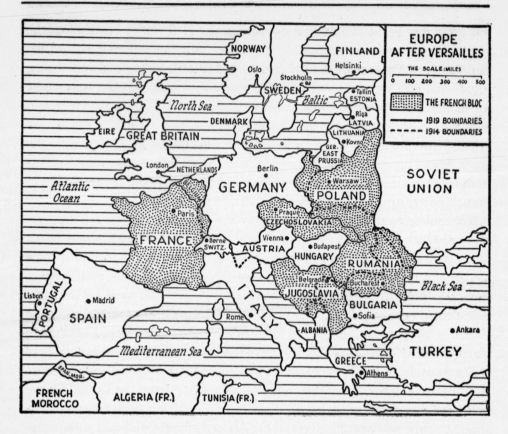

trate, for without capital and productive capacity no State can achieve military power or diplomatic influence. With this end in view, the French Government, between 1918 and 1924, insisted upon the full execution of the economic and financial clauses of the Treaty. A weak Germany could perhaps pay no reparations, but a strong Germany could threaten French security. Poincaré and his supporters preferred security to reparations. When payments were defaulted in 1923, French and Belgian troops occupied the Ruhr valley, industrial heart of Germany, as a means of coercing the Reich.

If these and similar measures were adopted to keep Germany impotent, corresponding measures were devised to keep France powerful. New fortifications were erected along the eastern frontier. The French Army, though reduced in numbers, was maintained at what was believed to be the highest possible level of technical efficiency. The French Government steadfastly refused to reduce its armaments further, except in return for an international police force or some alternative arrangement which would afford an equal degree of security. New allies were sought to replace the old. Tsarist Russia was gone, and French efforts during the Russian civil war to bring about the overthrow of the Soviet regime were fruitless. But Belgium and Poland became allies of France. In the southeast the Little Entente—Czechoslovakia, Jugoslavia, and Rumania—was no less resolved to maintain the *status quo*. All its members became allies of France, and under French guidance and with the aid of French loans they resolved to oppose all efforts to modify the existing distribution of territory and power, whether from Germany to the north, from Hungary or Austria within their midst, from Italy to the west, or from Russia to the east. These common interests stretched a broad cordon of French power around Germany's frontiers.

Not content to rely only upon this bulwark, the Quai d'Orsay sought overseas assistance from every possible source. In 1919 the French Cabinet reluctantly abandoned its plan for annexation of the Rhineland in return for a pledge of a Franco-Anglo-American security pact which never materialized. French interest in the League of Nations was largely inspired by the hope that it could be used to ensure enforcement of the peace treaties and place the power of all its members behind the victim of any aggression. The French Government attempted, without success, to secure a general British guarantee of European frontiers. Nothing would have been more welcome to it (or more improbable of attainment) than a pledge of support from the United States, in the event of any forcible effort at treaty revision. Despite failures and disappointments, post-war France and her eastern allies established such a preponderance of power on the Continent that the old equilibrium between opposing coalitions disappeared. For fifteen years, no aggregation of power emerged which could hope to challenge French ascendancy.

THE TRIUMPH OF FEAR

But this "security" was as uneasy as that of the proverbial head that wears a crown. Seventy million Germans remained in central Europe. It consequently seemed expedient to placate Germany to a certain degree. Following the failure of the Poincaré policy of coercion, the Herriot Cabinet of 1924 consented to the so-called Dawes Plan of reparation payments and to the evacuation of the Ruhr. Reparation obligations were further reduced in the Young Plan of 1930 and in the face of world-wide economic collapse were abandoned entirely in the Lausanne agreements of 1932. Under the leadership of Aristide Briand, a "new era" of Franco-German relations was inaugurated by the Locarno pacts of October, 1925, and by the admission of Germany into the League in 1926. The Rhineland was evacuated in 1930, five years before the required time.

Extreme French nationalists condemned these concessions as an indication of weakness and an invitation to Germany to make new demands for treaty revision. More moderate Frenchmen defended them as necessary steps toward security via conciliation. The "Locarno epoch" closed with the deaths of Briand and Stresemann. New friction developed over *Anschluss*, armaments, and treaty revisions in 1931–1932. French conciliatory gestures stopped at the point where equality in armaments and frontier revision began, for no French Government could permit any such enhancement of German power. Security demanded peace. Peace demanded the preservation of the *status quo* in its broad essentials. Preservation of the *status quo* demanded the maintenance of French hegemony. France was prepared to fight to maintain peace, *i.e.*, French ascendancy, rather than yield the fruits of victory.

Had this will to fight remained firm, all might yet have been well. Great Powers which show their willingness to fight usually preserve their security without having to fight. Only those unwilling to fight are condemned to fighting and defeat. The France of the 1920's was united in a resolve to fight the German Republic if Berlin should seek to rearm or to disrupt the French bloc on the Continent. The France of the early 1930's was willing neither to fight nor to make timely concessions to the crumbling democracy across the Rhine. Its leaders sought to substitute a hegemony of money for a hegemony of arms.

While German, British and American finances were tottering, France still had gold and a whip-hand in the money marts. The aging and feeble Briand was overshadowed by Pierre Laval, whose name, like his politics, read the same from left to right as from right to left. In 1931 this wealthy adventurer, who had the face and breadth of view of a sly pirate, helped to veto an Austro-German customs union. He haggled and quibbled over the suspension of German reparation payments, thereby discrediting Chancellor Brüning and driving desperate Germans to further desperation. By the middle 1930's the power which Paris had once wielded with so little wisdom was all but completely dissipated. Frenchmen, moreover, were hopelessly divided and paralyzed in their attitudes toward the militant Nazi despotism.

The Frenchmen of the Right who feared the poor admired Hitler and Mussolini for fighting "Communism" and keeping the poor in their place. The Frenchmen of the Left who feared the rich were sworn to "peace" and filled with deep suspicion of the wealthy. When either group urged action to protect

French interests, the other accused it of "interventionism," "war-mongering" and "treason." All were agreed that France must fight if France were invaded. But all could see that France behind the Maginot Line was as safe from invasion as America behind the Atlantic Ocean. All were equally agreed that enforcement of the Treaty of Versailles was not "worth a war." Nor Locarno. Nor Ethiopia, nor Spain, nor Austria, nor Czechoslovakia, nor Danzig. These were "other people's wars." In the end, with hearts heavy with doubt and fear, they decided (too late) that the blind, corrupt and divided Poland of Smigly-Rydz and Beck was "worth a war"—provided the war should be cheap and safe. The coroner of history could give but one verdict: death by suicide.

THE VICTORY OF DEFEATISM

The year 1933 inaugurated an epoch of disaster in French diplomacy. French refusal to act against the Third Reich drove Pilsudski into his nonaggression pact with Hitler in January, 1934. An unstable balance between political extremes in parliament rendered difficult the development of any strong French policy. A desire to secure British and Italian support against Germany inhibited action likely to alienate London or Rome. The rise of Fascism in France, represented in the *Croix de Feu* of François de La Rocque, in the followers of the renegade Communist Jacques Doriot, and in a variety of other groups, was a further source of confusion, as was the delayed but nevertheless damaging impact of the Great Depression on French economy.

The great issue before the Republic was no longer that of keeping a weak Germany in subjection, but that of preserving the remnants of security and checkmating a strong, rearmed, and defiant Reich. Could liberal France prevent the establishment of Nazi hegemony over the Continent? Could liberal France protect itself from domestic Fascism? Upon answers to these questions depended the future of the French position in the game of power and the future of the Republic itself as a democratic State.

La grande nation moved hesitantly and without clear guidance amid its new difficulties. Some positive steps were taken toward an affirmative answer to the questions posed. The "Maginot line"—a wall of steel and concrete, dotted with subterranean batteries and machine-gun nests—was rushed to completion along the German frontier. The Fascist riots in Paris on February 6, 1934, drew the powerful Socialist and Communist parties together into an anti-Fascist coalition, joined in January, 1936, by the large liberal party of the Radical Socialists. This "People's Front" frustrated the internal Fascist danger, at least temporarily.

In the diplomatic field, Foreign Minister Louis Barthou had moved to counterbalance the possible defection of Poland and the new might of Germany by a *rapprochement* with the U.S.S.R. In May, 1935, Franco-Soviet and Czech-Soviet mutual assistance pacts were signed. In the elections of April and May, 1936, the People's Front parties won a sweeping victory and put in power a Left Cabinet headed by the Socialist leader, Léon Blum. French democracy was apparently saved. French security was apparently assured. In August, 1936, General Gamelin, Chief of the French General Staff, visited Warsaw. In September, General Edward Smigly-Rydz, who had succeeded Marshal Pilsudski (d. May 12, 1935) as dictator of Poland, visited Paris. The alliance was reaffirmed in the face of Polish fears of Nazi militarism and French promises of new loans. Perhaps Poland was to be saved for the French bloc. The U.S.S.R. was a new ally. Belgium and the Little Entente seemingly remained bulwarks of French power.

But on October 9, 1934, Barthou and King Alexander of Jugoslavia had been assassinated at Marseille by a Croatian terrorist. This tragedy left France's ally on the Adriatic with a boy king, Peter II, and removed from the scene the only French foreign minister of great ability during the period of crisis. Pierre Laval, brought back to the Quai d'Orsay by Barthou's death, hesitated to ratify the Soviet Pact until Germany's *démarche* in March, 1936, compelled such action. Laval sought to conciliate Britain and Italy on the assumption that these Powers could be counted upon for support against Berlin. In order to placate Downing Street and "preserve peace," he acquiesced in German rearmament and supported Britain in imposing sanctions on Italy. In order to placate Rome and "preserve peace" he acquiesced in Italian designs on Ethiopia and undermined the League system of collective security. In the execution of this devious course, Paris fell between two stools. Rome and London were both alienated, Berlin was strengthened, and French power and prestige were diminished.

When on March 7, 1936, Hitler repudiated Locarno and remilitarized the Rhineland, the French General Staff perceived that effective military aid to Czechoslovakia or the U.S.S.R. in the event of Nazi aggression would be rendered impossible if Berlin were allowed to fortify the Rhine frontier. It urged French military occupation of the Rhineland, as was permitted by the Treaty of Versailles. But such a step would require expensive mobilization and would seem to threaten war. It would be highly unpopular in France and might lead to an open break with London. Weak-willed Gen. Maurice Gamelin did not insist. The Sarraut Cabinet consequently took no military action but limited itself to protests in accordance with the example set a year previously when the French Government acquiesced in Hitler's repudiation of the military clauses of the Treaty. The Blum Cabinet continued the same policy, hoping that French inaction in the Rhineland and French support of British initiative in deserting Ethiopia and abandoning sanctions against Italy would at least preserve an Anglo-French-Italian common front against Germany. Again the hope was vain. Britain refused to accept any commitments in central or eastern Europe. Mussolini at once reached an understanding with Hitler. The Quai d'Orsay was again betrayed by its own illusions.

The Little Entente was weakened by Czechoslovakia's relatively defenseless position and by growing German influence in the Balkans. On August 29, 1936, Nicholas Titulescu, for many years Rumanian Foreign Minister and a staunch advocate of solidarity with France, was forced out of office. The Jugoslav Government was also passing out of the French into the German orbit because Germany could supply a market for Jugoslav exports as France could not. Despite the efforts of President Eduard Beneš of Czechoslovakia, the Little Entente continued to languish. Belgrade and Bucharest, united to Prague only by fear of Hungarian revisionism, began to spin a web of pro-German and anti-Soviet intrigue. French power on the Danube was rapidly becoming a memory. That it survived at all was due to Mussolini's championship of Magyar dreams of *revanche*. Meanwhile, Belgium was also lost. On October 14, 1936, King Leopold, in response to pressure from Flemish sources and from the Fascist followers of the "Rexist" leader, Léon Degrelle, announced the termination of Belgium's military alliances and her return to pre-war neutrality. A Belgium rendered defenseless by French acquiescence in Nazi remilitarization of the Rhineland could scarcely be expected to remain France's ally. The French bloc was thus on the point of collapse before the Fascist diplomatic offensive.

BETRAYAL BY BLUM

If Laval personified the blindness of the conservative French plutocracy in the face of mortal danger from the Caesars, Blum personified the paralysis of French liberals and radicals in the face of the same danger. The Right would do nothing to halt the aggressors because it feared the Left more than it did the aggressors and hoped to make appeasement the means of protecting the class interests it represented. The Left would do nothing to halt the aggressors because its spokesmen were pacifists more interested in "social reforms" than in national security. The Right, moreover, threatened civil war if the Left should venture either to attack the privileges of the wealthy "200 families" or to translate its anti-Fascist convictions into diplomatic and military action.

On June 4, 1936, Léon Blum, leader of the French Socialist party, became Premier in a "People's Front" Cabinet of Radical Socialists and Socialists, supported in parliament by these parties plus their Communist allies against Fascism. When the Spanish "Popular Front" was violently attacked by the generals and the propertied classes, aided by the Axis, the Socialist deputies in the French Chamber declared their solidarity with the Loyalists on July 24. On the next day, however, Blum and Foreign Minister Yvon Delbos persuaded the Cabinet in the name of "peace" and "nonintervention" to forbid all arms shipments to Spain. In deference to Tory Britain and the pro-Franco parties of the Right, Blum appealed to the Powers on August 1 to adopt "common rules of nonintervention." On August 15, Britain and France put a formal arms embargo into effect at once. Other States adhered with a variety of qualifications. The farcical London "Nonintervention" Committee was set up. The betrayal of the Spanish Republic was launched. Blum's own followers protested bitterly and demanded, "Planes for Spain!" But Blum was imperturbable.

He told his supporters on September 6: "There is not a single piece of circumstantial evidence to show that the [nonintervention] agreement has been violated. Do you think my heart is not torn when I think what is happening down there in Spain? Undoubtedly the legal government that has arisen from the expression of universal suffrage, the government of the Spanish Republic, would assure us complete security on our Pyrenees frontier, while it is impossible to foresee the ambitions of the Rebel generals. On the one hand, safety; on the other, danger. But should we undertake a competition of armaments on Spanish soil? If certain Powers furnish arms and planes to the Rebels, should France furnish them to the Popular Front? . . . No."

FROM MADRID TO MUNICH

This decision was fatal not only to the Spanish Republic but to the French Republic. France was to fall not because of the People's Front "reforms," but because the diplomacy of the People's Front was identical with that of the extreme Right. The ensuing collaboration with the Axis in conquering Spain drove more nails into the coffin of France's eastern alliances and left *la grande nation* discredited. It also strengthened enormously the pro-Fascist element within France. In the autumn of 1937 a series of outrages revealed the existence of a "Secret Committee of Revolutionary Action," popularly known as the "*Cagoulards*," or Hooded Men, who were securing arms and money from Berlin and Rome to set up a Fascist Directory—to be headed by Jacques Doriot, Jean Chiappe, Pierre Laval, Maxime Weygand, and Henri Philippe Pétain. Exposure of the plot was hastily hushed up. Too many "respectable" personages in the army and in high finance were implicated.

Blum had been succeeded in the Premiership in June, 1937, by anti-Socialist Camille Chautemps of the Radical Socialists. To the Finance Ministry went the sly and sinister figure of Georges Bonnet. The Chautemps Cabinet fell on March 10, 1938. Blum tried in vain to form a new Ministry. On March 12 Hitler took Austria. Blum formed a cabinet on March 13—and did nothing. On April 8 he resigned once more. He was succeeded by the weak and ignoble leader of the Radical Socialists, Edouard Daladier who, like so many French politicians, began his public life as a radical (he was a baker's son) and finally acquired wealth and "wisdom" and therewith became first a conservative and later a reactionary. Daladier was to remain Premier of France until March, 1940. Although brought to power by the People's Front, he kept power with the support of the Right. His Foreign Minister (April 8, 1938–September 13, 1939) was Georges Bonnet. These two men were destined to bring France and the Republic to destruction.

Munich was the symbol of their folly. They made the Quai d'Orsay completely subservient to Chamberlain's designs. They dreaded war or threats of war to save Czechoslovakia because any such war would have to be fought against Fascism in the name of democracy and the People's Front and, *horrible dictu*, in alliance with Moscow. Bonnet publicly pledged support of Prague and privately worked for an entente with Hitler at Prague's expense. He denied (falsely) that France could rely on British support. He exaggerated the weakness of the French Army to London. He alleged (falsely) that Litvinov was abandoning Beneš. He cooperated with Pierre Etienne-Flandin (who sent Hitler a congratulatory telegram after the "peace") and with the defeatest press of the Right, much of it in the pay of the Axis. Bribed journalists denounced Prague and Moscow, and shouted over and again to a befuddled public, "No war for Czechoslovakia."

On his return from Munich, Daladier feared that the crowd at the airport might denounce him for betraying France. But it had come to cheer the "savior of peace." He was joined by Bonnet and Gamelin. All were praised as heroes for having thrown away the victory of 1918 for which a million and a half Frenchmen had died. Gamelin was silent when a visitor remarked, "General, you have just lost 35 divisions!"—the Czech army. "I accept my popularity," declared Daladier, "with the modesty that is only one of the forms my duty takes." Blum, in a mood he admitted was "cowardly relief," rejoiced that "peace was saved." Winston Churchill's judgment was more accurate: "France and Britain had to choose between war and dishonor. They chose dishonor. They will have war."

TOWARD WAR

Bonnet and Daladier moved after Munich to surrender the Continent to Hitler's fancied *Drang nach Osten,* to wage war at home against "Communism," and to undermine the social reforms of the French "New Deal." Labor resisted and ordered a one-day general strike on November 30. It was broken. Daladier declared he had saved France from Bolshevism. On December 6, 1938, Bonnet signed with Ribbentrop a declaration of "pacific and good neighborly relations." "It is the struggle against Bolshevism," wrote Bonnet a week later, "which is essentially at the basis of the common German and Italian political conception and, without saying so formally, Ribbentrop perhaps wished to give us to understand that there is no other objective to be attributed to it. In regard to Spain, it is again the struggle against Bolshevism which alone has inspired the German effort from the beginning." Ambassador Robert Coulondre in Berlin agreed: "To secure mastery over Central Europe by reducing Czecho-Slovakia and Hungary to a state of vassalage and then to create a Great Ukraine under German control—this is what essentially appears to be the leading idea now accepted by the Nazi leaders" (*French Yellow Book of* 1939, No. 33). Bonnet and Daladier were willing.

When Hitler yielded Carpatho-Ukraine to Hungary on March 16, 1939, immediately after the occupation of Prague, the last leaders of a doomed nation awakened belatedly to their error. "Will the Führer," asked Coulondre on March 19, "be tempted to return to the idea expressed by the author of *Mein Kampf* which, be it said, is identical with the classic doctrine held by the German General Staff, according to which Germany cannot accomplish her high destiny in the East until France has been crushed and, as a conse-

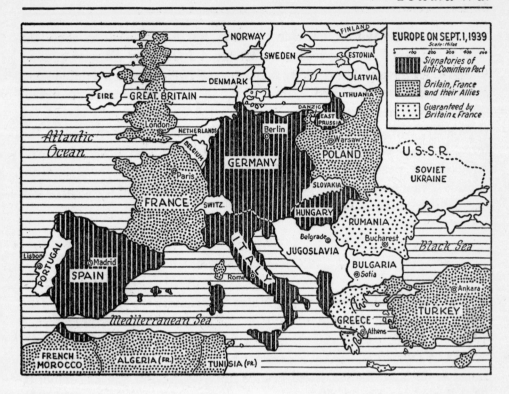

quence, Britain reduced to impotence on the Continent? . . . The Reich will
first turn against the Western Powers" (*ibid.*, No. 80). Paris joined London in
belated effort to reconstruct the coalition which had been thrown away. The
result was reaffirmation of the Polish alliance, support of Britain in guaranteeing Rumania and Greece, and the conclusion on June 23, 1939, of a
French-Turkish alliance, paid for by the cession of Hatay to Ankara.

But many of the Rightists were furious at such moves. "Danzig," screamed
Marcel Deat in the bought Paris press, "is not worth a war." "Danzig," wrote
Flandin on May 7, "is merely an episode of the revision of the peace treaty. If
there were a new world war, in which Germany would doubtless be defeated,
the German people would probably become Communist. If the present crisis
continues, revolution will come." The Quai d'Orsay, no less than Downing
Street, was unwilling to pay Stalin's price for a new alliance against the Reich.
The result was the collapse of the "peace front," followed by the Nazi-Soviet
Pact and the coming of war.

At the end, Bonnet made one last effort to arrange another Munich. On
September 1–2, 1939, he accepted Italian proposals for "peace" through a
conference, with German troops remaining where they were on Polish soil.

He declined to join London in a common warning to Berlin and insisted upon separate action. Daladier vacillated but told Parliament on Saturday afternoon (September 2) that France must not abandon its ally. The Chambers voted a war budget and gave the Cabinet implied authority to declare war. Halifax insisted that there could be no conference without a cessation of the *Blitzkrieg* and German evacuation of Poland. The French Cabinet agreed. Bonnet reluctantly assented. Ciano replied that, since Hitler was unwilling to accept the condition, no further action could be taken.

At 10.20 Sunday morning, Bonnet wired Coulondre of "the decision of the French Government" and instructed him to present an ultimatum at noon and to inform the Wilhelmstrasse in the event of a negative reply that Paris would be "compelled to fulfill as from today September 3 at 5 p.m. the engagements France entered into towards Poland." The British ultimatum was delivered at 9 and was followed by war at 11 a.m. At 11.20 Ribbentrop submitted a contemptuous note of rejection to Henderson. At 12.30 the Nazi Foreign Minister received Coulondre and told him that if France attacked the Reich "this would be on her part a war of aggression." At 5 p.m., September 3, 1939, war began between France and Germany. Bonnet had failed. He was obliged to yield the Quai d'Orsay to Daladier ten days later and content himself with the Ministry of Justice.

DÉBÂCLE

The Third French Republic entered upon its last war under leaders who were utterly inept. Its citizens were confused, baffled, and hopelessly divided against themselves. "Passive defense" was thought to be cheap in money and lives and was expected to save the State. No one was enthusiastic for war against the foe across the Rhine. Daladier, however, developed much enthusiasm for war against radicalism at home. On September 26, he decreed the dissolution of the Communist party and thereafter devoted much energy to combatting the "Reds." Bonnet schemed with Laval and Adrien Marquet to end the war and resume appeasement. After the outbreak of fighting in Finland, Daladier, Gamelin, and Weygand laid plans for war—not against Germany, but against the U.S.S.R. The collapse of Allied policy in Finland, however, led to a parliamentary vote of nonconfidence on March 19, 1940. Daladier resigned but retained the Defense Ministry in the new cabinet of Paul Reynaud. Bonnet was out. Reynaud had long been anti-Munichois and therefore anathema to the Right and to many of the Radical Socialists. "I have come too early," he remarked. He secured a majority of only one vote in his first test in the Chamber on March 21. He nevertheless decided to carry on.

In reality, Reynaud had come too late. Even he was self-defeated. He realized Gamelin's incompetence but was obliged by political considerations to keep Daladier in the Cabinet—and Daladier insisted on Gamelin's retention. Reynaud's friend, the Countess Hélène de Portes, moreover, was a defeatist and a friend of Munichman Paul Baudouin. Reynaud and Daladier quarrelled violently during the Nazi conquest of the Northlands and the Low Countries. Gamelin had no plan for meeting the *Blitzkrieg* save "Win or Die." All his calculations were based on the belief that the Maginot Line was impregnable. Years before, Reynaud had urged in vain the thesis of Charles de Gaulle, an obscure officer who had been denied promotion by the conservative General Staff, that German tanks and planes could break through the line near Sedan and that France must have armored divisions and a powerful air force to meet the threat. They were not available.

On May 18, Reynaud formed a new cabinet, putting Daladier at the Quai d'Orsay and appointing as Vice Premier the eighty-four-year-old Marshal Henri Philippe Pétain. He also took into the Cabinet the ultra-Rightists Louis Marin and Jean Ybarnégary, Vice President of the Fascist *Croix de Feu*. On May 19, he dismissed Gamelin and made seventy-three-year-old General Maxime Weygand Commander in Chief. These men were all clerical reactionaries, Anglophobes, anti-Bolsheviks, enemies of the Republic, and warm admirers of Franco and Mussolini if not of Hitler. If France was to be saved, it would not be by such artisans of disaster as these.

But France was now beyond saving. On June 5, as the full force of the invaders struck south from the Somme, Reynaud dropped Daladier and named Charles de Gaulle as Undersecretary at the War Ministry. Hélène persuaded him to name Baudouin as Undersecretary at the Quai d'Orsay. Weygand was baffled. His armies were overwhelmed. "A modern retreat," he observed, "has no limits." The Cabinet fled to Tours (June 11–14) and then to Bordeaux. Weygand alleged (falsely) that Communists were "rioting" in abandoned Paris prior to the German occupation and that the Cabinet must surrender to "save France from Bolshevism." Pétain, Chautemps, Baudouin agreed, as did Bonnet, Laval, and Flandin. To move to London or to North Africa, to carry on the war with the fleet and the colonies and the unbroken might of the British Empire would have been quite feasible. But the Munichmen gave Britain up for lost and preferred surrender for reasons of class interest.

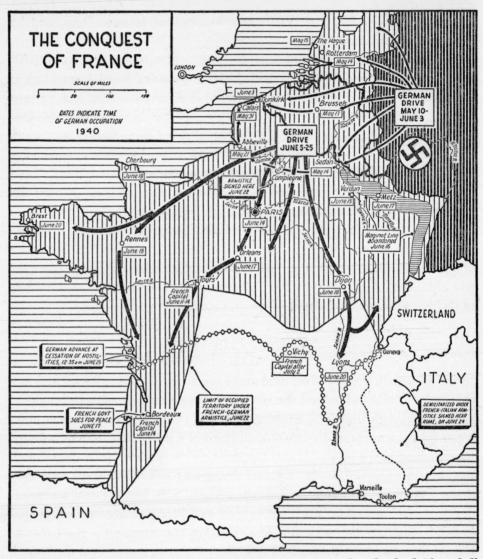

THE CONQUEST
OF FRANCE

SCALE OF MILES

DATES INDICATE TIME
OF GERMAN OCCUPATION
1940

Reynaud appealed in vain for immediate American aid and asked Churchill to release France from the engagement of March 28 not to make a separate peace. Churchill asked that the French fleet should first be dispatched to British ports. On June 16, he offered "Union Now" to Reynaud. But the capitulators won a majority in the Cabinet at Bordeaux the same evening. Reynaud resigned. He was later injured and Hélène killed in a motor accident. In August, he was arrested and imprisoned, along with Daladier, Gamelin, Blum, Mandel, and others, to be tried for "treason" by those who had betrayed France. Meanwhile, President Albert Lebrun named Pétain Premier,

Baudouin Foreign Minister, and Laval Minister of Justice. They sued for peace at once through Franco.

The anemic France of 1940 died with little bloodshed. Perhaps 150,000 French soldiers were slain or wounded by the foe—and by their own lack of weapons, by the incompetence or treason of their commanders, and by their own unwillingness to fight for a cause already betrayed by their leaders. Under the machine-guns and bombs of Nazi flyers some tens of thousands of civilian refugees—who will ever know how many?—perished when they abandoned their homes in panic flight and jammed the roads that should have been kept clear for the defenders of France. Despite these horrors, the Blitzkrieg was sparing in lives. The conquest of France was less the work of Nazi arms than of the poisoned words of the French preachers of "peace" in the years before the storm. The France of 1914–1918 lost a million and a half of its sons. But it saved its soul. The France of the appeasers, long before the war of 1940, sold its birthright and its heart and mind for the counterfeit coin of its own illusions.

PEACE BY PÉTAIN

In the aftermath the Republic died and France perished as a Power and as a free State. Pétain authorized the signature of an armistice with Germany on June 22 and with Italy on June 24. At Vichy, to which the Cabinet moved, a rump Parliament committed suicide in favor of a projected "totalitarianism." Pétain assumed the powers of the President and became "Chief of State" with Royalist trappings. *Liberté, Egalité, Fraternité* were outlawed. The very name "Republic" was abolished. Laval became Vice Premier and successor-designate in a triumvirate with Weygand and Marquet. He was committed to full "collaboration" with the Axis. Fearing the worst with good reason, Churchill ordered the British fleet to destroy the principal units of the French navy at Oran, Morocco, on July 3. Vichy severed diplomatic relations with London. On October 22, 1940, Hitler and Ribbentrop conferred with Laval near Paris and on October 23 with Franco near the Spanish frontier. Pétain, accompanied by Laval, conferred with Hitler, Ribbentrop, and Keitel at Montoire near Tours on October 25. On the next day, Pétain made Laval Foreign Minister and announced "collaboration" with the Reich.

Thanks to continued British resistance, however, there were difficulties. Laval overreached himself and failed to convert Pétain and Weygand (who went to North Africa) to his view that Vichy should join the Axis in war

[155]

against Britain. On December 13, Pétain dismissed Laval from all his posts and named Flandin Foreign Minister. Otto Abetz, German Commissioner to France, went to Vichy to demand "explanations" but received little satisfaction despite threats of a Nazi military occupation of all of France. Berlin had ample means of carrying out such a threat but hesitated to do so lest the remnants of the French fleet and the French forces in Africa might openly join the British cause.

What future awaited the strange regime at the *Hotel du Parc* amid Vichy's bubbling waters? What future awaited France? "What we ask at this moment," said Churchill in a broadcast to the French people in October, "in our struggle to win the victory which we will share with you, is that if you cannot help us, at least you will not hinder us. Remember, we shall never stop, never weary, and never give in, and that our whole people and Empire have bowed themselves to the task of cleansing Europe from the Nazi pestilence and saving the world from a new Dark Ages."

Most of the honest and simple people of France prayed in secret for a Nazi defeat. But in the anguish of their black despair, many were ensnared by the propaganda of their own betrayers. And the "government" of France was a committee of traitors, each of whom knew full well that his very life depended upon a Nazi victory over Britain.

THE WAY OF THE VICHYMEN

This stark fact of political biology was the clue to all of Vichy's acts. Pétain's crew of Munichmen did not debate among themselves as to how far they ought to go in resisting Nazi demands, for most of them had long been Hitler's bondsmen. They debated only how far they could dare to go in asking their bewildered subjects to fight Britain at Hitler's behest. Laval urged full military collaboration. Pétain and Weygand felt that economic collaboration would win them comparable benefits in the Führer's New Order with less risk of disrupting from within the Fascist France they were trying to build. Under German pressure the vain and bigoted Marshal conferred in January with the greasy Laval. But their "reconciliation" was brief. Laval asked too much. Pétain established a "National Council" of stooges, each personally answerable to the Chief of State, and created a totalitarian *Rassemblement Nationale* to supersede the political parties.

After some weeks of obscure intrigues, Pétain dismissed Flandin on February 9, 1941, and named his Naval Minister, Jean François Darlan, as Vice-Premier, Foreign Minister and successor-designate to the Chief of State. This Anglophobe Admiral was more useful to Berlin than was Laval. He could manage the doddering "hero of Verdun" more gracefully. He and his colleagues lost no time in pressing on with their task of undoing the work of the Great Revolution. They made clericalism, totalitarianism and anti-Semitism the pillars of their domestic program. As for foreign affairs, their watch-words were "economic collaboration" with the Reich in "the spirit of Montoire." French industry passed into Nazi hands, completely as to control and partially as to ownership, and was geared to the war machine of the conqueror.

London and Washington long closed their eyes to the ultimate consequences of this course. Neither Churchill nor Roosevelt was prepared to grant recognition to De Gaulle and his aides as the government-in-exile of the true France. They preferred a mixed policy of appeasement and threats to minimize (so they hoped) Vichy's collaboration with Hitler. Admiral William Leahy, United States Ambassador, warned and pleaded. Robert Murphy, first secretary of the American Embassy, visited Weygand in Africa and promised food for Algeria and Morocco if Weygand and Pétain would resist Nazi demands. When Darlan threatened to use his navy to convoy foodstuffs unless the British blockade was relaxed, Washington sent food cargoes to Marseille. Even oil was permitted to flow to Vichy territory. Here, as always, the fruits of appeasement were bitter.

PUPPET DANCE

The game of the Vichymen was to deceive London and Washington as long as possible and then join Hitler in striking blows against Britain and America. Deception, if successful, would bring to French ports Allied and American shipments useful to the Reichswehr. It would also enable Vichy to buttress its colonial outposts for eventual attack against the Führer's foes. Collaboration would lead Hitler to curb Mussolini's anti-French ambitions and would bring the reward of a favored place in a Nazi world.

In a radio plea for unity early in April, 1941, Pétain solemnly avowed that "honor" forbade any action against "our former allies." A month later Darlan conferred with Nazi envoys in Paris and returned full of plans. Berlin graciously agreed to relax restrictions on traffic between the two zones, to reduce by 25% the costs ($8,000,000 per day) of maintaining the forces of occupation, and to release 100,000 of the almost two million French war prisoners held by the Reich. No *quid pro quo* was announced. But certain articles of the armistice, said Vichy, would be modified "in a spirit of mutual comprehension."

This mystery was not long left unsolved. Veteran Munichman Fernand de Brinon, Vichy's emissary to the German authorities in Paris, warned American pressmen early in May that any United States occupation of Dakar would be resisted. "It is the common duty of the European nations to organize for the defense of the common interests of Europe." Three days later Darlan saw Hitler and Ribbentrop. Plans were perfected. Pétain gave his blessing and ignored warnings from Washington. "For you, French people," he told his subjects, "it is simply a question of following me without mental reservations along the path of honor and national interest. If through our close discipline and our public spirit we can conduct the negotiations in progress, France will surmount her defeat and preserve in the world her rank as a European and colonial Power."

Roosevelt replied at once with an appeal to the French people not to support Vichy in its course: "It is inconceivable that they will willingly accept any agreement for so-called 'collaboration' which will in reality imply their alliance with a military Power whose central and fundamental policy calls for the utter destruction of liberty, freedom and popular institutions everywhere." But the Vichymen were not to be moved by words from Washington. In Syria General Henri Fernand Dentz welcomed Nazi flyers on their way to Iraq. Vichy hinted at armed action to recover the African colonies held by the forces of De Gaulle. Darlan defended collaboration in the "New Order" but denied that Hitler had asked for the French fleet or for colonial territories or for a declaration of war on Britain. In Paris, which resembled Coleridge's haunted ocean where "slimy things did crawl with legs upon the slimy sea," Laval publicly warned the United States not to enter the war.

HESITATION WALTZ

In the sequel to the May days of 1941, however, the Vichy apostles of "honor" shrank from doing what they had originally planned. Darlan was opposed by Weygand, warned by Hull, threatened by Churchill, and doubtless advised to make haste slowly by his lord and master. Hitler was preparing to defer his proposed campaigns in Africa and the Near East in favor of his assault on Russia. When British and Free French forces invaded Syria in June, Vichy asserted that it would defend the mandate, but gave assurances via Madrid that it would not spread or aggravate the conflict with Britain. Darlan denounced De Gaulle and the Communists and insisted that Vichy's task was to "prepare for France's future in a new Europe" and to "create an atmosphere favorable to the establishment of an honorable peace."

But Pétain, like his good friend Franco, was a ruler of a vanquished and embittered people. He could not risk general war with Britain and open defiance of America so long as Hitler's men and machines were busy in eastern Europe. The Syrian hostilities were accordingly "localized." Vichy's chagrin at the eventual loss of the mandate was assuaged by new anti-Semitic measures at home and by ardent support of the Führer's crusade against Moscow. Diplomatic relations with the U.S.S.R. were severed. Some thousands of "volunteers" were recruited and armed to join Hitler's divisions in "saving Europe from Bolshevism." But this, as Vichy well knew, was collaboration *Ersatz*. Genuine collaboration against Britain and America must wait upon Russia's defeat.

Vichy's cup of shame was meanwhile filled anew to overflowing. Despite loud outcries that all French colonies would be defended to the death against all comers, another colony was yielded abjectly to the aggressors at Berlin's behest. Northern Indo-China had been occupied by Japanese forces—at Berlin's order and with Vichy's "consent"—in September of the year of defeat. At the end of July, in the year of disgrace, Vichy surrendered the rest of the colony to the Tokyo warlords behind a thin façade of "temporary" occupation and the alleged need of "defending" Indo-China against Anglo-American "aggression." The bought press of occupied Paris, reflecting the views of Laval, Ribbentrop & Co., demanded that French Africa be similarly "defended" by an agreement providing Nazi "protection."

INTO THE NIGHT

When, in the second year of the conquest, the leaves began yellowing and falling one by one into the melancholy streets of Paris, the men of Vichy found their prospects growing bleak. They dared not act as Hitler's open allies. They dared not refuse to act. They gave feeble explanations to Washington and pondered how best they could serve the Reich. And then, of a sudden, they heard an all but inaudible whisper from the grave. They sensed with dread that the people of their desolate land were at last beginning to stir from their coma and to give new voice to the spirit of the France of old.

On the 12th day of August Pétain named Darlan Minister of National Defense, the better to "protect" France and the colonies. The Marshal simultaneously issued a long appeal for support, deploring "unrest" and "confusion," and demanding "unity" and "obedience." Collaboration and the "National Revolution," he conceded, had not yet borne their full fruits. Germany was busy in the east "in defense of civilization." He denounced Freemasonry and the political parties. He declared their leaders would be "decimated." He attacked "trusts" and "capitalism" and "the most despicable tutelage of money." Public opinion, he complained, "is today divided" and is not always "favorable or fair" to Darlan. But "authority no longer emanates from below. Today I wish to save you from yourselves."

Parties were forbidden to hold meetings. Payment of members of Parliament was suspended. High degree Masons were banned from public functions. The police were reinforced. "Commissars of public power" were named to ferret out secret societies and oppositionists. Special courts were set up for political offenders. All higher officials were required to swear an oath of fealty to Pétain. He opened the ranks of the "French Legion of War Veterans," now groomed as the tool of one-party rule, to all who would support his regime. "The only authority," he said, "is that which I entrust or delegate. Those who are not with me are against me."

But repression bred resentment. Acts of sabotage increased. Rioting broke out in Paris. A German officer was stabbed to death in a subway. Thousands of Jews and "Communists" were arrested. In the unoccupied zone Darlan's minions copied the deeds of the Gestapo and the Schutzstaffel. By imperceptible stages the Vichy rule of fraud became a rule of terror, for a people no longer willing to be drugged with lies must be kept in chains by force.

Force was available in abundance, for the Nazi conquerors could not allow the authority of their puppets to be openly flouted. But the timeless France of yesterday and tomorrow is brave and proud, even in defeat. She responds badly to those who show their love by beating her. Vichy, moreover, had value to Berlin only as a symbol to make the work of subjugation and exploitation easier. A Vichy ruling only by violence would be useless. The "correct" behavior of the Reichswehr and the "honor" of Pétain would alike fail to win allegiance if any considerable number of Frenchmen became hopeful of an eventual Nazi defeat.

The tragic farce of the 26th of August sounded the somber notes of a larger drama. At Versailles the "French Legion of Volunteers to Combat Bolshevism," to which a few thousand young men were drawn by good pay, held a morning parade and rally. Its members were soon to depart for Poland where the Reichswehr would provide training for service on the Russian front. Prominent Nazis, both German and French, took part in the ceremonies at the barracks, among them Pierre Laval, Fernand de Brinon and Marcel Deat, leader of the Nazified Paris press. As the gathering dispersed, after the supreme mockery of singing the Marseillaise, five shots rang out. Laval and Deat were gravely wounded. The would-be assassin was Paul Colette, a volunteer from Normandy, who explained that he had joined the Legion to "bring down some collaborationist, no matter who."

German surgeons saved the lives of the victims. Pétain in Vichy did not hear the news till evening. He was attending a performance of "The Damnation of Faust"—who alone among the many old men who have sold their souls to the devil received the reward of the restoration of his youth. All the Vichymen trembled, while Darlan's men and Himmler's men rounded up other members of the Legion and alleged the existence of a terror-plot on the part of Jews, Bolshevists and De Gaullists. The guillotine and the firing squad were soon at work. The Gestapo executed innocent hostages for every new attack on German troops. But the attacks increased in a rising rhythm of vengeance and terror.

In France, as in Poland, Czechoslovakia and Jugoslavia, the victors and their stooges were slipping toward a morass of murders, reprisals, tortures and executions, generating such hatred for all things German, and for all who served the Germans, as even France had never known before. In the fury to come the hopes of the "National Revolution" and of the Nazi "New Order" might both be lost—unless Britons and Russians could be brought to swift defeat.

THE REBIRTH OF FRANCE

Whatever the final fate of Hitler's dreams might be, the regime of the Vichymen, with its aura of cheap lies copied feebly from Berlin, was but a passing phantom. Would the Nazi Reich win its war and conquer the planet? France would then become a German province. Pétain's fawning sycophants, then no longer useful to the Führer, would be dismissed and perhaps jailed for their pains. Would the Reich be ultimately crushed by Britain, Russia and America? The Vichy traitors would then be shot by outraged Frenchmen.

The vision of the France to come was obscured by the fog of war and all but lost in the long anguish of a people who had permitted their isolationists and appeasers to bring them to ruin. Yet one symbol of hope stood high and clear: General Charles de Gaulle. During World War I, this tall young soldier from Lille was thrice wounded while serving in Pétain's regiment before Verdun. He was once captured and several times decorated for character and valor. After serving under Weygand in Poland in 1920 he taught military history at Saint-Cyr and later at l'École de Guerre where he developed with prophetic genius his theories of mechanized warfare. He predicted in 1934 exactly how and where the Reichswehr would outflank the Maginot Line and conquer France if France should fail to acquire armored divisions and bombing squadrons. France failed. "The defender," he had written, "who limits himself to resisting in a fixed position with antiquated weapons is doomed to disaster."

When disaster arrived, De Gaulle was called by Reynaud (too late) to become Undersecretary of War. When he failed in his efforts to prevent the capitulation, he went to London and became leader of the "Free French"— for which Vichy condemned him to death in absentia. His mission was to rally Frenchmen everywhere to his banner (the tricolor with Jeanne d'Arc's double-barred cross of Lorraine) and to win as many of the French colonies as possible to his cause. In the summer of 1940 Tahiti and the New Hebrides in the far Pacific rallied to his leadership, as well as the Cameroons and French Equatorial Africa from Lake Chad to the Congo. His attack on Dakar in late September failed, thanks largely to British bungling in permitting the passage through Gibraltar of Vichy warships for Dakar's defense. But his troops fought well and tasted victory in the Libyan, East African and Syrian campaigns. By mid-summer of 1941 Syria was in his hands and his scattered forces numbered 50,000 men, 20 warships and 60 merchantmen.

Around this modest fighter France itself might rally when and if the hour of French deliverance should strike. Perhaps he was destined to found the Fourth French Republic. If not he, then some civilian leader of a resurrected democracy, aided by his troops. But before resurrection would be possible, before France could again become a united nation, worthy of its past, a great cleansing would be needed, probably by blood and fire. From the ashes might arise a new France. Meanwhile, in the long darkness of defeat, the men and women of the dead Republic drank shame and tasted despair. They had loved peace not wisely but too well. They had cherished their way of life too little to risk their lives to keep it. They had abandoned Europe to save France. They had therefore lost France and lost peace and their happiness as well. Only when they should again rediscover their souls and relearn the duties of wisdom and courage would France deserve a future.

"Flamingoes and mustard," said the Duchess, "both bite. And the moral of that is—'Birds of a feather flock together.'" "Only mustard isn't a bird," Alice remarked. "Right, as usual," said the Duchess: "what a clear way you have of putting things!" "It's a mineral, I think," said Alice. "Of course it is," said the Duchess, who seemed ready to agree to everything that Alice said. "There's a large mustard-mine near here. And the moral of that is—'The more there is of mine, the less there is of yours.'" "Oh, I know!" exclaimed Alice, who had not attended to this last remark. "It's a vegetable. It doesn't look like one, but it is." "I quite agree with you," said the Duchess; "and the moral of that is—'Be what you would seem to be'—or, if you'd like it put more simply—'Never imagine yourself not to be otherwise than what it might appear to others that what you were or might have been was not otherwise than what you had been would have appeared to them to be otherwise.'"

NOT TO BE

The agony of England, like the martyrdom of France, was self-inflicted. It flowed from a long series of tragic blunders and dishonesties on the part of the business men and land-owners who ruled the kingdom. They sought peace and prosperity (and lost both) by "minding their own business" and "keeping out of other people's wars." They thus proved incapable either of understanding their own interests or of defending the nation they were sworn to protect. If Waterloo was "won on the playing fields of Eton," it was no less true a dozen decades later that Madrid, Vienna, Prague, Warsaw, Oslo, Paris, Dunkirk and Athens were lost there. The short-sightedness of the "upper classes," and of the sons of the wealthy who came from the highly private "public schools," was far more responsible for what befell the realm than the ignorance or provincialism of the poor. "Petty minds and a great empire," once observed Edmund Burke, "go ill together."

In England there was not, as in France, any colorful Communist movement to frighten people of means. There was no important Socialist movement, for the Labor party remained politically impotent after its betrayal by Ramsay MacDonald. The forces of political Liberalism were feeble. During all of a dismal decade, Britain's destiny was entrusted by a confused electorate to the ultra-Tory wing of the Conservative party which dominated without challenge the catastrophic "National Government" of 1931. This regime of blind men made way for other leadership only on the brink of irreparable disaster in May, 1940. The disaster was the fruit of its toil.

The central error of Tory politics was to ignore a principle to which all wise British statesmen had adhered for many centuries: that of preserving a balance of power on the Continent by giving diplomatic and military support to the neighbors and possible victims of the most powerful Continental State. To permit any one Power to control the Continent had always been deemed highly dangerous to the British Isles and to its far-flung colonies and dominions. To prevent any such development, England had waged war upon the Spain of Philip II, the France of Louis XIV and Napoleon I, and the Germany of Wilhelm II. Only when a stable equipoise of rivals prevailed across the Channel could Britain safely follow a course of "splendid isolation." Such was the case between 1815 and 1904. When the growing power and ambition of the Second Reich threatened domination of the Continent, Britain joined forces with France and Russia to checkmate Berlin. This combination, even when joined by Japan and Italy, proved inadequate to defeat Imperial Germany. Only the addition of the United States made possible the victory of 1918. In the twenty years which followed, the leaders of Britain threw that victory away and finally permitted the Third Reich to enhance its power to a point at which it was able to conquer the Continent and menace Britain with destruction.

The question of why Britain's leaders so completely forgot the lessons of the past and brought upon their people so painful an aftermath of folly admits of various relevant answers, none of them having much relationship to the "explanations" offered by the chief actors during the years of retreat. In terms of *Realpolitik*, Britain after Versailles could have found security either by putting an end for all time to the Continental and world balance of power through giving full support to an effective League of Nations or by reverting to a policy of supporting the weaker Continental Powers against the stronger. The former policy would have required the assumption of far-reaching commitments of collective security and a firm resolve to honor all such obligations. The latter policy would have required enforcement of the military clauses of Versailles to prevent the rebuilding of a German war machine or, if this was not to be, then at least full British support of France, Poland, and the Little Entente and a *rapprochement* with the U.S.S.R. as a means of checkmating the Axis. Downing Street followed neither of these courses. It supported the League in a halfhearted manner and finally sacrificed it on the altar of appeasement. It supported Republican Germany in feeble fashion against the France of Poincaré and subsequently supported the Third Reich against the France of Barthou and Blum, meanwhile alienating the Soviet Union and firmly declining all obligations to defend Vienna, Prague, or Warsaw.

This policy, suicidal in its consequences and mad or muddled in its motivation, was not primarily a product of popular isolationism or pacifism, although these sentiments won public support for a program which otherwise might have been repudiated. The Tory line had a logic of its own in *Realpolitik*, albeit one seldom acknowledged. That logic presupposed that the great protagonists of the future would be Japan and the U.S.S.R. in Asia and the Reich and the U.S.S.R. in Europe. If these Powers were likely to checkmate one another and ultimately engage in a death grapple, Britain could well afford to stand aloof and to protect itself from involvement by pressing France to abandon the allies which stood in the way of the German drive to the East. If world revolutionary Communism, moreover, was the gravest of menaces to the British ruling classes and to the integrity of the Empire, and if the Fascist Triplice promised to hold the menace in check, Britain could well afford to boycott the U.S.S.R. and lend comfort to Hitler, Hirohito, and Mussolini. If the Triplice should attack and conquer the Soviet Union, it might, to be sure, become a danger to the Empire. But this danger was envisaged as negligible by comparison with the danger to the Empire of any extension of Communism beyond the Soviet frontiers or any major enhancement of the power of the Soviet State. Hence the wisdom of appeasement.

DEVICES OF COLONEL BLIMP

The only difficulty with this logic was that its premises were tragically false. If it be asked how so experienced and astute a group of men as ruled the world's greatest empire from Downing Street could have been so completely mistaken in their basic presuppositions about world politics, the only answer is that this group had come by the 1930's to reflect not the high political wisdom which had so often in the past enabled Britain to survive and prosper, but rather the narrow provincialism, class prejudices, and naïve ignorance of Tory squires, international financiers, and business men from the Midlands. David Low's immortal cartoon character, Colonel Blimp, thought of *Weltpolitik* as a cricket game or a bargain counter. That it might be a fox hunt with himself as the fox never occurred to him. He was for "peace," against "foreign entanglements," apoplectic about Russia, half envious of Mussolini and Hitler, contemptuous of all "nonsense" about "collective security," and whole-heartedly devoted to "muddling through," Scotch and soda, and "business as usual." He loved pudgy Stanley Baldwin with his pipe and pigs. He respected lank and cadaverous Neville Chamberlain who left his father's screw business in Birmingham to bring balm to a troubled world. He stoutly and stubbornly denounced all those who argued that these attitudes would spell the ruin of his nation and his class in a world vastly changed and increasingly dominated by ruthless demagogue-despots whose fondest secret dream was the destruction of the British Empire.

Colonel Blimp found the atmosphere congenial in such places as Cliveden, country estate of Lord Astor who owned *The Observer* (edited by J. L. Garvin), whose brother Major John Jacob Astor owned the *Times,* and whose wife, Lady Nancy, sat in Commons and entertained other lords and ladies, along with "interesting" foreigners and intellectuals, at luncheon parties and pleasant week-end gatherings. Sir Montagu Norman, Governor of the Bank of England, was of like mind. So were many of the greater industrialists of the Midlands and the financiers of the City. So were the magnates of the yellow press, Lord Beaverbrook and Lord Rothermere. (The latter for a time openly championed Sir Oswald Mosley's British Black Shirts.) So were Dean Inge of St. Paul's, the Archbishop of Canterbury, many High Churchmen, Anglo-Catholics, and a host of others. "I often think," sighed Lord Halifax, "how much easier the world would have been to manage if Herr Hitler and Signor Mussolini had chanced to have been at Oxford." Multitudes of "Little Englanders" and isolationists cherished a picture of the world which led to similar conclusions. Such Laborite pacifists as George Lansbury and James Maxton helped to educate the masses to the necessity of seeking peace with tyrants through appeasement. Of such materials was Britain's bitterest tragedy fabricated.

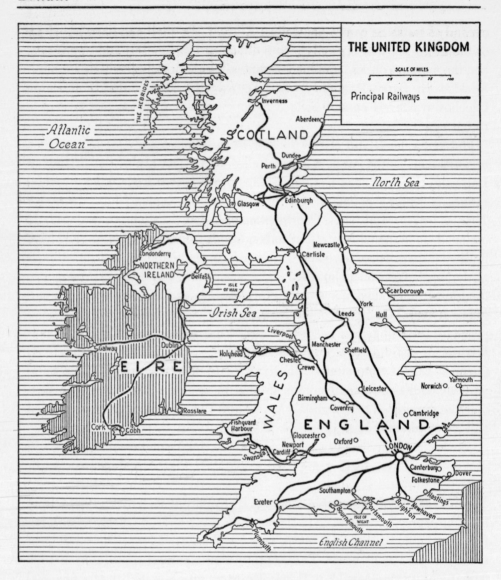

Tory politicians, large and small, looked without seeing and listened without hearing. Said Sir Thomas Moore, M.P. for Ayr Burghs, in 1933: "If I may judge from my personal knowledge of Herr Hitler, peace and justice are the key-words of his policy. Germany should be given back her old colonies in West Africa." Sir Arnold Wilson, M.P. for Hitchin, said in 1934: "There is no militarism in Germany. There is almost no Great Power with which we are less likely to become involved in war than Germany." Thus Annesley Somerville, M.P. for Windsor, after the fall of Prague: "Let Herr Hitler expand as far as he can in South-East Europe. We shall still have our share of the trade. He will certainly create difficulties for himself and opposition, and the more we oppose him the less difficult that opposition will be for him." Admiral Sir Barry Domvile quoted approvingly Mussolini's comment on Czechoslovakia: "I cannot believe Europe will set itself on fire to cook a rotten egg."

Plutocrats, lords and clerics flocked with dignified enthusiasm into such organizations as the Anglo-German Fellowship, "The Link," the Friends of Italy, and the Friends of National Spain. Opined Lord Redesdale: "General Franco is leading a crusade for all that they in England hold dear." Sir Thomas Inskip, Minister for Coordination of Defense, held that Britain should not insist upon the withdrawal of Italian troops from Spain "before they have finished the work they were sent there to do." Lord Mount Temple, at a dinner of the Anglo-German Fellowship: "Unity is essential and the real danger to the world today does not come from Germany or Italy but from Russia." Major Astor's *Times* contended in 1937: "The peace-minded can best serve peace for the moment by ceasing to agitate themselves and others with morbid fancies about corrupt understandings, trampled Austrians, and bartered Czechs." Lord Londonderry, Minister for Air, was "at a loss to understand why we could not make common ground in some form or other with Germany in opposition to Communism. The anti-Communist platform was (and still is) invaluable."

BLIND LEADERS OF THE BLIND

The devious and dishonorable course of British diplomacy in the 1930's, from Sir John Simon's connivance in the rape of Manchuria to Chamberlain's betrayal of Ethiopia, Spain, Austria, and Czechoslovakia, was the product of the Tory mind at its worst. The second Labor Cabinet, constituted in 1929 with Ramsay MacDonald as Prime Minister, disintegrated in the financial crisis of August, 1931, and gave way to a coalition "National Government," predominantly Conservative but still headed by MacDonald and his "National Laborites." The latter had no following and were expelled from the Labor Party as traitors, with Labor and part of the Liberals going into opposition. The National Government won an overwhelming victory in the election of October, 1931, and carried on with the renegade MacDonald at its head. He resigned on June 7, 1935, and was replaced by the Conservative leader, Stanley Baldwin.

The new Prime Minister, a kind of reduced British edition of Herbert Hoover, was far more interested in morals (Victorian) than in politics (Hitlerian). His greatest triumph was the abdication of King Edward VIII, who succeeded his father, George V, in January, 1936, and left his throne to his brother, George VI, in December when Baldwin forbade him to marry the American divorcée, Mrs. Wallis Simpson. Baldwin's next greatest triumph was his successful befuddlement of the British public regarding all issues of war and peace during the course of his diplomatic muddling in dealing with Hitler and Mussolini. "I should like to express the hope," he said on the eve of Hitler's repudiation of the military clauses of Versailles, "that Herr Hitler will soon be in full possession of his normal strength." On the same occasion he observed piously: "One of the greatest perils that have met democracies in the past, and meets them today, is when their leaders have not the courage to tell them the truth."

But in November, 1936, a year after he had won an election through misrepresentation, he confessed: "I put before the whole House my views with an appalling frankness. From 1933 I and my friends were very worried about what was happening in Europe. You'll remember that at that time the Disarmament Conference was sitting in Geneva and there probably was a stronger pacifist feeling running through this country than at any other time since the war. My position as head of a great party was not altogether a comfortable one. Suppose I had gone to the country and said that Germany was rearming and that we must rearm. Does anybody suppose that this pacific country would have rallied to that at that moment? I cannot think of anything that would have made the loss of the election from my point of view more certain."

At the end of May, 1937, Baldwin was succeeded as Prime Minister by Neville Chamberlain. Eden carried on as Foreign Minister until his belated disgust at appeasement led him to resign in February of the following year. His place was taken by Edward Frederick Lindley Wood, third Viscount Halifax, who (as Baron Irwin) had been Viceroy of India in the late 1920's. Chamberlain's principal advisers, aside from Halifax and such confidants as Sir Horace Wilson, were Hoare and Simon. He himself was an enlarged edition of Calvin Coolidge, albeit less taciturn and less honest than his American prototype. Like his father, Joseph Chamberlain, he served as a more or less enlightened Mayor of Birmingham before entering national politics. But he was essentially a cold and funereal business man who made screws, nuts and guns. His passion was peace—to be achieved by selling lesser peoples

into bondage to the Caesars. His political technique, like Baldwin's, was one
of spreading confusion in order to secure support for purposes which the
nation would never have approved had they been clearly stated. The betrayal
of China was "business." The desertion of Ethiopia and the League was
"peace." Connivance in the murder of the Spanish Republic was "non-intervention." Cooperation in Fascist aggression was "appeasement."

Chamberlain's oratorical style in Parliament was depicted accurately by
Alexander Glendinning in *The Nineteenth Century and After*, May, 1939:
"I have heard Mr. Chamberlain accused of fiddling while Rome burns; but
I do think that if he were in Nero's position Mr. Chamberlain would fiddle. *Not*
I think he would make a speech, and that it would go something like this:
'The fact, which I think I may say has been established beyond question,
that the greater part of this city is now in flames, will cause, I have no doubt,
the feelings of profound uneasiness and even alarm among those inhabitants
who are conscious of the possibility of a threat to their security. The question we have to ask ourselves is whether this conflagration has not now
created a situation which is incompatible with the safety of the community
as a whole. I am sure that it will be generally agreed that the collapse of most
of our public buildings, so far from relieving the apprehension which has
been widely felt, has served only to increase anxiety and to administer a
further shock to confidence. If the city is on fire, and if the lives of its inhabitants are in danger, then I confess that I find it difficult to reconcile this
state of affairs with the view that there is no cause for misgivings in a situation which, if permitted to develop, may prove detrimental to the well-being
of all concerned. It has been suggested that the Fire Brigade be called, and
I have no hesitation in saying that this suggestion is one which deserves the
most serious consideration, and I may add that we are keeping in close touch
with representatives of the Fire Brigade, with a view to such measures as
it may be necessary to take in pursuit of our general aim to restore the confidence we all so earnestly desire.' "

Of Britain's sorry leaders in the 1930's could be said, with doubled force,
what Ralph Waldo Emerson said of their predecessors in the 1880's: "Truth
in private life, untruth in public, marks these home-loving men. Their political
conduct is not decided by general views, but by internal intrigues and personal and family interests. They cannot readily see beyond England, nor in
England can they transcend the interests of the governing classes. 'English
principles' mean a primary regard to the interests of property. Their mind
is in a state of arrested development. There is cramp limitation in their habit

of thought, sleepy routine, and a tortoise's instinct to hold hard to the ground with his claws, lest he should be thrown on his back. There is a drag of inertia which resists reform in every shape."

APPEASING THE CAESARS

The *Leitmotifs* of appeasement have already been suggested. In the end the British public acquiesced in this policy in the mistaken conviction that it provided the only hope of escape from the war which the policy itself had made inevitable. But the electorate had not at the outset sponsored any such course and was in fact tricked into supporting those who did. In 1934-1935 the British League of Nations Union, under Lord Robert Cecil, conducted a "National Peace Ballot" in which no less than 11,500,000 votes were cast, giving an overwhelming majority for support of the League and disarmament and a heavy majority in favor of economic and military sanctions against aggressors. Accepting this result as an accurate index of what British voters wanted, Baldwin declared, "We value this support. The League of Nations remains, as I said in a speech in Yorkshire, 'the sheet-anchor of British policy.' " The National Government's election manifesto of November, 1935, asserted, "The League of Nations will remain as before the keystone of British policy. We shall continue to do all in our power to uphold the Covenant. There will be no wavering."

An election poster of the Conservative party showed Baldwin's fist squarely planted on the Covenant over the caption, "Our word is our bond." In the polling of November 15, 1935, the Government won 431 out of 615 seats in Commons. This was a popular endorsement not of appeasement but of collective security to which the Government had pledged itself. The voters did not know that Hoare and Laval had made a secret pact at Geneva in September to betray Ethiopia and the League, and that an even more shameful bargain between them was to leak out three weeks after the election. It is fair to say that for the next four years a group of leaders, placed in power by a public convinced it was supporting the cause of world order and resistance to Fascist aggression, pursued a policy of connivance in aggression which was certain to produce world anarchy. These leaders progressively "sold" this policy to the public in the name of "peace."

The precedent established in dealing with Japan in China was faithfully followed in dealing with Italy in Ethiopia, Germany in the Rhineland, and the Axis in Spain. At each step, one eloquent voice was raised in protest and warning. Each time it was ignored by those who knew better. It was the voice of one of the rarest of animals, a Tory dissenter—Winston Churchill. At each step the appeasers told Parliament and public that their decisions would insure peace. Once the new St. George had slain not the dragon but the Abyssinian maid (and the League which might have protected her from the dragon) the Tory leaders explained that the League was "too weak" to be relied upon. Finally they argued that support of the League was not to be thought of since it might mean "war"—*i.e.*, Mussolini might "attack" the British Empire, France, Jugoslavia, Greece, Turkey *et al*. "Is it not apparent," asked Chamberlain on June 10, 1936, "that the policy of sanctions involves a risk of war? There is no use for us to shut our eyes to realities."

Eden announced the abandonment of sanctions on June 18, 1936, one hundred and twentieth anniversary of Waterloo and first anniversary of the Simon-Hoare-Ribbentrop naval accord by which Britain had granted to the Reich 35 per cent parity in sea power and full parity in submarines. Simon asserted, "I do not think there is a single member of the League which is prepared to use force. I am not prepared to see a single ship sunk even in a successful naval battle in the cause of Abyssinian independence." Government supporters shouted at the Labor opposition, "Do you want war?" Lord Cecil wrote in the *Times*, "We cannot escape war by running away from it. There is no escape from blackmail by submission." But his voice was as lonely as Churchill's.

"PEACE FOR OUR TIME"

The formula thereafter was "no commitments" and "no entanglements." A clear indication was given to Berlin that Downing Street would not resist German expansion to the East by Anthony Eden's address to his constituents at Leamington on November 20, 1936:

"These [British] arms will never be used in a war of aggression. They may, and if the occasion arose they would, be used in our own defense and in the defense of the territories of the British Commonwealth of Nations. They may, and if the occasion arose they would, be used in the defense of France and Belgium against unprovoked aggression in accordance with our existing treaty obligations. They may, and if a new Western European settlement can be reached, they would, be used in the defense of Germany were she the victim of unprovoked aggression by any of the other signatories of such a settlement. These, together with our Treaty of Alliance with Iraq and our projected treaty with Egypt, are our definite obligations. In addition our armaments may be used in bringing help to a victim of aggression in any case where, in our judgment, it would be proper under the provisions of the Covenant to do so. I use the word 'may' deliberately, since in such an instance there is no automatic obligation to take military action. It is, moreover, right that this should be so, for nations cannot be expected to incur automatic military obligations save for areas where their vital interests are concerned."

On March 3, 1937, in Lords, Lord Halifax asserted that although the Government did not disinterest itself in these areas, "we are unable to define beforehand what might be our attitude to a hypothetical complication in Central or Eastern Europe." Eden and Halifax were thus in agreement, at a time when Eden was Foreign Minister and posing as the champion of collective security, that Britain should assume no commitments to defend victims of aggression in eastern or central Europe. This was the only assurance which the leaders of the Third Reich required. It meant that, so far as London was concerned, they had a free hand in the East. Then and later, the only stipulation insisted upon by Downing Street was that Nazi imperialism must achieve its purposes without war, since war might involve Britain by involving France.

By 1938, more than passivity was required. After *Anschluss,* which had been passively sanctioned by persistent British refusal to come to Austria's defense, Halifax cried, "Horrible, horrible, I never thought they would do it!" But when Litvinov warned on March 17 that Czechoslovakia was in danger, London declined his proposal for a conference of League members and the United States to consider collective means of "checking the further development of aggression and eliminating an aggravated danger of a new world massacre."

Chamberlain spoke to Commons on March 24, 1938: "Should we forthwith give assurance to France that in the event of her being called upon by reason of German aggression on Czechoslovakia to implement her obligations under the Franco-Czech treaty we would immediately employ our full military force on her behalf? Or should we at once declare our readiness to take military action in resistance to any forcible interference with the independence of Czechoslovakia and invite any other nations which might desire to associate themselves with us in such a declaration?

"From consideration of these two alternatives it clearly emerges that under either a decision as to whether or not this country should find itself involved in war would automatically be removed from the discretion of His Majesty's

Government and the suggested guarantee would apply irrespective of the circumstances by which it would be brought into operation and over which His Majesty's Government might not have been able to exercise any control. This position is not one which His Majesty's Government could see their way to accept in relation to an area where their vital interests are not concerned in the same degree as they are in the case of France and Belgium. It certainly is not a position that results from the Covenant. For these reasons His Majesty's Government feel themselves unable to give the prior guarantee suggested.

"His Majesty's Government will at all times be ready to render any help in their power toward the solution of questions likely to cause difficulty between the German and Czechoslovak governments. In the mean time there is no need to assume the use of force or, indeed, to talk about it. Such talk is to be strongly deprecated. Not only can it do no good; it is bound to do harm."

There followed in logical order the Ciano-Perth Accord of April 16 for appeasing Italy, Mr. Chamberlain's friendly gestures toward Japan, the Runciman mission to Prague, the ultimatum of September 19 to Beneš, and the "peace" at Munich. Chamberlain, like Daladier, was welcomed on his return from the *Führerhaus* as a conquering hero. Only one member of his Cabinet resigned in protest: Alfred Duff-Cooper, First Lord of the Admiralty. He said in Commons, "It was not for Serbia or Belgium we fought in 1914, though it suited some people to say so, but we were fighting then, as we should have been fighting last week, in order that one Great Power should not be allowed, in disregard of treaty obligations and the laws of nations and against all morality, to dominate by brutal force the continent of Europe. I tried to swallow the Munich terms, but they stuck in my throat. I have perhaps ruined my political career, but I can still walk about the world with my head erect."

Churchill also spoke: "We have sustained a total, unmitigated defeat. We are in the presence of a disaster of the first magnitude which has befallen Great Britain and France. Do not let us blind ourselves. Do not suppose that this is the end. It is only the beginning. It is only the first foretaste of the bitter cup which will be proffered to you year after year unless by a supreme recovery of moral health and martial vigor we rise again to take our stand for freedom, as in olden times." No one cared. By a vote of 366 to 144, Commons upheld the Prime Minister who went to Scotland to fish. Mahatma Gandhi commented, "Europe has sold her soul for seven days of earthly existence."

[*175*]

DISENCHANTMENT

The early events of 1939 did not change Mr. Chamberlain's view of the future. He observed with some anxiety the Japanese occupation of Hainan and Spratley Island. Earl Plymouth warned Tokyo in December of the "incalculable consequences" of closing the Open Door and paved the way for the granting of credits to China in March. Downing Street welcomed the reciprocal trade agreement of November 17, 1938, with the United States and looked with approval on the death of the Spanish Republic. Mussolini's demands for French territory, which Chamberlain and Halifax failed to satisfy by their January journey to Paris and Rome, were disturbing. Also disturbing were German proposals to build submarine tonnage up to the British level. Yet this, obviously, was a means of meeting the "Soviet menace." Wilhelmstrasse said so. The Nazi leaders, however, were slow in showing gratitude for appeasement. "I am still waiting for a sign," said Chamberlain in mid-December, "that they are prepared to make their contribution to peace." They were still slower in pushing toward the Ukraine. Montagu Norman visited Schacht early in January, but the safe and conservative President of the Reichsbank was unfortunately displaced a few weeks later by Walter Funk. Yet Chamberlain still had hopes.

His hopes were not at once shattered by Hitler's seizure of Prague in the Ides of March. This was doubtless the first step toward Kiev and the Caucasus. Halifax asked the press on March 13 not to "propagate rumors or spread distorted views." Bonnet and Sir Eric Phipps in Paris agreed that the Anglo-French "guarantee" to Czechoslovakia did not apply. "The proposed guarantee," explained Chamberlain, "was one against unprovoked aggression. No such aggression has yet taken place." When Ellen Wilkinson asked in Commons whether it was "unprovoked aggression for a country to provoke secession," the Speaker ruled her question out of order.

On Wednesday, as Hitler entered the Hradcany in triumph, Chamberlain declared that this had not been contemplated by any of the signatories of the Munich agreement, but "I do not wish to associate myself today with any charges [of bad faith]. It is natural that I should bitterly regret what has occurred. But do not let us on that account be deflected from our course." Simon urged sympathy toward Czechoslovakia but said the guarantee did not apply. "It is really essential that we should not enter into any extensive, general and undefined commitment." The *Daily Mail* opined, "The final disintegration of Czechoslovakia was almost inevitable. It was due to an internal split up, not external aggression."

On Thursday, March 16, Hitler gave Carpatho-Ukraine to Hungary. On Friday, at Birmingham, Chamberlain publicly denounced him for a breach of faith. Munich had been right but the Führer was now violating Munich and the principle of self-determination. "Is this the last attack upon a small State or is it to be followed by others? Is this, in fact, a step in the direction of an effort to dominate the world by force? I am not going to answer tonight but I am sure these questions will require grave and serious consideration. While I am not prepared to engage this country by new and unspecified commitments operating under conditions which cannot now be foreseen, yet no greater mistake could be made than to suppose that because it believes war to be a senseless and a cruel thing, this nation has so lost its fibre that it will not take part to the utmost of its power in resisting such a challenge if it ever were made."

STRAW WITHOUT BRICKS

There followed belated and hesitant efforts to rebuild a coalition against the Reich upon the ruins of appeasement. On March 31, 1939, Chamberlain informed Commons that the British Government, pending the conclusion of the extensive negotiations under way, would give Poland all the support in its power "in the event of any action which clearly threatened Polish independence, and which the Polish Government accordingly considered it vital to resist with their national forces." At the conclusion of Beck's visit to London (April 3-6), it was announced that "the two countries were prepared to enter into an agreement of a permanent and reciprocal character to replace the present temporary and unilateral assurance." Meanwhile Poland would consider itself "under an obligation to render assistance to H.M. Government under the same conditions as those contained in the temporary assurance already given by H.M. Government to Poland."

For the first time in twenty years, Downing Street had entered into a bilateral pledge of mutual defense with an eastern European State. On August 25, 1939, a formal five-year Anglo-Polish alliance was signed, pledging the parties to give one another all the support in their power in case of either "becoming engaged in hostilities with a European Power in consequence of aggression by the latter against that Contracting Party" or in consequence of a direct or indirect threat to the independence of either, requiring resistance. Provision was made for military consultation. In the event of hostilities, the signatories would conclude no armistice or peace save by mutual consent.

On April 13, 1939, following the Italian annexation of Albania, Chamberlain told Commons that he was "disappointed" but that "nothing that has happened has in any way altered my conviction that the policy of H.M. Government in signing the Anglo-Italian agreement a year ago was right." He announced, however, that the Government was prepared to lend Greece and Rumania all the support in its power "in the event of any action being taken which clearly threatened the independence of either, and which the Greek or Rumanian Governments respectively consider it vital to resist with their national forces."

On May 12, Chamberlain told Commons that, pending the conclusion of a definite alliance with Turkey, "H.M. Government and the Turkish Government declared that in the event of aggression leading to war in the Mediterranean area they would be prepared to cooperate effectively and lend each other all aid and assistance in their power." On October 19, 1939, Turkey signed a fifteen-year treaty of mutual assistance with Britain and France who pledged aid to Ankara in case of attack by any European Power. All agreed to aid one another in case of aggression by a European Power leading to war in the Mediterranean. Article 3, declared: "So long as the guarantee given by France and the United Kingdom to Greece and Rumania by the respective declarations on April 13, 1939, remain in force, Turkey will cooperate effectively with France and the United Kingdom, and will lend them all aid and assistance in its power, in the event of France and the United Kingdom being engaged in hostilities in virtue of either of the said guarantees."

This presumably meant that Turkey was pledged to keep open the Straits if France and Great Britain should be obliged to go to Rumania's aid. But a supplementary protocol asserted, "The obligations undertaken by Turkey in virtue of the above-mentioned treaty cannot require that country to take action having as its effect or involving as its consequence entry into armed conflict with the U.S.S.R." Moscow was thus left with a veto over Turkish policy if it chose to threaten war. Should Italy enter the war, Turkey would aid the allies, but only on condition that the guarantees to Greece and Rumania remained in force and that aid involved no conflict with Russia. This last success of Allied effort to complete the "peace front" was to prove as futile as earlier steps. The Italian declaration of war coincided with the collapse of France and the Rumanian repudiation of the British guarantee. Turkey remained neutral.

On other fronts, this intended coalition failed completely of its purpose. It neither deterred the Axis from risking war nor did it afford to the Western Powers any allies sufficiently powerful to save them from defeat. Poland was to be crushed like an eggshell. Rumania and Greece had assumed no reciprocal obligations to come to the aid of France and Britain. The Allied guarantee to Bucharest proved wholly illusory. The kingdom was partitioned and its remnant occupied by the Reich without resistance in the autumn of 1940. When Italy invaded Greece, Britain was able, thanks to naval control of the Mediterranean, to come to the aid of Athens and strike heavy blows at the foe from Greek bases. Even the attack upon 'Greece did not move Turkey to enter the war. All the Balkans were lost in the sequel.

FOLLY IN MOSCOW

The central difficulty in the projected coalition was that it bore no relationship to the obvious rules of arithmetic in the game of power. Poland, Rumania, and Turkey could be protected against the Reich only by the U.S.S.R. The considerations which prompted Chamberlain to guarantee Warsaw and Bucharest before opening negotiations with Moscow, and to refuse Stalin's price for an alliance until it was too late, were legacies of "appeasement" which proved fatal to the whole enterprise. As failure became apparent in the summer of 1939, the Tory leaders, far from adopting a more realistic program, sought to revert to appeasement. British spokesmen reiterated their willingness to settle all differences through "negotiation." In May, Chamberlain and Simon permitted the Reich, through the Bank of International Settlements, to secure control of £6,000,000 in Czech gold held in London. In July, Sir Horace Wilson and Robert S. Hudson entered into discussion with Hitler's economic adviser, Dr. Helmuth Wohltat, for a British "disarmament loan" to Germany of a billion pounds sterling. Chamberlain declared the discussions wholly "unofficial." Nothing came of them, but they revealed a state of mind which brought no comfort to those who hoped for the establishment of a firm and powerful anti-Nazi coalition. Downing Street, moreover, would not even lend money to Poland unless Warsaw agreed to spend it in Britain. On July 24, Chamberlain recognized that "the Japanese forces in China have special requirements for the purpose of safeguarding their own security and maintaining public order in the regions under their control and that they have to suppress or remove such causes or acts as will obstruct them or benefit their enemies. British authorities and British nationals in China should refrain from such acts and measures."

That the British negotiations with the only Power which could have served as an adequate counterweight to the Axis should have come to nothing was not unnatural, given such leadership as this. Lloyd George, Churchill, and other realists issued repeated warnings during the last spring of peace that all the Cabinet's efforts would be vain unless the Soviet Union were enlisted in the coalition. But Chamberlain and Halifax could never bring themselves to a realization of the urgency of securing Moscow's collaboration. They were therefore unable to overcome their chronic anti-Soviet prejudices and strike a viable bargain with the Kremlin. Litvinov's plea of March for a conference was rejected, as his similar plea after *Anschluss* had been. Not until mid-April were any negotiations undertaken. London desired no alliance and no offense to the anti-Comintern Powers. Litvinov's resignation on May 7 produced no awakening.

In the tedious discussions which dragged through five months, Moscow demanded a binding alliance for mutual defense against any attack on the signatories or any attack or indirect aggression against the Baltic States. Moscow also demanded, as an elementary strategic necessity, military access to Polish territory if the U.S.S.R. was to assume obligations to defend Poland. Chamberlain and Halifax, however, having lightly sacrificed China, Ethiopia, Spain, Austria, Czechoslovakia, and Albania to the Fascist aggressors, now became inflexible champions of the "rights of small nations." Since the Baltic States wanted no guarantee, London would make no pact with Moscow granting them one. Since Poland's leaders would rather see their State perish at the hands of Hitler than accept military aid from the hands of Stalin, London could not or would not meet the terms of Molotov and Voroshilov.

When the diplomatic discussions got nowhere, Chamberlain sent as special envoy to assist Ambassador Sir William Seeds one of his most devoted Munichmen, William Strang. When the *Strang nach Osten* also produced no results, an Anglo-French military mission (of wholly undistinguished personnel) was sent in August. In all cases, however, London and Paris would not meet Stalin's terms. But beggars cannot be choosers. Stalin, not being a beggar, had no need to conclude a pact with the Western Powers on conditions he regarded as strategically unworkable and highly dangerous to the U.S.S.R. Hitler was quite willing to grant him, in exchange for mere neutrality, what Chamberlain would not grant in exchange for an alliance. Despite their denials, Chamberlain and Daladier knew this early in May and throughout June. They still preferred to reject the Kremlin's terms. Stalin therefore made the obvious choice. His nonaggression pact with Berlin of August 23 left the Western Powers isolated in the face of a formidable foe.

FROM DANZIG TO DUNKIRK

Never did modern Britain embark upon a war under such perilous circumstances as prevailed in 1939. The cause had already been all but lost at Madrid and Munich and Moscow. To fight the Reich with no allies save a feeble Poland ruled by a Beck and a defeatist France ruled by a Daladier and a Bonnet was to invite disaster. Yet not to fight was to invite destruction, for even a Chamberlain was now dimly aware of Hitler's objectives and methods. After two days of doubt, due primarily to Bonnet's intrigues to desert Warsaw, the Prime Minister did what had to be done. At 11.15 a.m. on September 3, Halifax delivered a note to German Chargé Kordt, informing him that, since no reply had been received to the British ultimatum, the two Powers were at war as of 11 a.m.

Chamberlain told Commons: "When I spoke last night to the House I could not but be aware that in some parts of the House there were doubts and some bewilderment as to whether there had been any weakening, hesitation, or vacillation on the part of H.M. Government. In the circumstances, I make no reproach, for if I had been in the same position as hon. members not sitting on this Bench and not in possession of all the information which we have, I should very likely have felt the same. The statement which I have to make this morning will show that there were no grounds for doubt. This is a sad day for all of us, and to none is it sadder than to me. Everything that I have worked for, everything that I have hoped for, everything that I have believed in during my public life, has crashed into ruins. There is only one thing left for me to do; that is, to devote what strength and powers I have to forwarding the victory of the cause for which we have to sacrifice so much. I cannot tell what part I may be allowed to play myself; I trust I may live to see the day when Hitlerism has been destroyed and a liberated Europe has been reestablished."

When the Chinese Ambassador in London, Dr. Quo Tai Chi, who was later to become Foreign Minister at Chungking, was asked for his comments on the outbreak of war between Britain and the Reich, he observed: "The sky is black with chickens coming home to roost."

Poland perished at once. For eight months thereafter the Tory Munich-men in London clung tenaciously to their posts and directed the war under the slogan of "business as usual." In the War Cabinet of September were included two major critics of their policies: Anthony Eden as Dominion Secretary, and Winston Churchill in his 1914 post of First Lord of the Admiralty. But no Liberals or Laborites would serve in any government headed by Chamberlain. Save for the displacement of Leslie Hore-Belisha by Oliver Stanley as War Secretary in January, 1940, no major changes took place in the Cabinet until the advent of catastrophe.

The armaments with which Tory leadership had supplied Britain fell as far short of the requirements of waging effective war as Tory diplomacy had fallen short of the requirements of defending peace. Only the Navy remained in a high state of efficiency. The Royal Air Force, though qualitatively excellent and growing in size, was pitiably small. As for the Army, conscription had not been introduced until April, 1939. The B.E.F. in France was to find that it had no armored divisions capable of coping with the *Blitzkrieg* and no commanders who would have known how to use them had they existed. Yet Chamberlain expressed imperturbable confidence and held that Hitler had "missed the bus."

The débâcle of British arms in Norway foreshadowed what was to come. On May 7, 1940, the Prime Minister weakly defended his course in Commons. But it was clear that he was losing the war as he had lost the peace. Leopold S. Amery, rebel Conservative, drew cheers when he quoted Oliver Cromwell: "You have sat too long here for any good you have been doing. Depart, I say. Let us have done with you. In the name of God, go." But Chamberlain had no desire to go. His Tory majority, as always, voted "confidence." But the vote was 281 to 200. A majority of 81 was a defeat in a house normally conservative by a margin of 210. For two days Chamberlain sought in vain to persuade the Labor leaders to join the Cabinet. At dawn of May 10 the Nazi hosts struck at the Low Countries with irresistible force. Chamberlain resigned that night. He remained in the new Cabinet as Lord President of the Council but fell ill and resigned on October 3. On November 9, 1940, he died.

CHURCHILL'S HOUR

If England still lived, the credit for survival was due to Winston Churchill and to the millions of men and women whom he rallied to devotion and sacrifice in a cause they had all but forgotten under his puny predecessors. "He is a man," wrote Harold Nicolson years before, "who leads forlorn hopes, and when the hopes of England become forlorn, he will again be summoned to leadership." The coming to power of this pudgy descendant of the Duke of Marlborough symbolized the end of the rule of business men and the ascendency in the face of doom of an élite of fighters and intellectuals. He was proud, he said, to be a member of "one of the few hundred great families who had governed England for so many generations." His mother was an American beauty, Jennie Jerome. A mediocre student at Harrow, Oxford and Sandhurst, he became in his youth a war correspondent in Cuba, in India, in the Sudan, and in South Africa where he was captured by the Boers and escaped from jail. In the course of his stormy political career he deserted the Conservatives to join the Liberals in 1906. After 1915 he suffered eclipse because of the blame put upon him for the failure of the Dardanelles expedition.

In the 1920's he wrote biographies and histories. In the 1930's, back as a Cassandra in the Conservative camp, he warned his countrymen, always in vain, of their need to arm and to fight before the Nazi Reich should overwhelm them. In the 1940's he saved England. All his days he wrote, painted, played at sports and relished the life of an epicure. "Churchill's tastes are simple," said Lord Birkenhead. "He is easily contented with the best of everything."

No less than the best in leadership could rescue Britain from the consequences of the long retreat which began on the plains of Manchuria and culminated on the beaches at Dunkirk. In Churchill's first Cabinet, formed while the Nazi hordes were pouring into the Lowlands, Eden was War Secretary and Alfred Duff-Cooper Minister of Information. Liberal Sir Archibald Sinclair and Laborites Clement Attlee, Albert Alexander, Herbert Morrison, Ernest Bevin, and Arthur Greenwood all secured posts. Churchill told Commons on May 13: "I have nothing to offer but blood, tears, toil, and sweat. Our policy? It is to wage war by land, sea, and air. War with all our might and with all the strength God has given us, and to wage war against a monstrous tyranny never surpassed in the dark and lamentable catalogue of human crime. Our aim? It is victory. Victory at all costs—victory in spite of all terrors—victory, however long and hard the road may be, for without victory there is no survival."

On June 18, 1940, 125 years after Waterloo and immediately after the fearful débâcle on the Continent, Churchill warned his countrymen: "What

General Weygand called the Battle of France is over. The Battle of Britain is about to begin. On this battle depends the survival of Christian civilization. Upon it depends our own British life and the long continuity of our institutions and our empire. The whole fury and might of the enemy must very soon be turned upon us. Hitler knows he will have to break us in this island or lose the war.

"If we can stand up to him all Europe may be freed and the life of the world may move forward into broad sunlit uplands; but if we fail, the whole world, including the United States and all that we have known and cared for, will sink into the abyss of a new Dark Age made more sinister and perhaps more prolonged by the lights of a perverted science.

"Let us therefore brace ourselves to our duty and so bear ourselves that if the British Commonwealth and Empire last for a thousand years, men will still say 'This was their finest hour.' "

THE RAIN OF FIRE

After a summer lull in which military operations paused and obscure peace overtures came to nothing, Göring's *Luftwaffe* opened an "all out" assault on London in the hope of "softening England for invasion." Endless relays of hundreds of bombers made day and night hideous, slaying thousands and tens of thousands of civilians, burning whole blocks of houses, smashing factories, schools, churches, palaces, tenements, and many of the architectural treasures of the centuries. The world's greatest city suffered a fate far worse than that of Barcelona. Coventry was blasted as completely as Guernica and probably by some of the same aviators. Manchester, Liverpool, Southampton, Birmingham, and a dozen lesser towns knew horrors hitherto known only to the people of Shanghai, Addis Ababa, Madrid, and Warsaw.

British aircraft production and shipbuilding were retarded. But the people of Britain refused to be terrorized into submission. Their resistance hardened to steel, for they followed a great leader who promised them no comforts and told them no lies. "Death and sorrow will be our companions on the journey, hardship our garment, constancy and valor our only shield. We must be reunited, we must be undaunted, we must be inflexible. Our qualities and deeds must burn and glow through the gloom of Europe until they become the veritable beacons of its salvation."

To such summons the people of Britain and of all the Empire (save only neutral Eire) responded with a vigor and courage which caused Axis jour-

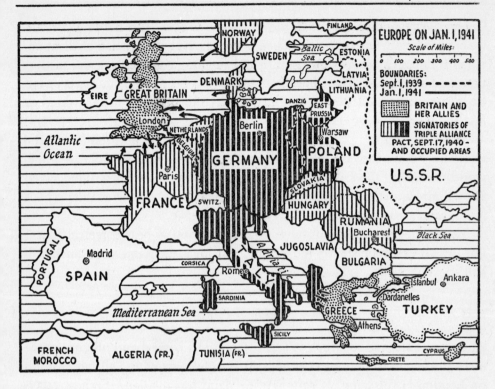

EUROPE ON JAN. 1, 1941

Scale of Miles:
0   100   200   300   400   500

BOUNDARIES:
Sept. 1, 1939 – – – – –
Jan. 1, 1941 ———

▦ BRITAIN AND HER ALLIES

▥ SIGNATORIES OF TRIPLE ALLIANCE PACT, SEPT. 17, 1940 – AND OCCUPIED AREAS

nalists to wonder anxiously whether their last unconquered foe consisted of "47 million Churchills." Faith begot works. Faithful work, inspired by new foresight and able leadership, begot staunch defense and a will to victory. The Royal Air Force won the Battle of London and made invasion too hazardous to attempt. Never before, said Churchill, had so much been owed by so many to so few. With the Army unable to carry the war to the Continent during the long slow process of rearming and expansion after Dunkirk, the civilians of England became the victims of Nazi fury and the actual defenders of the realm. With cries of "Thumbs up!" they acquired strength through misery and carried on undaunted. By mid-summer of 1941 some 50,000 of them had lost their lives in air raids. But all the rest fought on in ten thousand unsung deeds of courage.

THE BATTLE FOR BREAD

"Without victory," Churchill warned his countrymen, "there is no survival." Without control of the seaways linking the British Isles with the outer world, there could be neither survival nor victory. Two-thirds of England's millions lived week by week only by foodstuffs brought from abroad in the holds of a thousand ships. The waging of war on far-flung fronts and the ultimate hope of liberating the Continent depended even more on shipping and on protection of the precious freighters from the foe.

In the ghostly battle of the sea, the Royal Navy was able to cut off the Axis Powers from most of their sea-borne trade. But it was scarcely able by its own devices to defeat the Nazi counter-blockade of Britain. In the few spectacular sea fights which now and then took place, it vanquished the enemy as it had done of old. In mid-December of 1939 three British cruisers drove the formidable pocket-battleship *Admiral Graf Spee* into the harbor of Montevideo where her captain scuttled his vessel and took his life rather than renew the engagement. Sir Andrew Cunningham's Mediterranean squadron smashed Italy's dreadnaughts at Taranto in November of 1940. Off Cape Matapan at the end of the following March more of Italy's ships were liquidated. In May of 1941 the raiding *Bismarck*, after having destroyed the *Hood,* was similarly trapped and sunk. But in the narrow waters off Norway and Greece the great gray ships of war were checkmated by the Luftwaffe. And in the restless wastes of the North Atlantic Britain's Navy faced a task almost beyond its powers.

Between September and May, 1939-1940, sinkings of cargo ships averaged less than 200,000 tons per month—roughly 1% of the merchant fleet of the Empire. But after the establishment of Nazi bases for U-boats, aircraft and surface raiders in France, the Low Countries and Scandinavia, the rate of losses doubled, with 500,000 tons sunk in April, 1941, and almost 600,000 tons in May. The 7,000,000 tons of ships already lost were almost made up by acquisitions from the Axis and its victims. But with new losses approaching 6,000,000 tons per year, three ships were going down for every new one being built in British and American shipyards combined. Britain's destroyer fleet of some 240 ships (compared with over 800 available to the Allies in 1918) was too small for the job of protecting cargoes against Germany's 200 submarines and Italy's 100, despite the addition of 50 American destroyers under the agreement of September, 1940. Even were all the 160 destroyers of the United States to be added to the total (an impossible contingency, since it would immobilize the American battle fleet), the task would still have seemed hopeless by the summer of 1941 by any purely mathematical calculation.

Yet the grim logic of numbers could be beaten at sea, as it had been beaten in the air, by British stubbornness and courage. Losses were reduced by increased output of destroyers, corvettes and long-range bombers. As the war's third year began, American patrols off Greenland and Iceland were at last given "orders to shoot" in their mission of keeping open the sea-lanes. The construction of ships and of yet more ships in all the yards of the Empire and of the New World offered promise of ultimately overtaking the enemy's work of destruction. Above all, the daring and endurance of Britain's sailors in defying the Nazi menace in a thousand dark encounters offered promise to beleaguered Britain of sustenance, survival and possible triumph.

VICTORY IN EAST AFRICA

Rome's little Caesar, like the men of Vichy, guessed wrong as to the aftermath of Dunkirk. Churchill and his people refused to admit defeat. Mussolini's Abyssinian empire was therewith doomed, for neither he nor Hitler possessed means of defending it.

At the outset, to be sure, the troops under the command of the Duke of Aosta, Viceroy of Ethiopia, were able to invade Kenya and the Sudan and to overrun British Somaliland in August of 1940. But on the fringes of the Ethiopian plateau the foe which Rome had challenged gathered men and weapons with slow and methodical British patience. Britain's commander-in-chief in the East African arena was Lieut. Gen. Allan Gordon Cunningham, brother of the commander of the Mediterranean fleet. His task was to conquer the Italian colonial empire between the Red Sea and the Indian Ocean.

The campaign which he was to carry forward brilliantly began with the capture of Kismayu, southernmost Italian port, in mid-February, 1941. Modagiscio, capital of the colony, fell ten days later. By the end of the first week of March Italian Somaliland was cleared of Fascist forces. The invaders pushed northward into Ethiopia while other columns from the Sudan ascended the Blue Nile and summoned the black warriors of the exiled Haile Selassie to join their cause. A third force, coming by sea from Aden, retook Berbera in mid-March. A fourth army from the north invaded Eritrea and took the mountain stronghold of Cheren after a siege of seven weeks.

By the 1st of April Asmara, Eritrean capital, was in British hands, as well as Harar, south of the railway from Jibuti to Addis Ababa. Italian resistance disintegrated under swift British blows. On April 6 Addis Ababa was abandoned. A month later, on the 5th anniversary of Mussolini's vaunted victory, Haile Selassie re-entered his capital. A fortnight later the Duke of Aosta yielded his last great stronghold at Amba Alagi—on the day on which his

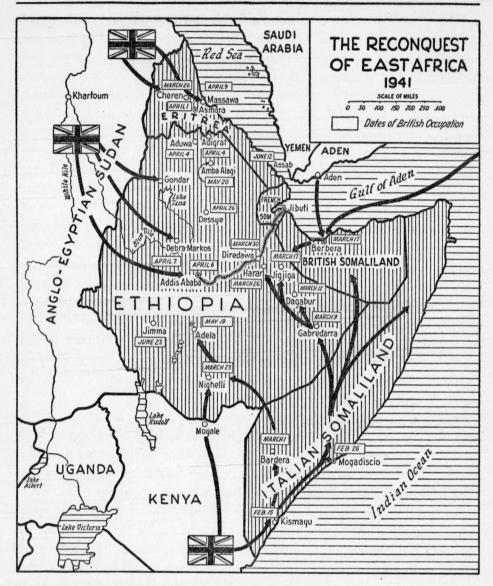

brother accepted the tinsel crown of Croatia. Save for the pursuit of scattered bands of Italian stragglers through the wilderness of the Ethiopian highlands, the war in East Africa was over.

THE STRUGGLE FOR ISLAM

British arms fared less well in the widely scattered conflicts of 1940-1941 around the rim of the Eastern Mediterranean. These Arab lands of palm

and desert were all once vassals of the Osmanli Turks and part of the great
Mohammedan realm of the Sultans which stretched in its heyday from the
gates of Vienna to the frontiers of India and from Gibraltar, the Sahara and
the Sudan to the Caucasus and the Crimea. The Arab periphery of this imposing empire had long since passed into the hands of Britishers, Frenchmen
and Italians. At the outbreak of World War II only three of the Arab States
were free of alien rule: Saudi Arabia, Oman and Yemen, all in the great
sandy peninsula between the Red Sea and the Persian Gulf. Two more
enjoyed nominal independence under British treaties of protection: Egypt
and Iraq. Here Britain and the Reich waged war for the mastery of the Near
East.

In the Moslem arena the balance of forces obliged the British to remain
largely on the defensive against Axis efforts to reach the great base at Alexandria and the vital waterway of Suez. General Sir Archibald Wavell's "British
and Imperial Army of the Nile" had first the task of beating back Graziani's
invaders from Libya who had reached Sidi Barrani in September, 1940. By
mid-December the defenders were able to attack. With the aid of tanks,
trucks and planes, and the support of the Mediterranean fleet, they staged
a Blitzkrieg of their own, taking in rapid order Sidi Barrani, Bardia, Tobruk,
Derna and Bengazi. Here they were stalled in turn and unable to cross the
wastes of sand to far-off Tripoli.

The strategic keystone of the East was Turkey. This once proud realm,
originally master of all the Arab world, had lost the last of its non-Turkish
provinces by sharing in the defeat of the Kaiser's Reich. The young Republic
of Ataturk, born out of the ruin of the Sultanate, had become in turn, by
1939, little more than a buffer between Russia, the Axis and the Allies. Each
belligerent strove to use the Turks against its foes.

Nazi control of the Straits and Anatolia would enable the Reichswehr to
dominate the Levant and to descend on Egypt by way of Iraq, Syria and
Palestine. British control of Turkey would insure protection of Egypt and
the Bible lands and perhaps help to save the Balkans from Nazi domination.
Turkey was "allied" to Britain, but guns speak louder than treaties. Had
Wavell possessed sufficient forces to come at once to the defense of Greece
in the fall of 1940 and to buttress strongly Turkish arms in Thrace, Ankara
would doubtless have honored its alliance. But Wavell's armies were weak
and far away. Had Keitel's forces had the means of conquering Turkey
swiftly and countering a possible Russian attack on their flank, Ankara
might well have yielded to Papen's pleas and joined the Axis. But neither

contestant was in a position to occupy Turkey at a blow or to offer the Turks plausible promises of protection against the other. Ankara therefore clung to "neutrality" and frustrated the hopes of London and Berlin alike.

In late February, 1941, Downing Street sought to counter the blandishments of Wilhelmstrasse by dispatching to the Turkish capital Sir Stafford Cripps, British Ambassador in Moscow; Sir John Dill, Chief of the Imperial General Staff; and Anthony Eden, who had succeeded Halifax as Foreign Minister a month before. "Complete agreement" was announced. In mid-March Eden conferred again with Saracoglu on the island of Cyprus. "Identity of views" was announced. But in truth the Turkish leaders would commit themselves to nothing beyond defense of their own territories.

BENGAZI–BAGDAD–BEIRUT

Under these circumstances the war for the Moslem world became a series of campaigns around the rim of a circle with Ankara at its center. With the coming of spring in 1941, Nazi forces gathered in Hungary, Rumania and Bulgaria to strike toward the Aegean. Other Nazi forces moved stealthily across the Mediterranean, via Sicily and perhaps via Tunis, to reinforce the vanquished Italians in Libya. Wavell was obliged by political considerations to weaken his Egyptian army in order to undertake a token defense of Greece. Early in April, only a few days before the Blitz against Belgrade, Lieut. Gen. Erwin Rommel ordered his North African Panzer divisions to attack. Bengazi and Derna were quickly retaken, along with many prisoners, including three British generals. By mid-April Axis troops had again reached the border of "neutral" Egypt at Fort Capuzzo, Halfaya Pass and Solum. British fighters in Tobruk were invested by land and subjected to a long and inconclusive siege. Hitler had saved Libya. But his troops were unable to push on to the delta of the Nile.

This blow was timed to coincide with the Nazi conquest of Jugoslavia and Greece, and with an Axis putsch in Iraq. On April 4 Regent Emir Illah and Premier Taha Al-Haschimi were ousted from power in Bagdad by the followers of Rashid Ali Beg Gailani who proposed to "liberate" his land from British influence by delivering it to the Axis. He ordered his troops to surround the British airport at Habbaniya. He appealed for German aid and protested the landing of British forces at Basra. Haj Amin el Husseini, exiled Mufti of Jerusalem, issued a summons from Beirut for a Holy War by all of

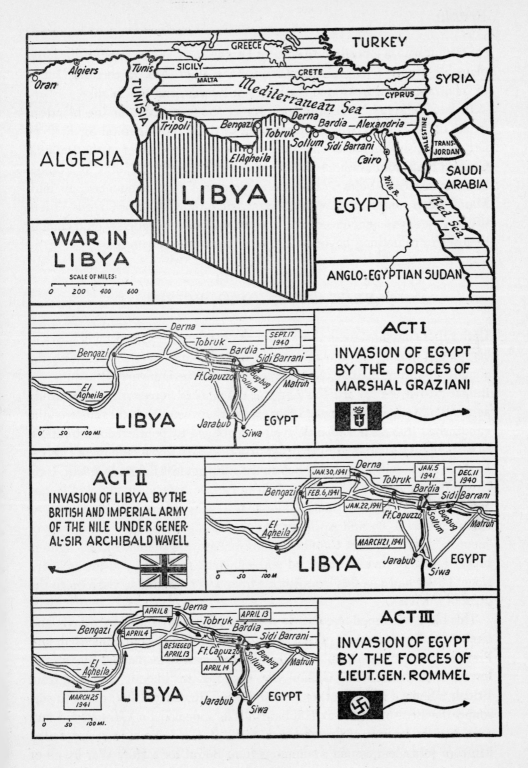

WAR IN LIBYA

SCALE OF MILES:
0 200 400 600

ACT I

INVASION OF EGYPT BY THE FORCES OF MARSHAL GRAZIANI

ACT II

INVASION OF LIBYA BY THE BRITISH AND IMPERIAL ARMY OF THE NILE UNDER GENER-AL-SIR ARCHIBALD WAVELL

ACT III

INVASION OF EGYPT BY THE FORCES OF LIEUT. GEN. ROMMEL

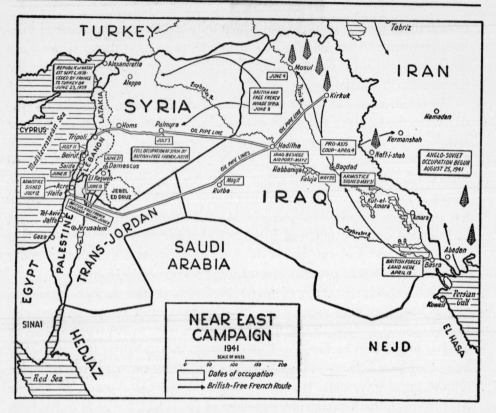

NEAR EAST
CAMPAIGN
1941
SCALE OF MILES
0   50   100   150   200
Dates of occupation
British-Free French Route

Islam on behalf of Gailani's regime. Berlin and Rome sent military missions to Iraq while the Luftwaffe traversed Syria, occupied the Mosul district and moved toward Bagdad.

Prompt British action saved the day. Early in May the R.A.F. began bombing Gailani's forces and lifted the siege of Habbaniya. Turkish offers of mediation were spurned by London, and similar Egyptian offers by Bagdad. Up the Tigris-Euphrates valley moved British columns. By the end of May Bagdad was theirs. Gailani fled to Iran, along with the Mufti and the Axis diplomats. With the signature of an armistice, Regent Abdul Illah returned to rule in the name of six-year-old King Feisal II. Göring's airmen hastily left Mosul.

In the course of these operations the Vichymen in Syria had given full support to the Axis. The R.A.F. accordingly bombed Syrian airports where Axis planes had fueled. The specious protests of General Henri Dentz were ignored. Early in June Lieut. Gen. Sir Henry Maitland Wilson, aided by General Georges Catroux, commander of the Free French in the Near East, invaded Syria from Palestine, with other British forces striking westward from Iraq. In the comic-tragic war which followed Dentz's men offered stubborn resistance to "enemies" who had no desire to fight them. Hitler (and therefore Vichy) was obliged to abandon Syria to its fate in order to launch his invasion of Russia.

The result was an Anglo-Free French victory. Damascus was taken on the day when the forces of the Reich crossed the Soviet frontiers. Other columns attacked Beirut on the coast and approached Homs and Aleppo in the north. On the 9th of July Vichy authorized Dentz to seek an armistice. General Wilson offered generous terms, but Pétain decided that any dealings with agents of De Gaulle would damage his highly sensitive "honor." He therefore left Dentz free to make what terms he liked. An armistice was signed at Acre, in Palestine, on the evening of July 12. Vichy ratified it on the ground that it was "military" and not "political." Syria and Lebanon thus passed under Allied rule. Six weeks later British and Soviet forces occupied Iran.

By the second anniversary of the outbreak of hostilities the British position in the Near East thus seemed secure, despite the loss of the Balkans and Crete—at least so long as the Reichswehr was busy in Russia. The fate of Turkey might well be fixed by Russia's fate. And upon the fate of Turkey hung the future fortunes of British arms in the Levant and the Mediterranean. On the 1st of July, 1941, Wavell exchanged posts with General Sir Claude Auchinleck, hitherto commander-in-chief of the British forces in India. Both were silent as to the reasons for the shift. Both were equally silent as to plans and prospects on the Africasian fronts. But both were agreed that the winning of the war would ultimately require an American expeditionary force.

MUDDLING THROUGH

When spring turned to summer in 1941 the British Commonwealth of Nations was fighting alone against the most formidable military Power of all time. It was too good to be true (and yet it was true) that no British territories anywhere in the world, save only the Channel Islands, were held by the enemy. But it was too true to be good that Britain had no allies anywhere in the world, while Hitler had two other Great Powers and a score of lesser vassals bound to his cause. Such was the penalty of the weakness of British arms which had suffered total defeat in every single encounter on the European Continent against the armies of Germany. Such was the penalty of the folly of British diplomacy which had brought the Reich to hegemony, appeased

Italy to the end, appeased Japan until after the end, and appeased Vichy and Madrid forever.

The heroic defenders of democracy might have been expected (by the naïve) to translate democracy's embattled faith into new deeds of liberation. But even as democratic Britain fought for its life, its rulers kept 30,000 men and women in the jails of India for demanding democracy and withholding support from democracy's war until democracy should be granted them. To complete the paradox, most of these prisoners, including Jawaharlal Nehru, serving four years at hard labor, were leaders of the Indian National Congress who asked no more than a chance to join the British cause as equals in fighting the hosts of tyranny. The rulers of a world empire might have been expected (by the naïve) to take a world view of their destiny and to appreciate the need of a program for a democratic new world order as the only possible means of combatting effectively the program of the Triplice. But even as they struggled to defend their far-flung domains, they saw the world through the eyes of the dead past.

Even Churchill, apart from his tragically belated offer of "Union Now" to defeated France, could not or would not see that victory might never be won by arms alone but only by imagination to revolutionize and remake the world. On the day when Athens fell he predicted that Britain, with American aid, would pass through the "long, stern, scowling valley" of war to victory. But "the war may spread to Spain and Morocco. It may spread eastward to Turkey and Russia. The Germans may lay their hands for a time on the granaries of the Ukraine and the oil wells of the Caucasus. Who can tell? We shall do our best to meet them and fight them wherever they go." Against 200,000,000 Britishers and Americans "there are less than 70,000,000 malignant Huns, some of whom are curable and others killable."

But killing alone would cure nothing. And curing required measures which Britain's rulers seemed unwilling to take, even in their darkest hour—measures to remake democracy, and measures to remake the world. On the 11th of May the Luftwaffe destroyed the House of Commons, damaged "Big Ben," and wrecked Westminster Abbey and Westminster Hall. On the 31st of May the Luftwaffe bombed Dublin, capital of neutral Eire. De Valera and his Irish compatriots would learn nothing. Churchill and his British colleagues would learn little. Their program appeared to be one of enlisting American aid to defeat Hitler and then putting Humpty-Dumpty back on the wall.

On June 12, 1941, representatives of Belgium, Czechoslovakia, Greece, Luxemburg, The Netherlands, Norway, Poland and Jugoslavia, all in exile, met with representatives of Free France and of Britain to adopt a resolution: "They will continue the struggle against German or Italian aggression until victory has been won. The only true basis for enduring peace is the willing cooperation of the free peoples in a world in which, relieved of the menace of aggression, all may enjoy economic and social security. It is their intention to work together with other free peoples both in war and peace to this end." Churchill in his address to Britain's allies-in-exile bespoke good cheer: "Lift up your hearts, all will come right. Out of depths of sorrow and sacrifice will be born again the glory of mankind."

But the words of Britain's valiant leader and the words of exiled politicians brought no balm to the peoples who knew, for all of their hatred of their Nazi masters, that the Europe and the world of 1939 (or of 1919) could never be restored and did not deserve restoration. An ounce of deeds was worth a ton of words, provided the deeds should shine with a vision of the unity of Man. Hitler's vision of a humanity united under the heel of the German "master race" could be beaten only by a nobler vision of a mankind united in the service of Liberty, Equality, Fraternity, with national sovereignty abolished in a democratic federation of the world. But such a vision was still beyond the ken of Britain's rulers as spring turned to summer in 1941.

STALIN'S ALLY

On the first summer Sunday of the year Hitler presented Churchill's Britain with a mighty ally. This ally had long been spurned by Chamberlain's Britain and had in turn spurned Churchill's Britain and pursued a course of suicidal neutrality and appeasement. Yet the alliance which democrats and Communists were never quite willing to make was at long last consummated by Nazi fury.

On the very day on which Hitler's robots were ordered to march against Moscow, Churchill broadcast to the world: "We have but one aim and one irrevocable purpose. We are resolved to destroy Hitler and every vestige of the Nazi regime. From this nothing will turn us. Nothing. We will never parley; we will never negotiate with Hitler or any of his gang. Any man or State who fights against Nazism will have our aid. Any man or State who marches with Hitler is our foe. We shall give whatever help we can to Russia and the Russian people. If Hitler imagines that his attack on Soviet Russia will cause the slightest division of aims or slackening of effort in the great democracies who are resolved upon his doom he is woefully mistaken. His invasion of Russia is no more than a prelude to an attempted invasion of the British Isles. The Russian danger is therefore our danger and the danger of the United States just as the cause of any Russian fighting for his hearth and home is the cause of free men and free peoples in every quarter of the globe."

Sir Stafford Cripps, who had come home in despair but a fortnight before, returned to Moscow with a British military mission. Said Eden on the 5th of July: "We are not in any circumstances prepared to negotiate with Hitler at any time on any subject. We are all out to beat him." After quibbles and quarrels among his Tory colleagues, Churchill at length acknowledged that the Soviet Union was Britain's ally. On July 12 an Anglo-Soviet agreement was signed by Cripps and Molotov in Moscow: "The two Governments mutually undertake to render each other assistance and support of all kinds in the present war against Hitlerite Germany. They further undertake that during this war they will neither negotiate nor conclude an armistice or treaty of peace except by mutual agreement."

BEYOND SURVIVAL

What British arms could not do, the Red Army did—at least temporarily. For the first time Hitler's Blitzkriegers were stopped short of speedy victory. Churchill and Roosevelt both conceded that Russian resistance was "magnificent." "The United States," declared the Prime Minister at the end of July, "is giving us aid on a gigantic scale and is advancing in rising wrath to the very verge of war." But "it would be madness to suppose that Russia or the United States are going to win the war for us." Yet he refused to restate Britain's purposes in any terms save those of restoring what was forever lost. And he refused to name a Minister of Production to meet criticisms of lagging output.

After two years of war effort, Britain still had no means of taking advantage of the conflict in Russia by invading the Continent from the west. The R.A.F. heavily bombed the "invasion ports" in France and plastered Bremen, Hamburg and the cities of the Ruhr. During the last week of July it resumed its long interrupted bombings of Berlin. The Luftwaffe was too busy over the steppes to retaliate effectively. The "V for Victory" campaign, launched in mid-July, represented the best that Britain could do to rally the conquered peoples against the Reich. Hitler's war was still a one-front war.

As the third year of World War II began, Britain's best in the war of nerves, like Britain's best in the war of weapons, still fell far short of what was needed for the winning of victory. Russia's resistance and American aid promised to protect the British Isles from starvation or successful invasion. But if the Reich were to be vanquished and the Continent liberated, much more than this was called for. Churchill's Britain lacked nothing in dogged courage and full willingness to endure all and dare all to the end. But it still lacked vision. And where leaders lack vision, the people perish.

A globe-girdling empire, assailed by a ruthless and imaginative conqueror bent upon subduing the planet, can survive and triumph only by dedicating itself to a dream of a world-wide commonwealth of freemen. Only such a dream would inspire the vanquished peoples to deeds of daring and ultimately win Germans and Italians to freedom's cause. Moscow had its dream of world revolution, albeit a tarnished one which had lost much of its magic. America, greatest of the Powers, shrank from its destiny of leadership in the creation of a new world order. Would America at length rise to the task? Would Britain's leaders follow or lead or stubbornly stand for the *status quo*? Could the war be won without such a vision?

RENDEZVOUS IN ATLANTIS

Both Churchill and Roosevelt acted as if they thought so. On August 9-11, in deepest secrecy, they met for the first time in a northern harbor "somewhere on the Atlantic." The American President was on his fishing yacht, accompanied by the cruiser *Augusta* and other ships of war. The British Prime Minister travelled on the new battleship *Prince of Wales*, protected by a squadron of destroyers and planes. Roosevelt brought with him Harry Hopkins, lend-lease administrator; W. Averill Harriman, lend-lease coordinator in London; Admiral Ernest J. King, commander of the Atlantic fleet; Admiral Harold Stark, Chief of Naval Operations; Sumner Welles, Undersecretary of State; Gen. George C. Marshall, Chief of Staff; and sundry other officials. Among Churchill's diplomatic and military advisers were Admiral Sir Dudley Pound, First Sea Lord; Gen. Sir John G. Dill, Chief of the Imperial General Staff; Sir Alexander Cadogan; and Lord Beaverbrook, Minister of Supply, who proceeded from the meeting place to Washington.

The communiqué issued in London and Washington on August 14, when the fact of the conference was first officially confirmed, declared that "the whole problem of the supply of munitions of war, as provided by the lease-lend act, for the armed forces of the United States and for those countries actively engaged in resisting aggression has been further examined. The President and the Prime Minister have had several conferences. They have considered the dangers to world civilization arising from the policies of military domination by conquest upon which the Hitlerite government of Germany and other governments associated therewith have embarked, and have made clear the steps which their countries are respectively taking for their safety in the face of these dangers." The anti-climax of the announcement was a statement of ultimate purposes:

"The President of the United States of America and the Prime Minister, Mr. Churchill, representing His Majesty's Government in the United Kingdom, being met together, deem it right to make known certain common principles in the national policies of their respective countries on which they base their hopes for a better future for the world.

"First, their countries seek no aggrandizement, territorial or other.

"Second, they desire to see no territorial changes that do not accord with the freely expressed wishes of the peoples concerned.

"Third, they respect the right of all peoples to choose the form of government under which they will live, and they wish to see sovereign rights and self-government restored to those who have been forcibly deprived of them.

"Fourth, they will endeavor, with due respect for their existing obligations, to further the enjoyment by all States, great or small, victor or vanquished, of access, on equal terms, to the trade and to the raw materials of the world which are needed for their economic prosperity.

"Fifth, they desire to bring about the fullest collaboration between all nations in the economic field with the object of securing, for all, improved labor standards, economic advancement, and social security.

"Sixth, after the final destruction of the Nazi tyranny, they hope to see established a peace which will afford to all nations the means of dwelling in safety within their own boundaries, and which will afford assurance that all the men in all the lands may live out their lives in freedom from fear and want.

"Seventh, such a peace should enable all men to traverse the high seas and oceans without hindrance.

"Eighth, they believe that all of the nations of the world, for realistic as well as spiritual reasons, must come to the abandonment of the use of force. Since no future peace can be maintained if land, sea, or air armaments continue to be employed by nations which threaten, or may threaten, aggression outside of their frontiers, they believe, pending the establishment of a wider and permanent system of general security, that the disarmament of such nations is essential. They will likewise aid and encourage all other practicable measures which will lighten for peace loving peoples the crushing burden of armaments.

> "[Signed] Franklin D. Roosevelt.
> "[Signed] Winston S. Churchill."

By a few Britons and Americans this declaration was hailed as a charter of Anglo-Saxon solidarity, beckoning the peoples of the world to a bright future of freedom. By the majority it was assessed for what it was, in the respective idioms of the two countries: a "damp squib" and a "flop." Compared to Wilson's "fourteen points" of 1918, the "eight points" of 1941 were but pious irrelevancies and stale platitudes. The signers apparently assumed that their own peoples were too stupid to face realities or too timid to accept responsibility for a new world order.

To the victims of international anarchy, who knew that peace-on-earth would remain a mirage so long as States retained their "sovereignty," Churchill and Roosevelt promised a restoration of sovereignty. To nations which had learned in tears and blood that no nation can any longer live safely if it lives for itself alone, they pledged "the means of dwelling in safety within their own boundaries." To a world in dire need of an effective international army, navy and air force to impose justice and protect the rights of all through the united action of all, they offered national "disarmament"— first of aggressors and then presumably of the victors. To a humanity eager for a new and positive vision of hope and order in the family of nations, they gave negative assurances of non-aggrandizement, self-determination and freedom of the seas, all reeking of the rancid memories of 1918. Those who asked guidance for the building of the world of tomorrow were offered the hollow phrases of a yesterday which all men of wisdom knew could never be recaptured. Those who needed leadership in creating a federation of mankind were dismissed with an empty reference to "a wider and permanent system of general security." Those who asked bread were given a stone.

Never before in a supreme crisis in human affairs had spokesmen upon whom millions pinned their hopes said so little in words so dead. If President and Prime Minister hoped by their vacuous verbiage to pave the way for some later statement with content, they would have been well advised to recall a comment made years before by Lloyd George: "There is nothing more dangerous than to leap a chasm in two jumps." Here, as always, when words are counterfeit, silence is golden. The "Declaration of the Atlantic" lacked even the negative merit of being "innocuous," for it played directly into Göbbels' hands. It demonstrated anew that in psychological warfare, as in military warfare, the great democracies were still hopelessly outdistanced by the totalitarian tyrannies.

TOWARD TOTAL WAR

More promising for freedom's cause was the circumstance that the statesmen in whose name the "eight points" were issued were accompanied by their principal diplomatic and military advisers. Unless these dignitaries were brought together merely as "window-dressing" for shoddy goods, they presumably discussed, earnestly and in detail, the problems of grand strategy on a world scale which confronted the English-speaking Powers and their Russian and Chinese allies. Those incapable of fighting effectively with ideas must put their hope in weapons.

On the day following the release of the Joint Declaration, Churchill and Roosevelt submitted a public message to Stalin proposing a conference in Moscow among high officials to plan the allocation of resources among the foes of the Axis. They had consulted together, declared the joint invitation, "as to how best our two countries can help your country in the splendid defense that you are making against the Nazi attack. Already many shiploads have left our shores and more will leave in the immediate future. We must now turn our minds to the consideration of a more long term policy, since there is still a long and hard path to be traversed before there can be won that complete victory without which our efforts and sacrifices will be wasted." Stalin accepted at once and promised to make arrangements for the conference in the immediate future. London forthwith announced a £10,000,000 credit to the U.S.S.R.

Two months after the outbreak of the Nazi-Soviet war and six weeks after the signature of the Anglo-Soviet alliance, London and Moscow took their first joint military step. Its purpose was to thwart new Nazi designs in the Near East and to establish a direct line of communication and supply between Soviet and British forces. Early in August Downing Street and the Kremlin warned the government of Iran that they could not tolerate the presence of some hundreds of German "tourists" on Persian soil. With a view toward reassuring Ankara, an Anglo-Soviet declaration was handed to Turkish Foreign Minister Saracoglu on August 12, pledging respect for Turkish integrity and for the Montreux convention, which guaranteed Turkish control of the Straits, and promising Turkey "every help and assistance in the event of her being attacked by a European Power." The replies submitted to Moscow and London by the Ministers of Shah Riza Pahlevi were evasive and unsatisfactory. With a speed unusual in British diplomacy, the Allies decided upon action.

At dawn of August 25, 1941, Soviet troops from the north and British troops from the south crossed the Iranian frontiers. Both governments issued statements explaining the necessity of military action and pledging respect for Iranian independence and integrity. The southern oil fields were occupied by forces from the Persian Gulf and Iraq, while Russian troops took Tabriz. The Iranian Army offered only "token" resistance. On the 27th the Shah accepted the resignation of Premier Ali Khan Mansur. His successor, Ali Furanghi, at once ordered resistance to cease and asked for peace terms. In mid-September the Shah abdicated in favor of his son, Mohammed Riza Pahlevi. Anglo-Soviet forces occupied Teheran and cleansed the land of Axis agents. This quick victory vastly improved the Allied position with respect to Turkey and furnished a safe and open southern road for the shipment of troops and supplies to Russia.

If Vladivostok and Murmansk could also be kept open; if the Red Army could hold the line of the Don or the Volga; if arms and men could be sent to hold the eastern front through the winter; if the people of America could bring themselves to do their full share in the common cause; if the leaders of both of the English-speaking democracies could develop imagination and dare to use it; then England and all the world of freemen could look forward hopefully to victory. And if none of these things should come to pass, then would surely fall "this earth of majesty, this seat of Mars, this blessed plot, this realm, this England," carrying with it to defeat and bondage the Americas, and Asia, and all the hopes of the years ahead. Seldom did so many depend for safety on so few.

Before so grave and grim a burden Britons did not flinch. If others would but give their all to crush the foe and help reshape the earth-wide mansion of mankind, Churchill's prophecy might well come true: "The Old World and the New will join hands to rebuild the temples of man's freedom and man's honor upon foundations which will not soon or easily be overthrown. We shall draw from the heart of suffering itself the means of inspiration and survival, and of a victory—one not only for ourselves but for all; a victory won not only for our own time but for the long and better days that are to come."

"If everybody minded their own business," the Duchess said, in a hoarse growl, "the world would go round a deal faster than it does." "Which would not be an advantage," said Alice. "Just think what work it would make with the day and night! You see the earth takes twenty-four hours to turn round on its axis—" "Talking of Axes," said the Duchess, "chop off her head!" Alice glanced rather anxiously at the cook, to see if she meant to take the hint; but the cook was busily stirring the soup, and seemed not to be listening, so she went on again: "Twenty-four hours, I think; or is it twelve? I—" "Oh, don't bother me!" said the Duchess. "I never could abide figures!"

LOVE THY NEIGHBOR. . . .

"Appeasement," as practiced in politics, if not as defined in the dictionary, means to seek peace by sacrificing others to aggressors. Since peace is only to be had by joining with others to prevent and suppress aggression, appeasement invariably leads to war and brings the appeasers to ruin. During the 1930's the non-Fascist States of the world had to choose between hanging together or hanging separately. In the name of "peace," "neutrality" and "nonintervention," the leaders of each shunned common action with others, lest they involve their people in "other people's wars." The Fascist hangmen were thus enabled to dispatch each victim separately, while future victims supplied the rope and observed with sympathetic interest the rites of execution. Only one Great Power spoke out against the folly of this course and repeatedly urged united action for joint defense. That Power was the Union of Socialist Soviet Republics.

After mid-summer of 1939, however, the U.S.S.R., in the name of "peace," "neutrality" and "nonintervention," pursued exactly the same course toward the Nazi menace which Chamberlain and Daladier had pursued so long and with such bitter results. There was a slight difference of vocabulary: the Western Munichmen praised Hitler early for saving Europe from "Bolshevism," while the Eastern Moscowmen praised him late for fighting the Anglo-French "plutocrats" and "imperialists." There was also a slight difference in geography: the Anglo-French appeasers sought safety by turning Hitler against Russia, while the Muscovite appeasers sought safety by turning him against the Western Powers. Downing Street and the Quai d'Orsay failed miserably in their enterprise. The Narkomindel, or Soviet Foreign Office, succeeded brilliantly.

But successful appeasement is as fatal as unsuccessful appeasement. For appeasement is weakness, and the wise aggressor will always attack the weak first and leave the strong to be dealt with later. Power, moreover, is relative, and the aggressor who is aided by one of his neighbors to destroy another is thereby strengthened to destroy the neighbor who has helped him to his first success. France, Britain and all the lesser States of the Continent learned this lesson too late. Russia and America learned it even later, to the vast delight of the Führer and his allies. Isolationism is the pleasant drug with which aggressors dope and dupe their victims. The drug is fatal, whether taken with vodka or with wine or Scotch or cocktails.

THE BIRTH OF BOLSHEVISM

From Brest-Litovsk to Brest-Litovsk stretches Red Russia's epic over the steppes of time. In the beginning was the Great Revolution. The defeat of Tsarist Russia by Imperial Germany made the Revolution possible. The defeat of Germany by the Allies, and the subsequent defeat of the Allies by the Soviets, enabled the Revolution to survive. Nations and governments, like individuals, are often marked for life by the circumstances of their birth and by the experiences of their infancy. So it was here.

In March of 1917, in the wake of military disaster, Nicholas II, last of the Romanovs, was forced to abdicate in favor of a "Provisional Government" composed of bourgeois democrats and moderate Socialists. This Government, under the leadership of Alexander Kerensky, sought to continue the war and to pave the way for a constituent assembly which would make Russia a middle-class parliamentary democracy. While its supporters deliberated and debated, however, peasants seized the estates of the nobles. Workers occupied factories. Soldiers deserted from the front to share in the new freedom. Real power throughout the country passed to spontaneously organized councils, or *soviets*, of workers', soldiers', and peasants' deputies, who spoke for the war-weary masses and insisted upon an end of the "imperialist" war, the partition of the landed estates, and the socialization of industry.

The Russian Social Democratic Party had been split since 1903 into a moderate minority (Menshevik) group and a radical majority (Bolshevik) group. The latter was led by Vladimir Ilytch Ulianov, alias Nikolai Lenin. His brilliant collaborator, Lev Davidov Bronstein, alias Leon Trotsky, oscillated between the two camps but ultimately joined Lenin's cause. These men and their comrades, many of whom went into Russia in the spring of 1917 via the Reich because the German High Command was sure they would complete Russia's disintegration, won the support of millions of workers, peasants and soldiers for their program of all-out revolution.

The impotent Kerensky regime tottered to its doom, unable either to carry on the war or to withdraw from it, helpless either to avert social revolution or to accept it. With their slogans of "All Power to the Soviets" and "Peace, Land, and Bread," the Bolshevik leaders secured ascendancy in the soviets and organized the new "proletarian" revolution. On November 7, 1917, the Provisional Government was overthrown by the armed workers of Petrograd, and the Second All-Russian Congress of Soviets approved the creation of a Council of People's Commissars, of which Lenin became president. The Soviet Government, thus established, proceeded at once to expropriate the landlords and the bourgeoisie, to abolish private property in real estate and the means of industrial production, to distribute the land to the villages, to establish workers' control in the factories, mills, and mines, and to lay plans for a socialized economy.

In 1918 the Bolsheviki changed their name to the Communist party, in order to distinguish themselves from the "Reformist" Socialists. The former ruling classes were deprived of their wealth and power and replaced by workers and peasants, under the leadership of the middle-class intellectuals who spoke in the name of the proletariat. The Communist party, organized as a highly disciplined brotherhood of revolutionary crusaders, brushed aside the constituent assembly, assumed a "monopoly of legality" in the Soviet Government, and ruled in the name of "the dictatorship of the proletariat"—a form of political authority intended to prepare the way for a Communistic social order and a classless State.

WAR AND PEACE

The foreign policy of the new workers' republic led to immediate friction with the bourgeois governments which were the allies of the old Russia. The Communists regarded their revolution as but a step toward a world revolution of the international proletariat, leading to the universal overthrow of capitalism, nationalism, and imperialism. The bourgeois governments regarded the Communists as a group of dangerous fanatics, whose subversive assault on the existing order must be met by ruthless suppression at the hands of the "sane" elements in Russia, *i.e.*, the expropriated classes, aided by the outside world. There were also specific grievances which impelled the Allies and the United States to move against the proletarian dictatorship. The Soviet Government at once opened peace negotiations with the Central Powers. When the Allies refused to participate, the Communists published the secret treaties, in order to reveal to the masses the imperialistic war aims of the Entente. An armistice was concluded on the eastern front in December, 1917. In March, 1918, the humiliating peace of Brest-Litovsk took Russia out of the war. The Soviet Government, moreover, repudiated the public debts contracted by Tsarist and Kerensky regimes, including both the pre-war government bonds, held in enormous quantities by French and British investors, and the huge war loans extended by the governments of Great Britain, France, and the United States. It likewise confiscated foreign property and private investments in Russia, along with the holdings of the Russian bourgeoisie. It summoned the workers of the world to revolt against the war and to overthrow the "capitalistic" governments which were directing it. The Central Powers seized upon the opportunity presented by the revolution to make an advantageous peace in the East. But between the Soviets and the Allies there could be no peace.

In August, 1918, Soviet Russia was subjected to an Allied blockade and to military intervention, participated in by Czechoslovakian, British, French, American, Japanese, and other Allied troops. The intervention coincided with counter-revolutionary uprisings within Russia, subsidized and supported by the Allied Governments, and with the beginning of the civil war. The moderate Socialist enemies of the Communist dictatorship played into the hands of the counter-revolution and were soon swept aside by Tsarist reactionaries, or "Whites," who rallied to their cause the former landowners and business classes. Blockade, intervention, and revolt were supplemented by terrorism and sabotage as weapons against the Soviets. In Finland the workers' government was drowned in blood by Baron Mannerheim's White terrorists, with German support. In the north, Allied and American troops seized Archangel and advanced southward toward Vologda and Moscow. In the Caucasus and the Ukraine, Denikin's White Army, with Allied support, prepared to invade central Russia. In Siberia, Kolchak's White Army, with Allied support, prepared to do likewise, while Japanese, American, and British troops occupied the Maritime Provinces. In Estonia, Yudenitch's White Army, with Allied support, prepared to take Petrograd.

The Soviet Government was assaulted on all sides from without and menaced by counter-revolution from within. It met these threats to its existence by suppressing the opposition parties, by inaugurating the Red Terror as a reply to the White terrorism of its enemies, and by organizing the Red Army to defend the revolution. In March, 1919, the Communist, or Third, International was established, with its headquarters at Moscow, as an international federation of the revolutionary Communist parties throughout the world. It was designed to replace the bankrupt Second International of the moderate Socialist parties and to serve as the general staff of the "world revolution" which would attack from the rear the bourgeois governments seeking to strangle the Russian proletarian dictatorship.

The civil strife which followed was long and bloody, for it was not only an international conflict between Soviet Russia and the Allied and Associated Powers, but a class war between the Russian nobility and bourgeoisie on the one hand and the proletariat and peasantry on the other. In the end the Red Army, under the direction of Trotsky and his comrades, finally proved more than a match for its enemies, domestic and foreign. Kolchak's forces were driven back from Kazan in the spring of 1919. The Allied and American invaders from the north were finally stopped and later compelled to withdraw. In October, 1919—the darkest month of the Revolution—Denikin's divisions approached Moscow from the south, while Yudenitch, with British support, attacked Petrograd. Both offensives were beaten back. Kolchak's army was crushed in central Siberia, and he was captured and executed in February, 1920. The other White Armies were similarly destroyed, despite desperate Allied attempts to save them.

Peace seemed in sight in the spring of 1920. But the armies of the new Poland invaded the Ukraine in a mad endeavor to restore the Polish frontiers of 1772. Kiev fell to the invaders. In the summer of 1920, however, the Polish forces were pushed back. The Red Army approached the gates of Warsaw and threatened to carry revolution into central Europe. British and French assistance enabled the Poles to counterattack successfully under the direction of General Maxime Weygand. The war closed in October. Meanwhile, a new White leader, Baron Wrangel, had seized the Crimea, invaded the Ukraine, and secured diplomatic recognition and military and financial support from France. His troops were speedily dispersed by the Red Army in the winter of 1920–1921. The civil war came to a close with the defeat of intervention and counter-revolution.

RECONSTRUCTION

The year 1921 marked a definite turning point, both in the internal policies and in the foreign relations of the Soviet Government. The end of the assault from abroad left Russia economically prostrate as a result of six years of almost uninterrupted hostilities. Lenin executed a temporary "strategic retreat toward capitalism" in the New Economic Policy of March, 1921, which permitted a certain amount of individual trade for private profit. At the same time, Great Britain granted *de facto* recognition to the Soviet régime by concluding a trade agreement. The blockade was broken. The *cordon sanitaire* was at an end. A truce prevailed between the proletarian dictatorship and the bourgeois States. The Communists could turn at last to the difficult task of laying the foundations of Utopia.

The restoration of trade relations with the outside world was an integral part of the process, for economic rehabilitation required the importation of machinery, manufactures, and foreign technical skill to be paid for by the export of grain, oil, timber, and other Russian raw materials. At the Genoa Conference of 1922, Georges Chicherin, Commissar for Foreign Affairs, met the representatives of the other European Powers in a general conference for the first time. They demanded payment of Russia's debts and compensation to expropriated investors as the price of recognition, credits, and trade relations. Their bill of 13 billion dollars was met by a Soviet counterclaim of 60 billions for damage done during the intervention. Neither side would yield, and no general agreement was possible. But Chicherin struck a bargain with the new Germany in the Treaty of Rapallo, whereby all claims were cancelled and mutually advantageous commercial relations were restored. Other States could not afford to ignore the Soviet market. Great Britain extended *de jure* recognition in February, 1924. France, Italy, Japan, and a dozen lesser States followed suit within the next eighteen months, with the United States alone among the Great Powers persisting in its refusal to restore diplomatic relations until 1933. The revolutionary outcast was received again into the community of nations, and a growing foreign commerce hastened the work of internal reconstruction.

Meanwhile the frontiers of the new Russia had been redefined and a territorial reorganization of the Soviet State effected. The Treaty of Brest-Litovsk was liquidated by the defeat of Germany in the Great War and by the express provisions of the Treaty of Versailles. During the intervention, Great Britain and France sought to acquire spheres of influence in southern Russia, for reasons of strategy, oil, and high politics. Japan seized eastern Siberia. Poland cast covetous eyes on the Ukraine. The United States opposed these territorial acquisitions by championing the integrity of Russia—of a capitalistic "national" Russia, which Washington hoped would emerge. But the Red Army ousted the invaders, and Moscow pursued its own policies. In accordance with its principles of national self-determination, the Soviet Government was quite prepared to recognize the independence of Finland, Estonia, Latvia, Lithuania, and Poland, with boundaries corresponding to the lines of language. The Baltic States became independent. Their boundaries were fixed in a series of treaties of 1920 and 1921.

Poland and Rumania, however, were determined to seize Russian territory. Rumania occupied Bessarabia in 1918, with the approval of the Allied Powers, and held it thereafter in the face of the persistent refusal of Moscow to concede the legality of this action. The Polish invasion of 1920 was driven back. But the boundary drawn in the Treaty of Riga of March, 1921, transferred several million Ukrainians and White Russians to Polish rule. Still unsatisfied, Poland seized Vilna from Lithuania in October, 1920. But in this chronic quarrel between her western neighbors, Soviet Russia took no sides save for a certain moral support given to the Lithuanian claims. In the Caucasus the old boundaries were substantially restored by agreements with Turkey and Persia.

On the Pacific coast the continued Japanese occupation was met by the creation of the "Far Eastern Republic," a semi-independent Soviet buffer State which was reabsorbed in 1922. In 1925, Japan extended full recognition to Moscow and evacuated all former Russian territory in return for oil and fishing concessions. The agreements with China of 1924 provided for joint ownership and management of the Chinese Eastern Railway across north Manchuria. Outer Mongolia became a Soviet dependency, and Chinese Turkestan was penetrated by Soviet influence. Within Soviet jurisdiction, cultural autonomy was granted to the linguistic minorities. Under the constitution of 1923, creating the U.S.S.R., the Soviet State became a federation of seven units.

"SOCIALIST FATHERLAND"

The interests of the U.S.S.R. in international politics, like those of all other States, reflected the attitudes and values of its ruling class. While "capital-istist" States were dominated politically by nationalistic businessmen or landowners, moved by patriotism and by profit motives, these classes were destroyed in Russia and replaced by a new political élite consisting primarily of middle class intellectuals, but speaking in the name of the proletariat. For the Communists, lines of cleavage and conflict based on language, race, and nationality were effaced by the universal class war between the workers of the world and their exploiters. The Soviet State was composed of numerous linguistic and national groups. It was regarded by its builders, not as a national entity, but as the socialist fatherland, as the citadel of the world proletariat, as the precursor of that world federation of Soviet republics which would follow the world revolution. Its historic mission was the creation of a socialist society and the organization of the class-conscious workers of all countries for the revolutionary seizure of power on a world scale. Its foreign policy was necessarily dominated by the exigencies of this mission.

In view of the "temporary stabilization of capitalism" following the Great War, the U.S.S.R. directed its energies toward building socialism on firm foundations in Russia, rather than toward working for an immediate world revolution. The view of 1917–1919 that a single socialist State could not sur-vive in a hostile capitalistic world was abandoned in favor of the view that political and economic relations with the bourgeois States could be advan-tageously employed to contribute toward the immediate task in Russia. The world revolution seemed imminent in 1919, with Soviet governments estab-lished in Bavaria and Hungary, with all of central Europe in turmoil, and with working-class unrest prevalent throughout the world. By 1921, these hopes had faded. Soviet support was given to the Kuomintang, or revolu-tionary Nationalist party, in China, but the party came to be dominated by bourgeois and militarist elements and expelled its Soviet advisers in 1927.

Lenin's disciple, Stalin, held that the final cataclysm of capitalism was in the future and that the world proletarian revolution would perhaps come only in the wake of the next great war. The Communist International and its national sections—the Communist parties of the various countries—continued to lay their plans in anticipation of this final event. But, for the present, the greatest service to the international proletariat was envisaged as the strengthening of socialist economy in the U.S.S.R.

The decision to "build socialism" in one country was not reached without sharp conflicts of views among the Soviet leaders, reflected later in foreign policy and in the strategy of the Comintern. The disastrous famine of 1921–1923 and the restoration of productivity achieved by the N.E.P. led to general acceptance of Lenin's tactics of retreat. Following his death in January, 1924, Stalin and Trotsky became rivals, with the latter insisting on world revolution, the immediate liquidation of the kulaks, or wealthy peasants, and the suppression of all private trade. Stalin's control of the party machine and Trotsky's infractions of party discipline led to the latter's dismissal and exile in 1927. He denounced Stalin as a betrayer of the revolution and sought to organize ultra-revolutionary Communists abroad into an anti-Stalinist "Fourth International."

After the restoration of production to its pre-war level, Stalin launched the first Five Year Plan in 1928. The N.E.P. was abolished, and a huge program of industrialization was embarked upon. Private trade was suppressed. The kulaks were liquidated with the collectivization of agriculture in 1931–1933. This gigantic agrarian revolution, which abolished individual peasant farms in favor of cooperative collectives and state farms, led to much injustice and suffering, approaching the proportions of famine in some areas. But it was ruthlessly pushed through to a successful conclusion. Industrial and agricultural production rose steadily and paved the way for the second Five Year Plan (1933–1938).

With land in process of socialization and bread of dubious quantity and quality during the transition, Moscow's greatest desire was for peace. Foreign Commissar Chicherin and Maxim Litvinov, his able aide and successor after 1930, bent all their energies toward ensuring peace, securing recognition, fostering trade relations, and forestalling dangers of new attacks on the U.S.S.R. These objectives seemed at times to create a divergence of purposes between the Soviet Foreign Office (the Narkomindel) and the Comintern. Soviet diplomats offered cooperation, but Comintern agents preached revolution. Acute friction with Britain in 1927–1929, controversies with France in 1929–1930, and continued non-recognition by the United States were in part a result of this dualism of Moscow's attitude toward the world. After the Sixth Congress of the Comintern in 1928, no Congresses were held for seven years. Trotsky's fulminations in exile went unheeded. Litvinov gave qualified diplomatic support to the German Republic and to Turkey, Hungary, Italy, and the "revisionist" cause in general against the French bloc, preferring to aid weak potential enemies against strong ones. He championed disarmament, hailed the Kellogg Pact (which the Soviet Union ratified before any of the other Great Powers), and negotiated a series of neutrality and non-aggression agreements with other States.

AGAINST FASCISM

The triumph of Hitler in Germany in 1933 altered fundamentally the peace problem of the U.S.S.R. The German Communist party, largest in the world outside of Russia, had gone down to defeat without a struggle. To the end, it had fought bitterly the largest of Socialist parties. Both had been destroyed, along with German Liberalism and the Weimar Republic. The Nazi leaders were loudly committed to conquest in the East and to an armed crusade against Bolshevism. Militant Fascism threatened Moscow with armed attack and promised to destroy Communists, Socialists, and liberals in other States. To prevent assault from Berlin, Moscow must arm to the teeth and find allies. To prevent destruction of the Communist movement throughout the world, Moscow must cooperate with Socialists and liberals against Fascism. The Narkomindel and the Comintern faced the new task realistically. The result was a revolution in Soviet diplomacy and a reorientation of international Communism.

The Franco-Soviet nonaggression pact of 1932 was supplemented by a commercial treaty in January of 1934, following a *rapprochment* during the year of the Nazi seizure of power in the Reich. Agreements of April and May with Poland and the Baltic States extended these nonaggression pacts to 1945. Closer relations were cultivated with Turkey and Great Britain. In June, 1934, Czechoslovakia and Rumania, on the advice of Louis Barthou, recognized the U.S.S.R., following the example of Hungary in February. On September 18, 1934, the Soviet Union became a member of the League of Nations. Efforts to conclude a nonaggression pact with Berlin and to induce the Reich to enter into an "eastern Locarno" failed. Litvinov strove for a defensive mutual assistance pact with France and the Little Entente, including Germany if she would enter, against Germany if she refused. Tukhachevsky, Vice Commissar of Defense, announced in January, 1935, that the Red Army had been increased from 562,000 to 940,000 and that planes, tanks, and artillery had been multiplied many fold. Under the impact of Hitler's repudiation of the disarmament clauses of the Treaty of Versailles, Paris signed a mutual assistance pact with Moscow on May 2, and Prague followed suit on May 16, 1935. The U.S.S.R. thus became the ally of France and Czechoslovakia, within the framework of the League, to resist Nazi aggression.

In midsummer, 1935, the Seventh Congress of the Comintern met at Moscow. The old slogan of world revolution—"Turn imperialist war into civil war" —was replaced by a call for union against Fascism. The Comintern resolved to discontinue, or at least defer, its assaults on Socialists and liberals and its efforts to overturn bourgeois democratic governments. The new policy of the "united front" contemplated a strategic retreat toward the right and loyal cooperation not only with Socialist parties but with bourgeois groups opposed to Fascism. Even the Roman Catholics in Germany were invited to join in opposing Nazi rule. An appeal was addressed to the Second International of Socialist Parties at Amsterdam to participate in the new alliance. This policy met with bitter condemnation on the part of Trotsky and his disciples as a fresh betrayal of the world revolution and a new compromise with capitalism. By Socialists and liberals, it was greeted with suspicion, since the plea of the "united front" (from below) had been made before for the purpose of "boring from within" and seeking to place the organizations which cooperated under Communist domination. Amsterdam spurned fusion with Moscow or even general collaboration. British Laborites as well as Socialists in Czechoslovakia and America likewise declined to cooperate. But in France and Spain, liberals and Socialists joined Communists in Popular Front movements to resist Fascist attacks on democracy.

Other defensive measures had long since been devised to meet the danger of Japanese attack in the East. Recognition by the United States on November 16, 1933, was to some degree motivated by common suspicion of Japan. Moscow made repeated but vain efforts to conclude a nonaggression pact with Tokyo. As further conciliatory gestures the U.S.S.R. sold the Chinese Eastern Railway to Manchukuo in March, 1935, and in the autumn of 1936 proposed to extend Japanese fishing and oil concessions in eastern Siberia— until the announcement of the German-Japanese anti-Communist accord of November 25 caused a reversal of policy. Japanese penetration of Inner Mongolia, which might place Japanese forces in a position to attack Ulan Bator and the Lake Baikal area, was met by a mutual assistance pact with Outer Mongolia, in force since 1934 and incorporated in a formal agreement on March 12, 1936.

More important, a self-sufficient Far Eastern army of 250,000 troops under General Bluecher was established in the Maritime Provinces ready to invade Manchukuo should Japan attack. A thousand warplanes were poised at Vladivostok to give Tokyo pause. The Trans-Siberian Railway was double-tracked and supplemented by a road north of Lake Baikal to Komsomolsk and Nikolaevsk. Fears of a combined Nazi-Japanese attack, with possible Finnish and Polish support, led to strengthening frontier fortifications in the east and the west. By January, 1936, the Red Army numbered 1,300,000 men and had some 6,000 tanks and 7,000 warplanes. Every effort was made to increase the output of mechanized armaments. In reply to Hitler's verbal assaults at Nürnberg, Defense Commissar Voroshilov declared on September 17, 1936, "When the enemy attacks the Soviet Ukraine or Soviet White Russia or any other part of the Soviet Union, we will not only prevent his invading our own country, but will defeat him in the territory whence he comes."

The new dispensation was accompanied by plans for liberalizing the Soviet regime. In July, 1934, the O.G.P.U., or secret political police, was abolished and its functions transferred to the Commissariat of Internal Affairs. After long deliberation a new Union Constitution was announced in June, 1936, and adopted in November. It created a Parliament or Supreme Soviet of two chambers, one—the Council of the Union—elected by direct and secret ballot every four years with the franchise restored to the former "enemy" classes, and the other—the Council of Nationalities—consisting of elected delegates from the constituent republics, which were increased from seven to eleven. An elected judiciary was also provided, and more adequate protection of individual rights was pledged.

PURGATORY IN UTOPIA

This evolution away from dictatorship, however, was transitory. On December 1, 1934, Sergei Kirov, aide of Stalin, was assassinated in Leningrad. Within a few weeks thereafter, 117 persons were executed as terrorists. Zinoviev and Kamenev, former Soviet leaders and once supporters of Trotsky, were implicated and sentenced to prison. In August, 1936, they, along with 14 others, were charged with conspiring with Trotsky, in his Norwegian exile, to slay Kirov, Stalin, and other Communist functionaries in a Trotskyite-Fascist murder plot. The accused confessed. Trotsky denied all. The defendants were found guilty and shot. Paradoxically, this act—representing a complete break between the Stalin leadership, which was committed to the united front and to the soft-pedaling of world revolution, and the Trotsky opposition, still bent on proletarian revolt everywhere—antagonized foreign liberals who otherwise were sympathetic with Stalin rather than Trotsky. As in all dictatorships, ruthless means were held to be justified by ideal ends. But to critics the ends seem to be destroyed by the means.

"The tyrant, if he means to rule," wrote Plato, "must get rid of those who speak their minds until he has made a purge of the State. And the more detestable his actions are to the citizens, the more satellites and the greater devotion in them will he require." In January, 1937, in a further trial of Trotskyites (who confessed to attempted assassination, sabotage, espionage, counter-revolution, and conspiracy with Trotsky to aid Germany and Japan in war on the U.S.S.R.), Karl Radek and Gregory Sokolnikov were sentenced to ten years' imprisonment and thirteen other defendants were sentenced to death, including Gregory Piatakov and L. Serebriakov, both former prominent officials. Trotsky, then in Mexico after expulsion from Norway, again denied all and cried "frame-up." In April Henry Yagoda, head of the "reformed" G.P.U., was arrested. In June Marshal Tukhachevsky and seven other high officers were court-martialed and shot for treason. In December Leo Kharakhan and other diplomats were reported to have been executed for allegedly treasonable dealings with Tokyo. In March, 1938, Bukharin, Yagoda, Rykov, Krestinsky, and fourteen other former leaders were tried, found guilty, and presumably put to death, while Christian Rakovsky and two other defendants were given prison terms.

Apart from celebrities, thousands and possibly tens of thousands of humble men and women lost their liberties or their lives. There was little publicity given to the proceedings, save in the case of the "Old Bolsheviks"—and of these only those who agreed to confess were given public trials. When asked by Lady Astor how long he proposed to keep shooting people, Stalin replied imperturbably: "As long as necessary." The victims doubtless included many actual or potential Fifth Columnists and Trojan Horses. Unlike the leaders of the democracies, Stalin believed in placing such figures not in Cabinet posts or in army commands, but in prison or in the cemetery. The victims also included many who were honest critics of the despot in the Kremlin and many who were liquidated out of personal malice. The principal scapegoat, Leon Trotsky, was assassinated in his home near Mexico City on August 21, 1940. Trotskyites said the killer was a Stalinist tool. Stalinists said he was a disgruntled Trotskyite who felt that Trotsky had betrayed Trotskyism.

THE FAILURE OF THE "POPULAR FRONT"

These developments had consequences in terms of the hidden calculations of the Fascist Caesars which were widely misunderstood in the democracies. They demonstrated to Hitler and to the warlords of Tokyo that the U.S.S.R. was not a weak State but a strong one. The result was a slow and secret abandonment of Nazi and Japanese dreams of conquest at the expense of the Soviet State and a reorientation of aggressive designs against the Western Powers. Since Western leaders continued to practice appeasement, however, on the assumption that a Fascist-Communist clash was "inevitable," the Caesars found it advantageous to denounce Moscow on all occasions. With each passing year, they took their own threats less seriously, and the Kremlin became less concerned with them. Fascist mouthings of "anti-Bolshevism" were intended for ears in London, Paris, and Washington where they were taken quite seriously.

Under these conditions, Soviet hopes of a "united front" with the West against the Triplice, and Communist hopes of a "united front" with Socialists and liberals against Fascism, were alike doomed to frustration. Without the support of the Western Powers, Moscow could not thwart Fascist aggression. Without the support of Western democrats, Communists could not combat Fascist tactics of disintegration in other States. When the U.S.S.R. sought to use the League to save Ethiopia from Mussolini, London and Paris preferred to save Mussolini at the cost of destroying Ethiopia and the League. When the U.S.S.R. sought to save the Spanish Republic by observing the "non-intervention" agreement only in the measure to which it was observed in Rome and Berlin, the Western appeasers preferred to cooperate with the Axis in destroying the Republican regime. The Spanish People's Front died. The French People's Front followed it to the grave.

After *Anschluss*, Litvinov proposed a conference to consider ways and means of halting Hitler. Downing Street and the Quai d'Orsay refused. When Litvinov proposed joint defense of Czechoslovakia in 1938, Chamberlain and Halifax, with the support of Daladier and Bonnet, preferred to abandon Prague. After Munich the *Journal de Moscou* asked, "What now is the value of France's word? What now is the value of the French-Soviet pact since France has just torn up her treaty with Czechoslovakia—a treaty that bound her much more strongly?" Immediately after the fall of Prague in March, 1939, Litvinov proposed a conference to consider joint action to halt aggression. London and Paris refused.

STALIN'S CHESTNUTS

Correct conclusions were drawn from these events in Rome and Berlin. Correct conclusions were also drawn in Moscow. On March 10, 1939, Stalin spoke at length to the Eighteenth Congress of the Communist Party of the U.S.S.R. He ridiculed the Western Munichmen and bespoke friendship with the Caesars:

"The majority of the non-aggressive countries, particularly England and France, have rejected the policy of collective security, the policy of collective resistance to the aggressors, and have taken up a position of nonintervention, a position of 'neutrality.' The policy of nonintervention reveals an eagerness, a desire, not to hinder the aggressors in their nefarious work: not to hinder Japan, say, from embroiling herself in a war with China, or, better still, with the Soviet Union; not to hinder Germany, say, from enmeshing herself in European affairs, from embroiling herself in a war with the Soviet Union.

"Far be it from me to moralize on the policy of nonintervention, to talk of treason, treachery and so on. It would be naïve to preach morals to people who recognize no human morality. Politics is politics, as the old, case-hardened bourgeois diplomats say. It must be remarked, however, that the big and dangerous political game started by the supporters of the policy of nonintervention may end in a serious fiasco for them. . . ."

Stalin bespoke peace with all countries and pledged support of nations resisting aggression. He added that new dangers imposed new tasks: "To continue the policy of peace and of strengthening business relations with all countries; to be cautious and not allow our country to be drawn into conflicts by war-mongers who are accustomed to have others pull the chestnuts out of the fire for them; to strengthen the might of our Red Army and Red Navy to the utmost; to strengthen the international bonds of friendship with the working people of all countries, who are interested in peace and friendship among nations." The crucial question as to which chestnuts were whose remained unanswered—until Hitler supplied the answer two years later.

THE ALLIANCE THAT MIGHT HAVE BEEN

Within a week after Stalin's words were spoken, Hitler liquidated Czecho-Slovakia, gave Carpatho-Ukraine to Hungary, and finally convinced the

Western Munichmen that their States, rather than the U.S.S.R., were "on the list and would never be missed" when the Reich should be ready to strike. They accordingly sought to rebuild a coalition against Germany. The enterprise required Soviet collaboration. Moscow was willing to be wooed and even to be won—for a price. But most of the Western leaders were still motivated by abhorrence of Bolshevism and were by no means convinced that the Nazi threat was so grave as to require acceptance of Moscow's terms. This attitude confirmed the Kremlin's distrust. In the absence of mutual respect, an equal sense of common danger, and a willingness to compromise in order to face it, the obvious logic of *Realpolitik* led nowhere. British willingness to guarantee Poland, and even Rumania and Greece, before coming to terms with the U.S.S.R. evoked contempt in Moscow. *Pravda's* cartoon of April 4, 1939, showed a silk-hatted British lion in a boat extending a rock-loaded life-belt to small nations struggling in a stormy sea swarming with sharks.

When Anglo-Soviet negotiations were initiated in mid-April, Moscow asked a binding alliance. London refused, preferring some more "flexible" formula which would not offend the "anti-Comintern" States and would leave Britain and France free if the Reich after all should attack the U.S.S.R. On May 3 Litvinov resigned his post as Commissar for Foreign Affairs in favor of Premier Vyasheslav Molotov. Chamberlain drew no conclusions from this event, although four days later the French Ambassador in Berlin began a series of ominous reports on the possibility of a Soviet-Nazi *rapprochement* to be followed by a new partition of Poland (*French Yellow Book of* 1939, No. 123*f.*). British counter-proposals of May 8 contemplated Soviet aid to Britain and France should they be obliged to fight in defense of Poland or Rumania. Moscow asked Anglo-French aid to the U.S.S.R. should it be attacked or be obliged to fight in defense of the Baltic States. All three Powers should agree to defend one another and should guarantee all the border States between the Reich and the Soviet Union, as well as the border States (Switzerland, Belgium, and The Netherlands) between the Reich and the Western Powers. Churchill and Lloyd George urged acceptance of Molotov's terms. Chamberlain and Halifax refused. The Baltic States worshiped "neutrality" and desired no international guarantee participated in by the U.S.S.R. Downing Street would not guarantee States unwilling to be guaranteed. It proposed "consultation" in the event of any Nazi aggression in the Baltic. But Moscow knew that this was a formula to evade any commitment.

At the end of May Molotov publicly declared that Moscow would make no pact save on the basis of "reciprocity and equality of obligations" and that this required (1) a binding alliance; (2) a joint guarantee of all European countries bordering the U.S.S.R.; and (3) a concrete agreement for mutual aid and defense of the guaranteed States in the event of attack by aggressors. London and Paris now accepted (1) but balked at (2) and (3). The negotiations dragged on inconclusively. At the end of June, Andrei Zhdanov, Leningrad party leader, wrote in *Pravda* that he did not believe that the British and French Governments desired an equal treaty with the U.S.S.R. At the end of July Chamberlain announced that Anglo-French military missions would go to Moscow to initiate staff talks, pending conclusion of a definitive agreement which had been held up by differences of views on the proper definition of "indirect aggression." The missions made a leisurely trip to the Soviet capital. Molotov, Voroshilov, and Stalin expected that they would have authority to sign a pact giving the U.S.S.R. the right to decide when the Baltic States were threatened, to act to meet the threat, to have necessary military access to the Baltic States and Poland, and to summon Britain and France to its support. They had no such authority. Deadlock was complete.

There thus failed of completion the only alliance which could have halted Hitler's career of aggression by threatening him with a two-front war and swift defeat. Moscow blamed London and Paris for the failure, and with much reason. London and Paris, with less reason, blamed Moscow. But assessment of blame was futile. Hitler was the victor. He had once more succeeded in dividing his victims against one another and isolating them, one by one, for the kill. London, Paris and Moscow alike were pulling Nazi chestnuts from the fire.

"NONINTERVENTION" BY MOSCOW

A complete revolution in Soviet diplomacy followed the failure of the Anglo-Russian discussions. Ribbentrop came to Moscow on August 23 and signed a German-Soviet nonaggression pact. Voroshilov declared that the U.S.S.R. could not defend Poland unless the Red Army were permitted to enter Polish territory. Neither Warsaw, Paris, or London had been willing to grant such permission. Molotov told the Supreme Soviet on August 31, when the pact with Hitler was ratified, that the Western Powers had "plotted to involve us in war" without being willing to see the Soviet Union strengthened. Germany had dropped its anti-Soviet policy. The U.S.S.R. had no need to join either side. It would remain at peace. After several weeks of confusion, due to obvious ignorance of the Kremlin's new decision, the Communist parties of France, Britain, and America dropped all slogans of "People's Front," "Unity against Fascist Aggression," and the like; denounced as an "imperialist war" the new conflict which the pact of Moscow enabled Hitler to unleash; and developed a line of "revolutionary defeatism" which admirably served the purposes of Stalin—and of Hitler.

The Kremlin's policy after the outbreak of hostilities was strict neutrality, tempered by a firm determination to sell nonintervention to Hitler at a price which would greatly strengthen the defenses of the U.S.S.R. against the Reich. The first step was to seize the former Russian territories of Poland and to reach an agreement with Berlin on the division of the carcass of the victim of the *Blitzkrieg*. On September 17, 1939, Moscow declared that the Polish State had "virtually ceased to exist" and that the Red Army must undertake the protection of its abandoned "blood brothers," the Ukrainians and the White Russians. Soviet troops were already on the march. They rapidly occupied all eastern Poland not yet in the hands of the Reichswehr. German and Russian troops met at Brest-Litovsk. Ribbentrop flew again to Moscow. On September 28 a new German-Soviet agreement partitioned Poland along the ethnographic frontier, the Reich taking the Polish areas and the U.S.S.R. the White Russian and Ukrainian areas, including western Galicia which had been part of Austria-Hungary before 1914. This extension of Bolshevism 250 miles westward was but the first of Stalin's victories and the initial installment of the price paid to Moscow by Berlin for "reinsurance" in the East.

The Kremlin's next step was the imposition of protectorates on the Baltic States. Hitler acquiesced not only in Soviet military control of the ancient realm of the Teutonic Knights but in the "voluntary" evacuation to the Reich of the Germans who had lived on the Baltic shore for seven centuries. By a combination of trumped-up accusations, invitations, and threats of invasion, Moscow induced Estonia (September 28), Latvia (October 5), and Lithuania (October 10) to sign mutual assistance pacts pledging common defense "in the event of a direct aggression or threat of aggression on the part of any European Great Power" against the Baltic frontiers of the signatories. Moscow acquired the right to establish garrisons on Baltic territory and to maintain naval and air bases at Paltiski, Oesel, Dagoe, Libau, and Windau. The Baltic Republics secured in return a short-lived "protection" of their "integrity" and their "sovereign" rights. Lithuania was granted the long-coveted city and region of Vilna.

Moscow now gave moral support to Berlin's bid for "peace" in October,

1939. "One cannot destroy any ideology by fire and sword," said *Izvestia.* "One may respect or hate Hitlerism, just as any other system of political views. This is a matter of taste. But to undertake war for 'annihilation of Hitlerism' means to commit criminal folly in politics. For whose benefit is this war waged for domination of the world? In any case, not for the benefit of the working class. The working class can only suffer in such a war." This attitude, far from being indicative of the Soviet desire to see the Reich win the war, was inspired by the conviction that a "negotiated" settlement on the basis of the new *status quo* would leave the U.S.S.R. secure in its new outposts. Such a development would also save the Western Powers from possible destruction and compel their discredited leaders to seek a new *rapprochement* with the U.S.S.R. on Moscow's terms as the only means of future protection against the victorious Reich. These strictly *Realpolitik* desiderata were rationalized by Communists everywhere in terms of stereotyped eulogies of peace and denunciations of Anglo-French "imperialism." But London and Paris were committed to restoring the *status quo ante bellum* and would neither recognize Moscow's title to the new Soviet territories nor consider peace with Hitler. Stalin therefore considered what further measures he should take to strengthen his State against the bourgeois Powers.

BLOODSHED IN FINLAND

Efforts to negotiate a mutual assistance pact with Turkey failed in the autumn of 1939 because of Ankara's reluctance to meet Soviet terms and Turkish determination to remain faithful to the Western Allies. Moscow acquiesced in the Turkish refusal. But when Finland rejected Soviet demands, the Kremlin resorted to force. In mid-October Molotov received a Finnish delegation in Moscow and asked a thirty-year lease for a Red naval base at Hanko and cession to the U.S.S.R. of part of the Karelian Isthmus north of Leningrad, several islands in the Gulf, and a strip of coast near Petsamo on the Arctic in exchange for a larger area of central Karelia midway between Lake Ladoga and the Arctic. Helsinki refused, since the proposals involved the abandonment of the Mannerheim line of fortifications on the Isthmus. Each side was willing to compromise. But Moscow would not relinquish demands for Hanko, for the removal of the alleged "threat" to Leningrad, and for effective military control of the Gulf of Finland and the entire northwestern frontier. Helsinki would not yield to demands which it regarded as incompatible with Finnish security, "neutrality," and "independence." The result was deadlock.

On November 26, 1939, Molotov alleged that Finnish frontier guards had fired on Soviet troops. He demanded that Helsinki withdraw its forces on the Isthmus a distance of twenty to twenty-five kilometers. Finland denied the charge and agreed to withdraw troops from the frontier only if Moscow did likewise. Molotov retorted by denouncing the Soviet-Finnish nonaggression pact of 1932 and ordering Soviet troops and air forces to attack Finland on November 30. On December 1, Moscow granted diplomatic recognition to a "People's Government of the Democratic Republic of Finland," established in the isthmian frontier village of Terijoki and headed by Otto Kuusinen, a Communist refugee from Finland. The U.S.S.R. herewith committed an act of flagrant aggression motivated by strategic considerations regarded as paramount. It sought to imitate the Fascist technique of intimidation and disintegration through support of a puppet regime. The expectation apparently was that Helsinki would yield at the first blow or that the Finnish masses would rally to Kuusinen, with whom Moscow concluded a treaty of mutual assistance (December 2) granting all the Soviet military and territorial demands.

These assumptions were completely mistaken. The Finns rallied to the defense of their country and inflicted heavy losses on the inferior Soviet troops sent against them. Over 100,000 lives were lost in bitter fighting in subzero weather amid the frozen marshes and forests of the sub-Arctic wilderness. During December and January the defenders more than held their own. Early in February, however, the invaders launched a frontal offensive against the Isthmus fortifications with first-class troops under General Gregory Stern. Marshal Gustav Mannerheim's "line" was broken by massed artillery and tanks. His troops were forced out of the island stronghold of Koivisto on February 26 and out of the suburbs of Viipuri (Viborg) on March 5. He had estimated in January that successful defense against the Red giant could be continued if 30,000 foreign troops were available by May. In February, he felt he would need 50,000 foreign troops by April. By early March, he conceded that 100,000 reinforcements were needed at once. Since they were nowhere to be had, he and his colleagues decided to sue for peace.

Meanwhile Finland had appealed to the Western Powers and to the League. On December 14, 1939, the Assembly and Council at Geneva condemned Soviet aggression and for the first time (and the last) expelled an aggressor from membership. Moscow scoffed. The League died. The Council and Assembly never met again. As for aid to Finland outside of the League, Sweden gave generously of arms, supplies, and volunteers but always within the limits of "neutrality." The United States, with nothing to fear, was likewise hypnotized by its own mythology. Private relief funds of more than a million dollars flowed from American pocketbooks to Finland. All Americans loved Finland as the only one of the war debtors to meet its obligations to the United States in full. All Americans hated Bolshevism. On December 10 the Export-Import Bank (created, by a curious irony, to help finance Soviet-American trade) opened a $10,000,000 credit for Finnish purchases. But the Finns were permitted to buy only "nonmilitary" supplies. Congress failed to act upon the President's plea for further credits until it was too late, when $20,-000,000 were made available—also for "nonmilitary" supplies, of which the Finns had little need. Although the "Neutrality" Act was not applied, congressional solicitude for "neutrality" forbade any effective assistance.

London and Paris were paralyzed for other reasons. The mad Munichmen relished the thought of fighting the U.S.S.R. far more than that of fighting the Reich. Gamelin and Weygand, then in Syria, made plans for bombing the Baku oil fields, less to aid Finland than to interrupt German imports of Soviet oil. But Turkey would not cooperate. Chamberlain and Daladier made plans for an expeditionary force to cross Scandinavia and go to Finland's support. But Norway and Sweden would not cooperate, lest this departure from "neutrality" provoke a German invasion to forestall Allied control of Scandinavia. After long hesitation the Allied Governments on March 2 formally requested Norway and Sweden to permit passage of Allied troops. Oslo and Stockholm both refused. While Chamberlain and Daladier, primarily for the purpose of cutting the Reich off from iron-ore shipments (via Narvik) from the mines of northern Sweden, contemplated forcible measures to induce compliance, the Finnish Government decided that its situation was hopeless. It asked Moscow for terms. Stalin recognized the error of his original calculations. He had no desire to be involved in hostilities with the Allies. He therefore agreed to drop Kuusinen and grant peace on "moderate" terms. Even after the peace in Finland, the Allied High Command toyed with plans for bombing Baku until the western Blitzkrieg put an end to all such schemes.

On March 12, 1940, a Finnish delegation in Moscow signed a peace treaty with the U.S.S.R. Helsinki was obliged to cede without compensation the entire Karelian Isthmus and the shores of Lake Ladoga, most of the Gulf islands, and a strip of northern territory near Petsamo, not including the port, however, or the near-by nickel mines. Moscow secured the right to build a railway in the north, along with free passage to Norway and Sweden. Hanko was leased for thirty years at an annual rental of $330,000. Molotov reaffirmed Soviet neutrality and denounced the Anglo-French "imperialists."

The ultimate irony of the Finnish war became apparent only later. Stalin had infuriated the rulers of Finland and then failed to deprive them of their power to take revenge. Had he imposed a conqueror's peace on the vanquished, Western democrats would have denounced him even more bitterly. His reward for moderation was to have Helsinki join Hitler in assaulting the U.S.S.R. in June of 1941. The reward of the Western democrats for their half-hearted help to Finland was to have Mannerheim ally himself with the Nazi Reich and place at Hitler's disposal the ambulances, motor cars, canned foodstuffs and other supplies which generous liberals had sent to help the Finns against Soviet aggression. And the moral of this is that in power politics there are no morals.

THE DIPLOMACY OF DOUBT

When Comrade Stalin discarded the rapier of Litvinov in favor of the umbrella of Chamberlain he hoped that the Nazi-Western war, which he thereby helped unleash, would become a stalemate. As a sensible man, familiar with Western ways despite his disinclination for travel, he knew that France and Britain unaided could never defeat the Reich. He also thought he knew that the Reich could never defeat the Western Powers, for such a defeat he knew full well would inevitably be followed, as promised in *Mein Kampf,* by a Fascist assault on the U.S.S.R. To prevent such an assault by appeasing Hitler was safe only so long as Hitler's legions were entangled in dubious battle along the Rhine.

The fall of Copenhagen, Oslo, The Hague, Brussels and Paris in the terrifying spring of 1940 raised questions in the Kremlin as to the correctness of the logic behind the Nazi-Soviet pact. The men of Moscow still took it for granted, as did all the world, that the Führer would never move east so long as Britain still fought a good fight. But if Britain should fall . . . ? Or if the Reich, in the name of fighting Britain, should try to encircle Western Russia via Scandinavia and the Balkans? These dangers might be met by a secret Anglo-Soviet pact. Churchill might have been willing, given a suitable *quid pro quo.* But Stalin was hypnotized by his own vocabulary. He decided upon further seizures of territory and upon a kind of diplomatic passive resistance to the Axis.

EXPANSION
OF U.S.S.R.
1939-1940

SCALE OF MILES:
0   100   200   300

Petsamo
MARCH 12, 1940

White Sea

SWEDEN

FINLAND

Gulf of
Bothnia

Ladoga

Viipuri

MARCH 12, 1940

Helsinki

Leningrad

Hanko

Stockholm

Tallinn

PROTECTORATE
SEPT. 28, 1939 -
ANNEXED ON
JULY 21, 1940

ESTHONIA

30 YEAR LEASEHOLD TO
U.S.S.R. UNDER PEACE
TREATY, MARCH 12, 1940

PROTECTORATE
OCT. 5, 1939 -
ANNEXED ON
JULY 21, 1940

Riga

LATVIA

Moscow

LITHUANIA

PROTECTORATE
OCT. 10, 1939 -
ANNEXED ON
JULY 21, 1940

Kaunas

SEPT. 17-28
1939

Warsaw

JUNE 28
1940

Rostov

AUGUST 30, 1940

No. BUKOVINA

Budapest

No. TRANSYLVANIA

BESSARABIA

HUNGARY

RUMANIA

Belgrade

Bucharest

JUGOSLAVIA

SO. DOBRUDJA

Black Sea

Sofia

AUGUST 21, 1940

BULGARIA

[225]

On June 15-17, 1940, Soviet troops abruptly occupied all of Lithuania, Latvia and Estonia. Following local "elections," the three Baltic Republics were formally incorporated into the Soviet Union. On June 28 the Red Army occupied Bessarabia and Northern Bukovina after Rumanian acceptance of a Soviet ultimatum.

These further enhancements of Soviet power had perforce to be "approved" with good grace by the Fascist Caesars. Stalin, unlike Mussolini, knew that an alliance with a stronger Power to despoil a third can only lead to ruin. He was confident, moreover, that the United States would not permit British defeat. On this assumption, he could afford to pursue "neutrality" with a vengeance, meanwhile taking care that the Reich did not install its forces in areas where they might prove menacing to the U.S.S.R. Despite its saving clause in Article 5, the Triple Alliance Pact of September 27, 1940, was not comforting to the Kremlin. The swift German occupation of Rumania in early October apparently caught Moscow unawares. A Tass communiqué asserted that reports abroad to the effect that the U.S.S.R. had been consulted and had approved in advance of the German action "did not correspond to the facts." Later reports that Moscow had approved Hungarian adherence to the Triplice elicited the comment that they "did not correspond to the facts to any degree."

Molotov visited Berlin in mid-November, 1940, doubtless seeking some "clarification" of Hitler's purposes. What was said by whom to whom is still a secret. The Führer probably sought to quiet the fears of his guest, for his warrior-hordes must first conquer the Balkans before they could tackle the Russian bear. If his purpose was to insure Soviet inaction while he devoured and digested Balkania, he was successful. If his purpose was to secure Soviet adherence to the Axis, as Moscow later alleged, and to arrange therewith a partition of Turkey and Iran, he failed.

According to the labored "explanations" of Hitler and Ribbentrop the following June, Molotov proposed a Soviet-Bulgarian mutual assistance pact and also asked Berlin's assent to the acquisition of Soviet bases on the Straits —an allegation, said Lozovsky, "as much like truth as Göbbels is like Apollo." The Soviet Premier (said Ribbentrop and Hitler) also demanded cessation of German support of Finland and asked whether the German "guarantee" to the rump of Rumania was directed against Russia. Molotov got no satisfaction. Hitler's satisfaction was incomplete in the face of what he termed "continually renewed extortions." But Soviet oil, grain and lumber continued to flow to Germany. "Business as usual" is not a slogan reserved for capitalists.

Molotov went home, resolved to speak softly and keep his powder dry. Officially the Kremlin remained on the best of terms with the Reich. It concluded a new trade agreement in January, reiterated its devotion to "neutrality" and "friendship," and denounced Anglo-American "plutocracy" and "imperialism" with all the passion of Hitler himself. All loyal Communists in Britain and America brought comfort to the Führer by following the party line of "revolutionary defeatism." But the "underground" Communist movements on the Continent gave little support to the Nazi New Order. And unofficially the Kremlin permitted itself occasional expressions of disapproval of the Reich's course.

In the strange duel in which Berlin and Moscow engaged during the first six months of 1941, each capital carefully refrained from any diplomatic complaints or protests to the other. Wilhelmstrasse gave no clue to its plans until after the last moment. The Nazi press was equally silent, save for periodical denials of "foreign" rumors of German-Soviet friction. The Narkomindel pursued a similar course. But the Soviet press, and particularly the Soviet news agency, Tass, was now and then allowed to hint obliquely that the Nazi-Soviet marriage of convenience was no longer in the honeymoon stage.

Thus Tass denied in mid-January that Moscow had approved of rumored German troop movements into Bulgaria. Moscow had no information of any such German project, since neither Berlin nor Sofia had consulted Moscow on the matter. Following the German occupation of Bulgaria, Vice Commissar for Foreign Affairs, Andrei Vishinsky, dispatched a formal note of protest. But it was addressed not to the aggressor but to his victim! Sofia was told that Moscow "cannot render any support" to a policy which "does not lead to consolidation of peace but to the extension of the sphere of the war." And on the 24th of March Moscow made the gesture of a pact with Ankara: "If Turkey be attacked and be obliged to enter the war for the purpose of defending her territory, she can rely upon the complete neutrality and understanding of the Soviet Union, based on the existing treaty of friendship between the two countries."

WATCHFUL WAITING

When Simovitch ousted Cvetkovitch in Belgrade, Moscow extended congratulations. When Berlin prepared to chastise the Serbs, Molotov and Minister Milan Gavrilovitch, on the day before the Blitz blow was struck, signed a treaty of friendship and nonaggression, pledging mutual respect for the independence, sovereignty and integrity of Jugoslavia and the U.S.S.R. When Hungary joined the Axis plunder raid, Vishinsky told the Magyar envoy that "a particularly bad impression is produced upon the Soviet Government by the fact that Hungary commenced a war against Jugoslavia but four months after she concluded with the latter a pact of eternal friendship."

Such insults from "Bolshevist sub-humanity" were as intolerable to Hitler as Hitler's rape of Balkania was to Stalin. Yet neither tyrant was yet prepared to defy the other openly. Each manoeuvered for position. German troops moved toward the new frontiers of conquered Poland running along the Rivers Bug and San. Soviet troops moved to the Bug and to the Balticum and Bessarabia. Yet each dictator held his diplomats and journalists to a line of "correct" relations. Whether the Japanese-Soviet nonaggression pact of April brought pain or pleasure to the Führer was known to no one outside the secret circles of the Reich—and least of all to Molotov and Matsuoka.

Pravda assailed the American commentators, including Walter Lippmann, who saw in the pact an anti-German gesture. Such interpretations, pontificated *Pravda*, "reveal the plans of certain American politicians who had hoped to get others to draw their chestnuts out of the fire for them." But Joseph the Georgian had long since begun to wonder about the chestnut game. By the end of April the Axis press was beginning to be critical of Soviet policy and *Pravda* was repeating, without comment (and to the tune of prompt denials from Helsinki and Berlin), that a German armored division had landed in Finland. How much longer?

Stalin's assumption of the Premiership on the 6th of May, with Molotov as Vice-Premier and Foreign Minister, was significant—but no one knew of what. Two days later Tass issued a categorical denial that any concentration of Red troops in the west "is taking place or is contemplated." Toward the end, the Kremlin, fearing the worst and hoping for the best, sought safety in new signals of appeasement. Diplomatic recognition was withdrawn from Norway, Belgium and Jugoslavia. "On May 16," announced Tass, "the Ambassador of the U.S.S.R. in Ankara, Sergei A. Vinogradov, and the Iraq Minister, Gailani, exchanged notes on the establishment of diplomatic, trade and consular relations between the U.S.S.R. and Iraq." To cultivate the Axis puppets and to spurn the governments-in-exile of the Axis victims might yet—who could say?—appease the Führer.

On the 13th of June, nine days before the final end of an unbeautiful friendship, the German Embassy in Moscow showed to a select audience a movie of the Nazi Blitz in the Balkans. This familiar technique of intimidation, involving the use of such Nazi cinema classics as *Feldzug im Polen* and *Sieg im Westen,* had been used before, in Copenhagen, Oslo, The Hague, Bucharest, Belgrade and elsewhere, always a few days before the arrival of the Stukas and the Panzer divisions. But Moscow was imperturbable.

A few hours later Tass issued a long communiqué, denying "obviously nonsensical" foreign rumors of German-Soviet tension. Such stories were but "clumsily concocted propaganda of forces hostile to the U.S.S.R. and to Germany and interested in further extension and unleashing of war." "Germany did not present any claims to the U.S.S.R. and does not propose any new, clear agreement. Germany abides by the provisions of the Soviet-German pact of nonaggression as unswervingly as the Soviet Union. Rumors of Germany's intention to disrupt the pact and undertake attack on the U.S.S.R. are devoid of any ground. The dispatching of German troops from operations in the Balkans to eastern and northeastern districts of Germany which now is taking place is connected, it should be assumed, with other motives having no bearing on German-Soviet relations. Rumors that the U.S.S.R. is preparing for war with Germany are false and provocational. Manoeuvers have no other purpose than the training of reservists. To present these measures as inimical to Germany is, to say the least, absurd."

APPEASER'S REWARD

On Sunday, June 22, 1941, Molotov in a choked voice broadcast an appeal to his countrymen: "Today at 4.00 a.m., without any claims having been presented to the Soviet Union, without a declaration of war, German troops attacked our country." Such perfidy was "unparalleled in the history of civilized nations." No demands were presented, no ultimatum was delivered, no complaints were made. At 5.30 a.m. Ambassador von der Schulenberg had simply announced war. "This war," said Molotov, "has been forced upon us not by the German people, not by German workers, peasants and intellectuals, whose sufferings we well understand, but by the clique of bloodthirsty Fascist rulers. Our entire people must now stand solid and united as never before. Ours is a righteous cause. The enemy shall be defeated. Victory will be ours."

Hitler had indeed given his Moscow friends no chance to accept or refuse demands. His object was not cooperation but the destruction of the Soviet Power. As always, he was first on the draw. Since he could not conquer Britain first and conquer Russia later, he decided to conquer Russia first and conquer

Britain later. The grandeur of this strategy lay in its daring simplicity and its utter improbability. Its danger lay in the circumstance that the Red Army bore no resemblance to the French Army or to the British or Polish or Jugoslav or Greek soldiery. The U.S.S.R., moreover, bore no resemblance to the Western democracies. This, at least, Stalin knew and Hitler dimly suspected. But he who would conquer the world must take great risks.

On the 12th day of the new war Stalin warned his people that "a grave danger hangs over our country." He defended his disastrous pact with Berlin with the feeble plea that solicitude for peace forbade refusal of a pact for peace "even with such treacherous fiends as Hitler and Ribbentrop." To thwart their troops in their deadly work, all Soviet citizens must unite and must steel themselves to guerrilla warfare and to a policy of "scorched earth." "The enemy is cruel and implacable. He is out to seize our lands watered with our sweat, to seize our grain and soil secured by our labor. He is out to restore the rule of landlords, to restore Tsarism, to destroy national culture, to Germanize the free peoples of the Soviet Union, to convert them into slaves of German princes and barons. Thus the issue is one of life or death for the Soviet State and for the peoples of the U.S.S.R. In this great war we shall have loyal allies in the peoples of Europe and America, including German people who are enslaved by Hitlerite despots. It will be a united front of peoples standing for freedom. Forward, to our victory!"

GRAND ALLIANCE

The desperate struggle across the vast Russian plains in the summer of 1941 was the bitterest and bloodiest combat thus far fought in World War II. Those abroad who assumed that the Red Army was worthless—and the members of the German General Staff were probably not among their number— were amazed at the vigor and tenacity of its resistance to the invaders. Those abroad who assumed, as Hitler and Rosenberg may well have done, that Russian workers, peasants and soldiers would fight listlessly and become demoralized with the first defeats were disillusioned. Stalin was able to recapture much of the fighting fervor of the Revolution and the Civil War. Beyond this, he evoked something far older and harder: the stubborn and fatalistic courage of a deeply patriotic people fighting for its land and its homes with the heroism of its ancestors.

The Teutonic flood poured quickly past Brest-Litovsk into eastern Poland,

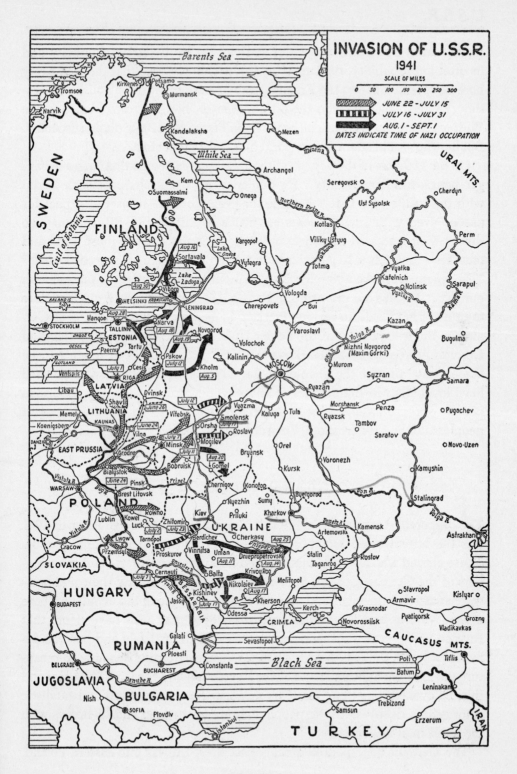

engulfed many defenders in the Bialystok-Minsk "pocket" and swept on to Vitebsk and Smolensk by mid-July. But beyond Smolensk its waves were beaten back. They dashed in vain against the defenders of Leningrad and Kiev. Here was no restoration of the superiority of fixed defense to attack, but a slowing and partial halting of the attackers by endless counterattacks around and among the strong points of the so-called "Stalin Line." On both sides were enormous casualties and costly confusion in a gigantic mêlée of infiltration, counter-infiltration, envelopment and counterenvelopment. After two months of unabated fury, hitherto unknown in the annals of warfare, the invaders were still pressing slowly forward. But their momentum was gone and each gain was costing them men and materials on a scale too great to be long endured.

On the political front supreme authority was vested in a Committee for State Defense with Stalin as chairman, Molotov as vice-chairman and Marshal Klementy Voroshilov, L. P. Berea and Georgi M. Malinkov as members. Voroshilov was given command of the armies defending Leningrad, while Defense Commissar Marshal Semyon Timoshenko commanded the central front, and Marshal Semyon Budenny directed operations in the Ukraine. Political commissars were restored to their positions in the Red Army in mid-July to seek out "cowards, panic-mongers and deserters."

On the diplomatic front a formal alliance was signed with Britain on July 12 with pledges against a separate peace. Stalin assured Inonu a fortnight later that Moscow had no designs on the Straits. In London Ambassador Maisky signed an agreement (July 30) with the Polish Premier, General Wladyslaw Sikorski, whereby the Kremlin renounced the territorial changes in Poland incorporated in the German-Soviet treaties of 1939, but left open the question of future frontiers. Poland-in-exile declared that it was not bound by any agreements with third Powers directed against the U.S.S.R. Diplomatic relations were restored and mutual aid was pledged "in the present war against Hitlerite Germany." Provision was made for organizing the 200,000 Polish troops interned in the U.S.S.R. since September, 1939, into a Polish Army under a Polish commander (Gen. Wladyslas Anders), subject to the Soviet Supreme Command. On the day on which this accord was signed, Harry Hopkins, emissary extraordinary of President Roosevelt, arrived in Moscow from London and conferred with Stalin on American aid to the U.S.S.R. By the end of September Anglo-American missions, headed by Lord Beaverbrook and W. Averell Harriman, had reached the Soviet capital to plan long-run collaboration against the common foe.

LIFE OR DEATH

Stalin's danger and Hitler's hope—i.e. Anglo-American aloofness toward the Nazi-Soviet war—was ended. But a danger equally grave confronted the U.S.S.R. Britain's war on Hitler was short of aid to Russia, while America's aid to Russia was short of war on Hitler. Litvinov's radio plea for a British attack on the Reich was echoed by many Britishers. But the British Command still had no means of invading the Continent and could do no more than intensify its bombing of German cities. If the full power of the Reichswehr continued to be thrown against the Soviet State, the Red defenders would ultimately be pushed back beyond Moscow and the Ukraine.

The course of the fighting during September revealed the scope of Russia's peril and the nature of the opportunity confronting the Western democracies. In the center Timoshenko's men recovered some lost territory and drove the Nazis back on Smolensk, but were unable to inflict any crushing blow on the foe. In the north the Red Baltic fleet was crippled by the Luftwaffe. Voroshilov's forces were pushed back by Leeb's armies, which reached the southern shore of Lake Ladoga early in the month and threatened to bomb and starve Leningrad into surrender.

In the south another major disaster overtook Budenny's armies in the wake of the loss of the Western Ukraine. Despite the destruction of the great Dnieperstroy dam, Reichenau's troops crossed the lower Dnieper and invaded the Crimea. Rundstedt's divisions meanwhile crossed the upper Dnieper at Kremenchug, midway between Cherkassy and Dniepropetrovsk, and drove northward. They effected a junction west of Kharkov with other armored forces under Bock which had smashed southward from Gomel to Chernigov, Konotop and beyond. Kiev was abandoned to the enemy on September 19. Berlin claimed the capture of 600,000 Soviet troops encircled between Kiev and Kharkov. The Donetz basin, Rostov and the rich North Caucasus region were all imperilled in turn.

These catastrophes were not fatal. But a series of them would enable the Reich to force Bulgaria and perhaps Turkey and even Japan into the war. The fruits of the Anglo-Soviet occupation of Iran might be lost. The whole British position in the Mediterranean and the Middle East might be jeopardized anew. Soviet losses of equipment and resources, moreover, might ultimately render doubtful the defense of Moscow. Russian tenacity and courage were not alone sufficient to hold the front indefinitely against the most formidable army of all time. Vast sources of new arms would be needed. Difficulties of supply, shipping and rail transport threatened to render Anglo-American aid inadequate to the task of furnishing what was required.

Early in October of 1941, in his first speech in five months, the Nazi Chancellor mouthed stale words and called on God. He claimed 2,500,000 Russian prisoners, 22,000 guns, 18,000 tanks, 14,500 planes captured or wrecked. "Everything has proceeded according to plan. We have, however, been mistaken about one thing. We had no idea how gigantic the preparations of this enemy were against Germany and Europe. The enemy does not consist of human beings but of animals or beasts. The enemy is fighting with a bestial lust of blood and out of cowardice and fear. But this enemy is already broken and will never rise again." Perhaps. And perhaps not . . .

Anglo-American hopes of survival and ultimate victory depended upon defense of the U.S.S.R. That defense promised to be effective, however, only if Britain and America could launch a large scale offensive against the Axis in some other theater of war: Scandinavia, Western Europe or the Mediterranean. Should such an attack be powerful enough to divert Nazi forces from the East, the Soviet Union would be able to fight on and perhaps inflict on Hitler the fate of Napoleon. Whether Britain's shortages of men and arms and America's shortages of a will to fight could be overcome in time was uncertain in the third autumn of the war for the world.

"Now! Now!" cried the Queen. "Faster! Faster!" And they went so fast that at last they seemed to skim through the air, hardly touching the ground with their feet, till suddenly, just as Alice was getting quite exhausted, they stopped, and she found herself sitting on the ground breathless and giddy. The Queen propped her up against a tree and said kindly, "You may rest a little now." Alice looked round her in great surprise. "Why, I do believe we've been under this tree the whole time! Everything's just as it was!" "Of course it is," said the Queen: "what would you have it?" "Well, in our country," said Alice, still panting a little, "you'd generally get to somewhere else—if you ran very fast for a long time, as we've been doing." "A slow sort of country!" said the Queen. "Now, here, you see, it takes all the running you can do, to keep in the same place. If you want to get somewhere else, you must run at least twice as fast as that!"

AMERICAN SCHISM

The hidden civil war within the Western soul which paralyzed France and Britain during the Great Depression and rendered them ripe for conquest had its counterpart in the North American Republic. Fear of Communism on the part of people of property was no less acute than in the Western European democracies, despite the political insignificance of the noisy American section of the Communist International. Admiration for Fascism was less widespread, doubtless because of the absence of any aristocratic tradition in American society and the greater devotion of all classes to democratic ideals of tolerance. The cleavage between "isolationists" and "interventionists," however, was deeper than in Western Europe—with a significant reversal of

[235]

roles. Anglo-French isolationists tended to be political conservatives or reactionaries, speaking for blue blood and large bank accounts, whereas proponents of collective security and world order were more frequently liberal or radical spokesmen for workers, peasants, and small business men. In America, conversely, "big business" was largely "internationalist" or "interventionist," whereas those who claimed to speak for urban workers, western farmers, and the lower middle class followed a tradition of liberalism or "Progressivism" which was heavily charged with xenophobia, isolationism, and fear of foreign entanglements.

Thus, charges of "dragging the country into war" were hurled by Anglo-French aristocrats and industrialists against liberals and radicals, and by American liberals and radicals against arms manufacturers, Wall Street, and the "international bankers." Another difference was that in France and Britain the politicians in power reflected the desires and prejudices of the monied élite, even during the interlude of the People's Front in France, whereas the American "New Deal" aroused bitter resentment among business men, large and small. The political scene in the United States was further confused by the circumstance that the isolationism of Harding, Coolidge, and Hoover was opposed by the business elements whose interests these Administrations favored and was approved by the farmers and wage-earners of the hinterland. The "internationalism" of Franklin D. Roosevelt, on the other hand, was approved by most of the business men who disliked him most cordially and was opposed by many of the provincial farmers and workers who elected him.

Such cleavages did not make for national unity until the eleventh hour. They served to obscure the central problem of American foreign policy in the 1930's and to prevent any relevant action until disaster was imminent. That problem was one of awakening Americans to the changed nature of the world and of their place in it. It was one of educating them out of the dangerous superstitions and delusions inherited from a past which few of them understood. It was one of moving them to support diplomatic and military policies which offered some hope of safeguarding the Republic from the designs of the world-conquering Caesars who had grown great through the indolence and paralysis of all the democratic States. Until the Year of Terror, 1940, most Americans reacted toward the challenge of the 20th century with nonrational stereotypes derived from the imagined experiences of their forebears in the 18th and 19th centuries. To discard old attitudes and habits was painful. To devise new ones based on a correct perception of external realities was difficult. Whether the transformation would take place in time to avert the fatal isolation of America in a dangerous world was anyone's guess.

SHADOW AND SUBSTANCE

All people possess some capacity to learn from experience. But when lessons once learned are embalmed in magic phrases which stir emotions deeply and thereby inhibit rational adjustment to new problems, then the products of experience are obstacles rather than aids to new learning. They render more difficult the task of facing emergencies and achieving that progressive adaptation to environmental change which is the prerequisite of survival for all living things. Still more is this the case when the magic phrases are not only irrelevant today and dangerous tomorrow but false as descriptions of yesterday.

In terms of techniques of communication, transportation, travel, and war, the entire planet on which Americans somewhat reluctantly found themselves in 1941 was a far smaller place than the thirteen states of the union in 1790. It is simple to say that America's dilemma of the 1930's was the result of the persistence of attitudes toward the world which were relevant and adequate a hundred years and more before but had ceased to be safe guides to action (or inaction) after the revolutionary transformation of the world society effected by science and technology. In terms of *Realpolitik*, however, "isolationism," with its corollary of security through nonintervention and nonentanglement, was never a reality.

America was settled by Europeans and was continuously a part of European civilization and of the European State System since the days of Columbus. The United States won its independence only because the rebels of 1776 made a military alliance with France, and because Spain and Holland also entered the fray. The Latin American Republics likewise won their independence in consequence of a European war. They preserved their freedom less because of the Monroe Doctrine of 1823, forbidding further European colonization, intervention, or interposition in the Western Hemisphere, than because Great Britain, for commercial reasons, favored independence and opposed attempts by Continental Powers to reassert their sovereignty over the New World. After 1815, following the failure of the American attempt to conquer Canada, there was uninterrupted peace between the United States and Britain—and a tacit agreement to abandon all efforts to play the game of power against one another.

For a hundred years thereafter all Americans, North and South, were the almost unconscious beneficiaries of a world balance of power which was unique and temporary but was confused in most American minds (when they were aware of it at all) with the unchanging pattern of the cosmos. The elements of that balance were three: (1) the preponderance of British naval power in the Atlantic and in most other seas; (2) the maintenance of a stable equilibrium on the European Continent by which no one Power could successfully threaten the others with subjugation or seriously endanger the British Empire; and (3) the inability of any Continental or Asiatic Powers, singly or in combination, to challenge the United States or menace Latin America.

The first element involved no danger to the Americas. British capitalists and imperialists, far from harboring territorial designs in the Americas or cherishing any desire to compete for power with the United States, were inspired by solicitude for Anglo-American collaboration on the basis of a common interest in preserving the world balance and keeping open the world channels of trade and investment. British sea power was therefore a shield between America and Europe rather than a sword pointed toward the New World. The second element in the balance was in part a product of a long-standing British policy of preventing the domination of the Continent by any one Power. The third element was a direct result of the first and second.

So long as Britain stood firm, Americans were safe in "splendid isolation." They could therefore engage safely in the periodic recreation of "twisting the lion's tail," and they could fancy that their security and prosperity were products not of the world balance but of their own wisdom in "minding their own business" and avoiding "foreign entanglements." They could imagine that the Monroe Doctrine kept Latin America free from the impact of European and Asiatic imperialisms. They could define American interests abroad in negative terms of neutrality and abstention from power politics and in positive terms of promoting commerce by championing neutral trading rights, freedom of the seas, most-favored-nation treatment, and the Open Door in the Orient. The underlying facts of power relationships which made these policies practicable were seldom perceived and little appreciated. The verbiage employed was harmless so long as the facts remained unchanged. It was potentially disastrous should the facts be altered and should Americans suppose that their safety was a result of the verbiage rather than of the facts.

WASTED VICTORY

The first serious Continental challenge to Britain after Waterloo put isolationism to its first major test. The outbreak of hostilities between the two European coalitions in 1914 caused the United States to proclaim its neutrality, as it had done in 1793 and in all subsequent European wars. An immensely profitable trade in munitions at once developed with the Allies. The effective Allied blockade of Germany prevented this trade from going to both sets of belligerents. But the continuation of this commerce was threatened by the efforts of the warring governments to cut off trade between the enemy and the outside world. The United States, in defending the liberty of its traders to do business of this kind, reverted to the principles of neutral rights and freedom of the seas, which it had evolved under comparable circumstances between 1793 and 1812. It protested the British contraband list, the British blockade, and the British interpretation of the doctrine of continuous voyage. It likewise protested the German submarine blockade of the Allies and was soon involved in acrimonious controversy with both sides.

In the sequel the United States leaned more and more toward the Allies, and this not for humanitarian or sentimental reasons expressed in war slogans, but for very tangible considerations connected with business and power politics. Allied defeat would probably mean Allied bankruptcy. American business had little to lose and everything to gain from Allied victory. A victory of the Central Powers would not only imperil these economic interests but would completely upset the balance of power and give Germany such a position of overwhelming preponderance on the Continent and throughout the world that even American security might eventually be endangered.

Circumstances permitted these economic and political interests to be presented on a high moral plane. Germany was an "autocracy," and the Allies and the United States were "democracies." The Allied cruiser blockade of Germany menaced American property and American legal rights, but the U-boat blockade of the Allies endangered American lives as well. Germany was ruthless, lawless, uncivilized. The Allies were considerate, law-abiding, and virtuous. When Germany announced the resumption of unrestricted submarine warfare, on February 1, 1917, President Wilson severed diplomatic relations. On April 6, 1917, the United States declared war on Germany. Other American States were induced to follow suit. The United States became an "Associate" of the Allies, not an "Ally." A large army was conscripted, and sent to France. A strengthened American Navy joined the Allied squadrons. Billions of dollars were raised and loaned to the Allied Governments. The immense economic power of the United States more than overbalanced the defection of Russia. Its support was sufficient to turn the scales. Neutrality had failed to protect American interests, and isolation was abandoned in favor of active participation in the European contest. Victory came in 1918, and the United States shared in the glory thereof.

The disillusioning aftermath produced a reversion to isolationism. Wilson went to the Paris Peace Conference, participated actively in the making of the treaty, took the initiative in the creation of the League of Nations, and committed the United States to cooperation with other Powers in preserving peace and dealing with post-war problems. On his return home he found himself a prophet without honor in his own land. The Treaty of Versailles failed of ratification. Its first 26 articles, comprising the Covenant of the League of Nations, was the chief target of attack—not on the reasonable ground that the League scheme of intergovernmental collaboration failed to limit national "sovereignty" sufficiently to offer hope of a workable world order, but on the unreasonable ground that American membership would destroy American "sovereignty" and "independence" and involve America in "other people's wars." Wilson and all his works were repudiated. He retired from public life a defeated and broken man. Narrow Republican partisanship and the personal animosity of Henry Cabot Lodge, Sr. (who had urged American membership in a league of nations in 1916) were responsible for his defeat, along with his own obstinacy and the doubtful wisdom of the founding fathers in requiring the approval of two-thirds of the Senate for the ratification of treaties. On March 19, 1920, the final vote was taken. It revealed 40 Senators "for" and 35 "against." The Covenant fell short by seven votes of securing the needed two-thirds.

Woodrow Wilson had warned his countrymen that if they rejected the League, they would be obliged to fight another World War in twenty years. He also told them: "I would rather fail in an enterprise that I know must some day succeed than succeed in an enterprise that I know some day must fail." They paid no heed. They had already forgotten why they went to war. In their flight from responsibility, they wanted no one to remind them of the price of peace.

NORMALCY

In the election of 1920 the Democratic ticket was headed by James Cox, publisher and editor, and Franklin D. Roosevelt, Assistant Secretary of the Navy in the Wilson Administration. They were overwhelmingly defeated by the Republican standard-bearers, Warren Gamaliel Harding and Calvin Coolidge. The way was thus paved for twelve consecutive years of Republican rule. In foreign policy, Republican rule meant isolationism with a vengeance. A separate peace was made with Germany on August 25, 1921. The League was first ignored, then recognized as a stubbornly irreducible fact, and later used, through its conferences and commissions, as an agency of cooperation—timidly at the outset and later with more confidence. American entrance into the World Court was pledged, but the pledge remained unfulfilled. The ill-fated intervention in Russia of 1918-1920 was abandoned, but diplomatic recognition was sternly refused to the Soviet Government. Immigration was cut off, and almost insurmountable tariff walls were erected, for isolationism and economic nationalism were opposite sides of the same coin. The Allies were required to sign on the dotted line for the repayment of their war debts. American dollar diplomacy in the Caribbean was continued in the best tradition, but Latin American sensibilities (which had a relationship to profitable trade) were soothed with assurances that the United States had no imperialistic designs and that the Monroe Doctrine was not what it seemed to be. The Open Door policy in Asia was reiterated. In short, the exclusive pursuit of American national interests was again couched in terms of long-established principles and policies.

During the 1920's the United States, as the wealthiest and most powerful of the Great Powers, helped to prevent the establishment of a viable world order to supersede the politics of power. Its tariff policies made impossible the payment of the war debts and insured the eventual loss of the billions of private capital which flowed into European investments. Its non-membership in the League was not in fact, whatever it seemed to be in form, a mere negation. The United States had fought four wars in defense of the right of its citizens to trade with belligerents. Should the League Powers commit themselves to an economic boycott of an aggressor, they would face the alternatives of seeing the boycott broken by American ships and goods, or of provoking sharp controversy with Washington by challenging the right of Americans to trade with a lawbreaker.

Secretary of State Charles E. Hughes and British Ambassador Sir Esme Howard discussed the issue in January, 1925, in connection with the implications of the Covenant, the Geneva Protocol, and the Locarno Treaties. Hughes declared "that there was one thing he believed could be depended upon, and that was that this Government from its very beginning had been insistent upon the rights of neutrals and would continue to maintain them. The Secretary did not believe any Administration, short of a treaty concluded and ratified, could commit the country against assertion of its neutral rights in case there should be occasion to demand their recognition." Under these conditions, it was easy for Anglo-French isolationists to repudiate, and later to betray, collective security on the ground that sanctions against aggressors would mean conflict with America.

Despite this obstructionism, the Republican Administrations made various gestures in the direction of peace, disarmament, and international cooperation. In 1921 the United States summoned the Washington Conference, where it secured naval parity with Great Britain in capital ships in return for a general reduction of naval armaments. It likewise secured a new recognition of the Open Door principle and Japanese withdrawal from Shantung and Siberia, in return for the abandonment of its bid for naval supremacy in the Pacific. In 1927, it sought to promote further naval disarmament in the abortive Coolidge conference at Geneva. In 1928, it sponsored the Kellogg-Briand Pact for the outlawry of war. In 1930, it participated in the five Power naval conference in London, where it acquired complete naval parity with Great Britain but no substantial reduction of naval armaments, because of Anglo-American differences regarding cruisers and Franco-Italian naval rivalry in the Mediterranean. In 1931, it cooperated with the Council of the League of Nations in the Manchurian crisis, though without tangible results. In 1932 the Hoover moratorium proposal for a one-year suspension of all reparation and debt payments was presented as a generous move toward world economic and financial rehabilitation.

The United States likewise participated in the General Disarmament Conference of the League of Nations and eloquently urged armament reduction, without being willing to commit itself to cooperation or even consultation with other Powers in the interests of peace. By all of these moves, national interests, moral principles, and humanitarian ideals were simultaneously served. And if none of them was served wisely or well in the long run, the cause lay in the refusal of Congress and the country either to implement power interests with Machiavellian diplomacy or to implement idealistic aspirations with concrete political arrangements contrary to past tradition. In world trade those who will not buy are finally unable to sell. In world politics those who give no help to others against aggression are finally helpless themselves against aggression.

NEW DEAL

In 1932-1933 the full impact of the Great Depression paralyzed American business and finance. Herbert Hoover and his party were swept from power by an impoverished and despairing electorate. Franklin D. Roosevelt, who promised reform, recovery and a "new deal" for the "forgotten man," entered the White House even as Adolf Hitler was establishing the Nazi dictatorship in the Reich.

This shift from Republicans to Democrats was more than a substitution of the "outs" for the "ins." Political power herewith passed—perhaps permanently—out of the hands of American Big Business into the hands of a new élite of liberal intellectuals (commonly termed "crack-pots" or "reds" by the disgruntled Bourbons) who envisaged themselves not merely as the champions of workers, farmers and the lower middle class but as the builders of a new American dream. A few of them believed that their social and economic objectives could be reached by "saving America first" without regard to the outer world. Most of them held, however, that America could enjoy political security, and Americans could enjoy economic and social security, only if America played a larger role in the world society and pointed the way toward a freer world economy and a more stable world polity.

In the field of foreign affairs the architects of the new dispensation were a variegated group of many minds. The President, with his background of inherited wealth and his genial nonchalance, was cordially detested as a traitor to his class by most Americans of means. Since he liked being liked, and feared being hated, he was ever tempted to trim his sails to the shifting winds of opinion, despite his earnest desire to build a better American society and a free world order. His Secretary of State was a shrewd judge and politician from Tennessee with limited imagination and a passion for free trade. Glacial and poker-faced Sumner Welles, who ultimately became Undersecretary of State, was, like Roosevelt, a son of the rich and a shrewd and polished product of Groton and Harvard. But no one ever accused him of betraying his class. And his class was not always overly bright in seeing its own interests or grasping the realities of world politics in the age of the new Caesars.

Lower posts in the Department of State and the Foreign Service were increasingly filled by professional diplomats rather than by deserving local politicians. The upper posts went chiefly to able career men or to prominent Democrats with money. To the London Embassy went wealthy Joseph Kennedy. To Moscow went wealthy William Bullitt, erstwhile friend of the Soviets, who later soured on his hosts and was transferred to Paris. Wealthy Joseph Davies replaced him at the Kremlin. Still later Davies gave way to career man Laurence Steinhardt. To Tokyo went Joseph Grew, and to Rome career man William Philipps. Two Embassies were filled with liberal scholars of moderate means: Claude Bowers to Spain (and later to Chile) and William E. Dodd to Germany.

Some of these men, particularly Ambassador Dodd, saw the world as it was and urged common action among the democracies to resist in time the rising tide of Fascism. Others were committed by prejudices of class or creed, or by deep devotion to Chamberlain's England, to a Tory course of appeasing the aggressors. A few gave almost open aid and comfort to the Fascist cause —e.g., Jefferson Caffery, Ambassador to Cuba and later to Brazil; Alexander Weddell, Ambassador to Franco; Breckinridge Long, Assistant Secretary of State, and a small but potent group of lesser bureaucrats who unwittingly saw the world as Hitler desired them to see it. Welles himself, the "icicle" of Oxon Hill, had helped (as Ambassador in Havana in 1933–1934) to deliver Cuban democracy out of the hands of dictator Machado into the hands of dictator Batista. He typified those in the diplomatic bureaucracy who sought to ape the snobbery of Downing Street at its worst. He was to bear a major share of responsibility for betraying the Spanish Republic, appeasing Japan, and cooperating with Europe's Munichmen and Vichymen to bring the cause of democracy to ruin.

But the chief obstacle in the way of a consistent American foreign policy after 1933, apart from these divergencies of attitudes and the chronic folly of London and Paris, lay in the fact that most of the national legislators and many of the voters of the United States, like the "Col. Blimps" of England, believed sincerely that safety and prosperity were to be had not by collaboration with other democratic nations but by scrupulous avoidance of all responsibilities, risks and entanglements. Roosevelt and his immediate advisers knew better. But the art of politics in a democracy is the art of compromise. So firmly did the leaders of Britain, France and America believe in the principle of compromise during the years of the Great Retreat that they compromised all their principles in its name. American foreign policy, in particular, was a product of checks and balances between the White House and Capitol Hill, and a reflection of the provincialism and pacifist escapism of the hinterland. The resultant confusion of thought and action on the part of the most powerful of the democratic Powers confirmed the hopes of the Caesars and served their purposes admirably.

IN QUEST OF PEACE AND PLENTY

The diplomatic problems of the first Administration of Franklin D. Roosevelt necessarily revolved around the tasks of restoring commerce in a world sorely afflicted with economic maladjustments, and of promoting peace in a world drifting toward war. As a satiated Power, the United States championed peace—and was willing to make minor sacrifices for its preservation within the limits of the isolationist tradition. As a commercial Power and a creditor nation the United States championed a restoration of international trade— within the limits of tariff protectionism. In both cases the gap between hope and achievement was due in part to conditions abroad over which Washington had no control and in part to attitudes and vested interests at home which required the adoption of policies that were emotionally acceptable and temporarily profitable rather than rationally relevant or permanently helpful.

In the quest for prosperity, the abandonment of the gold standard and the subsequent depreciation of the dollar by 41% stimulated exports to, and discouraged imports from, countries still on gold. Efforts to secure an international reduction of trade barriers at the London Economic Conference of June and July, 1933, failed because other Powers were unwilling to reduce tariffs without a guarantee against further depreciation of the dollar. Washington was unwilling to accept any agreement for currency stabilization. The abandonment of gold by France, The Netherlands, and Switzerland in September, 1936, was accompanied by provisional Anglo-French-American cooperation to prevent wide currency fluctuations. But no permanent stabilization was achieved. Secretary of State Cordell Hull, under authority of the Tariff Act of 1934, meanwhile negotiated a series of reciprocity agreements for mutual reduction of duties, with the benefits extended to all States not discriminating against American goods and having unconditional most-favored-nation clauses in their treaties with the United States. International trade recovered gradually from the low point of 1932. Total American foreign trade declined from $9,400,000,000 in 1929 to $2,800,000,000 in 1932 and then increased to $4,150,000,000 in 1935, and to $5,000,000,000 in 1938.

The quest for peace was more difficult. Logic posed three alternatives. The United States could protect its interests abroad in an insecure world by overwhelming armaments; it could abandon these interests, or refuse them protection, and retire into economic as well as political isolationism; or it could cooperate with other Powers interested in maintaining peace, either through alliances against potential aggressors or through participation in international organization and collective security. Unilateral protection of interests by force meant an arms race and eventually war, rather than peace. Complete abandonment of interests abroad was economically and politically impossible. Cooperation with other Powers was frustrated by the isolationist tradition and by the inability of other Powers to cooperate among themselves. Circumstances therefore dictated a policy of illogical compromise among the three possible courses.

Cooperation for peace was promoted by continued advocacy of general disarmament and occasional lip service to the Kellogg Pact and the Stimson Doctrine. The United States became a member of the International Labor Organization in 1934, but Administration efforts to achieve membership in the World Court were defeated by the isolationists. Membership in the I.L.O. was achieved by a Joint Congressional Resolution of June 19, 1934, authorizing the President to make the United States a member, provided that no obligations were assumed under the League Covenant. Since no formal treaty was necessary, it was impossible for one-third of the Senators to obstruct action.

For twelve years, every President, every Secretary of State, and a large majority in both Houses of Congress favored American membership in the Permanent Court of International Justice. But the isolationist Senators, loudly applauded by the Hearst press, the Chicago *Tribune*, Father Coughlin, and sundry superpatriots, had attached five reservations to the Protocols in January, 1926. The last of these forbade the Court to "entertain any request for an advisory opinion touching any dispute or question in which the United States has or claims an interest." Since this proviso, if interpreted broadly, would have given the United States a special veto enjoyed by none of the members of the League Council, whence requests for advisory opinions came, efforts were made by Elihu Root and others to secure agreement on an interpretation which would give the United States only a position of equality. The "Root formula" of 1929 solved the problem. The isolationists, however, had no desire to see it solved. On January 29, 1935, the final Senate vote showed 52 in favor of ratification and 36 opposed. The Protocols failed to secure the required two-thirds by a margin of 7 votes. Father Coughlin declared, "Our thanks are due to Almighty God that America retains her sovereignty. Congratulations to the aroused people of the United States who, by more than two hundred thousand telegrams containing at least one million names, demanded that the principles established by Washington and Jefferson shall keep us clear from foreign entanglements and European hatreds."

Yet the Administration found it possible to take certain limited steps toward joint action with other Powers. An obstacle to cooperation was removed by belated recognition of the U.S.S.R. On November 16, 1933, Litvinov and Roosevelt exchanged notes at Washington by which recognition was accorded. The two governments agreed to refrain from hostile propaganda. The religious and civil rights of Americans in the U.S.S.R. were elaborately safeguarded. Moscow waived all counterclaims arising out of American military activities in Siberia. Other claims were left for subsequent settlement. It was understood that American claims against the Soviet would be met by increased interest payments on credits extended by the United States to finance increased trade. In January, 1935, however, the claims negotiations which were expected to eventuate in a commercial treaty collapsed, owing to Moscow's refusal to meet claims except through repayments on a long-term loan and Washington's refusal to grant a loan on terms satisfactory to the U.S.S.R. But on July 13, 1935, Litvinov and Bullitt signed a one-year trade agreement which stipulated that Moscow would spend 30 million dollars for American goods. On August 25, 1935, and again on August 31, the United States protested emphatically at the Comintern Congress in Moscow as a violation of the propaganda pledge. The Narkomindel replied that it was not responsible for the activities of the Comintern. Despite this controversy, the trade agreement was renewed from year to year, with questions of loans, claims, and propaganda left in abeyance.

Widespread sentiment in favor of withdrawing diplomatic and military protection from American private interests abroad found expression in the "good-neighbor" policy and in the neutrality legislation. Americans were in effect told that their trade and investments in Latin America would not be protected by interventionist activities. They were forbidden to make loans or to sell arms to countries at war. Imperialism was renounced and protectorates over Cuba, Haiti, and other States were relinquished. Curiously enough, no steps were taken toward withdrawal of protection of American economic interests in the Far East, where trade and investments were negligible as compared with Europe and Latin America. In practice, this meant continued insistence on the Open Door in China and therefore friction with Japan.

The failure of disarmament led to intensified preparations for defense. The Vinson Act of March 27, 1934, contemplated building the American Navy up to full Treaty strength. The naval appropriation for 1936 was over half a billion dollars—a figure then regarded as staggering. The army and the air force were likewise enlarged. Total expenditures in preparation for war were approaching a billion dollars annually by 1937. The Anglo-French-American Naval Treaty of March 25, 1936, provided for qualitative limitation but not for reductions or even quantitative limitation of fleets. On December 31, 1936, the Washington and London naval treaties expired. No new agreement could be reached because of American unwillingness to grant Japanese demands for parity. A naval race ensued which augured ill for peace in the Pacific. The Japanese-German-Italian entente necessarily made impossible any separation of the problems of Japanese-American relations from those of European politics.

PAN-AMERICA?

The position of the United States in the Western Hemisphere gave rise to hopes that all the American Republics might evolve common policies toward Europe and Asia. Latin American resentment against the "Colossus of the North" was mitigated by the new orientation at Washington. Latin America's disposition to seek a counterweight to the United States by giving vigorous support to the League of Nations was weakened not only by the failure of League efforts to end the Chaco war between Bolivia and Paraguay but by the costly futility of sanctions against Italy and by the manifest unwillingness of other League members to create a system of collective security capable of preventing aggression. Brazil had withdrawn from Geneva in 1926. Guatemala, Honduras, and Nicaragua did likewise in 1936. Argentina's Foreign Minister, Dr. Carlos Saavedra Lamas, presided over the 1936 Assembly but was disappointed that no effective steps were taken toward League reform.

At the Seventh International Conference of American States, held at Montevideo, Uruguay, in December, 1933, a "Convention on the Rights and

Duties of States" pledged the American nations, including the United States, to non-intervention in one another's affairs and to non-recognition of titles secured by conquest. The Latin States responded favorably to President Roosevelt's invitation of January 30, 1936, to meet in a special Inter-American Conference for the Maintenance of Peace. The Conference program was approved by the Governing Board of the Pan-American Union in July. The delegates assembled in Buenos Aires on December 1, 1936, with the American President and Secretary of State both addressing the Conference in person.

Whether or not an "American League of Nations" might ultimately emerge from these efforts, the new regional peace system was certain to weaken Latin American ties with Geneva and to promote collaboration with Washington. Inter-American peace machinery was clarified and further developed. A joint neutrality policy, based on the Argentine Anti-War Pact and the legislation of the United States began to take shape. Commercial and cultural relations were strengthened. With Asia and Europe slipping toward war, Pan-Americanism breathed a new breath of life and offered new promise of pacific cooperation in the Western Hemisphere.

These aspirations were realized only in part. Friction developed between the United States and Mexico over expropriation of foreign-owned oil properties in 1938, although Washington scrupulously refrained from any threats of intervention. Franco's victories in Spain evoked sympathetic echoes among the propertied classes of the Latin American Republics. The establishment of a "totalitarian" dictatorship in Brazil by President Getulio Vargas in 1937 was not reassuring. Nazi and Fascist agents sowed the seeds of anti-Semitism, anti-Communism, and Yankeephobia.

The Eighth International Conference of American States met in Lima, Peru, in December, 1938. The United States sent a dozen delegates, including Secretary of State Hull and Alfred M. Landon, Republican presidential candidate in 1936. Hull declared that "an ominous shadow falls athwart our own continent" and pleaded for common measures to resist either military or ideological invasion. Foreign Minister Cantilo of Argentina, which had a large Italian population and was dependent upon European markets, opposed any binding commitments or formal treaty. Since unanimity was deemed essential, Washington compromised. The "Declaration of Lima" affirmed "continental solidarity" and "collaboration" but provided only for "consultation" among the foreign ministers, meeting "when deemed desirable and at the initiative of any one of them" whenever the peace, security, or territorial integrity of an American Republic should be threatened. They would use "the measures which in each case the circumstances may make advisable. It is understood that the Governments of the American Republics will act independently in their individual capacity, recognizing fully their juridical equality as sovereign States."

Despite suggestions from Washington, no action was taken in the direction of consolidating and simplifying the confusing array of inter-American peace treaties, such as the Gondra Conciliation Treaty of 1923, the Kellogg Pact, the Pan-American Conciliation and Arbitration Treaties of 1929, the Argentine Anti-War Pact of 1933, the Convention of Montevideo of 1933, and the Buenos Aires Conventions of 1936. Questions of defining aggression and organizing sanctions were also sidetracked. The Stimson Doctrine was reaffirmed, but all hopes of a Pan-American league or court went glimmering. Sundry innocuous resolutions were passed, but the record of positive achievement toward a genuine solidarity of interests and of deeds, rather than of words, was not impressive.

MAL DE MER BY WELLES

Following the outbreak of war abroad the foreign ministers met for the first time at Panama in late September, 1939. Sumner Welles asserted that the twenty-one American Republics could not permit "their security, their nationals, or their legitimate commercial rights and interests to be jeopardized by belligerent activities in close proximity to the shores of the New World." He proposed the establishment of a "safety zone." On October 3 a Final Act was approved, embodying sixteen declarations and resolutions. Most of them were clichés (*e.g.*, "maintenance of international activities in accordance with Christian morality") or routine pledges of collaboration. But the "Declaration of Panama" set up a "neutrality zone" including all of South and Central America and North America south of Canada and extending out to sea 300 to 1,000 miles. Within this vast area of ocean, covering more than 5 million square miles, the American Republics asserted "as of inherent right" and "as a measure of continental self-protection" that they were entitled to keep the waters "free from the commission of any hostile acts by any non-American belligerent nation."

That such an attack on belligerent rights and freedom of the seas should be made by twenty-one neutrals, led by the most powerful neutral, all of whom had always insisted on full respect for freedom of the seas and for their own neutral rights, verged upon the preposterous. To relinquish one's own recognized rights, as in the "neutrality" legislation, is in law and fact far different from denying the recognized rights of others, as was done at Panama. Both steps were motivated by an effort to escape involvement in war by fleeing from duty and danger into an imaginary isolationist haven. The President who had proposed on October 5, 1937, to "quarantine" aggressors in the name of upholding international law now sought to "quarantine" the American neutrals by a formula which violated international law in a fashion impartially damaging to aggressors and their victims alike. Wits referred to the zone as a "chastity belt" or a "prophyl-Axis" and predicted that it would fail of its purpose.

It did. The only major Anglo-German naval engagement in the first year of the war took place well inside the "zone." On December 13 the pocket battleship *Admiral Graf Spee* fled into the harbor of Montevideo after a sixteen hour running fight with three British cruisers. Four days later, following expiration of the time limit granted by Uruguay, the German commander scuttled his ship in the Rio de la Plata and took his own life. Two days thereafter the German freighter *Arauca* fled from a British cruiser into Fort Lauderdale, Florida. On the same day the liner *Columbus*, fleeing from Vera Cruz, encountered a British destroyer 400 miles off the New Jersey coast and was scuttled by her commander. In no instance did any of the belligerents pay the slightest attention to the Declaration of Panama.

On December 21, 1939, the twenty-one American Republics, acting through the President of Panama, protested to Britain, France, and Germany and hinted at barring from American ports belligerent vessels committing acts of war within these zones. London, Paris and Berlin all replied that the "zone" could not be imposed on belligerents by "unilateral action" and that they were not bound to respect it. When subsequent violations took place, the American Republics limited themselves to further verbal protests which had no basis in law or logic.

MODERNIZING THE MONROE DOCTRINE

The "Second Meeting of Ministers of Foreign Affairs of the American Republics" met in Havana, Cuba, July 21-30, 1940, on the initiative of the United States. In the face of the conquest of the Northlands, the Low Countries, and

France, accompanied by an alarming increase of Nazi activities in Latin America, the delegates were moved to consider countermeasures. On June 17, Hull had informed Berlin and Rome that "the United States would not recognize any transfer, and would not acquiesce in any attempt to transfer, any geographic region of the Western Hemisphere from one non-American Power to another non-American Power." The United States Congress had passed a "hands off" resolution, reaffirming the Monroe Doctrine and contemplating immediate consultation with the other American Republics on measures to protect common interests. Washington bespoke economic collaboration and urged common action to thwart all activity arising from non-American sources likely to imperil American economic or political freedom.

The Havana Conference approved a Convention and a Supplementary Act "continentalizing" the Monroe Doctrine and declaring that "when islands or regions in the Americas now under the possession of non-American nations are in danger of becoming the subject of barter of territory or change of sovereignty, the American nations may set up a regime of provisional administration," pending eventual independence ("provided they are capable of self-government") or restitution to their previous status, "whichever of these alternatives shall appear the more practicable and just." The provisional administration should be exercised for the "twofold purpose of contributing to the security and defense of the Continent, and to the economic, political and social progress of such regions." Arrangements were made to establish an emergency committee made up of one delegate from each of the Republics, to be deemed constituted as soon as two-thirds of its members should be appointed, to meet in a crisis at the request of any signatory, and to assume the administration of the threatened region with eventual transfer of authority to an "Inter-American Commission for Territorial Administration." The Convention of July 29, moreover, authorized any one of the Republics to act individually or jointly with others in an urgent emergency in order to safeguard its own defense and that of the continent. Somewhat sketchy resolutions were passed for further economic and financial collaboration. The widely publicized project for an intercontinental marketing cartel was dropped in favor of credits from the Export-Import Bank of the United States for industrialization, agrarian diversification, and holding or marketing of Latin American surpluses.

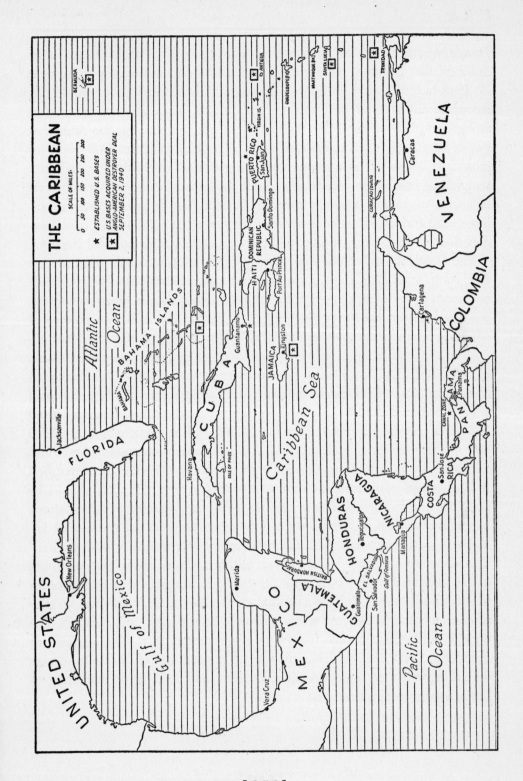

THE CARIBBEAN

SCALE OF MILES:
0   50   100   150   200   250   300

★ ESTABLISHED U.S. BASES

⊠ U.S. BASES ACQUIRED UNDER
   ANGLO-AMERICAN DESTROYER DEAL
   SEPTEMBER 2, 1940

HEMISPHERIC MIRAGE

Some North Americans hoped that such steps as these would eventuate in the creation of a solid "Western Hemisphere" or "continental" coalition which would erect impregnable barriers against foreign attack and successfully defend the ramparts of the New World against dangers from the Old. These hopes, however, had little likelihood of realization. The "Western Hemisphere" or the "American continents" do not constitute a unity, real or potential. Though "Latin America" itself is in no sense a unity, its peoples have much more in common with one another and with Europe than any of them has with the "Colossus of the North." Their ruling élites speak the tongues of Latin Europe and look for inspiration to Madrid, Lisbon, Rome, and Paris. Their masses consist of poor peasants, often bound by debt to the soil they till—Indian in race and culture (with a strong Negro strain in Brazil and the Caribbean), often illiterate, half-pagan, half-Catholic, and little touched, save in Mexico, by the tides of change that sweep so swiftly over much of the Western world. Except in Argentina and Chile, there is no middle class and therefore little social basis for democracy save as a form to disguise oligarchy or tyranny.

Latin American economy is a colonial economy, based upon crops, herds, and mineral wealth, all of which have value only when sold to the people of industrialized societies who can supply manufactures and capital in exchange. Latin America's great markets, without which no tolerable livelihood is possible for its inhabitants, lie in Western Europe rather than in the United States which has long excluded the basic Latin American exports competing with the products of Iowa farmers, Minnesota wheat growers, southern cotton planters, Michigan sugar producers, western cattlemen, and Chicago meat packers. Such imports as coffee, cocoa, bananas, tropical woods, oil, and minerals come into the United States chiefly from Mexico and the Caribbean. They furnish no basis for an exchange of commodities comparable to that which has long taken place between Latin America and Europe. Even in geographical terms, most of South America lies nearer to Eurafrica than to the United States. Most of its people have strong economic and cultural ties with Europe, not with English-speaking North America.

Latin American attitudes toward North Americans and Europeans are products of a century of experience. "Yanquis" and Britishers in the southlands have usually been traveling salesmen, unsympathetic with Spanish and Indian ways, living apart and eager to go home. Or they have been bankers or executives or technicians who touch native life either too lightly or too harshly to win good will. They have often symbolized foreign exploitation and "Yankee imperialism." Millions of Germans and Italians live in Latin America as farmers, workers, business men, and members of the professions. They are not insensitive to Axis efforts to rally their loyalties to the service of the Caesars. They are respected by Latin Americans, for they have made themselves useful citizens of the countries where they live and work. The native ruling classes, moreover, are insecure in the face of Anglo-American pressures from abroad and social unrest at home from the ranks of the Indian peasantry and proletariat. Despite lip service to democracy, they take kindly and quickly to totalitarian doctrines as conforming to their interests and needs. The preachers of anti-Communism, anti-Semitism, and anti-Yankeeism, whether they be native Fascists, Axis agents, or local members of the Spanish Fascist Falange, receive a ready hearing.

The imperatives of diplomacy and strategy are determined by such facts as these—not, to be sure, beyond all possibility of change, but beyond all probability of decisive change. The British blockade of the Continent after 1939 cut off much of the normal foreign market of Latin America. The United States could not or would not supply an alternative market to the detriment of its own producers, even though North American purchases of South American exports were more than doubled between 1938 and 1941. Once hostilities in Europe should cease, Latin America would inevitably resume broken contacts across the Atlantic. Axis defeat would mean that Latin America could remain secure behind the barrier of the British fleet and would cease to be in any sense the "Achilles' heel" of the United States. Peace by stalemate would mean eventual Axis victory. Axis victory would mean the domination of Latin America, economically, ideologically, politically by a Fascist Europe.

Neither guns nor planes nor battleships nor gestures of "good neighborliness" nor yet a resumption of imperialistic domination by the United States could possibly prevent this result. Nothing could prevent it save a crusading faith in democracy on the part of the United States, frankly and efficiently directed toward full support of such movements as the Mexican revolution, the People's Front in Chile, and the Apra in Peru, and toward the promotion of social revolution elsewhere in the southlands for the purpose of awakening and liberating the Indian masses and the lower classes and thus overthrowing the oligarchies who would at once embrace Fascism. Such a program is scarcely conceivable for the United States of America so long as the "Good

Neighbor" policy is administered by bureaucrats of Wellesian mentality whose conception of statesmanship is a series of "bargains" with clerical tyrants and purchasable dictators.

Without a Pan-American program of revolutionary democracy, the victory of the Caesars over Britain in the North Atlantic, and inevitably in Africa, would mean Axis victory west of the South Atlantic, followed by the swift penetration of the southern continent by the propagandists, diplomats, and strategists of triumphant Powers bent upon organizing Latin America against the United States and utilizing its resources and its bases to immobilize and possibly conquer the North American Republic. A United States unwilling to do so small a thing as buy Argentine beef or sell arms to the Spanish Loyalists was scarcely a nation capable of so large a mission as that of uniting the Western Hemisphere for its own protection.

THE NEW "NEUTRALITY"

To return to the early days of the New Deal: In the first year of Franklin D. Roosevelt's first term, most Americans permitted themselves to be persuaded that they could escape involvement in "other people's quarrels" by running away, by "minding their own business," and, if need be, by abandoning business which might "drag them into war." A few voices were from time to time raised in favor of abandoning "freedom of the seas" and "neutral trading rights" in such fashion as to cooperate with, or at least not impede, other Powers which might impose economic sanctions against States resorting to force in violation of the League Covenant or the Kellogg Pact. But all proposals to discriminate between law-enforcers and lawbreakers were shouted down by the champions of "impartiality" who urged restrictions on trade with all belligerents in the interest of avoiding "entanglements." That such a program was based upon a complete misconception of the position and interests of the United States in the world of the mid-twentieth century did not prevent it from being eagerly sponsored by millions who wished to believe that war could be escaped by a formula for abandoning rights instead of enforcing them and for insulating America from a dangerous world rather than organizing the world for collective security.

Discussion of these problems was revived by the diplomatic crises of 1935 and by the growing conviction that war abroad had become inevitable. The result was the emergence of a "new" American neutrality policy, largely dictated by isolationists and designed not to facilitate American cooperation with the League States or with the signatories of the Kellogg Pact in preserving peace and restraining aggression, but to ensure American noninvolvement in war when it should come. The complexities, confusions, and frustrations encountered in the course of this effort revealed the impossibility of achieving isolation in a world in which American trade and investments were scattered over the five continents and the seven seas.

The neutrality legislation of 1935-1939 was in part an outgrowth of the investigation of the munitions industry by a committee of seven senators, headed by Gerald P. Nye of North Dakota, pursuant to a Senate resolution of April 12, 1934. The investigators revealed, among other things, that private arms interests had repeatedly defied or circumvented governmental action designed to control the arms traffic; often promoted sales through bribery of foreign officials; employed American officials to secure contracts abroad; sold arms to both sides simultaneously in war; armed both factions in civil wars; stimulated armaments races; organized lobbies to oppose arms embargoes and to work for larger military and naval appropriations; reached agreements with foreign competitors for the division of markets and profits; and indulged in sundry other practices designed to enrich the "merchants of death." These revelations stimulated congressional and public interest in the double problem of the arms trade and neutrality, which were linked together in a somewhat artificial fashion.

In the subsequent consideration of the problem of keeping the United States at peace, it was generally assumed by Congress, the press, and the public that the United States becomes involved in war by virtue of damage to American interests resulting from hostilities among other States. It was assumed, secondly, that Americans become involved in European wars by virtue of the machinations of munition-makers, bankers, and exporters bent upon making blood money out of the world's woes and determined to make their own profits a national interest for which the United States must fight. It was assumed, in the third place, that the price of peace was the sacrifice of profits and that insurance against war was to be had by the abandonment of trade and investments abroad. It was assumed finally that true "neutrality" implied complete impartiality between belligerents, with no distinctions drawn between aggressors and victims of aggression. That all these assumptions were partly or completely false did not prevent them from being accepted and acted upon by those who preferred wishful thinking to a stern facing of facts.

The Neutrality Act of August 31, 1935, hastily formulated in the face of what looked like impending war in Africa and Europe, reflected the beginnings of confusion. The Senate and House resolved "that upon the outbreak or during the progress of war between, or among, two or more foreign States, the President shall proclaim such fact, and it shall thereafter be unlawful to export arms, ammunition, or implements of war from any place in the United States, or possessions of the United States to any port of such belligerent States, or to any neutral port for trans-shipment to, or for the use of, a belligerent country. The President may from time to time, by proclamation, extend such embargo to other States as and when they may become involved in such war." Violators were to be punished by forfeiture of property and by a $10,000 fine and/or five years imprisonment. The act further established a National Munitions Control Board, consisting of the Secretaries of State, Treasury, War, and Navy, with which all manufacturers, exporters, and importers of arms were obliged to register their names, goods, and places of business. A $500 fee was required for a five-year registration certificate. All arms exports from the United States were to be licensed by the Board. American vessels were forbidden under penalty to carry arms to belligerents. The President was authorized at his discretion to close American ports to belligerent submarines and to warn American citizens that travel on belligerent vessels was at their own risk.

The public registration and licensing of arms exporters gave rise to no immediate problem. There were difficulties, however, as to the arms embargo. Far from cutting off all trade with belligerents as a means of keeping the United States at peace, the act only banned arms exports, narrowly defined. The embargo, moreover, was to be applied "impartially" with no distinctions among aggressors, victims of aggression, and sanctionist States that might become involved in hostilities in their efforts to uphold international law through the League. The President was given no discretion. As was pointed out at the time, the United States would be bound to close the American arms market to both Italy and Ethiopia in the event of an attack by the former on the latter. This action would aid the aggressor since Italy, unlike Ethiopia, had no need for American arms. Should Britain or other League States subsequently become involved in hostilities with the aggressor in the course of enforcing League sanctions, the President was presumably bound to aid the aggressor once more by barring American arms to the League States. That such a result could help keep the United States out of war seemed most dubious. In signing the Act President Roosevelt asserted, "No Congress and no Executive can foresee all possible future situations. The inflexible provisions might drag us into war instead of keeping us out."

MAKING THE WORLD SAFE FOR AGGRESSION

Another feature of the Act not generally appreciated at the time was the circumstance that it involved the repudiation of the Kellogg Pact. If all belligerents were to be treated identically regardless of whether they had observed the Pact or violated it, then the pact and its corollary, the Stimson Doctrine—already quite sufficiently emasculated through lack of implementation—would cease to have any meaning at all. America seemed once more on the point of disowning its child. In July, 1935, in response to an appeal from Ethiopia, President Roosevelt had declared that "my Government would be loth to believe that either [Italy or Ethiopia] would resort to other than pacific means as a method of dealing with this controversy or would permit any situation to arise which would be inconsistent with the commitments of the Pact." On July 12, Secretary Hull announced that "the Pact of Paris is no less binding now than when it was entered into by the sixty-three nations that are parties to it." On September 12, as war approached, Mr. Hull said "the American Government asks of those countries which appear to be contemplating armed hostilities that they weigh most solicitously the declaration and pledge given in the Pact of Paris." Thus the Executive was clinging to the Pact, though not prepared to protest in its name against Mussolini's aggression, while Congress was destroying any practical value it might have by proposing to treat the lawless and the law-abiding alike.

On October 5, 1935, two days after the Italian invasion was launched, the President proclaimed that a state of war existed, that exports of American arms, munitions, and implements of war to both belligerents were illegal, and that Americans would henceforth travel on belligerent ships only at their own risk. He further warned that all transactions of any character with either belligerent was at the risk of the trader (Caveat Mercator) and thereby implied, though Congress had not expressly authorized such a step, that the United States would not defend its right as a neutral to trade with Italy in the event of a League blockade. But no mention was made of the fact that Italy had obviously violated the Pact as well as the Covenant. Since Ethiopia had no ships and carried on little trade with the United States, it was assumed that the President's warnings would redound only to the disadvantage of Italy.

[259]

The arms embargo, however, was a benefit to the aggressor. Ethiopia was penalized by the United States for having been attacked. A lively war trade with Italy soon sprang up in commodities other than arms. Congress had not banned such trade. The warnings issued during October and November by President Roosevelt, Secretaries Hull, Ickes, and Roper, and other officials had little effect. Exporters not trading in arms were not subject to punishment. American exports to Italian Africa jumped from a monthly average of $25,403 in 1934 to $367,789 in October and $583,735 in November, 1935. Crude-oil exports to Italy increased 600 per cent. Exports to Ethiopia declined. "Moral suasion" failed. Mussolini floated to victory on a sea of oil, much of which came from the United States. American business, as usual, was in the war for profit, and its activities were aiding the aggressor. Congress had obviously failed to build an adequate economic cyclone cellar into which America could flee from foreign hostilities. The isolationists had kept the United States out of a war in which it could never conceivably have been involved by a formula which penalized the victim of international gangsterism and rewarded the gangster—thereby promoting the kind of future war in which the United States would inevitably be involved.

Since the Neutrality Act was scheduled to expire on February 29, 1936, Congress began reconsidering it in January. The Administration surrendered to the isolationist forces in Congress on the issue of Executive discretion. Both the Pittman-McReynolds (Administration) bill and the Nye-Clark-Maverick bill sought to tie the President's hands completely. Both bills further sought to carry the cyclone-cellar theory of neutrality to its logical conclusion. The American Government, according to this theory, should itself destroy American foreign trade in order to prevent belligerents from destroying it and thus creating danger of American involvement. To cut off all American foreign trade with all belligerents was unthinkable, however, since it would mean a major economic catastrophe in a general war. The bills therefore sought to limit American trade to "normal" peacetime quotas. But this was seen to be administratively unworkable. The whole plan was dropped. On February 18 the Senate, following similar action by the House, adopted a joint resolution signed by President Roosevelt on February 28, 1936, amending the Act of the previous summer and extending it to May 1, 1937. The amendments tied the President's hands even more completely. The new Act also forbade all long-term loans and credits to belligerents and further specified: "This act shall not apply to an American Republic or Republics engaged in war against a non-American State or States, provided that the American

Republic is not cooperating with a non-American State or States in such war."

This statute left the situation even more confused than before. The United States would ban arms, ammunition, implements of war, and loans to all belligerents, but all other trade would go on unimpeded and would presumably create all the old problems again in the event of a general and prolonged conflict abroad. Aggressors, victims of aggression, and sanctionist belligerents would be treated alike. But should a Latin American State become involved in war with a non-American State, either as an aggressor or as a victim of aggression, the United States would impose its embargo only against the non-American belligerent—unless the Latin American States were cooperating in a League war in the enforcement of sanctions, in which case it would receive no preferential treatment. The States injured by such a policy might be tempted to undertake reprisals against the United States. To old sources of conflict, new ones would be added. Far from ensuring peace the new policy seemed likely to promote war by throwing the economic weight of America into the scales on the side of Covenant-breaking and Pact-breaking aggressors. In December, 1936, at Buenos Aires, Secretary Hull attempted, without success, to commit all the American Republics to a similar policy.

On January 8, 1937, by special amendment sponsored by the Administration, the existing legislation was amplified to extend the arms and loan embargoes to foreign States afflicted by "civil strife." The occasion for this move was the effort of some Americans to sell arms to the Spanish Loyalists. The sensitivity of the Administration to the desires of Downing Street and of the Roman Catholic hierarchy in the United States, reinforced by the sensitivity of Congress to isolationist demands for strict "nonintervention," led to a statutory prohibition on the lending of money or the selling of arms to either side in the Spanish conflict. The Republican regime, whose rights under treaty and customary international law were thereby ignored, was thus deprived of the means of defending itself. The Rebels received all the arms they required from Germany, Italy, and Portugal.

Drew Pearson pointed out a year later that American arms were being sold freely to Germany and that this was a violation of the German-American peace treaty of 1921, and therefore of the Neutrality Act which forbade arms sales contrary to treaty terms. Hull replied weakly that the sales to the Reich were small and that the treaty merely forbade Germany to import arms from the United States without forbidding Americans to export arms to Germany. By May of 1938 even Senator Nye was appalled at the consequences of the "new neutrality" for Spain. He proposed that the Spanish embargo be lifted.

But the Administration, more anxious than ever to placate Chamberlain and the Vatican, declined to act. The destruction of Spanish democracy was a direct consequence of "nonintervention" by the European democracies and of a specious "neutrality" on the part of the United States. American isolationists helped the Fascist Caesars to win another major victory.

Meanwhile the new dispensation had been put into "permanent" form. On May 1, 1937, the President, then fishing in the Gulf of Mexico, signed a new act passed unanimously in the House and by a vote of 41 to 15 in the Senate, following prolonged debate productive of much heat and little light. As before, Americans were forbidden by an impartial and mandatory embargo to sell arms or make loans to foreign belligerents or to factions in civil strife. Travel on belligerent vessels was banned. The arming of American merchant vessels was prohibited. The American Republics were favored. The N.M.C.B. was continued. Section 2, which expired on May 1, 1939, without renewal, gave the President discretionary authority to place trade with belligerents in commodities other than arms on a "cash-and-carry" basis— *i.e.*, specified goods might be sold only on condition that title pass to the purchaser in advance of shipment and that transport be in foreign vessels. This section was never applied, but it furnished a formula for later use. The entire act was not applied to the undeclared war between Japan and China (resumed in July, 1937), since its application would obviously injure China more than Japan. In the event of war in Europe, all belligerents would be denied American arms and loans. The United States would thus (in theory) avoid the "deadly parallel" and the "tragic fallacy" of 1917.

CONGRESS HELPS HITLER

Critics of the new course at once pointed out that if the Axis attacked Britain and France the application of the "neutrality" statute would be of incalculable assistance to Hitler and Mussolini. Their heavily armed States would be prevented from securing American arms by the British fleet and would have no need of them in any event. France and Britain might well have desperate need of weapons and money from America, but would be prevented from securing either by American legislation. The United States would thus once more become the economic ally of the aggressors and would contribute to the possible defeat of the Western European Powers whose survival against the Reich had been deemed a major American interest, well worth fighting for, twenty years previously.

In January, 1939, President Roosevelt urged repeal of the arms embargo and resort to methods "short of war" but "stronger than words" to deter aggression. Legislative progress toward this goal was impeded, however, by loud outcries from isolationists over the accidental revelation that the President had released to a French purchasing mission certain types of aircraft intended for the army. Cried Hiram Johnson: "Good God, do you not, Gentlemen, think the American people have a right to know if they are going down the road to war?" Herbert Hoover, speaking in Chicago, denounced the President for "his proposal that we make effective protests at acts of aggression against sister nations. The distinction between legitimate expansion and wicked aggression becomes confused." We must not "set ourselves up as an oracle of righteousness." We must not risk war by playing "world-wide power politics." Soon afterward, Roosevelt was quoted in other quarters as having said that the American frontier was on the Rhine. For three days the Anglo-French press rejoiced, only to have the President issue a denial. Moves in Congress to repeal the arms embargo lagged during February and March.

On March 21 Senator Key Pittman moved to amend the Neutrality Act by putting all exports to belligerents, including munitions, on a cash-and-carry basis. Increased military and naval appropriations were voted. Senate hearings on the neutrality legislation opened April 5. Borah argued that aggressors were not violating the Kellogg Pact. Amid confusion worse confounded, the Duce struck down Albania. Hull announced on April 8 that "the forcible and violent invasion of Albania is unquestionably an additional threat to the peace of the world. It is scarcely necessary to add that the inevitable effect of this incident, taken with other similar incidents, is further to destroy confidence and to undermine economic stability in every country of the world, thus affecting our welfare."

The visit to the United States of King George and Queen Elizabeth (June 7-12, 1939) strengthened rather than weakened the determination of isolationists and obstructionists to prevent any modification of the Neutrality Act. The Senate Foreign Relations Committee had concluded its leisurely hearings on May 8. Pittman's leadership in the upper chamber produced no results. Sol Bloom introduced a resolution into the House to put all trade with belligerents on a cash-and-carry basis. At the end of June, however, the House approved an amendment retaining the impartial and mandatory arms embargo. Hull appealed belatedly to Congress. But the President acknowledged defeat on July 18, 1939, when Vice-President Garner told him laconically at a White House conference: "Cap'n, you haven't got the votes." If war came in Europe, the United States would aid the aggressors and penalize their victims. Undeclared war was raging in Asia. Despite notice to Tokyo on July 26 of abrogation of the commercial treaty of 1911, the invaders of China continued to purchase 65 per cent of their imported oil, 65 per cent of their motor cars, 77 per cent of their aircraft, and 90 per cent of their copper, scrap iron, and steel from the United States. The aggressors concluded that the world was quite safe for further aggression.

CONGRESS REPENTS

The outbreak of hostilities in Europe found almost all Americans passionately devoted to two desires which were to prove incompatible: Allied victory and American neutrality. On September 5, 1939, the President issued a traditional neutrality proclamation along with a second proclamation under the "Neutrality" Act, imposing an embargo on exports of arms, ammunition, and implements of war to Germany, Poland, France, Britain, India, Australia, New Zealand, South Africa (September 8), and Canada (September 10). On September 8, he proclaimed a "limited" national emergency under the National Defense Act. Some 80 million dollars worth of war materials, ordered by Britain and France and already licensed for export, were held up in American harbors by the proclamation. On September 13 the President called Congress into special session. He deemed it expedient to ignore the central issue of aiding the Allies by "methods short of war." When the lawmakers assembled on September 21 the President appealed to the traditional American policy and to the international law which had been departed from in the "neutrality" statute. "I regret that Congress passed that act. I equally regret that I signed that act." He held that the arms embargo was "most vitally dangerous to American neutrality, American security, and American peace." He proposed repeal of the embargo and the substitution of prohibitions on travel by Americans in belligerent vessels, on entry of American vessels into war zones, on lending by Americans to belligerents, and on exports of arms other than those paid for in cash and carried away in foreign vessels.

These proposals were not at all a "return to international law." They constituted a complete abandonment of "freedom of the seas" and "neutral rights" for which America had fought in 1798, 1805, 1812, and 1917. Since isolationists and pacifists chose to believe that America had been "dragged into war" in 1917 by virtue of private loans to the Allies and German destruction of American goods, ships, and lives, the way to peace was obviously to ban loans and to keep American goods, ships, and lives out of danger. The President yielded to this sentiment and sought to make possible the shipment of arms to the Allies by agreeing to prohibit loans, shipping, and travel in the name of "cash and carry." The resultant legislation would aid the Allies so long as they had no need of American money and American shipping. Should Hitler's foes later require funds and vessels from the United States, their rights under customary international law to secure these services would be denied by statute to the immense advantage of the Reich. Under the conditions of September, 1939, however, the President felt that he could secure no more than "cash and carry."

The Senate discussion was tedious. Its low point was reached when Senator Lundeen of Minnesota urged that while the Allies "were pretty busy on the Western front" the United States should demand prompt payment of the war debts and, failing compliance, should seize the British and French West Indies. "Not a shot would be fired. Let us show that there is some red blood in us." The isolationists talked their case to death. Senator Nye agreed with Borah that "there is nothing ahead of America but hell if we repeal the arms embargo." He averred that "the assumption that the British fleet is our first line of defense" was "conceived in the brain of the Mad Hatter." He repeated his favorite thesis that munition makers had pushed America into the Great War, but this argument provoked a belated counterattack, joined by Senator George Norris, lone survivor among the Senators who had voted against war in 1917. Congressman Ludlow pleaded vainly for a total embargo on all trade with the belligerents. Senator Clark of Missouri branded Britain and France as "aggressors" for refusing to make peace on Hitler's terms and thus driving the Germans "into the bosom of Communism."

The President denounced those who were tearing their hair over "American boys dying on European battlefields" for indulging in "a shameless and dishonest fake." The bill was amended to lighten the restrictions on American shipping. On October 27, the Senate passed the bill 63 to 30. Eight Republicans joined 54 Democrats and 1 Independent in voting affirmatively, and 12 Democrats joined 15 Republicans, 2 Farmer Laborites, and 1 Progressive in the opposition. The House assented. After further minor revisions, the Senate voted approval on November 3, 55 to 24, and the House 243 to 172. This result was hastened by the capture of the British-bound American freighter *City of Flint* by the *Deutschland* on October 9. The captors took the vessel to Norway, then to Murmansk, and finally back to Norway where the local authorities interned the prize crew and released the ship. Such incidents would be made impossible by the new statute.

CASH AND CARRY

The act which the President signed on November 4, following adjournment of Congress, was entitled "Joint Resolution to Preserve the Neutrality and Peace of the United States and to Secure the Safety of Its Citizens and Their Interests." Its preamble asserted that the United States "waives none of its own rights and privileges, or those of any of its nationals, under international law." Its text abandoned neutral rights and freedom of the seas. The President was required to issue a proclamation naming belligerent States "whenever the President, or the Congress by concurrent resolution, shall find that there exists a state of war between foreign States, and that it is necessary to promote the security or preserve the peace of the United States or to protect the lives of citizens of the United States. It shall thereafter be unlawful for any American vessel to carry any passengers or any articles or materials to any State named in such proclamation," subject to a fine of $50,000, five years' imprisonment, or both. "It shall thereafter be unlawful to export or transport, or attempt to export or transport, or cause to be exported or transported, from the United States to any State named in such proclamation, any articles or materials (except copyrighted articles or materials) until all right, title and interest therein shall have been transferred to some foreign government, agency, institution, association, partnership, corporation or national." These prohibitions were not to apply, however, to shipments of goods other than arms by air or inland waters to lands bordering the United States or to ports in the Western Hemisphere south of 35° north latitude or north of 35° and west of 66° west longitude (thereby exempting Canada, except for Halifax, Newfoundland, and Labrador) or to ports in the Pacific or Indian Oceans or to Atlantic ports south of 30° north latitude (cutting across North Africa) unless such ports should be included in "combat areas" proclaimed by the President and barred to American citizens and vessels.

The Act also forbade Americans to travel on belligerent vessels or to arm American vessels. Loans and credits to belligerents were likewise banned. For the rest, the new Act varied little from the old. The clause relating to "civil strife" which had helped to destroy the Spanish Republic was omitted.

Solicitation and receipt of contributions for belligerent States (save for relief) were banned. American Republics engaged in war against non-American States were exempted from the prohibitions unless "cooperating with a non-American State or States in such war." The President was given authority to prevent the use of United States ports as bases of supply for belligerent war vessels and, at his discretion, to ban foreign submarines and armed merchant vessels from United States waters. The National Munitions Control Board was retained. The President at once issued proclamations lifting the arms embargo, banning belligerent submarines from United States waters, and defining a "combat area" including the North and Baltic Seas, the Bay of Biscay except for the north coast of Spain, and the eastern Atlantic beyond 20°. American ships and citizens were thus banned not only from European belligerent territories but from the then neutral ports of Eire, Sweden, Denmark, Belgium, The Netherlands, and Norway south of Bergen.

Twenty-two years previously the United States had gone to war rather than accept German terms which would have allowed one American vessel each week to go to Britain. Now the United States itself forbade all its vessels and citizens to go to any European belligerent port or war zone at any time during hostilities, thereby inviting the Reich to sink all neutral shipping on sight without fear of protest from Washington. Berlin at once took advantage of this opportunity. The Nazi leaders realized that the new statute was by no means an unmixed blessing for their enemies. Had it been applied to the wars in Finland and China, it would have aided the cause of the Soviet and Japanese aggressors. Wherever it might be applied, it sounded the death knell of the rights of neutrals to lend, sell, and ship goods to belligerent States —despite ardent defense of these rights by America for over 150 years.

THE SLEEPER WAKES

In the terrifying spring of 1940 the fall of Copenhagen, Oslo, Amsterdam, Brussels, and Paris confronted Washington with the necessity of making choices not foreseen in the formulae of 1939. Each new victim of Nazi aggression was dutifully punished by Presidential proclamations barring American ships, citizens, and money from its territory. At the same time the American bank balances of the victims were impounded, lest the victors seize the foreign assets of the vanquished. To Rome and Tokyo went warnings and pleas, necessarily unimplemented since Congress and public forbade "commitments" or "entanglements." Rome replied on June 10, Tokyo later. On April 13, five days after the event, Roosevelt condemned the German invasion of Denmark and Norway: "If civilization is to survive the rights of the smaller nations to independence, to their territorial integrity, and to the unimpeded opportunity for self-government must be respected by their more powerful neighbors." On April 17 Hull issued a statement declaring that America had an interest in the rubber and tin of the East Indies and that any violent alteration of the *status quo* would be prejudicial to the "stability, peace, and security" of the "entire Pacific region." He recalled that Japan had promised to respect the rights of The Netherlands. He urged that "policies of force be abandoned."

These lofty statements of aspiration produced no visible effect. On May 12 the President warned the American Republics that until recently "too many citizens believed themselves safe." A "definite challenge" had to be faced. "Can we continue our peaceful construction if all the other continents embrace, by preference or by compulsion, a wholly different principle of life?" The President's personal answer to his own question was clear. But his political answer had to be different, since millions of his fellow-citizens firmly refused to face the question or insisted upon answering it in a fashion more consonant with spiritual comfort than with mental clarity or moral courage.

On May 16 the President went before Congress to ask for huge defense appropriations and a plane-building capacity of 50,000 units per year. There was no notable dissent until Colonel Charles A. Lindbergh three days later demanded by radio that America "stop this hysterical chatter of calamity and invasion. No one wishes to attack us and no one is in a position to do so." There was little response, however, to the appeals of the man who had aided Hitler to prepare the "peace" of Munich and had subsequently accepted the Service Cross of the Order of the German Eagle with Star, second highest decoration in the Nazi Reich. The President had asked for a billion dollars for arms. A few days later, he asked for another billion. The Senate voted almost 2 billion dollars to the Army and 1½ billion dollars to the Navy, 74 to 0. The House approved, 400 to 1. Wendell Willkie commented on May 29 that Allied victory would save America "billions of dollars, billions of tons of armament, billions of hours of wasted and unfruitful work. Just on the most selfish basis, it is enormously to our advantage to have them win." Vandenberg demanded "insulation," but soon urged full aid to the Allies, "short of war" and "within international law."

AMERICAN NIGHTMARE

The collapse of France created the conditions necessary for the first step. William Allen White's "Committee to Defend America by Aiding the Allies" grew by leaps and bounds throughout the country and exercised vast influence in arousing the public and mobilizing pressure on Congress, despite the outcries of a few congressmen that it was a "committee to get America into war." Under its auspices, General John J. Pershing made a radio plea on June 8 for "unlimited quantities" of aircraft, guns, and munitions to the Allies. But Senator Claude Pepper's motion to authorize the immediate dispatch of army planes was voted down in the Senate Foreign Relations Committee, 22 to 1. Senator Key Pittman urged a month later that the British Government "end Hitler's ambition for world conquest" by abandoning the British Isles. After reflection and a talk with the President, however, he opined that an "understanding" between the British and American fleets might "localize Hitler in Europe." On June 6 a trickle of army planes to the Allies began by virtue of Presidential exercise of statutory authority to exchange old planes for new ones, with the manufacturers willing enough to sell the traded-in goods to new customers.

In his address at the University of Virginia on June 10, denouncing the Duce's "stab in the back," Roosevelt stated a new policy: "Some still hold to the now somewhat obvious delusion that we of the United States can safely permit the United States to become a lone island in a world dominated by the philosophy of force. Such an island may be the dream of those who still talk and vote as isolationists. Such an island represents to me and to the overwhelming majority of Americans today a helpless nightmare, the helpless nightmare of a people without freedom; yes, the nightmare of a people lodged in prison, handcuffed, hungry, and fed through the bars from day to day by the contemptuous, unpitying masters of other continents. It is natural also that we should ask ourselves how now we can prevent the building of that prison and the placing of ourselves in the midst of it. . . . In our American unity, we will pursue two obvious and simultaneous courses: we will extend to the opponents of force the material resources of this nation and, at the same time, we will harness and speed up the use of those resources in order that we ourselves in the Americas may have equipment and training equal to the task of any emergency and every defense. . . . Signs and signals call for speed—full speed ahead. I call for effort, courage, sacrifice, devotion.

Granting the love of freedom, all of these are possible. And the love of freedom is still fierce, still steady in the nation today."

Colonel Henry L. Stimson declared on June 18 that the world "cannot endure permanently half slave and half free. America can cling to the dreams of a mistaken fiction of neutrality no longer applicable to her interest or her safety; she can leave the British fleet to its fate and face the consequences of a future which may leave her virtually defenseless to a Fascist attack. Or she can frankly realize that now as for many years past our own immediate safety depends in part upon the continuance of British sea power, and she can lend her resources to make our joint sea power effective for that purpose." The former Secretary of State urged repeal of the Neutrality Act, full access to all American ports by British and French vessels, and prompt dispatch of planes and arms "if necessary in our own ships and under convoy." He also urged military conscription and condemned defeatism. "I believe that if we use our brains and curb our prejudices, we can, by keeping command of the sea, beat her [Germany] as we did in 1918." Wendell Willkie, also committed to aid to the Allies, asserted at the same time that "we must stay out of war. No man has the right to use the great powers of the Presidency to lead the people indirectly into war." When Roosevelt on June 20 named Stimson as Secretary of War and another distinguished Republican, Colonel Frank Knox, editor of the *Chicago Daily News,* as Secretary of the Navy, the Republican National Committee "read out" both men from the party.

In his plea to Roosevelt of June 10, Reynaud pledged continued resistance in the provinces and French possessions and asked for all aid "short of an expeditionary force." In his reply, released June 15, the President extended admiration and sympathy and promised "redoubled efforts" to give material aid. But "only the Congress" could make military commitments. Congress would commit itself to nothing beyond frantic rearmament. Most Republicans and many Democrats in both Houses gave aid not to the Allies but to the obstructionists who were bent upon preventing aid to the Allies. The President's efforts to transfer a number of small torpedo boats were abandoned after the Attorney General cast doubt on their legality and the Senate Naval Affairs Committee introduced a measure (passed June 28, 1940) designed to forbid any executive transfer of naval vessels. Democratic Chairman David I. Walsh of Massachusetts asked, "Who in God's name thought that these contracts for our own protection would be modified or changed in order to assist one side or the other, or all sides, of belligerents at war? The Committee has inserted into the bill every possible safeguard to see that there is not in the future any attempt made to lessen our defenses so far as the navy is concerned."

The handwriting on the wall was scrawled large enough for all to see across the ruins of Rotterdam, the deserted casements of the Maginot Line, and the bloody beaches of Dunkirk. But the inert mass of legislators and citizens, blinded by fear of war, believed that America was in no danger or could somehow be defended after the arrival of an invader.

AID TO BRITAIN

The President could either do nothing, apart from urging measures of defense which he knew could never by themselves defend America, or he could exercise his executive discretion without regard for Congress. He chose the latter course. On August 18 the President and Prime Minister Mackenzie King of Canada, attending army manoeuvers in northern New York, announced their agreement "that a permanent joint board on defense shall be set up at once by the two countries" to "commence immediate studies relating to sea, land and air problems" and "consider in the broad sense the defenses of the northern part of the Western hemisphere." Since public response was favorable, Roosevelt took another step which was kept secret until completed.

On September 3 he sent a communication to Congress: "I transmit herewith for the information of the Congress notes exchanged between the British Ambassador at Washington and the Secretary of State on Sept. 2, 1940, under which this government has acquired the right to lease naval and air bases in Newfoundland and in the Islands of Bermuda, the Bahamas, Jamaica, St. Lucia, Trinidad and Antigua and in British Guiana; also a copy of an opinion of the Attorney General dated Aug. 27, 1940, regarding my authority to consummate this arrangement.

"The right to bases in Newfoundland and Bermuda are gifts—generously given and gladly received. The other bases mentioned have been acquired in exchange for fifty of our over-age destroyers.

"This is not inconsistent in any sense with our status of peace. Still less is it a threat against any nation. It is an epochal and far-reaching act of preparation for continental defense in the face of grave danger."

Lord Lothian's note defined the leaseholds on the Avalon peninsula (on the south coast of Newfoundland) and in Bermuda, granted "freely and without consideration," as well as the West Indies bases, granted "in ex-

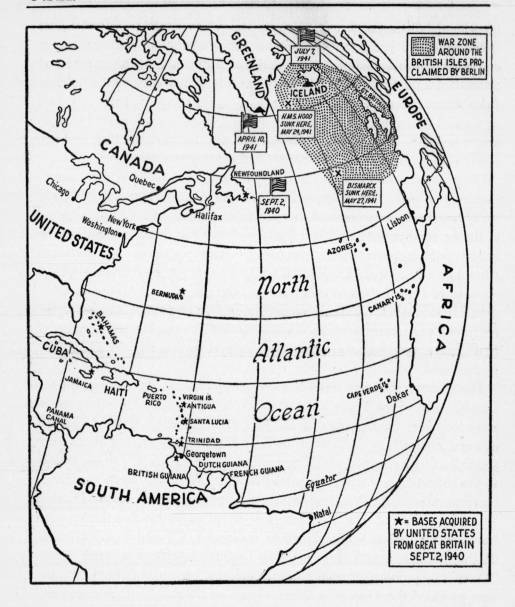

change for naval and military equipment and material." All the leases were for ninety-nine years and "free from all rent or charges" save compensations to owners of private property needed for the bases. Hull's note "gladly" accepted these "generous" proposals and agreed to transfer fifty 1,200-ton destroyers. Robert Jackson's opinion was a masterpiece of legal casuistry, interpreting statutes to mean things never intended by them and finding the transaction consonant with international law by the simple expedient of ignoring the distinction between private and governmental transfers of arms from neutrals to belligerents. A simultaneous exchange of communications conveyed renewed assurances that the British fleet would not be surrendered or scuttled if the British Isles became untenable. This pledge was of dubious value since a successful invasion of England would bring into power a Pétain or a Laval who would do the victor's bidding, and the demoralized seamen might be expected to do what was needful for the safety of their families rather than for the defense of a remote and neutral America.

Congress was outflanked. The bargain was an "executive agreement," requiring no legislation or appropriations. The anguished outcries of America's Munichmen were less loud than expected. Willkie endorsed the purpose of the agreement but found it "regrettable" that the President had not obtained prior approval from Congress. Britain registered joy, although Churchill warned that "it would be a mistake to try to read into the official notes more than the documents bear on their faces." The Axis press interpreted the bargain as a further step in the disintegration of the British Empire. No formal protest was made to Washington, despite the flagrant violation of traditional conceptions of neutrality, lest interventionist sentiment in America be increased.

The Caesars, however, retaliated at once by threatening war against the United States in the Triple Alliance treaty of September 27, 1940. Immediately following the signature of the Pact of Berlin, Hull asserted that the alliance "does not, in the view of the Government of the United States, substantially alter a situation which has existed for several years." On September 25 the Export-Import Bank announced another loan of $25,000,000 to China. On September 26 the President imposed an embargo, to be effective October 16, on all exports of scrap iron and steel except to Britain and the Western Hemisphere. Sumner Welles, however, declared in Cleveland on September 28 that the way was still open for an "equitable settlement" with Japan. "There is no problem presented which could not be solved through negotiation, provided there existed a sincere desire on the part of those concerned to find an equitable and fair solution which would give just recognition to the rights and the real interests of all concerned."

Americans eagerly applauded the pledges of "peace" which Roosevelt and Willkie both made in their bids for votes. "The Republican Party," declared its platform, "is firmly opposed to involving this nation in foreign war. The Republican Party stands for Americanism, preparedness and peace." Said the Democratic platform: "We will not participate in foreign wars, and we will not send our army, navy or air forces to fight in foreign lands outside of the Americas, except in case of attack." "I give you the pledge," said Willkie, "No American soldier boy will be sent to the shambles of any European trench." "Your boys," declared Roosevelt, "are not going to be sent into any foreign war. The purpose of our defense is defense." Hitler gave silent cheers.

LEND-LEASE

Yet the United States declined to be intimidated by the threats of the Triplice. Although both major candidates were in substantial agreement on foreign policy, President Roosevelt's unprecedented reelection to a third term was interpreted abroad as an endorsement of the policy of all aid to Britain. He moved cautiously to give further effect to the program laid down and to formulate national purposes in a more forthright fashion. Before the close of 1940, Congress had approved the expenditure of over $12,000,000,000 for "defense." By the President's "rule of thumb," half the new production of arms was allotted to Britain. The Compulsory Military Service and Training Law of September 16, 1940, introduced conscription for the first time during "peace" in the history of the Republic. The "Two Ocean Navy" bill of July 19 authorized a 70 per cent increase in sea forces. Early in the new year the Navy was reorganized into an Atlantic squadron, a Pacific squadron, and an Asiatic squadron in an unmistakable gesture of warning to Tokyo and the Axis. On January 6, 1941 (two days before proposing a 1941–1942 budget of $17,485,-528,000, of which $10,811,000,000 would go for armaments), President Roosevelt told Congress:

"Armed defense of democratic existence is now being gallantly waged in four continents. If that defense fails, all the population and all the resources of Europe, Asia, Africa and Australasia will be dominated by conquerors. And let us remember that the total of those populations and their resources greatly exceeds the sum total of the population and resources of the whole of the Western Hemisphere—many times over.

"In times like these it is immature—and incidentally untrue—for anybody to brag that an unprepared America, single-handed, and with one hand tied behind its back, can hold off the whole world.

"Let us say to the democracies: 'We Americans are vitally concerned in your defense of freedom. We are putting forth our energies, our resources and our organizing powers to give you the strength to regain and maintain a free world. We shall send you, in ever-increasing numbers, ships, planes, tanks, guns. This is our purpose and our pledge.'

"In fulfillment of this purpose we will not be intimidated by the threats of dictators.

"In the future days, which we seek to make secure, we look forward to a world founded upon four essential human freedoms.

"The first is freedom of speech and expression—everywhere in the world.

"The second is freedom of every person to worship God in his own way—everywhere in the world.

"The third is freedom from want—which, translated into world terms, means economic understandings which will secure to every nation a healthy peacetime life for its inhabitants—everywhere in the world.

"The fourth is freedom from fear—which, translated into world terms, means a world-wide reduction of armaments to such a point and in such a thorough fashion that no nation will be in a position to commit an act of physical aggression against any neighbor—anywhere in the world. . . .

"This nation has placed its destiny in the hands and heads and hearts of its millions of free men and women; and its faith in freedom under the guidance of God. Freedom means the supremacy of human rights everywhere. Our support goes to those who struggle to gain those rights and keep them. Our strength is our unity of purpose.

"To that high concept there can be no end save victory."

The Administration followed this appeal by the introduction of a "British Aid" bill (House bill 1776), giving the President emergency authority to make the United States the "arsenal of democracy" and to "sell, transfer, exchange, lease, lend or otherwise dispose of" or cause to be manufactured defense materials "for the government of any country whose defense the President deems vital to the defense of the United States." Wendell Willkie endorsed the principle of the bill and carried greetings from Roosevelt to Churchill on his visit to bomb-battered London at the end of January. The bill was attacked, on the ground that it would "lead to war" and create a "dictatorship," by an incongruous congeries of isolationists, Communists, superpatriots, Nazis, Socialists, pacifists, and Fascists.

After leisurely hearings and prolonged debate, the "lease-lend" bill was approved by the Senate, 60–31, and by the House, 371–71, with the addition of minor amendments. The Act was signed by the President on March 11, 1941. He therewith received the authority he sought, "notwithstanding the provisions of any other law," subject to termination on June 30, 1943, or earlier

by concurrent resolution of Congress. The Act declared that it did not authorize the convoying of vessels by naval vessels of the United States nor the
entry of American vessels into combat areas. But Congress and the public
were now apparently dedicated to the defeat of the Axis. All necessary means
toward the end in view would follow as a matter of course—unless Americans
should acquiesce in the failure of the enterprise to which they had put their
hearts and hands and thus invite disaster. The President at once asked and
received an appropriation of $7,000,000,000 to give effect to the new policy,
in addition to the $1,300,000,000 worth of defense articles, procured from
funds hitherto appropriated, which he was authorized to transfer by the Act
itself.

ARSENAL OF CONFUSION

For many months after the lease-lend bill became the law of the land, Washington's policy toward the war continued to mirror the hopeless cross-purposes
of a people who wanted to bring about the defeat of Hitler and his allies without committing themselves to any dangerous obligations. "Aid to Britain—
Short of War" was the formula of paradox whereby American politicians
adapted themselves to the schism in the American soul. Of the American
electorate in 1941 could be said what Arnold J. Toynbee said of the British
electorate in 1935: "It had come to believe that its talent for clockwork could
dispense it from the need of holding convictions and of summoning up courage to act upon them when the consequences were likely to be unpleasant.
It made its momentous choice neither on the absolute criterion of morality
nor on the relative criterion of expediency, but on that trivial distinction
between this moment and the next which keeps the sluggard cowering between the blankets when the house is burning over his head."

The task of the President and his advisers was to achieve a nice balance in
words and deeds between "aid to Britain" and "short of war," and at the same
time do something to prevent a British defeat. In deference to the keepers-
out-of-war the Administration alarmed and enraged the aiders-to-Britain by
continuing to enforce the "Neutrality" Act of 1939—save that the Red Sea
was declared no longer a "combat Zone" after April 11 and the "neutrality"
embargoes were not applied to the U.S.S.R. when the Reich invaded Russia
in June. In deference to the aiders-to-Britain the Administration enraged
and alarmed the keepers-out-of-war by ignoring completely all the cus-

tomary duties of neutrals toward belligerents. Whether the result was aid-short-of-war or war-short-of-aid no one could say with certainty.

In any event the result, as of mid-summer of 1941, was very strange indeed. With eager haste the American Government transferred money, arms and planes to Britain. The same American Government forbade American citizens, under heavy penalties, to lend money to Britain or to sell arms or planes on any basis other than cash-and-carry. American goods were pledged to Britain, but American ships were forbidden to carry them and the American Navy was forbidden to insure the arrival of the goods. "Freedom of the seas" was boldly championed, but American merchant vessels were forbidden to arm themselves for their own protection, and were denied protection by American warships, against those who made a farce of "freedom of the seas." American shippers could send their ships to the Red Sea and to Vladivostok, and to South Africa and Australia and New Zealand, but so long as they kept them under the stars-and-stripes they could not send them to any of the ports of the British Isles where they were most desperately needed.

Confusion was worse confounded in the Asiatic theater of war. For here the Administration gave aid to the Chinese against Japan and simultaneously encouraged American sellers and shippers to give aid to Japan against China. Exports of scrap iron and steel were embargoed in 1940, but finished iron and steel were still sold freely to Japan in 1941. Aviation gasoline was embargoed in 1940, but other forms of gasoline and oil, from which aviation gasoline could be refined, were sold in ever greater amounts in the early months of 1941. Americans gave generously to aid the Chinese victims of Japanese bombs which were dropped by planes made of American materials and flying on fuel sold by Americans.

After years of silence the President (July 24, 1941) explained, with the feeble logic and the doubtful ethics of all appeasers everywhere, why this policy had been pursued: "It was very essential from our selfish point of view of defense to prevent a war from starting in the South Pacific. If we had cut the oil off, the Japanese probably would have gone down to the Dutch East Indies. The policy has worked for two years." The wounded women and children of Chungking were thus told that America had helped the Japanese to bomb them in order to keep the Japanese from bombing the rubber and tin of the East Indies which Americans needed. War was very puzzling. But then the bombing of Chungking happily involved no "war," only an "incident." Anyway the policy "worked" by bringing the Japanese promptly to Indo-China, Thailand and the East Indies. A comparable policy on the part of Washington also "worked" in dealing with Vichy and Madrid. It was the same policy which Baldwin and Chamberlain, Blum and Daladier, had worked so successfully.

THE APPEASOLATIONISTS

For his halting and hazardous course the President won no thanks from the allies of the aggressors within the gates. His every move was on the contrary denounced most bitterly by America's Munichmen as evidence of a fiendish plot to "plow under every fourth American boy" (Burton K. Wheeler) on foreign battlefields for the benefit of Britain, Jewry and Wall Street.

The noisy minority that did so much to confuse thought and paralyze action during the time of America's greatest peril consisted, as in other democracies, of diverse elements united only by their determination to oppose and obstruct. The spectrum of divergency was broad. On the extreme Left marched the Communists who praised Hitler with faint damns and assailed all "capitalist war-mongers" with bitter invective—until the Nazi goring of the Soviet ox miraculously transformed the wicked "imperialist" war into a struggle for freedom against Fascist aggression. Next to the comrades, in self-righteous piety, marched the American equivalent of Ramsay MacDonald and Léon Blum, Norman Thomas, preaching heaven at home by abandoning all abroad to the hosts of hell.

Behind the knowing and high-minded Norman stood in valiant denseness of heart and mind a goodly throng of American "progressives," bespeaking the xenophobia and blind provincialism of many mid-western farmers and burghers. Here was Senator Wheeler, running mate of "Fighting Bob" La Follette in the lost cause of 1924. Here were "Fighting Bob's" two sons: Senator Robert and ex-Governor Philip. Here was California's windy champion of the common man, Senator Hiram Johnson, a survivor of the "irreconcilables" of 1920, and North Dakota's charming Senator, Gerald Nye, the nay-sayer. Here would have stood Idaho's William Borah had he not been called to his reward in January of 1940. Here too, curiously, was the greatest mind of the 13th century, serving as the President of America's greatest university, Robert M. Hutchins, whose love of "peace" was matched only by his solicitude for the sufferings of the poor.

In mid-parade marched Christian pacifists and the professional Anglophobes who wept for the victims of British brutality. Farther to the Right were the "America Firsters," following General Robert Wood and other men of means who favored appeasement because their only god was gold, or because (cf. John T. Flynn) everything British was bad and everything anti-British was good. Or because (cf. Herbert Hoover and Senators Taft and Walsh) they were simply muddled Tories. Near them stood the "Duke of Chicago," Col. Robert R. McCormick, who found all his prejudices fit to print in the news columns of his *Tribune*. Beyond the Duke stood Lindbergh, Knight of the German Eagle. By all but imperceptible gradations the Progressives and America Firsters shaded off into the fanatics of race and creed— the Christian Fronters, pro-Fascist Catholics, anti-Catholic fundamentalists, anti-Semites of all varieties, Bundsmen, Fascists, Quislings and quacks, mobilizing their fifth columns and training their Trojan horsemen for *Der Tag*.

Bedfellows make strange politics. All these groups were agreed upon the symbols with which the muddled public could best be befuddled. Their message was the home-grown American version of the earlier message of Europe's Munichmen and Vichymen. Americans should defend America or, at most, the Western Hemisphere. They had no concern with quarrels in far-away lands among people of whom they knew nothing. American democracy would be ruined by war and saved by peace. America was unprepared. America was too weak to "play God" in Europe or Asia. But America was so strong that no combination of Powers could ever attack it. Britain was already defeated. To aid Britain was to back a dead horse. To aid Russia was wicked. The Reichswehr was invincible, but the Atlantic Ocean was impregnable. Anyway, Hitler's victory was the wave of the future.

Göbbels agreed. On the 1st of May, 1941, he told ex-Ambassador John Cudahy, champion of a "negotiated peace," that Britain would be beaten by summer and that "the German General Staff has made an estimate of the situation from every military angle and has reached the conclusion that any invasion in sufficient numbers to occupy and hold any territory of the Western Hemisphere is impossible." Three weeks later the Führer assured Cudahy in Berchtesgaden that an invasion of the Western Hemisphere would be as fantastic as an invasion of the moon. Thus were America's Munichmen vindicated.

From this it followed that all who urged resistance to the Triplice were tools of Downing Street, or of the Kremlin, or of the Jews, or of the "international bankers." The members of the Cabinet were evil old men, thirsting to taste the blood of other men's sons. Mr. Willkie was a stooge of Roosevelt, and Roosevelt was a stooge of Churchill and King George. The advocates of a large armed force were plotters scheming to send the youth of America to horrible deaths on alien shores. "Interventionists," "alarmists" and "war-mongers" were imps of Satan, conspiring to wreck America. Americans should fight only on American soil. America first. Women and children first. Heil Hitler! Should America be wrecked, the identity of the wreckers would at least be clear.

THE BATTLE OF THE ATLANTIC

That the Administration could make any headway at all against this raucous chorus of defeatism was due to the fact that most Americans, for all their indecision, retained some vestiges of common sense. They feared and hated Hitler and all his works and insisted on all-out aid to Hitler's foes even at the risk of war. If the Administration supplied little leadership, fearing by too rapid moves to throw the doubters into the enemy camp, it at least followed its followers and somehow managed to act, albeit at a pace of one step forward and half-a-step back.

In his plea of mid-March for an all-out effort in production the President told his countrymen that aid to Britain and China would be "increased and yet again increased until total victory has been won." By the end of the month Churchill and Ambassador John G. Winant were signing an elaborate accord for American use of the bases acquired from Britain, and the President was ordering the seizure of Italian, German and Danish ships in American ports to protect them from sabotage. Early in April Washington asked Rome to recall its naval attaché. Axis protests over the seizure of the ships were rejected. Welles denounced the "barbaric invasion" of Jugoslavia. Ten coast-guard cutters were transferred to Britain.

More vigorous measures followed. On April 10 Hull and Danish Minister Henrik de Kauffmann, "recognizing that there is danger that Greenland may be converted into a point of aggression against nations of the American Continent," signed a pact whereby the United States secured the right to establish bases on Denmark's Arctic island. Danish sovereignty was fully safeguarded and appropriate mention was made of the Monroe Doctrine and the Act of Havana. Both diplomats ignored orders from Nazi-held Copenhagen "voiding" the pact and "recalling" De Kauffmann. Manhattan's Mayor La Guardia, American Chairman of the Canada-United States Joint Defense Board, declared two weeks later that the waters of the North Atlantic would be defended a thousand miles from shore. The President asserted that the "neutrality patrol" would be extended and that American warships would be sent wherever needed for "hemisphere defense."

Since these steps met with public support, Roosevelt marched on. On May 1st fifty oil tankers were placed at Britain's disposal by the Maritime Commission and plans were announced for a shipping pool. A fortnight later Vichy's ships in American ports were seized and the President reminded the press that the United States had fought two undeclared wars in defense of freedom of the seas. In his radio address of May 27 he championed this ancient cause more firmly, with pointed references to Dakar, the Azores and the Cape Verde Islands. He further proclaimed an "unlimited national emergency." On the next day, however, he explained that he was not planning convoys nor any change in the "neutrality" legislation, though Stimson, Knox and Willkie had long demanded both.

The torpedoing in the South Atlantic on May 21 of the *Robin Moor,* first American vessel to be sunk by the Nazis, led to a sharp diplomatic protest to Berlin. On June 14–15 Washington ordered the "freezing" of all Axis funds in the United States, the closing of all German consulates (and, as of June 21, Italian as well) and the withdrawal "for improper and unwarranted activities" of the German Library of Information, the German Railways Office and the Transocean News Service. In his message to Congress regarding the *Robin Moor,* Roosevelt called the Reich an "international outlaw" and "pirate." Said Sumner Welles on June 23: "If any further proof could conceivably be required of the real purposes and projects of the present leaders of Germany for world domination, it is now furnished by Hitler's treacherous attack on Soviet Russia. Any defense against Hitlerism, any rallying of the forces opposing Hitlerism, from whatever sources these forces may spring, will hasten the eventual downfall of the present German leaders, and will therefore redound to the benefit of our own defense and security."

Iceland was next. On the 3rd of July Senator Wheeler predicted its occupation. Churchill accused him of endangering British lives. In his Independence Day message President Roosevelt restated his stand: "We are in a serious, in a mighty, in a unified action in the cause of the defense of the hemisphere and the freedom of the seas. I tell the American people solemnly that the United States will never survive as a happy and fertile oasis of liberty surrounded by a cruel desert of dictatorship." On the 7th he told Congress that Iceland was occupied: "The United States cannot permit the occupation by Germany of strategic points in the Atlantic to be used as air or naval bases for eventual attack against the Western Hemisphere." A German seizure of

[*281*]

Iceland would threaten Greenland and North America as well as North Atlantic shipping and "the steady flow of munitions to Britain." He submitted the texts of letters exchanged on the 1st of the month with Iceland's Premier, Hermann Jonasson, safeguarding Iceland's independence and sovereignty and granting the needed facilities to the American forces sent to replace the British. "As commander-in-chief I have issued orders to the Navy that all necessary steps be taken to insure the safety of communications in the approaches between Iceland and the United States, as well as on the seas between the United States and all other strategic outposts."

THE AGONY OF INDECISION

Despite these moves and others which followed them, the Great Republic of North America was still irresolute and disunited as World War II entered its third year. Few Americans favored active participation in hostilities. Few opposed aid to the Allies. But almost all were at war within themselves, for they desired the defeat of the Axis without desiring to pay any part of the price in struggle and pain. Most of them approved the President's policies only because those policies seemed to offer hope of victory without war.

By the approach of autumn of 1941 the United States of America was engaged in fighting the Triple Alliance on a dozen far-flung fronts. In order to confer with Churchill and Stalin on American aid Harry Hopkins made a midsummer flight on a bomber to London and thence to Moscow. Nelson A. Rockefeller, "Coordinator of Commercial and Cultural Relations between the American Republics," announced in August a blacklist of 2,000 Latin American firms and individuals charged with aiding the Axis. The President froze their funds in the United States and put all inter-American trade on a license basis. Washington gave encouragement to efforts in the Argentine to uncover and suppress Nazi subversive activities; extended moral support to President Enrique Penaranda de Castillo of Bolivia in his expulsion of German Minister Ernst Wendler in mid-July for plotting a Nazi putsch; sought peace in the border war between Peru and Ecuador; sent Owen Lattimore to Chungking; and froze all Japanese assets, restricted trade, and warned of worse to come when Japan moved into southern Indo-China. Arms and other supplies were given or "loaned" to Britain, dispatched to China on credit and sold to Russia for cash.

In early August Sumner Welles and Constantine Oumansky exchanged notes renewing the annual Soviet-American trade agreement and pledging full material support by the United States to Russia's war effort. Oil shipments for Vladivostok moved across the Pacific even as Roosevelt and Churchill met in the Atlantic to plan further steps in common to aid the U.S.S.R., immobilize Japan and bring about "the final destruction of the Nazi tyranny."

But no American guns were fired, no American troops were ordered into action, no American planes attacked the enemy, no American ships of war sought out the foe on any sea. America was still "at peace," albeit engaged to the hilt in a mighty effort to defeat the Triple Alliance.

This strange state of affairs was not unprecedented. Hitler's Reich, Mussolini's Italy and Hirohito's Japan had been "at peace" for the better part of a decade while their leaders inspired their subjects with martial fervor, built up the greatest war machine of the ages, conquered China, Ethiopia, Spain, Austria, Czechoslovakia and Albania, and prepared the "New World Order." Could America "at peace" perform comparable miracles while Chinese, Russians and Britons fought her battles for her? If so, victory might be won by measures short of war. If not, the entire enterprise might fail and lead to ultimate defeat.

The answer hinged on the magic potency of words. The Caesars had abolished all distinction between peace and war and pursued their goals by force and fraud with no regard to the niceties of law and ethics. But most Americans still chose to believe that "peace" and "war" were different and that citizens' duties under each were not the same. So long as obsolete distinctions hypnotized the American public mind, so long would millions oppose their Government's every move on the plea of "keeping out of war." And so long as this was possible, there could be little hope of achieving that united national effort without which the war could not be won. Totalitarian States can suppress dissent and imbue their subjects with eager willingness to sacrifice and with a dynamic will to deeds without the ancient ritual of declaring war. Democracies cannot.

The leaders of the Triplice were too shrewd to provoke America into open war. And in the absence of a major provocation, the leaders of America were too timid, too hopeful, too "democratic," too politically minded to risk a plea to Congress for a declaration of war, or to wage actual war without declaring it. They feared a disunited nation if "short of war" should be transmuted into acknowledged "war." Yet the longer they hesitated and waited for unity, the graver grew the danger that the disunion fostered by the appeasolationists would grow to a point at which "short of war" would fail and war itself, embarked upon too late, would mean defeat. Here once more was Hitler's highest hope.

This hope rested on careful observation of the American public mind. The Führer's assumption that his invasion of Russia would further confuse and paralyze American opinion was partially vindicated. The Republican leaders repudiated the position of Willkie, Stimson and Knox and sought to make political capital, as their predecessors had done so successfully in 1920, by championing isolationism. Typical of the clichés they used to win support were the words of a statement issued early in August by Hoover, Dawes, Lowden, Hutchins, John L. Lewis and other oppositionists: "It is not purely a world conflict between tyranny and freedom. The Anglo-Russian alliance has dissipated that illusion. Insofar as this is a war of power politics, the American people want no part in it. We maintain that American lives should be sacrificed only for American independence or to prevent the invasion of the Western hemisphere. Freedom in America does not depend on the outcome of struggles for material power between other nations."

Most Republicans and some Democrats spoke and voted in Congress as Hitler hoped they would. By mid-August the national law-makers, for the first time since the outbreak of European hostilities, were showing reluctance to approve all the requests of the armed services for further appropriations. The question of retaining under arms the new conscripts whose year of service would soon expire precipitated acrimonious controversy. The Administration contended that the nation was in graver peril than ever before. Gen. Marshall argued convincingly before Congressional committees that the new army would disintegrate if the service of draftees was not extended. Yet extension was favored by a bare half of the citizenry. Many of the men in camps wondered, not unnaturally, why they should be expected to make further sacrifices when their country was not at war. On August 12, 1941, the House of Representatives voted to extend military service of the conscripts another eighteen months. Of the Republican members, 21 voted in the affirmative and 133 in the negative. The total vote was 203 to 202.

The disease of national morale reflected in these figures could be cured neither by such hollow words as were to be found in the "eight points" nor yet by reassurances from the President after his meeting with Churchill that the United States was "no nearer war." At the end of August Tokyo was hopefully soliciting further appeasement from Washington while the Nazi armies completed their conquests of the Baltic and the western Ukraine.

Hitler and his faithful lackey, Mussolini, met on Russian soil and replied to the Roosevelt-Churchill declaration by pledging themselves to victory and to European peace on the basis of "the destruction of the Bolshevist danger and of plutocratic exploitation." Americans looked upon all these events in the role of observers rather than participants. Roosevelt quoted Lincoln's comment of 1862: "The people have not yet made up their minds that we are at war. They have no idea that the war is to be carried on and put through by hard, tough fighting, that it will hurt somebody; and no headway is going to be made while this delusion lasts."

The Americans of the 1920's had been slightly hurt in winning a war which they forthwith repudiated. They were so anxious to avoid being hurt again that they threw their victory away and helped the aggressors to hegemony over Europe and Asia. In the face of dangers grown to terrifying proportions, the Americans of the 1940's were still so bent on pursuing pleasure and avoiding pain that they would risk nothing beyond their pocketbooks (and those grudgingly) in what most of them still believed were "other people's wars." This delusion would be fully dispelled only when the bombs should begin falling on their heads out of their own skies. Should they persist in their irresolution up to the hour of assault upon their shores, they would inevitably share the fate of other peoples similarly doomed to defeat and subjugation by their own irresponsibility.

Wars in our time are commonly lost long before the test of battle by the refusal of the losers to fight them until the hour of possible victory is past. In seeking victory without fighting Americans might well find themselves in the end alone, fighting without victory. For here, as elsewhere, there is in truth "a tide in the affairs of men which taken at the flood leads on to fortune," and, neglected, causes those who wait to spend all the balance of their lives in grief and vain regret.

AMERICAN CENTURY?

Thus was the mightiest of the Great Powers all but self-defeated by the painful vacillation of its people. Their resolution, like Hamlet's, was "all sicklied o'er by the pale cast of thought." Their endless debate, though they knew it not, was in fact over the question of: to be or not to be. But they believed they were debating simpler questions: How to eat one's cake and have it too? How to spend money and wax fat in safety while one's friends spent blood and tears? How to keep out of "foreign quarrels" in the name of "America First" while others suffered and died in halting a foe on whose list America was last? Eventually Hitler or Hirohito might solve the American dilemma as the Reich had solved a similar dilemma for the Soviet Union. Eventually Americans might reason themselves, or frighten themselves, into a willingness to fight. By then, however, the Triplice might have won its war, or at least made itself so formidable that the stoutest hearts might quail at the cost of bringing it to defeat.

President Roosevelt's words and deeds during September showed evidence of a growing determination, in the White House if not in Congress, to do what was necessary before the hour for action had passed. The strategy of intimidation so long and successfully practiced by the Tokyo warlords was at long last met by defiance and threats of force. The warriors of Righteous Justice were given to understand, secretly but surely, that any Japanese assault on Thailand or the Dutch East Indies or any interference with shipments of war supplies to Soviet Siberia, would bring the American and British Navies into action in the Pacific. With his bluff called, Premier Konoe submitted a confidential message to the President through Ambassador Nomura, soliciting "negotiations." In the ensuing discussions, the President delayed a reply and stood firm. Tokyo ceased beating the war drums and resolved to bide its time—pending a resumption of American appeasement or a hoped-for collapse of Soviet and British resistance to the Axis.

On Labor Day of 1941 the President asserted: "Our fundamental rights, including the rights of labor, are threatened by Hitler's violent attempt to rule the world. We cannot hesitate, we cannot equivocate, in the great task before us. Forces of insane violence have been let loose by Hitler upon this earth. We must do our full part in conquering them. There are a few appeasers and Nazi sympathizers who say it cannot be done. They even ask me to negotiate with Hitler, to pray for crumbs from his victorious table. They do, in fact, ask me to become the modern Benedict Arnold and betray all I hold dear. This course I have rejected. I reject it again. We shall do everything in our power to crush Hitler and his Nazi forces."

Three days later, on September 4, as the first American tanker reached Vladivostok, the destroyer *Greer*, en route to Iceland, was attacked by a Nazi submarine. It replied by dropping depth bombs. The President ordered the Navy to track down and "eliminate" the attacker. In the waters between Greenland and Iceland three merchant vessels, all of United States ownership and Panamanian registry, were torpedoed: the *Sessa* on August 17, the

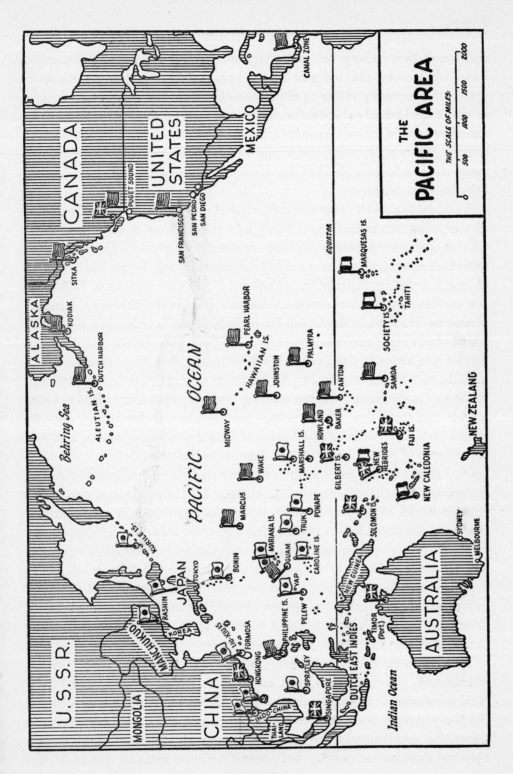

THE

PACIFIC AREA

THE SCALE OF MILES:

0   500   1000   1500   2000

CANADA

UNITED STATES

MEXICO

CANAL ZONE

ALASKA

PUGET SOUND

SAN PEDRO

SAN DIEGO

SAN FRANCISCO

SITKA

KODIAK

DUTCH HARBOR

ALEUTIAN IS.

Behring Sea

PACIFIC OCEAN

PEARL HARBOR

HAWAIIAN IS.

JOHNSTON

PALMYRA

MIDWAY

WAKE

MARCUS

MARSHALL IS.

HOWLAND

BAKER

CANTON

GILBERT IS.

NEW HEBRIDES

FIJI IS.

SAMOA

SOCIETY IS.

TAHITI

MARQUESAS IS.

EQUATOR

NEW CALEDONIA

NEW ZEALAND

KURILE IS.

JAPAN

TOKYO

BONIN

MARIANA IS.

GUAM

YAP

PELEW

TRUK

PONAPE

CAROLINE IS.

NEW GUINEA

SOLOMON IS.

AUSTRALIA

SYDNEY

MELBOURNE

U.S.S.R.

MONGOLIA

MANCHUKUO

RASHIN

KOREA

CHINA

LIU-KIU

FORMOSA

HONGKONG

PHILIPPINE IS.

SPRATLEY

INDO-CHINA

THAI-LAND

SINGAPORE

DUTCH EAST INDIES

TIMOR (Port.)

Indian Ocean

[287]

Montana on September 11, and the *Pink Star* on September 19. In a radio address of September 11 the President announced that the Navy would defend freedom of the seas "no matter what it costs." "From now on, if German or Italian vessels of war enter the waters, the protection of which is necessary for American defense, they do so at their own peril. Our patrolling vessels and planes will protect all merchant ships of any flag engaged in commerce in defense waters." Five days later a "shoot first" order went into effect. Secretary Knox declared that the Navy was now using all possible means to protect shipping, including convoys. By the end of September the President indicated that he would ask Congress to amend the "Neutrality" Act to permit the arming of American merchant ships.

While an undeclared naval war with the Reich loomed in the North Atlantic, Washington ordered $100,000,000 worth of Russian metals and made an immediate advance against future delivery to speed the purchase of war supplies for the Soviets in the United States. On September 16 the President's second quarterly report on the lease-lend bill showed that almost all of the $7,000,000,000 originally appropriated had been "allocated," but that actual exports under the Act to nations fighting the Axis totalled only $190,447,000 in the first six months. Of this, $110,600,000 consisted of foodstuffs and other agricultural products. Two days later Roosevelt asked Congress for an additional $5,985,000,000. If the mountain in labor had thus far brought forth only a mouse, there was promise at least of a volcanic eruption of planes, tanks and guns during 1942–1943—if only Russian and British resistance allowed time for full American production to affect decisively the fortunes of war. American opinion approved these steps. But a large segment of the citizenry continued to demand "peace."

The Americans who could not decide whether they wanted to defeat the Triplice at the cost of war were also unable to decide whether they wanted future security at the cost of reordering and policing the world. The price of victory and survival was not only willingness to fight at a time and place offering prospects of success. It was willingness also to confront the "New World Order" of the Caesars with a Newer World Order of freemen. Among the foes of the Triplice, only America had the resources and the prestige required for a role of world leadership. But even the Americans who saw most clearly the need of defeating the Triplice shrank back from the task of remaking the world society—some because they would not or could not see the world as one community, others because they feared to drive their fellow-citizens back into the burning barn of isolationism.

The America of 1941 had neither war aims nor peace aims. Since its people would not be moved to action by any positive purpose or any hope-inspiring vision, their leaders sought to move them by fear and by negative objectives of "defense." The great goal, said Sumner Welles (July 22), was security for all, and a peace which would "establish fully and adequately the natural rights of all peoples to equal economic enjoyment." The means thereto? Perhaps "the great ideal" of an "association of nations" for the "abolition of offensive armaments and the limitations and reduction of defensive armaments through some rigid form of international supervision and control." Such echoes of empty words doubtless caused Woodrow Wilson to turn unhappily in his grave. The Americans of 1916 saw the world, and America's role therein, more clearly. The Americans of 1941 saw all as through a glass darkly, without vision and with little desire for truth. So at least their leaders believed.

Great nations unwilling to face their destiny have no future. Whether America deserved a future depended upon the capacity of Americans to awaken and prepare themselves for the tasks of tomorrow—in war and peace alike. If they continued to close their eyes and minds, the Nazi Reich would rule the world, America included. If they would finally see reality through the fog of their own delusions, America would unite and reshape the world into a fit dwelling place for freemen. How soon? How late?

"Cheshire-Puss," she began, "would you tell me, please, which way I ought to go from here?" "That depends a good deal on where you want to get to," said the Cat. "I don't much care where—" said Alice. "Then it doesn't matter which way you go," said the Cat. "—so long as I get somewhere," Alice added as an explanation. "Oh, you're sure to do that," said the Cat, "if you only walk long enough." Alice felt that this could not be denied, so she tried another question. "What sort of people live about here?" "In that direction," the Cat said, waving its right paw around, "lives a Hatter; and in that direction," waving the other paw, "lives a March Hare. Visit either you like: they're both mad." "But I don't want to go among mad people," Alice remarked. "Oh, you can't help that," said the Cat: "we're all mad here. I'm mad. You're mad." "How do you know I'm mad?" said Alice. "You must be," said the Cat, "or you wouldn't have come here."

THE WORLD'S DISEASE

The gentle reader who has come thus far in these ungentle pages will doubtless by now be weary and not a little puzzled. A story of grief and pain seven times told is tiresome and baffling. No sane man or woman relishes any such morbid preoccupation with crime and folly. Yet our epoch drives its children, willy-nilly, on a doleful voyage. Those who still survive its miseries are all alike sucked into a giant whirlpool of evil and weakness which draws its victims down to doom ever more quickly even as they struggle for freedom.

"How the world has fared," wrote Dante Alighieri in another age of frustration, "we may read in books; would that we might not see it with our eyes. Oh, race of mankind! What storms must toss thee, what losses must thou endure, what shipwrecks must buffet thee, as long as thou, a beast of many heads, strivest after contrary things. Thou art sick in both thy faculties of understanding; thou art sick in thy affections."

Sick indeed are those who worship vice, despise virtue, love lies, hate truth and banish beauty from their lives in favor of a hideously "heroic" delirium of war and death. Sick also are those who seek "peace" by hiding their heads or by bribing evil-doers. Anguish of spirit and torment of flesh are ever the penalties of such misdeeds.

Yet in the middle decades of this, our century, such behavior is all but universal. Lunatics and paralytics compete for mastery of the future. Mad players of the game of power, hate-crazed and swollen with bloated ambition, play checkers on the squares of the world against opponents who play give-away because they are fear-crazed and possessed by an irresistible urge to flee from life.

Why are these things so? What can the sane still do to keep their sanity and restore some measure of mental and moral health to a species thus afflicted? Many answers float about amid the havoc wrought by man's inhumanity to man. To add to their number may be pure presumption. Not to add, however, may be worse. For here as elsewhere the sins of silence and inaction are often blacker than the sins of words and deeds.

LESSONS FROM LUNATICS

Consider then, in all seriousness and with all sympathy, the ways of madmen. These unfortunates, broadly speaking, differ from the sane in one (or more) of four respects. They are blind and deaf to their surroundings, living in a darkness of their own devising, beyond love or rage or fear. Or they rule the world in wildly exciting fantasy, and in their imagined roles of potentates and conquerors impose their will upon all by sly deceptions or by violence. Or they seek love insistently in orgies of brutality toward others or of pity for themselves, and they nourish fierce suspicions and spites against those they accuse of denying them affection. Or, finally, they cultivate abjectness and docility and find peace within by submitting utterly to the will of others.

What do such sufferers, apparently so different, have in common? Each is engaged in escaping from the torture of worry. Each is fleeing from a world which, he is sure, has brought intolerable pain upon him. Each fears, and therefore hates, the world. Hatred flows from thwarted desire. Bitterness toward others is often but admiration turned to envy by failure, or hidden love turned to rage by fear. Rage and fear are ancient habits of nerves and glands and blood, useful for survival in the face of threatening dangers. But these elixirs of life become poison when they are too long fixed in living tissue. They must explode into sudden action—by flight from what is feared or by force against what is hated. Fear and hatred then subside. When they are pent up and denied discharge, they drive their victim to a frantic quest for relief. The very madness of the mad has method in it, for it is a mode of escape from inner tensions too painful to be endured.

Retirement into oneself provides escape: those who quit the world, physically by suicide or psychically by retreat into a self-induced coma, can no longer be injured and have no further need to hate or fear. Power to subdue the world also provides escape: those whom one dominates cannot do one harm. Love provides escape: those who love one will not hurt one. Submission likewise provides escape: docility prevents punishment for insubordination and frees one from the painful need of taking thought. Each in his way finds relief from his torment. Each thus adjusts himself to an environment which is terrifying and hateful because he has projected onto it his own fears and hatreds.

THE FRONTIERS OF SANITY

Now go outside the private worlds of the demented. Consider the conduct in our time of those throughout the public world who are alleged (by themselves) to be sane. "Having been in international politics for most of the time since the war," said Stanley Baldwin in 1935, "I will not write myself down a pessimist, but I will say that at times I feel that I am living in a mad-house." The behavior of the inmates is but a milder form of that observed in lunatics. For all sanity is but insanity held in check by those who are slightly better "balanced" than the "unbalanced."

Here, in the capitals of the new despotisms, are the remorseless power-seekers, merciless and cruel, fearing and hating all alien tribes of men and seeking frantically to protect themselves from their own diseased desires by conquering others. This they must do in order that they may have the world at their mercy. Only thus can they avoid the danger of having the world treat them as they deserve, or the painful humiliation of having the world deny their importance.

Some of the Caesars, like the first Napoleon or Benito the Little, seek surcease from their lack of self-assurance in endless *amours*, ever repeated and forever unsatisfying. From these endless disappointments they flee to politics and war, for those who can find no peace in love often find joy in hatred and violence, and in the drunkenness or tears which they inflict upon their followers or victims. Some, like the son of Schicklgruber, are incapable of personal love, whether normal or compulsive, and find their souls only in public frenzy. All are miserable unless they have victims to flay, foes to slaughter, followers to command and mobs of howling slaves to applaud their every act.

Here, in the lands the Caesars rule, are the thousands of petty despots and madmen, tortured by fears of punishment and by dreams of power. They see themselves alternately as objects of fearful persecution or as noble saviors of the race. These deluded ones have the double joy of subordinating themselves utterly to Duce, Führer or Mikado and of lording it over those below them in the pyramid of power. At the bottom of the hierarchy are the millions of escapists and submitters who have gladly abdicated, leaving their rulers to think for them while they merely believe, obey and fight. In herd-like multitudes these millions discharge their fears and hatreds upon foreign enemies or upon helpless victims within their midst. Through brutality they inflate their sick souls. Through the wanton cruelty of the impotent, they make themselves heroic members of a master-nation or a master-race.

Yonder, in the America of the isolationists, in the recent Britain of the appeasers and in the lost France of yesterday, are other disciples of escape through submission. These find comfort in abnegation. They would crawl into their psychic cyclone-cellars. They seek safety through withdrawal from danger. They fancy that security will be theirs if only they will shun all responsibilities and risks beyond their Maginot Lines, their Atlantic Oceans, their walls of ships and gold, their "Western Hemispheres" or their supposedly impregnable frontiers. The pain of hidden doubt, gnawing unceasingly at their vitals, is eased by the verbal drugs of endless rationalizations, by which they convince themselves and others of the wisdom and rectitude of their ways. Their buried fears are conquered by discharging their hatreds not on aggressors abroad but on their fellow-citizens at home who warn of mortal peril and plead for relevant action. Their foes are the "interventionists," the "internationalists," the "bankers," the "Jews," the "Reds," the "warmongers." Against these foes they aid their conquerors. They unconsciously admire their own destroyers. When conquest is complete, they drink to defeat, they rejoice in submission, they become the Quislings and the Vichymen of the doomed.

ESCAPE FROM WORRY

This conduct, to be sure, is that of politicians rather than that of humble men and women lacking power. It is an article of liberal faith that the Common People can do no wrong and can never lose its Common Sense. But in truth most people receive the kind of leadership they deserve. Even in tyrannies politicians represent the masses and lead them by following their desires. All politicians differ from non-politicians in that they find no psychic fulfillment in purely private work or in private love but only in the applause of crowds. In an age when masses are moved to escapism or submissiveness, or to a mob-quest for mastery through intertribal theft and murder, only those politicians remain in power who meet their needs.

The needs themselves are products of successive failures and fears, many times multiplied and suffered by millions. Frustration begets aggression. If the victim is not to turn his aggressions against himself, and thereby court despair, madness and suicide, he must turn them outward against others. In dealing with family, friends and neighbors, worriers are typically either subdued, submissive and resigned, or irritable, quarrelsome and inconsiderate, depending upon whether their worry is best assuaged by punishing themselves or by punishing others. Epochs of anxiety are rich in divorce, crime, suicide, cruelty, venery, asceticism, alcoholism, drug-addiction, neurasthenia and insanity.

When these private devices for escape from fear prove insufficient, they are often followed or replaced by public aggressiveness or submissiveness, political fanaticism, assassinations, riots, revolutions and wars. These responses to frustration are readily rationalized in the name of the "public good." They therefore render it easy for the victim of fear to externalize his aggressions and to escape the shame and disgrace he would feel at private exhibitions of his hostilities. No man truly enjoys the "loss of face" which goes with bullying his wife, beating his children, fighting with the neighbors or taking to drink, drugs or delinquency. But all men share joyously in the inflation of the collective ego which goes with communal acts of inebriation and brutality.

Sex, religion and politics are the forms of human communion which enable the largest number of victims of worry to enjoy the largest measure of escape from fear. In the shared excitement of great emotional debauches insecure personalities most easily find themselves by losing themselves. This man (or

woman) finds solace in illicit love. The next is "converted" and "saves his
soul." The third becomes a revolutionist or a "red-baiter" or an impassioned
reformer who damns loudly and long the bosses or the Communists or the
Catholics or the Jews or the Nazis, as the case may be. Each of these experiences provides intimate identification with fellow-sufferers and sanctifies
attitudes and actions which each man alone would condemn as immoral but
which all men together praise as heroic or divine. Periods of general insecurity therefore drive men and women to morbid eroticism; to religious revival-
ism and persecution; and to revolution, Caesarism and "total war." All are
roads toward self-assurance. The terror of loneliness is vanquished by these
various means of merging the self with others. Escape from worry is the
reward of the passionate, the pious and the power-seekers.

ANATOMY OF FRUSTRATION

But why, asks Everyman, is the 20th century so poor in fulfillments and so
rich in insecurities and frustrations? Because, to begin with, the millions who
suffer have obviously been denied by the world the things the world has led
them to expect. The unhappiness of those who get less than they need is as
nothing compared with the unhappiness of those who get less than they think
they are entitled to. Slow disappointments, small and oft repeated, allow time
for adjustment through reduction of expectations. Sudden deprivations lead
to frantic fear and hot resentment. With startling suddenness the maladjusted
world of our time has over and again denied to its children not only jobs and
bread but sundry intangible goods of greater worth: safety, dignity, hope
and self-assurance—all things they had been led to expect as their heritage by
virtue of the long "progress" of the recent past toward a more secure and
abundant life for all.

Aristocrats with lands and titles, plutocrats with bank accounts and bonds,
have everywhere stared blankly into the face of ruin. In fear of loss of privi-
lege they have nurtured rage in their hearts—not against the blind, impersonal
forces which have wrecked their fortunes, for these cannot be hated, but
against labor leaders, reformers, radicals and "crack-pots." In many lands
they have hired private thugs or political gangsters to give them "protection."
And commonly, like the Fritz Thyssen who put Hitler in power, they have
become the victims of their protectors. As for the millions everywhere who
live by the sweat of honest toil, they have often, when faced by joblessness

and hunger, embraced the creeds of class war and revolt, thereby finding spiritual peace through a "cause" but frightening their social superiors almost out of their wits. This social schism is inherent in the structure of modern industrial communities. Successive economic "crises," breeding acute and widespread deprivations, have everywhere rendered the schism chronic and desperate, destroying the peace of mind of masses and classes alike and adding to the insecurities out of which the schism itself was born.

When such a cleavage not only turns one class against another, but turns a single class against itself, even in terms of single families and individuals, the result is not social war but a kind of collective neurosis. Such has long been the affliction of that stratum of modern societies which has been least well-defined and most insecure: the middle-income millions of salesmen, technicians, small business men, once well-to-do farmers, and sundry professional people living by expensively acquired skills. These are the little men who recently climbed from the ranks of poor peasants and wage-earners toward the happy ranks of the leisure class. They cannot endure the end of their hopes of riches. They are horrified at the black prospect of being ground down between the upper and nether mill-stones of the social machine to the humble level of their forebears.

Hence their hatred of "capitalists" and "radicals" alike. Hence their eager support, long before World War I, of Populism, Progressivism, Reform, New Freedom, moderate Socialism and a dozen other nostrums for their ills. Hence their support more recently of Anti-Semitism, Fascismo, National Socialism and all the frenzied folly of totalitarianism in some countries and appeasolationism in others. From the fermenting depths of this unstable middle class have come the new élites of our time, and many of the leaders of causes, old and new—the Mussolinis and Matsuokas, the Hitler and Arakis, the Lenins and Kerenskys, the Roosevelts and La Follettes, the Blums and Lavals, the Chamberlains and Attlees, the Willkies and Lindberghs, the Darlans and De Gaulles, and a host of others, all seeing the world through different eyes and often utterly at odds with one another, but all alike reflecting in their various ways the world-wide worries of the class from which they sprang.

THE WORLD'S DESIGN

Why these worries? Because of hunger and humiliation caused by the sickening dips of waving lines on statisticians' charts. And why this "business cycle," this slow paralysis of trade, these repeated paroxysms of the body economic, breeding fear and friction in the body social, producing fever and delirium in the body politic? Because, answer many of the victims, there is "lack of confidence," "public extravagance," "unbalanced budgets," "governmental meddling," etc. But these are results, not causes, of the economic malaise. Because, argue the doctors on the Left, "capitalism" is "inevitably" doomed to "collapse" á la K. Marx, because of "shrinking markets," the "expropriation of surplus value," the "contradictions of the profit system." But these phrases ring hollow.

If truth be told, however unpalatable it may be to those who prefer their grand illusions or their petty lies, the world's disorder stems from a source at once simpler and more baffling than these attempted explanations would suggest. The malady has many symptoms, each of which is often mistaken for its "cause." The actual cause, at bottom, is the tyranny of time and the difficulty of spanning the chasm between yesterday and tomorrow. Modern man is like a boy who has grown up too soon and is forced to face the responsibilities of manhood with the outlook of a childhood which he has no wish to leave behind him. His anguish springs from his attempt to live with his body and mind in the future while his heart and soul are trapped in the past. Men and women as citizens still live throughout most of the modern world amid the social attitudes and political habits of the 18th century. But the same men and women as producers and consumers are living (or trying to live) amid the stream-lined gadgets of an ultra-modern industrial civilization, created by the Machine and spanning all the planet.

The Machine has long since made of all the world one market, one workshop, one playground, one Great Neighborhood whose people are everywhere dependent one upon another all over the globe for their livelihood and their security. The new Great Neighborhood of the 20th century is much smaller in travel-time than any of its nations were in 1800, for the traveller can now fly half-way around the earth in the hours then needed by horse and coach to journey from one province or county to the next. As for the minutes or seconds needed to send spoken or written words from one point to another, the Great Neighborhood of the world is infinitely smaller than was any tiny town of Europe or America a century and a half ago. Even the poorest of its peoples, moreover, are blessed with the fruits of a world-wide division of labor. They enjoy, as "necessities" of life, such comforts and luxuries of daily living as were beyond imagining by the wealthiest kings and conquerors of the days before man's conquest of steam and electricity.

This scheme of 20th century living was scarcely planned. Sight unseen, it grew from the separate deeds of tens of thousands of inventors, manufacturers, merchants and bankers. It grew from the daily buying and selling through the years of millions of producers and consumers. Unwittingly they made the world a unity by exchanging across all the lands and seas of the earth the goods and services which the new technology made possible. An "invisible hand" perhaps controlled all these manifold acts which together revolutionized the world. But the actors themselves had in mind no world purpose or plan. Their motives were curiosity and a desire for adventure and wealth. Most of them hoped and believed that the greatest good of the greatest number would somehow be brought about by each serving his own good first through the virtues of thrift, industry and foresight.

And indeed it was. In the end all the world's children awakened to discover that the Machine had made them all one family, united and indivisible, with its members linked by ties of trade, travel and investment into a World Society where the weal and woe of each affected in a million hidden ways the weal and woe of all.

This result was clearly not a curse but a boon for the race. The seeds of tragedy lay only in this: that men did not awaken fully to the New World created by their handiwork but continued, in their sleepy, muddled way, to perpetuate another world's design inherited from their ancestors. The old design, unlike the new, was one of local loyalties and local market-places in a pre-industrial civilization divided politically into "sovereign" and "independent" States pursuing their narrow purposes in an ancient competition for power and prestige. The very business men who wove the new pattern for living in the Great Neighborhood were more often than not ardent patriots who insisted that each of the linguistic tribes of Western mankind was rightfully entitled to political "self-determination" and all the trappings of "sovereignty." The practices of men in earning a living knit the world together. But the practices of the same men in preaching patriotism tore the world apart into an ever larger number of political entities, waging tariff wars and currency wars and diplomatic wars and military wars one against another.

THE POLITICS OF POWER

This familiar game has often been played for centuries in civilizations whose peoples have been politically divided against themselves by the rival ambitions of dynasts or by the clashing cults of language and race. Wherever the design becomes fixed, each "Great Power" must play the game or surrender its rights to "independence" and "sovereignty." Its leaders and people cannot choose between playing and not playing. They can only choose between playing well and playing badly. Those too weak to play become provinces or protectorates of their rivals, or else enjoy a precarious "neutrality" as buffers among more powerful neighbors. Those able to play and yet unwilling to play lose the game and forfeit their fortunes and their lives as well.

The rules are simple. Each player strives to increase his power and to enhance his "prestige," which is nothing more nor less than reputation for power. Here, as in all politics, power is ability to win friends and influence people to do one's bidding. And here, as in all politics, the implements of power are force, fraud and favors. But since there is no central authority in the unruly family of nations to enforce justice and keep the peace, no rules save the "international law" of custom and treaty, and no police or courts to compel obedience to law, the players of necessity play against one another under the law (or lack of law) of anarchy. Hence force is the most effective tool of sovereignties in bending other sovereignties to their will. The measure of power becomes the measure of a State's capacity to win its case in trial by battle.

The players therefore strive, above all else, to add to the arms at their disposal in order to overawe and threaten their neighbors, for the player who cannot coerce others is all but certain to become a victim of coercion. Force depends for its successful use on weapons and men. It also depends on goods and gold. As Machiavelli once put it: "Men, yron, money, and breade be the strengthe of the warre, but of these fower, the first two be most necessarie; because men and yron find money and breade; but breade and money fynde not men and yron." Effective force depends on possession of land and of rivers and harbors and seaways and islands from which men can use weapons and ships for attack or defense.

These things are therefore the stakes of diplomacy. For control of them nations fight, each fighting out of fear that by not fighting it may lose its power for future fighting and thereby be subjugated. War is less the fruit of the greed or wickedness of men than of the circumstance that men who live in rival nation-states must, if they would have their States survive, strive for mastery of the means of coercion. Armed violence among nations is not at all the "inevitable" product of "human nature." But it is assuredly the "inevitable" product of the division of coercive authority among rival sovereignties.

Diplomacy, properly understood, is but war carried on by "peaceful" means —that is, by trickery and bargaining, supported by threats of force. War is but diplomacy conducted by the open use of arms. In both phases of the game rivals can best be checkmated and often rendered ripe for defeat by operations of outflanking or encirclement. This requires allies. As a rule, therefore, every State is the potential enemy of its neighbors and the potential ally of its neighbors' neighbors. Coalitions arise out of these relationships, and counter-balance one another in ever larger arenas of possible conflict. The politics of the balance-of-power flows from the effort of each player to protect his independence by finding adequate allies against some bloc of potential foes.

But each player, if he plays for the highest stakes, strives to preserve the balance only when he is weak or satisfied. When he is strong and ambitious, he strives to upset it to his own advantage. If he succeeds, he strives for further upsets in order that he may extend his power as widely as possible over as many rivals as possible. His rivals and victims combine for self-defense in successive coalitions, designed to beat down the strongest among them who threatens all. But in the end, at least in all earlier State Systems, the strongest player ultimately succeeds in his purpose and extinguishes the independence of the rest—first of his enemies, then of appeasing "neutrals," and finally of his allies. When this occurs (and it has always sooner or later occurred in every earlier civilization), the game of power ends and men at long last enjoy the peace of a world imperium.

THE POWER OF POLITICS

This game is a relatively harmless sport of kings, politicians and patriots so long as people live simply and poorly on their local lands with little business across frontiers. In such a world few are affected by the intrigues of diplomats, the ambitions of generals and the vicissitudes of alliances and counter-alliances. When latent war becomes open war, many share vicarious glory but few suffer loss of livelihood or limb or life. In such a world professional armies are small and soldiers fight with circumspection. Civilians go undisturbed about their daily tasks, little touched by the deeds of the high and mighty.

But when people live abundantly and precariously in a World Society, then power politics becomes a formula for universal ruin. In the name of "defense," each Power strives for self-sufficiency and thereby hampers trade. Each sovereignty harnesses industry and commerce to the chariot of Mars and thus renders the profitable exchange of goods and services across frontiers ever more difficult. Each player of the game, in striving to win the stakes of diplomacy, encourages dubious investments and deflects the flow of imports and exports into doubtful channels in order that some allegedly higher purpose of *Realpolitik* may be served. Every phase of life, within States and between States, is more and more dominated by the politics of nationalism and imperialism. The world-wide net-work of trade and finance upon which millions depend for their security is more and more ruptured and broken. Countrysides suffer from a glut of goods which cannot be sold while hunger stalks the streets of the great cities. Fears and hatreds spread in ever-widening circles from the moves and counter-moves of the diplomats and strategists.

When war breaks out among Great Powers under such circumstances as these, the everyday lives of all the world's two billion people, in belligerent and neutral States alike, are exposed to dangers and worries of appalling scope. Millions die. Millions more are wounded in body or soul or both. Further millions lose their homes, their fortunes and their hopes—if not at once in the fury of fighting, then later in the course of post-war miseries. Through sudden panic on a world-wide scale, or through the slow corrosion of despair, tens of millions are driven to acts of aggression or abnegation with results which all may see.

In this vale of sorrow vanquished hope weeps in vain for lost and buried yesterdays. Reason perishes. Kindness dies. Brotherhood becomes a mockery. Religion itself is prostituted to the service of mass murder and theft, for all the tribes of men plead passionately with their common Creator in words as terrible and bitter as those of the "War Prayer" of Mark Twain: "O Lord our God, help us to tear their soldiers to bloody shreds with our shells; help us to cover their smiling fields with the pale forms of their patriot dead; help us to drown the thunder of the guns with the cries of the wounded, writhing in pain; help us to lay waste their humble homes with a hurricane of fire; help us to wring the hearts of their unoffending widows with unavailing grief; help us to turn them out roofless with their little children to wander unbefriended through the wastes of their desolated land in rags and hunger and thirst, sport of the sun flames of summer and the icy winds of winter, broken in spirit, worn with travail, imploring Thee for the refuge of the grave and denied it—for our sakes, who adore Thee, Lord, blast their hopes, blight their lives, protract their bitter pilgrimage, make heavy their steps, water their way with their tears, stain the white snow with the blood of their wounded feet! We ask of One who is the spirit of love and who is the ever faithful refuge and friend of all that are sore beset, and seek His aid with humble and contrite hearts. Grant our prayer, O Lord, and Thine shall be the praise and honor and glory, now and ever. Amen."

TO HAVE OR HAVE NOT

The issue posed to modern Man by these man-made holocausts of force and fear is starkly plain—or would be if men had vision and courage to face it. Whether faced or not, the issue cannot be evaded, for it is both the shadow and the substance of today's dilemma. Western mankind has the choice of reshaping its old design for politics to fit its new design for living, or of abandoning its modern design for living in order to continue playing the ancient game of power. If Man clings stubbornly and past all learning to his 18th century pattern for chaos, he must expect his 20th century world economy to perish and to carry its impoverished survivors back to a simpler, poorer and cruder level of life. If he would preserve his 20th century World Society and enjoy the fruits thereof, he must renounce the politics of power. This cannot be done—alas!—by any firm resolution to avoid entanglement and mind one's own business, for those who are thus resolved become the victims of those who are not. Neither can it be done by breaking up nations and empires into smaller and weaker units on the model of feudal times. It can only be done by replacing anarchy by government in inter-state relations.

Anarchy in world politics is incompatible with unity and order in world business and world civilization. One or the other must go. The political unification of the Great Neighborhood, on a scale commensurate with the social and economic interdependence of its members, spells security and promise and an end of the bitter anxieties which rot the souls of men. Continued anarchy and the quarrelling of warring sovereignties spells maddening poverty and grief, driving men to ever more vicious acts of violence and cruelty. For under anarchy, in the words of Thomas Hobbes, human life is "solitary, poor, nasty, brutish and short." The cure for anarchy is order. And the price of order is government with power sufficient to impose peace and protect justice by a force which none can challenge.

What choice will be made? Perhaps none, since men in misery often fail to see the true nature of their alternatives. But no choice will also be a choice.

The forces of chaos will irresistibly trample down those who face them without any will to act. In all likelihood, however, a decision is imminent. And in all likelihood the decision will be in favor of order and against anarchy. For men, even when half-demented by misfortune, are still able to recognize dimly the sources of their suffering and to take action together for their own salvation.

THE GOVERNANCE OF THE WORLD

The prerequisites of world order are not mysterious. To grasp them requires neither Utopian speculation nor pious sentimentalism nor Herculean feats of mental or emotional gymnastics. The experience of the race supplies the answers. On the negative side of the ledger of cost, the price is first the abolition of the "balance of power." For so long as the building of hostile coalitions is possible in an uneasy equipoise of force, so long will periodical outbreaks of violence be inevitable. The next installment of the price is the abolition of the "sovereignty" and "independence" of States. For the unification of the world is unthinkable without an end of the ancient rules whereby the petty politicians of national land-patches can win the applause of their provincial patriots by subsidizing exports, taxing imports, barring immigrants, coining local money, sending diplomats abroad, maintaining national armies and navies, waging wars, making peace, and treating as they choose those who happen to live within their frontiers. In the third place, it is more than probable that any program of governing the world as one will require not only an end of political rivalries and wars for power between States but an end as well within States of the wars for profit and pelf among rival classes, factions and pressure groups.

On the positive side of the ledger, the achievement of world order requires first the permanent establishment of an overwhelming aggregation of power under a single direction, able and willing to crush at once by an invincible superiority of arms any hostile Power outside its borders and every attempt within by secessionists or rebels to restore the old disorder. Cultural independence of national tribes is compatible with the needs of a united world. Political independence is not.

Unity also requires that men be bound together by a common faith in a common destiny, whatever may be the symbols of love and hope in which that faith may find expression. Such a faith must be suitably implemented on a world scale by vigorous political leadership supplied by a new élite, the members of which have unshakable determination to refashion and govern the world. The rulers of the future must control and allocate labor, resources and money in such wise that social and economic security will be enjoyed by all, to the end that the expectations and the rewards of simple men and women will be brought into harmony. With an energetic and enlightened use of these tools of social engineering, international conflict and class conflict alike will cease, as they did in the empire of ancient Rome. With the removal of the causes of worry and fear, the neurotic desperations of the present time of troubles will pass away.

CANDIDATES FOR GLORY

What groups of power-holders or power-seekers in the world of today show promise of ability to accomplish these tasks? What groups are aware of the tasks that call for action? What groups are disposed to act? The answer is all too obvious. The ambitious Caesars of the totalitarian States, almost alone among contemporary rulers, have faced the problem of unifying the world and have acted to achieve a solution. Stalin's "World Revolution," to be sure, has failed and has small prospect of ultimate success. But Hitler's World Revolution, allied with Japan's New Order in Asia, has marched on from triumph to triumph.

The goal of the Nazi élite is the replacement of the balance of power by the undisputed hegemony of the "master-race" of Germans, organized as the guardians and governors of the world of tomorrow. Victims and allies alike have been deprived of their sovereignty in order that the earth may be ruled as one. A wild creed of racialism, fantastic in its logic but quite effective in its emotional appeal, has supplied the "royal lie" or myth in the name of which the new élite rules and gives its subjects peace of soul. Conflicts among classes and among nations are ended by force and fraud. Order is enforced. Social and economic security is achieved. Peace reigns—or will reign when the work of conquest is completed. It is possible, to be sure, that the Nazi ideals of intolerance, persecution and exploitation may in the end generate more insecurities and aggressions than they cure. But for the present and the immediate future the *Pax Germanica* beckons the majority of men, Germans and non-Germans alike, to a future more tolerable than the endless disorder and irresponsibility of the past. The very brutishness of the Teutonic madmen enables them to impose *Frieden* and *Ordnung* on peoples too feeble and feckless to command their own destinies.

[*304*]

Can lunatics and barbarians remake the world? Western sophisticates, addicted to wishful thinking, will readily answer "No." But the test of survival and of capacity to control the future is neither sanity nor civilization. Virtue without wisdom is helpless. Right without might is impotent. "Good" men lose the race to "bad" when the good are stupid or cowardly and the bad are clever and brave. Loyalty to Christian ethics, or to the creed of liberty by which Western Man has hitherto sworn, can never by itself insure success in a struggle for power over the souls of men. Fitness to survive and to rule the world is measured first by will to survive and to rule the world, and secondly by ability to meet men's needs. In an epoch of universal agony, men's first needs are order and security. For these they will gladly sacrifice an empty "freedom" and abandon whatever devotion they may still feel to piety and virtue. The change is easy if the new dispensation gives them self-assurance through a crusading faith and a daring vision of a new heaven and a new earth, in the creation and enjoyment of which they are invited to share.

Can paralytics remake the world? Can defeatists, escapists and appeasers save mankind or even save themselves? Can those who fight, however courageously, for mere survival or for a restoration of yesterday bring order and unity to the Great Neighborhood of the world? Events give answer. No law of nature decrees that the foolish or the blind shall inherit the earth, however noble their motives may be. Those who live in the past can never prevail against those who have met the challenge of the future. Those who are utterly lacking in imagination and ideas cannot conquer those gifted with both.

NEW WORLD ORDERS

The central issue of World War II is not the issue of whether the world of the 20th century shall achieve political unity. It is the issue of who will build that unity, on what foundations and for what purposes. The Fascist Caesars have not hidden their goals under a bushel. They and their fanatic followers propose to build by force and mysticism a new feudal realm of world-wide scope. This realm is to be elaborately and firmly governed through a hierarchy of rulers and races. Jewish scapegoats, Slavic pariahs and Negro "subhumans" will be at the bottom for all others to look down upon. A militant caste of Samurai and Teutonic Knights will be at the top for all to obey. Between these extremes in serried ranks will stand, in order of benefits received, the citizens of Germany and Japan, other "Nordics" (both Asiatic and European), allied peoples, erstwhile neutrals, vanquished enemies, backward peoples, and despised barbarians beyond the pale, all subjected to varying degrees of efficient exploitation but all enjoying some measure of security and more or less getting what they expect and deserve. Under penalty of starvation or torture, each man will obey his superiors in the hierarchy of power. And each man will externalize his aggressions and discharge his resentments not against his equals or superiors but against his despised and degraded inferiors in the pyramid of deference.

Opposed to this vision, which is relevant and quite workable for all its ugliness, is—what? The program (if any) of the English-speaking democracies, loosely allied with China and Russia and appealing for support to contemptuous Latin Americans, skeptical Moslems, cynical European neutrals and all the disillusioned peoples of the subjugated Continent. In human and material resources this coalition is invulnerable and irresistible. Or would be, if its members were able and willing to act together. But in ideas and in dynamic vision, it is incredibly poor. Its leaders and peoples have in truth no program of uniting mankind. They fight, it is true, for purposes which might well inspire all the world to deeds of devotion and victory. They fight for human dignity and freedom; for the brotherhood of Man; for the sacredness of the human spirit, with each man and woman equal to his neighbor and free under God to give his best; for soaring dreams of justice and reason in human affairs. But thus far they lack wit or will to proclaim the Parliament of Man. And without this their dreams are but the dust of a past forever lost.

Many among them would fight (or pray without courage to fight) for a return to the very causes of disaster: for national "sovereignty" and "independence," for a new balance of power, for the old design of anarchy in the family of nations, feebly diluted by a new League and by vague words about four freedoms or eight points or sixteen platitudes. Some would neither fight nor pray, but would surrender forthwith to the "wave of the future," hoping to hide in holes or caves from the ruthlessness of the Caesars, or perhaps to win the doubtful honors of puppet rulers. Others would fight—eternally too late—when their own lands are invaded, but would have no hand in the "dangerous" work of defeating the foe and reordering and policing the world. Still others would win their war wherever it needed to be won by sheer weight of metal and mass of men with no thought of the aftermath until some far-off "Peace Conference" should meet amid the ruins for the work of "reconstruction."

THE PRICE OF VICTORY

A future as improbable as this may conceivably be realized by new miracles of valor on the part of the soldiers and civilians of Russia and China. But those whose minds are blind and whose hearts are empty merit no miracles. There is no reasonable basis for belief that Americans and Britons can save themselves and win the world on any such terms as these. The task of their leaders is to inspire their peoples with a positive purpose worthy of sacrifice and devotion. Their task is further to inspire the vanquished with a vision of hope in a Free World Order, for without the aid of the vanquished the Continent can never be rewon. Their task is to give a pledge of pitiless punishment to Germans, Italians and Japanese so long as they follow their warlords, and an equal pledge of mercy and justice in a partnership of peoples if they will but raise the banner of rebellion. These prerequisites of victory call for daring dreams of reconstruction now—not alone in eloquent words but in concrete deeds as a token of earnest purpose and inflexible will to win the future.

Is the task too hard? Its fulfillment is simplicity itself, were there but a will to act. "We can answer now," writes Clarence Streit, "in a way that will speed catastrophe over there and over here, and be remembered to our everlasting dishonor. Or we can give an answer that will encircle the earth in a flash with a force as omnipresent, never-resting, invisible and acceleratingly powerful as gravity itself, a force that no army can keep out, that no dictator can put his finger on, and that yet comes sweeping on as does an avalanche. We can give an answer that will sow confusion and revolt among the enemies of freedom, and put new, invincible life in its beleaguered defenders. We can again give 'hope to all the world.' We, too, can answer in a way that will go shining through the ages to our undying honor, as the answer that turned lightning-shattered darkness into enduring sunny light for all mankind."

Let America unsheath the sword of liberty and silence its home-grown Quislings by the shame of disgrace. No democracy that fosters treason and tolerates the apostles of intolerance is worthy of respect or survival. Let America and the British Commonwealth at once proclaim a customs union now and invite all Latin Americans to join. Let America and the British democracies adopt a common currency and a common citizenship; create a common army, navy and air force under common command; and establish a provisional federal government with limited but adequate powers to provide for the common defense and the general welfare.

Such a federation could end forever the balance of power and make itself the nucleus of a federation of the world. Let America extend the hand of friendship to its Latin neighbors, not in glittering words but in generous deeds. Let Britain invite the leaders of the peoples of India to join her, not to achieve an empty "independence" which no nation henceforth may ever enjoy again, but to collaborate in war and peace in a federation of equals. Let Britain and America together issue a Declaration of the Rights of Man and proclaim an end of colonial imperialism and of every self-seeking aspiration at the expense of the colored peoples of the earth. Let them fix for the future their relations with Russia and China on a basis of mutual aid and collaboration for the welfare of the race. Let them carry liberty to weary Europe, cradle of our culture, on the banners of a federal army made up of convinced crusaders for freedom. Let them summon Germans, Italians and Japanese to insurrection against their tyrants and to membership as equals, if they choose to join, in the coming union of freemen. Let all frontiers inside the Union henceforth be stripped of barriers of arms and tariffs. Let all men trade and travel freely and in safety, protected not by national armies (which are the eternal symbols of international anarchy) nor yet by the fatuous will-o'-the-wisp of "disarmament" through treaty, but by the mighty weapons on land, sea and air of Federation of the Free.

Is all of this beyond the dreams and deeds of Americans and Britons? Do the peoples of the great democracies hope to win safety and victory by something less than this? If so, they are mortgaged to the worms. International anarchy will pass away in our time before the conquering arms of those who will its passing. If the freemen of the Atlantic world will not do what destiny demands of them, then the bondsmen of the Caesars will do what must be done in the service of their own dark cults. To be or not to be now means: to unite and police the world or to suffer extinction in a world demanding government and peace. The world will be federated because it must be federated if its people are to continue to live in a world civilization. It will be federated either by the Triple Alliance and its vassals, or by a dynamic Anglo-America supported by Latin America and by Russia and by a free India and China. Victory in war will be won by those most eager and anxious to perform this task, and bravest and wisest in carrying it forward now

OUTWARD BOUND

Power politics is approaching its twilight. The Great Neighborhood, already made one by scientists and engineers, will find rulers to give it unity and will move forward to a new millennium. This transition is as "inevitable" as any change in human affairs can be. For the alternative to union is the wrecking of the World Society and the descent of modern Man into an endless nightmare of savagery. Man still has a will to live. He will choose the way which offers hope of life.

The human denizens of the turning earth, warmed by a flaming star a hundred million miles away and fed by the lesser forms of life which flourish on the flowering planet, face a change that comes but once in the cycle of every culture. Of the distant origins of this, and of the other man-made mansions of men, little enough is known. Of ultimate destinations no man can speak. From its remote birth out of the loins of ape-like ancestors half a million years ago, and from the dim emergence of literate cultures some ten thousand years in the past, the species moves on toward unseen goals hidden in the dawns and dusks of countless days to come. But the social artifacts of men move now and then through streams of change which lie in charted waters between ports which are clearly seen. And from time to time in mid-passage comes an hour unlike all before when the vessel escapes the fury of storm and strife and enters calm seas between the sunset and the quiet night. Such an hour now draws near for the weary voyagers of our time.

The change that looms ahead is a change from an age of violence and an epoch of warring States to a time of peace under a government of all mankind. Such was the change which came under the law and the legions of Rome to the Mediterranean peoples two thousand years ago. Such is the change now overdue for the peoples of the 20th century, already united in a common civilization and waiting to be united under a government of all the planet. Embattled freemen will win mastery of tomorrow if they will but undertake this task. If they will not, they will fail and fall and yield the future to the hosts of the Caesars. The task of union is reserved for those who see its need and who act courageously to bring the gift of ordered peace to men. Let those most worthy take the helm.

WHERE'S WHERE

A List of Maps

[311]

WHAT'S WHAT

A Table of Nations

OCTOBER 1, 1941

N.B. *Order of States within each major group is by population. Order of sub-entries is chronological. Dates indicate time of conquest, annexation, occupation or "protection" of communities which were independent or under different sovereignty prior to the aggressions of 1931–1941. Colonies, mandates and other non-independent areas are not included. Figures are estimates where data are doubtful.*

STATES	CAPITALS	AREAS SQ. MI.	POPULA-TIONS
A. *Great Powers*			
GREATER GERMANY AND SUBJECT STATES			
The Reich (pre-Anschluss)	Berlin	182,000	69,000,000
Austria, March 12, 1938	Vienna	33,000	7,000,000
Sudetenland, October 1, 1938	Karlsbad	11,000	3,400,000
Bohemia & Moravia,			
March 15, 1939	Prague	20,000	8,000,000
Slovakia, March 23, 1939	Bratislava	14,500	2,500,000
Memel, March 22, 1939	Memel	1,000	150,000
Danzig, September 1, 1939	Danzig	750	415,000
Western Poland,			
September 28, 1939	Warsaw	70,000	22,000,000
Denmark, April 9, 1940	Copenhagen	16,500	3,800,000
Norway, April 9, 1940	Oslo	124,500	2,900,000
Luxemburg, May 10, 1940	Luxemburg	1,000	300,000
The Netherlands, May 15, 1940	The Hague	12,700	8,800,000
Belgium, May 28, 1940	Brussels	11,700	8,400,000
Occupied France, June 25, 1940	Paris	130,000	27,400,000

STATES	CAPITALS	AREAS SQ. MI.	POPULA- TIONS
Rumania,[1] October 8, 1940	Bucharest	74,000	13,870,000
Hungary,[2] Autumn 1940	Budapest	62,000	13,325,000
Italy,[3] 1940–1941	Rome	130,000	46,100,000
Bulgaria,[4] March 1, 1941	Sofia	44,000	6,560,000
Jugoslavia,[5] April 17, 1941	Belgrade	95,500	15,800,000
Greece, April-May, 1941	Athens	50,000	7,250,000
Finland,[6] June 22, 1941	Helsinki	135,000	3,700,000
Eastern Poland,[7] June-July, 1941	....	80,000	13,000,000
Bessarabia and No. Bukovina,[8] July, 1941	Kishinev	19,000	3,400,000
Lithuania,[9] June, 1941	Kovno	23,000	2,900,000
Latvia,[10] July, 1941	Riga	25,000	2,000,000
Estonia,[11] August, 1941	Tallinn	18,300	1,135,000
Total Greater Germany and Subject States [12]		1,384,450	293,105,000

[1] Exclusive of Bessarabia and Northern Bukovina (19,000 sq. mi., 3,400,000 pop.), occupied by U.S.S.R., June 28, 1940; Northeastern Transylvania (17,000 sq. mi., 2,370,000 pop.), ceded to Hungary, August 30, 1940; and Southern Dobruja (4,000 sq. mi., 360,000 pop.) ceded to Bulgaria, Sept. 7, 1940.

[2] Inclusive of Southern Slovakia (4,600 sq. mi., 1,000,000 pop.), annexed Nov. 2, 1938; Carpatho-Ukraine (4,700 sq. mi., 675,000 pop.) annexed, March 16, 1939; and Northeastern Transylvania (Cf. Note 1), but not including territories annexed from Jugoslavia, April, 1941.

[3] Including Albania (10,600 sq. mi., 1,100,000 pop.), annexed, April 9, 1939, when Italy still enjoyed *de facto* as well as *de jure* independence, but not including annexations to Albania and Italy at expense of Jugoslavia, nor the puppetries of Montenegro and Croatia, carved out of the remains of Jugoslavia in May, 1941.

[4] Including Southern Dobruja (Cf. Note 1), but not including territories seized from Greece and Jugoslavia in April, 1941.

[5] Including all territories of the former Kingdom, partitioned among Bulgaria, Hungary, Germany, Italy, Albania and the puppetries of Montenegro and Croatia, April-May, 1941.

[6] Including territories (12,250 sq. mi., 100,000 pop.) ceded to U.S.S.R., March 12, 1940, but not including formerly Soviet territories occupied by Finn-Nazi forces in the war of 1941.

[7] Annexed to U.S.S.R., Sept. 28, 1939.

[8] Annexed to U.S.S.R., June 28, 1940.

[9] Protectorate of U.S.S.R., Oct. 10, 1939; annexed to U.S.S.R., July 21, 1940.

[10] Protectorate of U.S.S.R., Oct. 5, 1939; annexed to U.S.S.R., July 21, 1940.

[11] Protectorate of U.S.S.R., Sept. 28, 1939; annexed to U.S.S.R., July 21, 1940.

[12] Exclusive of Unoccupied France, Spain and the occupied areas of the U.S.S.R.

STATES	CAPITALS	AREAS SQ. MI.	POPULA-TIONS
UNION OF SOVIET SOCIALIST REPUBLICS [13]	Moscow	8,100,000	171,800,000
UNITED STATES OF AMERICA	Washington	2,974,000	131,800,000
Commonwealth of the Philippines	Manila	114,000	16,000,000
Total [14]		3,088,000	147,800,000
JAPAN	Tokyo	148,000	72,750,000
Manchukuo	Hsingking	503,000	39,000,000
Total [15]		651,000	111,750,000
GREAT BRITAIN	London	89,000	47,500,000
SELF-GOVERNING DOMINIONS			
Canada	Ottawa	3,700,000	11,300,000
Union of South Africa	Pratoria	473,000	10,000,000
Australia	Canberra	2,975,000	7,000,000
Eire	Dublin	27,000	3,100,000
New Zealand	Wellington	104,000	1,700,000
Newfoundland	St. Johns	43,000	300,000
Labrador	St. Johns	110,000	4,800
Total [16]		7,521,000	80,904,800

[13] Exclusive of territories annexed 1939–1940 (Cf. Notes 1, and 6-11) but including areas (White Russia, most of the Ukraine, etc.) under Nazi military occupation.

[14] Exclusive of Alaska (586,400 sq. mi., 73,000 pop.). Hawaiian Islands (6,500 sq. mi., 415,000 pop.), the Panama Canal Zone (552 sq. mi., 52,000 pop.), Puerto Rico (3,400 sq. mi., 1,800,000 pop.), Virgin Islands (133 sq. mi., 23,000 pop.), Samoa (76 sq. mi., 10,000 pop.), and Guam (206 sq. mi., 21,000 pop.). Also exclusive of Greenland (736,500 sq. mi., 17,000 pop.) and Iceland (39,700 sq. mi., 120,000 pop.), both of which were occupied by U.S. forces in the summer of 1941 by agreement, respectively, with the Danish Minister in Washington and the Icelandic Government at Reykjavik.

[15] Exclusive of occupied provinces of China.

[16] Exclusive of mandates, protectorates and non self-governing colonies in Africa, Asia, Oceania and South America, and exclusive also of the largest unit of the Empire: India with 1,809,000 sq. mi., and 370,000,000 people.

STATES	CAPITALS	AREAS SQ. MI.	POPULA-TIONS
B. Secondary Powers			
China [17]	Chungking	4,000,000	428,000,000
Brazil	Rio de Janeiro	3,275,000	46,500,000
Spain [18]	Madrid	196,600	25,500,000
Mexico	Mexico City	764,000	20,000,000
Turkey	Ankara	294,400	17,840,000
Hatay, June 23, 1939	Alexandretta	200	273,000
Total		295,600	18,113,000
Egypt	Cairo	383,000	16,000,000
Thailand (Siam)	Bangkok	200,000	15,000,000
Iran (Persia) [19]	Teheran	628,000	15,000,000
Unoccupied France [18]	Vichy	83,000	14,500,000
Argentina	Buenos Aires	80,000	13,000,000
C. Minor Powers			
Colombia	Bogota	449,000	8,000,000
Afghanistan	Kabul	270,000	8,000,000
Portugal	Lisbon	35,500	7,000,000
Peru	Lima	482,200	6,600,000
Sweden	Stockholm	173,350	6,325,000
Nepal	Kathmandu	54,000	5,600,000
Chile	Santiago	295,000	4,680,000
Cuba	Havana	44,000	4,235,000
Switzerland	Bern	16,000	4,220,000

[17] Excluding Manchukuo (See Japan above) but including provinces under Japanese occupation, with a total population of perhaps 200,000,000.

[18] A persuasive case could be made out for including Franco's Spain and Pétain's France as German Subject States, along with Mussolini's Italy and Horthy's Hungary, but since Vichy and Madrid are supervised by the Reichswehr and the Gestapo to a slightly lesser degree than Rome and Budapest, France and Spain are here listed as "independent" Powers.

[19] Under Anglo-Soviet occupation since August, 1941.

STATES	CAPITALS	AREAS SQ. MI.	POPULA- TIONS
Saudi Arabia	Mecca	320,000	4,000,000
Iraq [20]	Bagdad	116,600	3,700,000
Yemen	Sanaa	75,000	3,500,000
Venezuela	Caracas	352,100	3,500,000
Bolivia	La Paz	537,500	3,450,000
Guatemala	Guatemala	45,450	3,100,000
Haiti	Port-au-Prince	10,000	3,000,000
Ecuador	Quito	276,000	3,000,000
Uruguay	Montevideo	72,000	2,100,000
Salvador	San Salvador	13,000	1,750,000
Dominican Republic	Ciudad Trujillo	19,300	1,600,000
Liberia	Monrovia	45,000	1,500,000
Nicaragua	Managua	60,000	1,170,000
Honduras	Tegucigalpa	44,300	1,000,000
Paraguay	Asuncion	321,000	1,000,000
Costa Rica	San José	23,000	625,000
Oman	Muscat	82,000	500,000
Panama	Panama	33,670	470,000
Iceland [21]	Reykjavik	39,700	120,000

D. The Microcosms of Sovereignty

STATES	CAPITALS	AREAS SQ. MI.	POPULA- TIONS
Monaco	Monaco	8	25,000
San Marino	San Marino	38	15,000
Liechtenstein	Vaduz	65	12,000
Andorra	Andorra	191	6,000
Vatican City	Vatican City	0.1	1,000

[20] Under British occupation since May, 1941.
[21] Under British occupation (May, 1940), followed by U.S. occupation, July 7, 1941.

WHO'S WHO

An Index of Persons

Abe, Nobukuyi, 27
Abetz, Otto, 156
Aimone, Duke of Spoleto, 77
Akiyama, Kunio, quoted, 34
Alexander I, Tsar, 127
Alexander, King, 55, 146
Alexander, Albert, 183
Al-Haschimi, Taha, 190
Aloisi, Baron, 60; quoted, 58
Amaterasu, 3
Amenokoyane, 27
Amery, L. S., 182
Anders, Wladyslaw, 232
Antonescu, Ion, 120; quoted, 131
Aosta, Duke of, 77, 187
Araki, Sadao, 26
Arita, Hachiro, 26, 27
Arminius, 79, 80
Astor, Lady Nancy, 167, 215
Astor, Lord, 167
Astor, John J., 167
Attila, 80
Attlee, Clement, 183
Attolico, Bernardo, 104
Auchinleck, Claude, 193

Badoglio, Pietro, 62, 64, 72, 75, 76, 77
Balbo, Italo, 52, 62, 65, 77
Baldwin, Stanley, 59, 167, 169; quoted, 170, 172, 292
Bardossy, Ladislaus, 123, 131
Barthou, Louis, 55, 146, 212
Baudouin, Paul, 71, 153, 155
Beaverbrook, Lord, 167, 197, 232
Beck, Josef, 60, 107, 108, 145, 177, 181
Beck, Ludwig, 93
Beneš, Edouard, 99, 101, 102, 103, 147, 149, 175
Beran, Rudolf, 101, 103
Berea, L. P., 232
Bevin, Ernest, 183

Birkenhead, Lord, quoted, 183
Bismarck, Otto von, quoted, 48
Bleucher, Vassily, 20, 21, 214
Blimp, Col., 166f., 244
Blomberg, Werner von, 90, 98
Blum, Léon, 61, 146, 147, 148, 149, 150, 154
Bock, Gen. von, 134, 233
Bonaparte, Napoleon, 119, 127, 129, 135, 165, 292
Bonnet, Georges, 68, 100, 102, 104, 149, 151, 153, 176, 181, 216; quoted, 150, 152
Borah, William, 263, 265, 278
Boris, King, 121, 123
Borodin, Michael, 20, 21
Bowers, Claude, 244
Brauchitsch, Walter von, 98, 114
Bredow, Gen. von, 90
Briand, Aristide, 85, 143, 144
Brinon, Fernand de, 71, 158, 161
Brüning, Heinrich, 87, 144
Budenny, Semyon, 232, 233
Bullitt, William, 244, 247
Burke, Edmund, quoted, 165

Cadogan, Alexander, 177
Caffery, Jefferson, 244
Caligula, 80
Cantilo, Señor de, 249
Carol, King, 120
Carroll, Lewis, quoted, 3, 44, 79, 138, 164, 203, 235, 290
Casado, Sigismundo, 69, 70
Catroux, Georges, 192, 193
Cavagnari, Domenico, 75, 76
Cavallero, Ugo, 76
Cecil, Robert, 172; quoted, 173
Chamberlain, Joseph, 170
Chamberlain, Neville, 60, 68, 69, 70, 100, 101, 103, 106, 108, 116, 149, 167, 169,

[*318*]

THANKS TO

A Note of Appreciation

To McGraw-Hill Book Company, for permission to reprint here, with sundry revisions, deletions and additions, various maps and passages which first appeared in the third edition of *International Politics: The Western State System in Transition*, published in May, 1941. . . . To Bella Brodsky and Lily Schuman, for patience, inspiration and useful suggestions. . . . To Leonard W. Stearns, for aid and counsel in terrestrial photography. . . . To Clare Boothe, for ideas and encouragement. . . . To Bernard Smith and Sidney R. Jacobs, for helpful advice at the eleventh hour. . . . To Lewis A. Dexter, for stimulating discussion of the politics of power and the psychology of insecurity. . . . To Agnes Whitmarsh, for cartographic courtesies. . . . To Lewis Carroll, for words of wisdom. . . . To Sally Carlton Foote, for assistance in research, typing and indexing. . . . Any resemblance between the contents of this volume, true or false, and the opinions of those named above is purely coincidental.

G. D. B.
F. L. S.

A NOTE ON THE TYPE

The text of this book is set in Caledonia, a Linotype face designed by W. A. Dwiggins, the man responsible for so much that is good in contemporary book design and typography. Caledonia belongs to the family of printing types called "modern face" by printers—a term used to mark the change in style of type-letters that occurred about 1800. It has all the hard-working feet-on-the-ground qualities of the Scotch Modern face plus the liveliness and grace that are integral in every Dwiggins "product" whether it be a simple catalogue cover or an almost human puppet.

The book was composed, printed, and bound by H. WOLFF, New York.